Praise for **Scorpion Tongues**

"In [President Clinton's] beach-bag this year he could tuck this hilariously readable book, which will reassure him that when it comes to scatological rumors about politicians, there is nothing new under the sun."
—*The Economist*

"Gossip has long been a staple of public life, Gail Collins reminds us in *Scorpion Tongues*, a breezy, timely history of political gossip."
—*The New York Times Book Review*

"[A] useful and amusing book . . . Collins dishes the dirt on just about every presidential candidate and explains the reasons behind the tall tales."
—*The Boston Globe*

"Gail Collins digs up plenty of scandalous stories in her history of American political gossip . . . a major public service . . . Besides demonstrating that gossip is transient and gossiping is eternal, Collins shows that political gossip has some useful functions."
—*Entertainment Weekly*

"An often entertaining account of political gossip in American history, collecting an ample supply of 'facts and near-facts about the great and near-great' from Thomas Jefferson to William Jefferson Clinton. It's not hot dish exactly—since many of the stories are at least several decades old—but it's tasty dish nonetheless."
—*Salon*

"A breezy, anecdotal look at American gossip's many forms, from whispers about George Washington's supposedly kingly ambitions to the media blitz surrounding Bill Clinton's zipper problems."
—*Time Out, New York*

"In the consistently fascinating and timely *Scorpion Tongues*, esteemed journalist and *New York Times* editorial-board member Gail Collins traces our sullied national history of tall tales, bogus boasts, tarnished truths, and outright lies . . . both an insightful investigation of moral turpitude and a gossip junkie's dream."

About the Author

GAIL COLLINS, a columnist for the *New York Times*, was the first woman ever to serve as editorial page editor for the paper. Previously, she was a member of the *Times* editorial board, and a columnist for the *New York Daily News* and *New York Newsday*. She is the author of *America's Women*.

Scorpion

Tongues

Also by Gail Collins

America's Women
The Millenium Book *(with Dan Collins)*

Scorpion
Tongues

Gossip, Celebrity, and
American Politics

New and Updated Edition

Gail Collins

HARPER PERENNIAL

NEW YORK ✦ LONDON ✦ TORONTO ✦ SYDNEY

HARPER PERENNIAL

First Harvest paperback published 1999.
First Harper Perennial edition published 2007.

Designed by Caroline Cunningham

The Library of Congress has catalogued the Harvest paperback as follows:

Collins, Gail.
    Scorpion Tongues : The irresistible history of gossip in American politics /
    Gail Collins.—1st Harvest ed.
        p.   cm.—(A Harvest book)
    Includes bibliographical references and index.
    ISBN 0-15-600650-2
    1. United States—Politics and government.   2. Gossip—Political aspects—United
States—History.   3. Political corruption—United States—History.   I. Title.
E183.C716   1999
306.2'0973—dc21   99-31817

ISBN: 978-0-06-113962-8 (pbk.)
ISBN-10: 0-06-113962-9 (pbk.)

        09   10   11   DIX/RRDH   10   9   8   7   6   5   4   3

To Dan

Contents

Introduction   xi

Chapter 1. The Road to Hillary's Lamp   1

Chapter 2. Public and Private Sinning,   1776–1830   23

Chapter 3. Gossip and Mutating Morals,
                                           1830–1880   45

Chapter 4. The Birth of the Celebrity Class,
                                           1880–1900   71

Chapter 5. The Anxiety of the Moment,
                                           1890–1920   95

Chapter 6. Political Gossip Goes Underground,
                                           1920–1945   123

Chapter 7. The Quiet Years, 1945–1964   155

Chapter 8. The Deluge of Defining Events,
                                           1964–1980   181

Contents

Chapter 9. **The Institutionalization of Gossip,**

                                           1980–1990 207

Chapter 10. **Endless Exposure,**   **1990–1999** 233

Chapter 11. **Millennial Politics**   277

                Bibliography   303

                Acknowledgments   341

                Index   345

The scorpion tongue of political slander assailed me.
—LOUISA ADAMS, 1797

Introduction

When I first agreed to write a book about the history of political gossip, Monica Lewinsky was still an unknown intern and my goal, to be honest, was to tell the world about what happened to Grover Cleveland. (It's taken me a long time to accept the fact that Grover is always going to be an acquired taste, and that no one is ever going to turn him into an HBO miniseries.) But as the Clinton administration rolled on, a bigger picture began falling into place. *Scorpion Tongues*—through no prescience on my part whatsoever—went off to the presses just days after the story about sex in the Oval Office first surfaced in the newspapers. It wasn't until the paperback version that I was able to retool the book a bit to reflect the fact that the American people turned out to be far more pragmatic about the President's wildly improper behavior than almost anyone had expected.

Looking back over what I had written, I realized that what had originally looked like a series of near-disasters on the part of misbehaving politicians was actually just the opposite. The American people had spent the last two centuries talking about "character" in their political leaders. But when it came to those same leaders' private behavior, they actually seemed, more often than not, to be stone cold indifferent. For all their willingness to be shocked, and titillated, by gossip over who was doing what in the bars and bedrooms and closets of after-hours Washington, their real bottom-line requirements for keeping someone in office were minimal: Their elected officials should do what they were hired to do. What they did on their own time generally had little or no bearing on the matter. "All they want is that you don't shove it in their faces," said the mayor of a particularly conservative big city when I asked her whether the fact that everybody in town knew that she was gay had posed any political problems.

During the Clinton impeachment, all the time I'd spent researching *Scorpion Tongues* really did turn out to be a gift that kept on giving. I was writing for the editorial board of the *New York Times,* and there were many, many days when it felt as if we'd said everything that could possibly be said about presidents and bad behavior. It was then that my capacity to compare whatever was going on to something that had happened to William Henry Harrison or Warren Harding really came into play. "Could you just write—one of those Grover Cleveland things?" my editor asked wearily, on more than one occasion.

When I was offered the chance to update the book for a new edition, it seemed like the least I could do in return. And so much had happened—a whole campaign full of rumors about George W. Bush's "reckless youth" and another that frequently appeared to be about nothing but John Kerry's war record. Rudy Giuliani had gone from being the guy who told a press conference he was getting divorced before he told his wife to the hero of 9/11. The governor of New Jersey announced he was gay, and it became clear that about half the state already knew the story, including the name of his lover. And there was Hillary Clinton, gearing up for a White House run while my own paper came up with an extremely well-researched estimate of exactly how much time she and Bill actually spent in the same residence. It had been fifteen years since we first got to know the Clintons, but we still couldn't quite put our finger on how that marriage worked. And we still wanted to know. Short of Franklin and Eleanor, there surely has been no other married political couple with the same ability to frustrate and fascinate.

This is not a story about the great issues in American government. While I was working on *Scorpion Tongues,* I had a colleague who was writing a book about the late nineteenth-century monetary crises that led to the creation of the income tax, and we realized that between us, we knew everything about fin de siécle American financial policy and high-level sex scandals. It was somewhat embarrassing to admit which one was my area of expertise. But the *Scorpion Tongues* story still touches on the things that move us and scare us most deeply— sex, race, religion, and sin. It's a chance to view American political history from the ground, and to get to know the American voter on a whole new level.

And in the end, we'll always have Grover.

Chapter 1

The Road to Hillary's Lamp

1. Hillary's Lamp

"Suspicions have already been, um, aroused . . ."

Inaugural week, 1993: Barbra Streisand led the Celebrity Salute to the new president. Barney the purple dinosaur was the star of the parade. The crowds were so dense that people tried to hoist their kids on the Portosans to get a better view. Bill Clinton, contrary to his supporters' worst fears, did not talk too long after he took the oath of office. The nation, which had been feeling a bit bedraggled both economically and emotionally, was unaware that it was on the edge of one of the biggest boom periods in history. The economic boom. The Internet boom. And a boom in political gossip. Michael Harrington, the editor of a magazine for the burgeoning talk radio industry, would later look back on the Clinton presidency as a Golden Era. "He's just a guy that has—I could go on for hours," Harrington enthused. "Bill Clinton is a package with *lots to talk about*. He embodied people's hopes. Brought them down. Raised them up.

1

Down. Up. The man's whole way of governing is similar to a talk radio program."

On the day it all began, the insiders exchanged inaugural rumors about who was getting what job and everyone else talked about who was going to what party. The gossip du jour, however, was the story of Hillary Clinton and the lamp. The First Lady, it was whispered, had thrown a lamp at her husband during a fight in the White House. Sometimes the argument was said to have started because the president-elect ogled one of the celebrities at the pre-inaugural show. Sometimes it was about whether or not Hillary Clinton's offices would be located in the critical White House West Wing. Frequently, the story included a subplot about the antagonism between Mrs. Clinton and her Secret Service guards. It remained confined to the nation's capital for about as long as it took to say "e-mail." Up in New York City, Hillary and the lamp were soon a big topic at a party for a retiring city detective. Investigators from the Treasury Department's Bureau of Alcohol, Tobacco and Firearms who had dropped by to wish the detective good-bye entertained the guests with the story, which they said they'd heard from friends in the Secret Service. "Those guys must really *hate* the Clintons," said a lawyer who had been at the affair, and then called his own circle of acquaintances to spread the tale along.

When it came to talk about the private lives of politicians, the Clinton administration was going to take the nation where no one had gone before. Before it was over, Americans would wind up knowing more about the sexual preferences of this president than many of them knew about those of their closest friends. The lamp story was an innocent tale compared to what was going to come later. But the speed with which it traveled across the country and the avidity with which it was passed around were a portent of things to come.

There were, of course, other rumors about the First Family's private life that cropped up during Bill Clinton's first days in office. The *Washington Monthly*'s "Who's Who" column tried to float a rumor that there was something more than economic indicators passing between the president and his new appointee to the Council of Economic Advisers. ("Suspicious have already been, um, aroused about one of Bill Clinton's better known weaknesses. Certain insiders say that . . . Laura Tyson has the ear and the eye of the president-elect, giving Hillary a new and compelling reason to sit in on all those top-level late night meetings.") There was some perfunctory talk about a woman on the transition team who was supposed to be having a liaison with the chief executive, but it faded away quickly, as would dozens of similar stories that sprang up over the next few years but failed to flower into serious gossip. And *The Washington Monthly* stampeded into retreat on its Laura Tyson rumor. ("The item was not intended to convey that anything more had happened or that Tyson had sought to use her physical charm to attract the president's attention. Indeed, from all we hear she is one of the more original intellects in his administration and deserves Clinton's attention strictly on the basis of merit.") But the lamp story endured. By March, major publications had begun printing it. By the summer it had achieved such legendary status that people were joking about it on network television. But long before the national media had decided the rumor was worth mentioning, people all across the country had picked it up through more informal communications networks. I went to Ohio for a family party in February, and when I was asked for inside Washington gossip, I offered up Hillary's lamp. But it was old news—my mother had already heard it on Rush Limbaugh's radio show.

Even before the birth of Web blogs, tabloid TV, and talk radio, it was possible to pick up quite a bit of gossip about the personal lives of important political figures, no matter where you lived or how communicative the newspapers were feeling. When Boston schoolteacher Barbara Wilson was a child and Dwight Eisenhower was president, she knew there were rumors his wife, Mamie, was a heavy drinker. "I must have heard it from my mother," she recalled. "She loved politics. Not in an active way, but she was a very big reader." How Wilson's mother picked up the information is a mystery. In the 1950s that sort of gossip had to be transmitted word of mouth—*The Boston Globe* didn't print it, and back then radio shows didn't encourage callers to phone in the latest rumors about the president's home life. Yet the Mamie-drinks rumor, like Hillary's lamp, had a remarkable ability to travel. One of the differences between that discreet age and today was that in the fifties and early sixties, people tended to hear only the gossip that appealed to their political prejudices, or their special interests. Steve Weisman, of *The New York Times*, grew up in Beverly Hills, where most of his junior high school class had heard that President Kennedy was having an affair with actress Angie Dickinson: "The hotel was right across from my old grade school." But back in Boston, the people in Wilson's neighborhood believed the nation's first Catholic president was a model husband. "He and Jackie had no faults. I couldn't imagine them fighting. I couldn't even imagine them brushing their teeth," she said. The entire Boston parochial school system, Wilson theorized, was out of the gossip loop on that one.

"Those pesky and unproved rumors"

It would have required an act of will to avoid the story about Hillary and the lamp in 1993. Everybody with even a remote interest in politics or the First Family knew it, although nobody actually knew if it was true. "I thought at the time it wasn't, but later I thought it probably was," said one highly placed member of the Clintons' 1993 political circle, hazarding a guess that might have been just as easily made by a waitress in Birmingham or a truck driver in Dubuque. Even after America had learned more than it wanted about the president's sexual practices, we were no more informed about the inner life of the Clinton marriage than we had been about relations between Dwight and Mamie Eisenhower. The communications network was getting thicker and faster every day, but not necessarily more accurate.

As the lamp saga spread through the dense, intertwining communications routes, people heard it again and again— on tabloid television shows, talk radio, through the Internet and Jay Leno jokes. The mere repetition made it seem true. The old-line media—newspapers, network news shows, newsmagazines—became less important as transmitters of gossip than as judges of credibility. By paying attention to a rumor, they could raise it to a new level of seriousness—a sort of official gossip.

In March of 1993, the conservative *Washington Times* became the first paper to print a variant of the lamp rumor, which had the First

Lady throwing a book (perhaps a Bible) at a Secret Service guard. Although "trustworthy sources" had discounted the tales, the *Times* added, the story had spread to papers in "Middle America and Europe." Most reports of gossip about political figures are accompanied by these two elements—an excuse for printing the story (the rumor has gotten so out of control it's being repeated in Berlin and Boise) and a denial. The most powerful denials are the ones from some variation on "trustworthy sources." (The inference is that the reporter has consulted people so reliable they're worth quoting even if their names can't be used.) The weakest come from the subject's spokesperson. (After all, what else would you expect a spokesperson to say?)

The critical point, however, was that the *Washington Times* story freed other publications from the onus of being the first to print the gossip, making everyone else more comfortable about leaping in. *Newsweek* ran a story about the rumor in which an angry First Lady threw "a lamp, a briefing book or a Bible" at the president, and added a new fillip—that Mrs. Clinton was rumored to have lit a cigarette to torture her smoke-allergic husband. (The writers personally deemed the cigarette story "outrageous" but simply quoted White House spokesman George Stephanopoulos as denying the thrown-lamp rumor.) White House correspondents asked Press Secretary Dee Dee Myers whether the lamp gossip had created a rift between the president and the Secret Service. Myers called the story "ridiculous" and urged the press to focus on the president's programs, not "the gutter." Her comments were part of a tradition that began with George Washington's wistful suggestion that newspapers should forget about scandal and concentrate on "the debates in Congress on all great national questions."

Myers's comments opened the way for *The Washington Post* to report, briefly and somewhat impatiently, that "the White House finally felt compelled to deny those pesky and unproved rumors involving all manner of domestic disputes between Bill and Hillary Clinton." (In a one-paragraph story, the *Post* also managed to move the rumor ahead a step by adding "punches" to the things that might have been thrown.) *The Washingtonian* weighed in with a conclusion that the throws-lamp-at-Bill part of the story began on Inauguration Day, when the Senate Republicans were penned up in a holding room next to one where the Clintons were fighting. "One prominent senator says he overheard Hillary shouting at Bill and threatening to throw something at him," the magazine reported. The Secret Service had been leaking stories of its own, *The Washingtonian* said, "including separate bedrooms and lots of loud talk and bad language including lots of the twelve letter 'm' word. One agent claims that Hillary threw her Bible at an agent who was driving too slow."

The Hillary-lamp saga became one of those stories that is so well known it can be referred to in shorthand, without explanation, in a David Letterman Top Ten list or *Saturday Night Live* skit. By June, when Mrs. Clinton was taking NBC's Katie Couric on a televised White House tour, Couric cheerfully asked her to "point out just where you were when you threw the lamp at your husband."

"Well, you know that's—I'm looking for that spot, too," the First Lady responded.

2. Deconstructing Political Gossip

"Such a filthy old man he had become!"

This is a book about American political gossip, a term that's been used to cover everything from the Clinton impeachment scandal to speculation about George Bush's drinking to conspiracy theories about "the missing day" in Dick Cheney's famous quail hunt. It covers such a sweeping variety of human behavior that we'll need to try to narrow it down. Many people, for instance, think of political gossip as shoptalk—rumors about who's going to get a certain nomination or why a bill was killed. But for our purposes, it will only refer to unverified information about a person's private life that he or she might want to keep hidden. This is the classic form of gossip, and passing it around has been one of our most popular social activities since privacy was invented. Politicians have been favorite targets throughout history. The ancient Greeks speculated that Pericles always kept his helmet on because he was embarrassed by his pear-shaped head. In

Rome, Mark Anthony spread the rumor that the future emperor Augustus jump-started his career by sleeping with Julius Caesar. Parts of Suetonius' *Lives of the Caesars,* one of Western civilization's most venerable histories, are pure gossip. Tiberius Caesar, Suetonius wrote, trained small boys to "chase him while he went swimming and get between his legs to lick and nibble them . . . such a filthy old man he had become!" Historically speaking, the anecdotes about American leaders have generally not been quite so colorful. (Except, perhaps, for the 19th-century presidential candidate who was rumored to have been a cannibal.) But the public has always passed around stories about their private lives, even though the newspapers have not always printed them.

One very American aspect of American political gossip is how often it culminates in an indictment. In a country that litigates everything, what starts as a whispered rumor can easily wind up before a grand jury. The mega-scandal of the 20th century, the Clinton impeachment, would probably never have occurred if Monica Lewinsky hadn't spent so much time on the phone with her alleged girlfriend, Linda Tripp. But the whole mess was pushed into the open through a complicated series of seemingly unrelated legal proceedings—special investigator, sexual harassment suit, Supreme Court ruling, presidential deposition and then perjury charges.

We'll call these moments defining public events, and they can also include anything from mistresses holding press conferences to police blotter reports linking famous names to solicitation of sexual services. In America, they often mark the point when the mainstream media feels free to jump in and report matters that were previously regarded as too uncertain or too unwholesome to put on the front page or the network evening news.

"I think my sainted mother told me that one"

For all its tawdry reputation, gossip performs many important functions. It makes the teller feel important. It bonds teller and listener together with a sense of sharing something that's slightly forbidden. By revealing behavior that's normally hidden, it helps people to understand how things really work in the mysterious world behind closed doors. (A young wife may figure out how to judge and deal with a husband's infidelity by listening to stories about other straying spouses.) People express their hidden fears through gossip, imposing on others the anxieties they haven't resolved in their own lives. They sometimes also use gossip to reaffirm their commitment to the social order. (Whispering about an acquaintance who wears sloppy clothes to Sunday services shows you still hold to the tradition of dressing up for church.)

But gossip has sometimes had a subversive role, too. For much of human history, it was one of the few weapons available to the powerless: servants who spread stories about their masters, serfs who irreverently speculated about the most private aspects of life in the manor. (The French peasants had a song about Louis XVI's penis that was popular as long as the king failed to produce an heir.) When the austere President Vladimir Putin urged his countrymen to start having more children in 2006, the much put-upon Russians immediately produced two satisfying, if deeply contradictory threads of gossip—that Putin himself was impotent (in truth, he had two adult children) or that he was hiding away a stable of mistresses.

Gossip has always been identified as a woman's vice, because from the time of the ancient Greeks, men realized that the really threatening stories were the ones their homebound, anonymous wives could tell if given the chance. Aristotle warned gloomily that democracy might lead to a society where women could seize the reins of domestic control and begin carrying gossip about their husbands to the outside world. In the Middle Ages, "gossip" was connected with midwifery, because the birthing room was one of the few places women gathered without supervision, free to make fun of the men in their lives and tell their most embarrassing secrets.

In American history, gossip has sometimes been a reaction against a heavily marketed politician who voters suspected was being thrust upon them against their will. Nineteenth-century presidential candidates promoted as war heroes were often gossiped about as cowards; paragons of virtue as "illegitimate" by birth. Even today, voters who pass around stories of a nominee's womanizing or drinking habits may

8

be attempting to show they aren't fooled by the barrage of commercials broadcasting his virtues.

Political gossip is, of course, very frequently a tactical weapon that supporters of one candidate use to try to weaken an opponent. It was obviously no coincidence that in the middle of the effort to impeach President Clinton, Republican members of the House Judiciary Committee suddenly discovered their own sexual indiscretions being leaked to the media. But while anybody can start a story, it isn't possible to force people to pick up on it and pass it around. The gossip that reverberates and endures isn't necessarily true, but it usually reflects something real about the target, or the national anxieties at a given point in time. When the recently widowed Woodrow Wilson suddenly married Edith Galt, people began to whisper that the two of them had murdered the president's first wife. That was a myth, of course. But the gossip did express people's discomfort with such stark evidence of a husband's ability to recover from his spouse's death, as well as the general impression that Wilson was something of a cold fish. More balanced citizens relieved their emotions by telling catty jokes about the second Mrs. W. The late columnist Murray Kempton remembered as a boy in the 1920s hearing that when President Wilson asked Mrs. Galt to be his wife, she was so excited she fell out of bed. "I think my sainted mother told me that one," Kempton said.

The lamp story grew and grew because Hillary Clinton's arrival as First Lady stirred up anxiety in many Americans, and the story about her smashed lighting fixture helped them express it without directly confronting the things that were bothering them. Mrs. Clinton made it clear she planned to have a policy-making role in the administration at a time when the nation was wrestling with its feelings about how women should mix the duties of career and marriage. The gossip reflected many voters' unresolved concerns about working wives and powerful women. By passing along the rumor that Hillary had physically attacked Bill Clinton, people were expressing their secret fears that she (and maybe by implication all women) would try to push her husband aside and run things herself.

3. The Three Great Eras of American Political Gossip

The Kaleidoscope Theory of History

The freedom with which people pass around rumors about their political leaders' private lives has changed dramatically over the past two hundred-odd years, but not necessarily in the way we imagine. We tend to think of history as a continuum, trending ever up or downward. We now know that John Kennedy invited his lovers to swim in the White House pool without fear of exposure, while the details of Bill Clinton's sex life got rehashed every day on talk radio and tabloid TV shows. So we assume that the nation was once discreet, concentrating on the political issues rather than scandalous secrets, until some very recent period when we lost our bearings and began obsessively speculating about the private vices of our leaders. But in fact the progress has been more erratic. We saw that in 2000 and 2004, when the many rumors about George W. Bush's forty-year-old youthful rebellion never really blossomed into a full-blown gossip extravaganza, and other candidates' unusual marriages or messy divorces slid under the national radar. Rather than a continuum, the interaction of gossip and politics is a sort of kaleidoscope, in which new patterns are created with every turn of the wheel. The national morality relaxes or stiffens. An irresistibly likable president is replaced by one with a downright irritating personality. A politician with a closet full of skeletons and an urge to party is followed by a string of men whose idea of a good time is taking a nap after dinner. Each year brings a new mix. The public is doomed to be shocked, hardened, and then reborn into hopeful innocence, over and over.

Still, we can divide the nation's history into three rough eras, depending on how freely people talked (and newspapers wrote) about their leading politicians' private lives. The era of the Founding Fathers was a sort of prologue. Our story really begins with the 1820s, when states began opening the elections up to all (white male) citizens. That was also the beginning of a long period, running through

10

most of the nineteenth century, in which average people were very interested in politics. They were wildly patriotic, but not particularly reverent about their elected officials. People thought nothing of spreading stories that a candidate had an illegitimate child, was concealing his "Negro blood" or Catholic faith. They jeered at Andrew Jackson as a bully and adulterer, passed around stories that Martin Van Buren wore women's corsets, distributed leaflets listing how Henry Clay had broken each one of the Ten Commandments ("spends his days at a gaming table and his nights in a brothel"), and accused Daniel Webster of being a drunken boor who couldn't keep his hands off innocent female clerical workers. Abraham Lincoln was rumored in the South to be a secret Negro ("Abraham Africanus the First") and in the North to be a war profiteer. The press compared Andrew Johnson unfavorably to Caligula's horse and speculated that Grover Cleveland would turn the White House into a bordello.

Then, around the turn of the century, things slowly began to quiet down. The nation no longer found politics fascinating—it had discovered movies and radio band singers and professional baseball. There was much less idle talk about politicians once people had the opportunity to speculate about the private lives of Mary Pickford and Babe Ruth and discuss the shocking rumors about what comedian Fatty Arbuckle did to the starlet Virginia Rappe in his hotel room. Political figures weren't entirely exempt, of course, particularly during election years. People whispered that Woodrow Wilson had an affair with a mystery woman named Mrs. Peck, that Warren Harding was the decendant of runaway slaves, that William McKinley beat his wife, and that Franklin Roosevelt and his entire family were alcoholics, as well as Theodore Roosevelt, and of course Mamie Eisenhower. But the media ignored this sort of talk. When one of Franklin Roosevelt's top officials got caught drunkenly propositioning the railroad porters on a train trip, the president confidently and accurately announced no newspaper would ever print the story.

This quiet and sometimes self-satisfied era ran from around World War I until the American involvement in Vietnam. Voters, if they chose, could easily convince themselves that the people running their government were faithful spouses and temperate drinkers, paragons whose public images were in perfect accord with their private behavior. "The fifties were a curious age," said Russell Baker, who covered Washington during the apex of that discreet period. "You'd go on vacation with Eisenhower, and the local people would come up and say: 'What sort of man is he?' And you'd say 'Well, he's rather cold.' They didn't want to hear that. They were convinced he was a great guy and they didn't want to be disillusioned or have fun made of him."

In the 1970s, things changed again. The public moved from disinterest in politics to something that bordered on contempt. There may actually have been less political gossip than ever, given the declining number of people interested in doing the talking. But what there was got printed, repeated, and, eventually, e-mailed, posted on the Internet, and masticated in talk radio and tabloid TV. The cynicism that began with scandals like Watergate and the disillusionment over the war in Vietnam prepared the public to hear almost anything—that the mayor of Seattle's wife had shot him when she caught him with another man, that the First Lady had murdered her lover, or that the Republican and Democratic candidates for president were each covering up an affair with a woman named J(G)ennifer. The politicians helped the process along by promoting themselves on television and radio in a manner guaranteed to remove any barriers the public felt to freely discussing their most personal secrets.

These shifts were created by all sorts of changes in the society and economy, particularly the development of communications technology, the decline of the power of political parties, and the growth of the entertainment industry. Of course, the deportment of the politicians mattered, too. If congressmen get shot by their mistresses, or a president is hit with a sexual harassment suit, people will talk, whatever the socioeconomic conditions. But when all the forces come together, like some sinister alignment of the planets, they can pull even the most discreet figures into the rumor mill.

The Media: "Important If True"

In the early years of American democracy, the salient fact about the newspaper business was that almost nobody made a profit at it. Most editors ran one-man shops, sold few ads, and usually boasted a readership of only a few hundred souls, almost all of whom were slow in paying for their subscriptions. "Subsisting by a country newspaper is generally little better than starving," said a New Jersey editor. Their brightest hopes lay in pleasing a successful politician and snagging a government printing contract or—better yet—a government job. Some of the best spots went to people who had printed the most outrageous stories. The editor who claimed that John Quincy Adams slept with his wife before they were married was made governor of Florida by the triumphant Andrew Jackson. Another who spread the story that Adams had been a pimp for the czar of Russia was made a senator and a member of Jackson's "Kitchen Cabinet." It's hardly surprising that most editors were ready, willing, and able to print any scandal about an opposition candidate that they could find or manufacture. Accuracy was not regarded as an important quality, anyhow. Editors of the era had no shame in admitting they were simply recycling rumors. ("Important If True" was a common headline.)

As technology improved and the population began to congregate in large cities, papers were able to make money from circulation and advertising. As long as production costs were still relatively low, even a small city could support a couple of profitable publications, along with a handful of fly-by-night competitors who might still be in the game of jockeying for political patronage. These smaller papers were the ones most likely to print shocking stories about government officials and election candidates. In 1881, for instance, a rumor went roaring through New York's state capitol in Albany concerning U.S. senator Thomas Platt. Platt's political enemies had discovered he was having an assignation with a woman in a local hotel, and arranged to watch the proceedings over the transom from an adjoining room. The *Albany Argus* promptly reported every detail: the conspirators' long vigil armed with "a stepladder, some whiskey, some crackers and cheese and cigars"; their three hours of amusement "taking turns mounting the stepladder and playing Peeping Tom"; the names of everyone involved except the woman. (It did report that she was "of engaging form but unpleasing features.") The other papers' more staid response must have sent readers racing out to look for a copy of the *Argus.* "A scandalous story affecting the private character of a prominent politician of this state was reported on the streets here and in Albany yesterday," announced the *New York Tribune,* with maddening discretion. "And full particulars were telegraphed to this paper, which we declined to print."

As newspaper chains grew and competition began to shrink in the twentieth century, the small, scurrilous papers died out and the surviving media tended to prefer less controversial family fare. That was the quiet era, bracketed by the Harding administration (extremely popular president makes love to his mistress in the Oval Office closet) and that of John Kennedy (extremely popular president makes love to rapidly revolving series of girlfriends just about everywhere but the White House press room). Newspaper editors, who were almost all men, found it distasteful to publicize the private misbehavior of politicians, who were almost always men, too. The periods in which newspapers did publish such personal revelations were generally marked by a strong female influence on the nation's social agenda. Women tended to focus on the problems of the family, and to regard male misbehavior in private life as a serious matter. Men tended to disagree.

Like all sweeping generalizations, the one that said newspaper readers could not pick up much about politicians' private misdeeds during this period didn't hold true, especially if a defining public event helped things along. But there's no question the overall tenor of the era was discreet—until the arrival of television news forced newspapers and magazines to give readers something they couldn't get from Walter Cronkite. By the 1980s, cable television, talk radio, twenty-four-hour news, and the Internet were creating an unprecedented competition for news consumers' attention. Because the old "scoops" of hard-news information could be transmitted so fast, the emphasis shifted to personality-driven stories that were more difficult for the competition to copy. With every public word recorded by TV and available on the Internet, reporters felt more pressure to learn things that were hidden.

While the nation's focus on politicians' personal misbehavior will always ebb and flow, it may never again reach the kind of perfect tsunami that occurred during the Clinton administration. Not much occurred between 1993 and 1999 that hadn't happened before. Presidents had conducted affairs in the vicinity of the Oval Office. Former mistresses had written tell-all accounts. There had been other, earlier eras in which the media had consisted of rapidly multiplying outlets competing desperately to see who could get the most attention with the loudest, shrillest and most scandalous reports. The political climate had been hyper-hot before, with partisans so intent on destroying the opposition they were willing to do anything, including underwrite investigations into a powerful man's darkest secrets. But the media had never been so hungry and salacious and the politics so mean and invasive at the same time that a president had been so randy and incautious.

Things calmed down considerably when Bill Clinton left the stage. The most important candidates seemed to have less dramatic bad habits; the media suspected that the public was exhausted with scandal in high places; politicians had learned that voters were unexpectedly willing to ignore bad behavior even if it was spotlighted, and therefore put less of a premium on revealing an opponent's personal sins. And when terrorists struck on September 11, the national dialogue shifted and focused on far more significant issues—at least temporarily. Michael Harrison believes the day the planes hit the World Trade Center, talk radio lost its interest in frivolous matters like sensational murders, runaway brides or politicians' personal lives. "When you have the issues of life and death, that stuff seems frivolous. It's not a growing up or maturation—it's just a different time."

The Parties: "If so, mention it modestly"

People used to *like* to belong to a political party. It was one of the ways they kept track of their own identities in a shifting, mobile society. It also greatly simplified the process of being a good citizen. If you knew you were a Democrat, you voted the party line and you did not need to study the League of Women Voters candidate summaries just to choose between two state senate hopefuls.

Even back in 1828, there were party image-makers who tried to maximize their candidates' good points. ("Does the old gentleman have prayers in his own house?" asked one of Andrew Jackson's handlers, Martin Van Buren. "If so, mention it modestly.") Their followers read newspapers that favored their party's side of things, and talked politics with people who shared their views. It was like belonging to a fraternal lodge or drinking club. That was one of the reasons that nineteenth-century voters turned out so eagerly for every election. They also happily spread rumors about the opposition candidates. It was part of the civic duty of preaching to the political heathen and helping the forces of justice to triumph.

The parties started losing their moral underpinnings around the turn of the century, when muckrakers published exposés about the corruption of the big-city bosses. Word got around that a really well informed citizen voted the man, not the party. Newspapers started to brag about being independent. Political gossip stopped being printed, and people stopped spreading it with quite as much avidity. Voter participation, unfortunately, plummeted.

A much bigger change occurred in the 1960s and 1970s, when Vietnam and Watergate left Republicans and Democrats—particularly Democrats—so alienated from their party bosses that they took away the power to nominate candidates. Instead of the smoke-filled room, there was the clean, well-lighted polling place. Nominating a president became a strange ritual that began years before the election, as hopeful politicians trotted out their wares before an indifferent nation. The real selection process telescoped into a few hectic months early in the election year, when candidates the public had hardly begun to focus on raced through a packed schedule of primary elections, most of which were conducted almost completely through TV ads.

The old system, under which political insiders picked the nominees, presumed that the decision-makers knew all the gossip about the candidates' personal lives and took it into consideration when they made their choices. It wasn't always true. (In 1920, when the party bosses asked Warren Harding if he had any secrets that might cause political problems, nobody seemed to think it was ominous that Harding thought for ten minutes before saying no.) But it was a sensible rationale for keeping rumors about candidates' private failings from the public. Once the voters took control of the nominations, however, it was inevitable that they would wind up being let in on the gossip, too.

Celebrity: Richard Gere and the Gerbil

Politicians are obviously not the only people whose personal lives get dissected by total strangers. For every story like that of Hillary's lamp there are a dozen popular legends about movie stars or rock singers or athletes, from the 1960s rumor that Paul McCartney was dead to the more recent one about Richard Gere and the gerbil. The gerbil story is a good example of the way gossip about entertainers has paralleled gossip about politicians. It also demonstrates the willingness of even family newspapers to print outrageous and unverified stories about famous people's personal lives. "Rumor: Richard Gere had a gerbil, the result of a bizarre sexual practice, removed from his rear end at a Los Angeles hospital in the mid-1980s" reported the *Indianapolis Star* in a sixteen-hundred-word rumor-roundup in 1997. "Fact: There has never been a verified medical case of a gerbil (or any other rodent) having been extracted from a patient's rectum."

The gerbil story's staying power was related to an anxiety as powerful as the one about overreaching women—fear of AIDS. It was basically a cautionary tale about unsafe sex, like the famous anti-hairspray legend from the 1960s about the girl with a lacquered beehive hairdo who died when poisonous spiders built a nest inside it. *Playboy* claimed the original gerbil story was a homophobic fable dating back to 1990 that was linked to Gere after "the actor had joked to a magazine writer about having performed some youthful indiscretion with a chicken." A *Los Angeles Daily News* columnist got it into print through the time-honored method of decrying the people who were spreading the gossip. A prankster then sent people in the Hollywood community a phony fax from the Association for the Prevention of Cruelty to Animals, attacking Gere for abusing a gerbil. Like the Hillary lamp story, the gerbil rumor reached a status where it could be referred to in shorthand. In a *Vanity Fair* profile of actor Keanu Reeves, author Michael Shnayerson claimed a rumor that Reeves was

17

having an affair with producer David Geffen "was everywhere. Like Richard Gere and gerbils."

The roots of American gossip about entertainment celebrities run back deep into the nineteenth century, when romantic schoolgirls used to fantasize about the brooding poet Lord Byron. After Byron's death, the writer Harriet Beecher Stowe started an incredible uproar by announcing that she knew for a fact Byron had slept with his own half sister. Stowe was trying to defend her friend, Byron's much-abused wife. But she soon discovered a lesson from the history of political gossip: There are some stories the public won't believe because they simply don't want to think prominent people *do* that kind of thing.

The class of entertainment celebrities that we know today was created around the 1880s, when people started moving to the cities, making money, acquiring leisure, and reading newspapers that celebrated the new heroes of sport and society and theater. In the early 1900s, movie stars were added to the mix. The public couldn't get enough information about these fabulous new creatures—even in the early years when the producers stubbornly refused to reveal their names. But the identities emerged, followed by movie magazines bearing information about their backgrounds, their romances, their hobbies and favorite foods and clothes.

This was a very important development for politics, which until then had been just about the only source of entertainment for most Americans, as well as the main provider of celebrities to talk about. For average people in the nineteenth century, being politically involved meant going to picnics, marching in parades, and drinking toasts to the party nominees, many of whom were depicted as cartoon-like embodiments of utter heroism or (to the opposition) utter depravity. Once times changed and the candidates were no longer connected to entertainment, they became more remote, more dignified, more boring.

In the 1920s, movie stars went through a sort of shakedown in which one scandal after another prompted newspapers to dump all the accumulated gossip about people like (accused killer) Fatty Arbuckle and (admitted drug addict) Wallace Reid onto the shocked readers. But once things quieted down, entertainers and politicians both sailed into that long period in which they were gossiped about in public only in the most harmless terms. Alcoholic senators would be described for public consumption as "colorful," even as the most dysfunctional of Hollywood marriages was referred to in euphemisms like "those battling Bogarts." While the plethora of movie magazines made it appear as if actors and actresses were perpetual gossip victims, the information that was actually printed was "totally sanitized," said gossip columnist Liz Smith, who started her own career writing for the magazines. "Louella Parsons might predict that if Clark Gable married Carole Lombard he'd be ruined, but there was enormous restraint," she said. "They'd never put in anything that reflected on the stars' morals."

The most important difference between the gossip about the two professions was that the public really wasn't much interested in the politicians anyway. That was an advantage in the 1950s, when entertainers were being tortured by scandal magazine exposés but politicians were deemed too uninteresting to humiliate. But with the advent of television, political candidates slowly tried to win the voters' attention and affection by sneaking into the world of entertainment. Each generation pressed the envelope a little further. The Richard Nixon who made the traditional, if somewhat bizarre, "Checkers" speech on television in 1952 became the Richard Nixon who tried to promote his presidential candidacy in 1968 with an appearance on *Laugh-In*.

When the studio system and the political parties broke down, both entertainers and politicians had to market themselves directly to the public—a process that involved embarrassment and ruined careers on both sides. But the same public indifference that protected politicians in the era of the scandal magazines forced them to expose themselves further and further in the eighties and nineties, as they desperately attempted to gain recognition. The deference bred by a combination of apathy and distance fell apart when presidential candidates began to appear on TV variety shows, when senators and governors vied to be interviewed by "shock-jock" radio hosts, and members of Congress volunteered to be "interviewed" on *The Colbert Report,* a parody of a conservative political cable show, in which the host barraged them with silly or hostile questions and commented on the quality of their toupees or hair-dos.

4. The Lessons of Political Gossip

A Gossip Theory of History

Viewing the history of American politics through the prism of gossip naturally tends to distort the perspective. We see Andrew Jackson without his war against the banks, Ulysses Grant without Reconstruction, and the Eisenhower administration with no Korean War. (The late nineteenth century, from our vantage point, is full of sex and devoid of the uproar over the silver currency issue, which some history students might see as an improvement.)

A great deal of the American experience is still there, however. The gossips of the pre–Civil War period would not have obsessed about politicians with black mistresses, whether real or imaginary, if the problem of slavery had not been reverberating everywhere. Public consciousness of the fight for women's rights expressed itself in a raft of rumors about wife-beating presidents. When the sexual revolution arrived after World War I, so did gossip about syphilitic politicians. Perhaps it was the ratcheting up of sexual awareness after World War II that created several generations of politicians, beginning with Adlai Stevenson, who managed to be gossiped about both as homosexuals and womanizers. Rumors about alcohol often mirrored the nation's hopelessly mixed feelings about drinking. The United States continually runs through cycles of heavy drinking, then temperance. When the country was on a backlash after a long period of enthusiastic imbibing, it tended to focus nervously on any signs of alcohol in the White House. Theodore Roosevelt, a modest social drinker, was tortured by stories that he was a drunkard in a period when temperance groups were trying to convince the nation that a single sip of beer was the first step toward perdition. Other presidents, from John Adams to Harry Truman, were permitted to enjoy their liquor in more relaxed eras, without setting off serious rumormongering.

Gossip about politicians provides an insight into what's bothering Americans—maybe not as precisely as a random cross-sample poll of the voting public, but with a little more flavor. Issues that create enormous anxiety in one generation may not even raise an eyebrow for another. For a long time, people regarded homosexuality as too awful even to be talked about. Our earliest gay politicians were protected from unfriendly gossip because people really couldn't connect the idea of homosexuality with the idea of a congressman or president. The very fact that rumors about which elected officials are gay are now tossed around so casually is an indication of how much more comfortable some parts of the electorate have gotten with the concept. On the other hand, in 1984 when Mississippi Republicans hired three black transvestite prostitutes to claim they had had sex with Democratic gubernatorial candidate Bill Allain, the public seemed to be adhering more to the earlier frame of reference. "The idea in Mississippi of a white gubernatorial candidate having sex with black transvestites just went beyond anything anyone was prepared to imagine," said a longtime student of state politics. Allain won the election.

"The iron had entered the soul and it rankled"

The most startling thing about gossip's impact on American politics is how seldom politicians' private behavior has mattered to the voters. When polls showed that the vast majority of people did not want to impeach Bill Clinton because of Monica Lewinsky, commentators on the Sunday morning talk shows moaned that the country had lost its moral compass. But they were poor students of history. The people who elected Thomas Jefferson president knew the stories about Sally Hemmings and chose not to act on them. In 1828, everyone knew that Andrew Jackson's wife had been a divorcee, and most knew that he had lived with her while she was still married to her first husband. Even so, Jackson was easily elected president. Rumors that Woodrow Wilson had broken his late wife's heart with his philandering may have cost him votes in 1916, but it did not cost him a second term. Voters made it clear during the Clinton impeachment trial that while they certainly didn't approve of their commander-in-chief having sex

21

with an intern, they didn't want to see him removed from office, either. A late-breaking revelation of a drunken driving incident came close to costing George Bush the presidency in 2000, but the drama of that election finale said much more about the near-even split in voters' political sentiments than any widespread revulsion against Bush's private character. Members of Congress have frequently survived what would appear to be disastrous personal scandals, from escapades with prostitutes to acute alcoholism to sex with a male Congressional page.

But the more lasting effect of a gossip-drenched political episode is the way it changes the targets of the rumors. A politician whose private life is subjected to whispering campaigns or media debate almost always emerges wounded, whether he or she is president or the humblest member of a city council. Some late-nineteenth-century scholars thought the effects of gossip on Andrew Jackson led directly to the Civil War. Grover Cleveland, who was not a warm public figure before his great gossip ordeal, became even less so afterward. "Made a victim of slander, the butt of scandal, his life belied, his character assailed, his habits misrepresented, his life explored even into the corners and accounts of it distorted, the iron had entered the soul and it rankled," wrote a friend.

In 1993, Hillary Clinton had been through a campaign in which her own marriage had been explored even into the corners, and she came to Washington with an intense distrust of the press and other outsiders. The fact that the newspapers had published the lamp story, the suspicion that the rumors had been started by members of the Secret Service assigned to guard her, the general feeling that everyone was *talking* about her private affairs, must have increased her sense of being surrounded by enemies. Soon, her concern for privacy would help propel the White House into its series of first-term disasters that often appeared to be cover-ups in search of a scandal.

As President Clinton was preparing for what then looked like a tough reelection campaign in 1996, his beleaguered wife went back on television to talk about what was by then a three-year-old rumor. "I mean, you know I have a pretty good arm," she told Barbara Walters. "If I'd thrown a lamp at somebody, I think you would have known about it."

Chapter 2

Public and Private Sinning

1776–1830

1. The Founding Fathers

*"Allowances must be made for occasional
effervescences"*

George Washington was a hero of almost godlike proportions to his
countrymen. "I could fall down on my knees before him," cried a
young woman in the crowd on his first Inauguration Day. In an age
before photography, Washington was the only major politician whose
features were familiar to the average citizen—cheap copies of his portrait hung in almost every American home, his face decorated por-
celain pitchers and bowls on every table. Unfortunately, since most
of the reproductions were terrible, his admirers probably weren't sure
of much beyond a large nose and receding hairline. But for average
Americans, his face was still as critical a unifying symbol as the flag.

Some of the other heroes of the Revolution, like John Adams,
couldn't understand why a man so ordinary, with no real intellect,
charm, or even all that much military talent, got such adoration. They

had done just as much to build the new nation, but *their* pictures weren't hanging in every American hut or mansion. Unsurprisingly, they enjoyed gossiping about his shortcomings. Washington, they sniped, was practically illiterate. He had been seen making a purchase in a shop, and was unable to count the change. He was so cheap he was practically a miser, and he had cheated a friend out of a piece of land. The last story upset Washington so much that he published a challenge daring his accusers to come forward and prove their charge.

Like human beings throughout history, Revolutionary-era Americans enjoyed hashing over the private failings of their acquaintances. But the Founding Fathers would not have connected that kind of talk with political gossip. (They wouldn't have thought of themselves as politicians, either.) The moral code they were concerned with was the one requiring that government be conducted at the highest ethical levels. The code was broken all the time, and *that* was shameful behavior a public man would want to keep hidden behind closed doors. So when Thomas Jefferson, that great cataloger, kept records of the political gossip of his era, he wrote about men acting out of selfish motives, going back on a bargain, lying about their intentions, or holding a secret sympathy for monarchism. In Jefferson's time, calling someone a self-interested politician was likely to lead to a challenge to a duel. No one regarded running the government as an amoral game of favor-trading. These people knew they were building a new nation, and they expected history to judge them on the basis of their public honor.

Even when they did dip into what we would think of as gossipy talk, it tended to reflect public concerns. Stories about John Adams often stressed his fondness for things British—a reflection of the ongoing dispute over whether the nation should side with Britain or France in international affairs. Perhaps the most inventive tale had him sending General Charles Pinckney to England to procure four beautiful mistresses for them to share. "I do declare on my honor, if this be true Gen. Pinckney has cheated me out of my two," retorted Adams. Imperious behavior was a favorite theme, reflecting the national fear of kings or dictators. Adams, who was naturally pompous, was always being accused of acting as if he had inherited the country, and newspapers printed rumors that he and his wife, Abigail, were plotting to marry off one of their sons into the British royal family. People were particularly keen on sniffing out any kingly pretensions on the part of George Washington. They knew the first president really could have made himself a monarch, and their gratitude to him for protecting the infant democracy was mixed with a certain amount of fear. The newspapers complained endlessly about the president's "court-like levees" and "queenly drawing rooms." But we have to look to the guests' private diaries and letters to get what a modern American might regard as the real dirt about Washington's social evenings, which was that they were very boring. ("Today I dined with the president and as usual the company was as grave as if at a funeral," wrote one of his supporters dolefully.)

Gossip about sex and private bad habits cropped up in daily conversation, of course. Wartime rumor gave Washington a Tory mistress in New Jersey, and his neighbors in Virginia regularly resurrected the story that he was the father of an illegitimate son. The boy in question was the offspring of an impoverished friend of the family. But in the eighteenth century whenever a great man took an interest in a youngster whose father was missing or unsatisfactory, rumors of illegitimacy were bound to follow. Washington, who was actually childless, once tried to float a rumor blaming his lack of progeny on his wife. He wrote friends that if Martha (who gave birth to four children during her first marriage) should die, he could easily produce heirs by marrying "a girl."

The governing elite might not have been seriously concerned with private morals, but they managed to make disagreements about things like tax policy or foreign affairs sound extremely personal. The newspapers favored a mad-dog rhetoric, like the *New England Courant*'s prediction that if Thomas Jefferson became president, "murder, robbery, rape and adultery and incest will be openly taught and practiced, the air will be rent with cries of distress, the soil soaked with blood and the nation black with crimes." By Washington's second term, he was no longer exempt from being called a "usurper with dark schemes of ambition." The president was even more sensitive about his reputation than most of his peers, and he privately regarded himself as more abused by the press than any man in history. (A remarkable number of his successors would lay claim to the same distinction.) "Allowances must be made for occasional effervescences," he wrote a friend gamely. But the assaults almost broke his faithful and unimaginative heart. He retired after his second term and was left mercifully alone until his death from pneumonia. The neighbors immediately speculated that the ex-president had caught the chill visiting a mistress on a rainy night.

"The intercourse with Mrs. Reynolds in the meantime continued"

The classic example of the Founding Fathers' concern with public honor came when Alexander Hamilton tried to acquit himself of charges of corruption by proving that he was an adulterer. In the 1790s, a journalist named James Callender was trying to demonstrate that Hamilton had abused his post as Washington's secretary of the treasury. He produced a mysterious correspondence between Hamilton and an embezzler named James Reynolds. The letters, Callender said, showed that the two men must have been plotting a raid on the public funds. Hamilton offered a different explanation: The suspicious letters actually referred to blackmail he was paying with his own money, to cover up his affair with Reynolds's wife.

The Reynoldses were shakedown artists who milked Hamilton for payoffs of more than one thousand dollars at a time when the average laborer made a dollar a day. The controversy over "the Reynolds affair" went on for a long time, and was distinguished by Hamilton's eagerness to broadcast the fact that he had repeatedly betrayed his much-admired wife, Elizabeth. Hamilton told his story privately to a delegation of congressmen, going into far more detail than the startled legislators said they required. But the disappointed Callender was determined to prove that "so much correspondence could not refer exclusively to wenching." He produced the lovely and extremely flexible Maria Reynolds, who weepily denied she had ever sinned with Hamilton. Ignoring his friends' pleas that he forget the matter, Hamilton insisted on proving his innocence as a public official and guilt as a private philanderer. So he produced a long pamphlet, giving all the details of his year-and-a-half-long affair.

"Some time in the summer of 1791 a woman called at my house in the city of Philadelphia and asked to speak to me in private," the confession began. Fascinated readers learned that the handsome Maria Reynolds described herself as a penniless, unprotected woman abandoned by a faithless husband. "I replied that her situation was a very interesting one," Hamilton understated. He offered to give her money, and added that it would be more "convenient" to deliver it to her home personally at a later hour. Mrs. Reynolds found it more convenient to receive Hamilton in her bedroom. "Some conversation ensued from which it was quickly apparent that other than pecuniary consolation would [also] be acceptable," he wrote. The meetings then shifted to his own house: "Mrs. Hamilton being absent on a visit to her father with her children . . . the intercourse with Mrs. Reynolds in the meantime continued."

The reaction of Hamilton's enemies was predictable. "Even the frosts of America are incapable of cooling your blood and the eternal snow of Nova Zembla would hardly reduce you to common propriety," thundered one editor. John Adams attributed Hamilton's overarching political ambition to "a super-abundance of secretions which he could not find whores enough to draw off." Less creative opponents never missed an opportunity from then on to refer to Hamilton as "Mrs. Reynolds's lover." Even Hamilton's friends believed he must have been in one of his not-infrequent states of hysteria when he decided to embarrass himself and his wife in such a dramatic way. But they understood his preference to be thought guilty of breaking his marriage vows rather than his public trust. Almost no one in Hamilton's circle would have prized family values nearly as much as public honesty. Benjamin Franklin's status never suffered because he had a common-law wife, or an illegitimate child by yet another woman. Benjamin Harrison, a signer of the Declaration of Independence, was known to be a regular patron of brothels and a seducer of slave women. He was also the author of a letter to George Washington that described his sexual adventures in a way that playfully suggested the general would want to be in on the action, too. The letter was captured by the British during the war and published, to Washington's utter humiliation. But Harrison went triumphantly on to be elected governor of Virginia and become the father and great-grandfather of two of America's most mediocre presidents.

"By this wench Sally our president has had several children"

James Callender's goal in humiliating Hamilton was typical for editors of his day: money or perhaps a no-show job in the bureaucracy like the one Thomas Jefferson got for his favorite editor, Philip Freneau. Callender was a bitter drunkard who left his family in miserable poverty in Scotland when he fled to America to escape imprisonment. He lived in the States only ten years before he drowned in three feet of water during a drinking spree in 1803. But in that time he made quite an impact, and was the source of much of the most sensational gossip we know about the Founding Fathers.

Callender first signed on with the pro-Jefferson faction and devoted himself to undermining Hamilton, Jefferson's political archenemy. But Callender's patrons soon decided that a smart, paranoid, undisciplined minion was likely to become far more trouble than he was worth. When he hinted he would like to be put up for a while at Jefferson's home at Monticello, Jefferson sent him fifty dollars and a suggestion that Philadelphia might be a good place to work. When he asked for a job as postmaster in Richmond, he was ignored. Frustrated, Callender switched sides. Moving south, he quickly discovered the omnipresent but unmentioned secret of miscegenation. He threw terror into Southern society by naming prominent gentlemen who had black mistresses or "dabble to some extent in African merchandize." The stories culminated in his famous charge that Jefferson kept the slave Sally Hemings as his mistress. "It is well known that the man, whom it delighteth people to honor, keeps . . . as his concubine, one of his own slaves. Her name is SALLY . . . By this wench Sally our president has had several children," the first article began. ". . . THE AFRICAN VENUS is said to officiate as housekeeper at Monticello."

None of the newspapers in Jefferson's time featured much in the way of reporting—they were more like a collection of editorials and vituperative essays. Callender was actually more diligent about the facts than many of his journalistic peers, and he was right in saying that the rumors about Sally were "well known" in the inner circles of Washington and Virginia society. Many prominent Americans and Europeans who had visited Monticello had taken note of the fact that some of Jefferson's young slaves looked a lot like their master. Callender didn't create the story, but he did spread the gossip to the outer loops of the political community—newspaper readers and the readers' own circles of friends. It spread so far that it reached thirteen-year-old William Cullen Bryant in Massachusetts. The precocious youngster published a long assault on the then-president that coupled foreign policy with sex. "And thou, the scorn of every patriot's name," he wrote,

> *Thy country's ruin and thy country's shame!*
> *Go wretch! Resign the Presidential chair*
> *Disclose thy secret measures foul and fair . . .*
> *Go scan, philosophist, thy [Sally's] charms;*
> *And sink supinely in her sable arms.*

Recent DNA tests of Sally's descendants indicate that the gossips—and Callender—were right. The stories, which were whispered before Jefferson became president and published before he was reelected in 1804, did not hurt his political career. But he was no doubt tortured by the newspaper articles, the pornographic songs, and the whispers that dogged him for the rest of his public life. "Of all the damsels on the green," sang the drinking men,

> *On mountain or in valley*
> *A lass so luscious ne'er was seen*
> *As Monticello Sally.*

> *Yankee Doodle, who's the noodle*
> *What wife was half so handy?*

> *To breed a flock of slaves for stock*
> *A blackamoor's a dandy.*

Callender helpfully printed the words in his newspaper.

2. 1828: The Scorpion Tongue of Political Slander

"The most bitter and wicked persecution in history"

The Adams family of Massachusetts had a tradition of setting standards so high that only one heroic heir per generation was able to meet them. As a result, the family tree contained a long line of superachievers with rigid personalities, as well as a quantity of suicidal alcoholics. John Adams, the second president of the United States, had three sons, two of whom wound up as pathetic failures. The other became John Quincy Adams, the sixth president of the United States and a paragon from the cradle whose childhood letters already read like little diplomatic reports. "I am," he wrote later in his diary, "a man of reserved, cold, austere and forbidding manners." John Quincy's rectitude seemed to infect everyone around him with a case of psychic frostbite. His youngest son, Charles, who would become the icy success story of the next generation, referred to his father as "the Iron Mask." Charles's older brother George suffered from a recurring nightmare in which his attempts at lovemaking were interrupted when John Quincy appeared above his head intoning: "Remember, George, who you are and what you are doing." Louisa Adams spent her White House years compulsively eating chocolates and writing an autobiography entitled *Adventures of a Nobody*.

Adams seemed like the most improbable candidate for a lead role in one of the most gossip-drenched presidential elections in history. The fact that he wound up being talked about as a pimp, gambler, and spendthrift was a tribute to the era's "Important If True" school of journalism, which never let lack of evidence stand between a newspaper and a useful rumor. But bad timing was what really betrayed him. John Quincy was a product of the Revolutionary Era, who was able to succeed in politics only as long as it remained an elitist game. He was elected in 1824 in the last of the old-time campaigns that were conducted through Washington dinner parties and gentlemanly deal-making. Even then, he nearly lost in a confusing one-party, four-way contest that wound up having to be resolved by Congress. The election was decided by a single vote, cast by an addled elderly representative from New York who saw a piece of paper bearing Adams's name on the floor and decided it must be a sign from God.

But four years later, almost all white male citizens were eligible to vote and the country was prepared for its first real mass popular election. The number of people voting for president would triple in 1828, and nearly half lived west of the Alleghenies. It was, an Illinois politician said sadly, the end of the good old days when candidates could travel around, meet the electorate personally, and "whisper slanders" about their opponents. To get to the hundreds of thousands of new voters, supporters of the presidential nominees were going to have to print the gossip they used to pass by word of mouth. And the East Coast traditionalists backing Adams were not sure what all these working men and subsistence farmers wanted to hear. Perhaps they didn't share the Founding Fathers' conviction that public virtue was far more important than private conduct. The common man's favorite author, Parson Weems (of George Washington's cherry-tree fame) had always said to look behind closed doors: "Public character is often an artificial one, and no evidence of true greatness."

If the fear of the new was not enough temptation to start a mud-slinging war, there was also the Adamsites' sinking realization that the opposition had the most charismatic candidate since George Washington. Andrew Jackson was a war hero, a man of the populous West, and even the possessor of the nation's first presidential nickname. His followers were organizing bonfires, barbecues, and torchlight parades in honor of "Old Hickory." The opposition could not exactly rally around the "Iron Mask." Winning the hearts and minds of more than a million common people was a whole new political game, and it became mean very fast. "The most bitter and wicked persecution in history," said Andrew Jackson, who was really not known for his sense of perspective.

Jackson had had a terrible childhood, even by eighteenth-century standards. His father died before he was born. Both his brothers died of illness and exposure while fighting in the Revolutionary War. Andrew, who was only fourteen, was taken prisoner. His mother caught cholera and died while nursing a nephew in a British prison ship. An angry child even before those multiple disasters, Jackson grew into an angry man, famed for his wild rages. As a young lawyer, he lost a case to a more experienced attorney, and immediately challenged his astonished opponent to a duel. He killed a man named Charles Dickinson in a duel over a horse-racing bet. Dickinson fired his single bullet first, wounding Jackson. Then he stood, quaking, while the bleeding Jackson calmly aimed at his chest and blasted a hole through his body. "I should have hit him if he had shot me in the brain," the winner muttered. He was, in a word, a person who tended to get talked about.

As he grew older, Jackson learned to use his temper as a tool, to terrify people into doing what he wanted. He was in his own way a cautious man, capable of enormous self-discipline. He settled in Tennessee, developed a thriving estate called the Hermitage, and made his name as commander of the Tennessee volunteers in the War of 1812. Jackson's victory at the Battle of New Orleans was such an enormous triumph—2,037 British dead, missing, or wounded, and only 71 American casualties—that it changed the nation's self-image. For the first time, Americans felt they were a major power, capable of handling the best Europe could throw at them. Old Hickory was a hero to the whole country, and the people of the West absolutely worshiped him. When he ran for president in 1824, Jackson actually came in first in the electoral vote. But it was a crowded race, with no one winning a majority. When Congress decided the runoff in Adams's favor, the general felt he had been swindled, and vowed revenge against the "corrupt bargain." The Adamses had barely moved into the White House before the Tennessee legislature nominated Jackson for president again in 1828.

It was the general's idea to turn that election into a referendum on character. He wanted to run against the "corrupt bargain" and the Washington establishment without making it clear where he stood on the big issues of the day—the tariff beloved by eastern manufacturers, or "internal improvements," the federal roads and bridges coveted by the underdeveloped West. "My real friends want no information from me on the subject of internal improvements and manufacturers, and I never gratify my enemies," he wrote to one of his organizers. But the problem with running on character is that it practically dares the opposition to prove you're a scoundrel, too.

"A convicted adulteress and her paramour husband"

When he was young, Andrew Jackson had fallen in love with Rachel Donelson Robards, his landlady's married daughter. They lived together while Rachel was still legally Captain Lewis Robards's wife. Her husband got a divorce on the grounds of adultery, and Rachel and Andrew were married in 1793. All that was fact, although the details of the story were the subject of gossip and speculation for the rest of Rachel's life. The illicit romance had been talked about all over Tennessee when it happened, and Jackson had fought duels with men who made remarks about his wife. Charles Dickinson, the man he killed over a racing bet, had made matters worse by sneering that the winning horse had run "about as far out of sight as Mrs. Jackson left her first husband when she ran away with the general." But by 1828, the Jacksons had been married thirty-five years. Rachel Jackson had become a "coarse-looking stout little old woman whom you might easily mistake for his washer-woman if it were not for the marked attention he pays her and the love and admiration she manifests for him," wrote the daughter of one of Jackson's officers. The young woman also reported that Mrs. Jackson appeared to great "disadvantage" in society, and that the ladies of Jackson's party kept close to her "apparently to save her from saying or doing anything which might do discredit to their idol."

Rachel hated politics and everything that kept her husband away from home—despite his legendary devotion, he spent three-quarters of their married life away from her. Childless, Rachel had raised many of her nieces and nephews as wards, as well as the children of friends and an orphaned Indian boy. (Jackson, who was always kind to people who were weaker than he was, had found the baby during his Indian campaigns, shipped it home to be raised as part of the family, and then returned his attention to wiping out the tribes east of the Mississippi.) Rachel seldom left Tennessee. Her life was the farm, her family, and religion—in her old age, she had become extremely pious. All in all, she was the worst possible candidate for bearing up under a campaign in which the opposition press demanded: "Ought a convicted adulteress and her paramour husband to be placed in the highest offices of the free and Christian land?"

Jackson's marriage was discussed only in whispers in 1824, when the general was a dark-horse candidate for president and Rachel actually went to Washington for a series of low-key social events. But during the trip a friend warned Jackson that the opposition had "papers" about his wife, and cautioned the general to be on guard.

"I know how to protect her," he growled. He didn't. Throughout the next campaign, Jackson would fume, fret, and predict dire consequences for the men who were defaming his wife's name. But he never challenged any of them to a duel, or even wrote an angry letter to the editor. The secret side of his nature—the cautious, ambitious side—knew silence was the best strategy.

The man most responsible for turning the Rachel story into a campaign issue was Charles Hammond, a Cincinnati lawyer and journalist. Hammond was a fierce Adamsite, but he was not the typical political hanger-on. He had once turned down a seat on the Supreme Court, and later he would face down a mob who came to tar and feather him over his abolitionist editorials. But Hammond's own well-loved wife had died in 1826, and the hard-drinking editor may have been unhinged by the loss. In 1827, he published his first exposé on the Jackson marriage in the *Cincinnati Gazette*. "In the summer of 1790, Gen. Jackson prevailed upon the wife of Lewis Roberts [sic] of Mercer County, Ky., to desert her husband and live with himself in the character of a wife," it began. His series of stories was reproduced in a pamphlet, "Truth's Advocate and Monthly Anti-Jackson Expositor." Jackson, stopping overnight in a Tennessee hotel, was serenaded by crowds waving banners that said: "The ABC of Democracy. The Adulteress, the Bully and the Cuckold."

"Oh, Andy, Andy," they sang,

> *How many men have you hanged in your life?*
> *How many weddings make a wife.*

John Eaton, Jackson's campaign strategist, prepared a defense. He wrote to the general's old friend John Overton, asking for information about Rachel's divorce, and for testimonials from local ministers. "Delicate as it may be to go into a man's family concerns, necessity demands that we should be at least possessed of the facts, that we may act defensively," he said. In a tradition of campaign aides that extends to the present, Eaton seems to have been willing to go to almost any lengths rather than ask the candidate himself for details of his sexual history.

The convoluted explanation Eaton and Overton produced was printed in the lead Jacksonian paper, *The United States Telegraph*: Rachel had fled from her abusive husband to Natchez, with Jackson going along to protect her during a dangerous journey. He left her there, but returned when he heard that Lewis Robards had been granted a divorce. They married, and returned to Nashville. Later, they discovered that Robards had only won permission to sue for divorce, a process that had taken two more years. The horrified couple then married legally. The story took up ten columns, but it still had some holes. Although probably not the best-read of lawyers, Jackson presumably knew enough law to understand how the divorce process worked. And his supporters had never been able to find any documentation of that Mississippi wedding.

The people spreading stories about Rachel were not concerned about evidence anyway. Thomas Arnold, a Tennessee congressional candidate, passed around a pamphlet describing the day Captain Robards "surprised Genl Jackson and his wife exchanging most delicious kisses." Over in Cincinnati, editor Hammond announced in his paper that "General Jackson's mother was a COMMON PROSTITUTE brought to this country by the British soldiers." Furthermore, Hammond claimed, "she afterward married a MULATTO MAN with whom he had several children, of which General JACKSON IS ONE!" Jackson's only public show of feeling came when his handlers let him out of Tennessee for a boat trip down the Mississippi to celebrate the anniversary of the Battle of New Orleans. When another steamboat attempted to maneuver in for a look at the war hero, Jackson tried to shoot the captain.

"The Pimp of the Coalition"

Duff Green, the editor of *The United States Telegraph*, was too ambitious to restrict his efforts on the general's behalf to a ten-column explanation of his marital entanglements. He prepared a counterattack, in the form of a story charging that John Quincy Adams had slept with Louisa before their marriage. "The whole Adams camp was thrown into consternation," he wrote Jackson proudly. (It was not for nothing that historian Frank Luther Mott called this period "the Dark Age of Partisan Journalism.") Jackson seems to have called him off, at least halfheartedly. "Female character should never be introduced by my friends, unless a continuation of attack should continue to be made against Mrs. Jackson. . . . I never war against females," he wrote. But after the election, Green was named the official printer for both houses of Congress. Later he was made governor of Florida and his son became minister to Russia.

Besides describing Louisa as a woman who slept with her fiancé before marriage, the Jackson forces also branded her a bastard. (Mrs. Adams's father, an American merchant living in England, had never mentioned having a wife until long after Louisa was born.) Some Adams paper actually picked the story up and spread it further, in a clumsy attempt to garner sympathy for the First Family. FATHERS! HUSBANDS! BROTHERS! bannered the *Marion* (Pa.) *Pioneer*.

READ. PAUSE. REFLECT. AND THEN
VOTE FOR JAMES BUCHANAN IF YOU CAN.

The paper accused Buchanan, then an up-and-coming Jacksonian politician, of gossiping "within the hearing of two or more respectable witnesses that Mrs. Adams, the wife of the chief Magistrate, was born out of wedlock." It had obviously been a slow news day.

Louisa Adams actually bore up better under these assaults than her thin-skinned husband. "Put a little wool in your ears and don't read the papers," she advised coolly when he moaned about the "public ridicule" after a paper claimed he frequently went to church barefoot. By middle age, Louisa was no longer the tender bride who wept about the "scorpion tongue of political slander" when a Boston paper described her as an Englishwoman. She had buried her only daughter, lived for decades with three generations of Adams men, and ridden across Europe in midwinter during the Napoleonic War, alone in a carriage with her small son, crossing icy fields littered with thousands of dead soldiers. These days she was a lot harder to upset.

Not to be outdone by Duff Green, Isaac Hill, the short, cranky, almost skeletal editor of the *New Hampshire Patriot*, came up with the story that Adams had served as a pimp for Czar Alexander of Russia. In a footnote to his glowing Jackson campaign biography, Hill charged that Adams was the "panderer of an Autocrat." It was a footnote heard round the world. Hill claimed that when Adams was minister to Russia, the czar had taken a fancy to the Adams children's pretty nanny, and expressed a desire to examine her as a potential addition to the imperial stable of mistresses. John Quincy, Hill said, obligingly sent the unknowing girl to walk where Alexander could watch her. Fortunately, "the lascivious monarch" judged the girl "less voluptuous than his gorged appetite could relish." But the depraved ambassador and his wife, Hill claimed, later freely recounted the "story of their shame."

The idea that Adams, who devoted much of his honeymoon to washing rouge off Louisa's cheeks, entertained his guests with the tale of how he set up the children's nurse with the czar of Russia was far-fetched even for 1828. But the story spread quickly through the chain of Jackson-supported papers, reaching almost every part of the country. Adams's skill as a diplomat was the great pride of his career—even today he is regarded as possibly the greatest American secretary of state. But Jackson's partisans happily said that Hill's footnote revealed the real secret of his success, and they dubbed Adams "the Pimp of the Coalition." After the election, Hill became a member of Jackson's "Kitchen Cabinet" of advisers and a U.S. senator.

But a rumor that did Adams the most damage involved a second-hand billiard table the workaholic president purchased under the delusion he might enjoy a relaxing game now and then. Senator Thomas Hart Benton wrote a much-quoted anonymous letter to *Ritchie's Enquirer* accusing Adams (who paid for the table himself) of spending twenty-five thousand dollars in public money on all kinds of gambling devices, including the billiard table, backgammon board, dice, chess, and—peculiarly—"soda water." Benton was a Jackson supporter. They had once been on opposite sides of a barroom brawl and shoot-out that left the general with a permanently crippled arm. But neither man regarded attempted murder as an excuse for permanent political rupture. As Benton's letter moved west through Jackson's string of papers, Adams was described as more and more of a profligate. "The people here think a less splendid establishment might do," warned an Ohio supporter, adding that Adams could not have chosen a sin more calculated to irritate the sensibilities of western voters.

The billiard table story reverberated more than any of the other gossip spread during the campaign, because it was what the voters in the newer parts of the country wanted to believe about the eastern establishment—that they were living in the lap of luxury off the taxes of virtuous and hardworking western farmers. The public was also picking up on something pinched about Adams's character, which made it pleasant to think he was trying to get the government to pay for his billiard balls and fizzy water. Adams's backers believed the rumor did him serious damage. Andrew Jackson, on the other hand, was inoculated against nasty personal stories by his own long-standing fame. He won the election, 647,276 votes to 509,064.

"In the presence of this dear saint . . ."

The attacks on Rachel Jackson had failed to make a dent with the public, but they had an enormous effect on Rachel, and the president-elect. It's not certain how much Rachel heard about the stories being spread about her during the campaign. But she probably knew—or suspected—plenty. "The enemys of the Genls have dipt their arrows in wormwood and gall and sped them at me," she wrote a relative. "Almighty God was there ever aney thing to equal it. My old acquentances wer as much hurt as if it was themselves or Daughters. To think that thirty years have passed in happy society, knowing and thinking ill of no one . . ." Rachel had no desire to be First Lady, and she agreed only reluctantly to go to Nashville and buy a dress for the inauguration. The story of that fateful shopping expedition has been passed down for generations like this: After purchasing her gown, Rachel stopped to rest at the office of the local newspaper editor while her friends continued their errands. While waiting, she chanced upon a copy of "Truth's Advocate" and discovered, for the first time, how vicious the stories about her had been. Her companions found her huddled in a corner of the office, weeping hysterically. On the way home she stopped to wash her face in a creek so her husband would not see she had been crying.

Whatever happened to Rachel in Nashville, it was quickly followed by an apparent heart attack. She recovered, then had a second attack three days before Christmas. Her maid found her sitting by the fire in the middle of the night, smoking her pipe and muttering an old refrain about the White House: "I'd rather be a doorkeeper in the house of God than to live in that palace." A few minutes later she collapsed and died. Jackson, inconsolable, refused to leave her side. The doctor ordered Rachel's body laid out on a table, and the president-elect told his servants to put four blankets down first. "Then if she does come to, she won't lie so hard on it," he told them. Visitors found him sitting by the corpse, stroking her hair.

Even Rachel's death did not quiet all her critics. "She was indeed a fortunate woman," sniped the *New York American*, which claimed Mrs. Jackson had expired just in time to save herself from the humiliations that would have greeted her in Washington. But ten thousand people came to the funeral, many of whom had loved Rachel for reasons totally unrelated to her husband's fame. She was buried in the white dress she had purchased for the inaugural. "In the presence of this dear saint," Jackson wept, "I can and do forgive my enemies. But those vile wretches who slandered her must look to God for mercy." He never recovered from her loss. During his presidency, Jackson was hosting a lively dinner at the Hermitage when the guests noticed the president had vanished. One of the women went to look for him, and found him stretched across Rachel's grave.

3. The Washington Gossip Wars

"Married his mistress—and the mistress of
eleven doz. others!"

President-elect Andrew Jackson arrived in Washington a crushed and bitter man, convinced that the campaign gossip had killed his wife. Incredibly, he was almost immediately confronted with an opportunity to defend a female friend whose chastity was being maligned in Washington society. Peggy O'Neale Timberlake was the beautiful and rambunctious daughter of a Washington innkeeper who had entertained Jackson during his brief career as a U.S. senator. Peggy, he had written to Rachel, "plays the Piano delightfully, and every Sunday evening entertains her pious mother with sacred music, to which we are invited." But Peggy had another side. Before she was married at sixteen, one man had committed suicide over her. One elopement had been prevented when Peggy accidentally knocked over a flowerpot, alerting her ever-vigilant father. Another was canceled by the bride-to-be herself when she grew cold to her beloved because of "a foolish speech he made upon returning my pocket-handkerchief."

Her husband, John Timberlake, was a Navy purser. While he was off serving his country, Peggy was often seen in the company of John Eaton, the Tennessee senator who helped run Jackson's campaign. Peggy denied to her death that she had ever been unfaithful, but Washington society was convinced she and Eaton were lovers. The gossip hit an absolute crescendo when word arrived that Timberlake had died at sea after cutting his own throat, and Eaton married the widow. (Peggy claimed that he killed himself during the delirium of an asthma attack.)

Whatever sins Peggy had committed, the gossip about her ran far ahead of her worst possible crimes. A Delaware senator reported Eaton had "married his mistress—and the mistress of eleven doz. others!" A prominent clergyman passed around the story that when Peggy was still Mrs. Timberlake, she had summoned a physician to the family home to treat her after a carriage accident. The minister told his friends that when the doctor arrived, Peggy and her mother laughingly announced that she had just miscarried "a little John Eaton." That the famously religious Mrs. O'Neale would make sport of her daughter's adultery and miscarriage is about as likely as John Quincy Adams pimping for the czar. But the gossip reflected the intense social anxiety in Washington about Jackson and his followers. The capital was only a few generations away from swampland and pig farms, and its society had always drawn assurance from the prestige of the president. Now, the son of an impoverished carpenter had arrived from the far West, leading a pack of riffraff that poured into the White House during his inauguration, breaking china and ruining furniture. The Jacksonians were just the sort of people to marry strumpets, Washingtonians told each other. The more they vented their fears, the more outrageous the talk about Peggy became. "Poor Eaton is to be married tonight to Mrs. T!" wrote a New York congressman. "There is a certain vulgar saying of some vulgar man, I believe Swift, on such unions. About using a [chamber pot] and then putting it on one's head."

There was nothing Peggy could have done to endear herself to the president more than becoming a social pariah. "I would rather have live vermin on my back than the tongue of one of these women on my reputation," he told her. Jackson sent a three-thousand-word handwritten letter to the gossiping clergymen arguing, with touching though lunatic reasoning, that Eaton could not have cuckolded Peggy's husband because both men were Masons. The letter was, people noted in awe, longer than his inaugural address. Jackson sent emissaries up the eastern seaboard, checking inn registrars to prove

Eaton and Mrs. Timberlake had never taken a room together. He amassed testimony from eighty-nine women who were prepared to swear Peggy was a faithful wife to Purser Timberlake. He got affidavits from former residents of the O'Neale hotel, from Timberlake's fellow navy officers. He called together the Cabinet and announced that he had gathered the nation's top officials "to obtain justice for her, for myself, and for our country." He ended the meeting by declaring Peggy O'Neale Timberlake Eaton was "chaste as a virgin."

The Peggy issue dominated the first part of Jackson's administration. He named Eaton secretary of war, and insisted that Peggy be given the social deference due to the wife of a Cabinet member. But the other Cabinet wives refused to speak to Peggy at balls, or attend her dinners, or include her in the endless round of afternoon visiting and card-leaving that formed a central part of their lives. "After a thousand rumors and much tittle-tattle and gossip . . . public opinion, ever just and impartial, seems to have finally triumphed over personal feelings and intrigues and doomed her to continue in her pristine and lowly condition," wrote Washingtonian Margaret Bayard Smith triumphantly. Andrew Jackson Donelson, the president's nephew and closest aide, was forced to retreat to Tennessee when his young wife, Emily, refused to socialize with Peggy.

What became known as the Ladies War reshaped the political landscape. Secretary of State Martin Van Buren, a canny widower, was free to follow the president's directives and make a fuss over the Eatons, thus nailing down his own future role as Jackson's successor. "The political history of the United States for the last thirty years dates from the moment when the soft hand of Mr. Van Buren touched Mrs. Eaton's knocker," wrote a Jackson biographer in 1860. He was one of the many nineteenth-century historians who looked at Peggy Eaton and saw the beginning of a road that stretched directly to the Civil War. That was because of the profound effect the affair had on Jackson's relationship with his vice president, John Calhoun.

Calhoun was a brilliant, humorless, and wildly ambitious ex-senator from South Carolina, a man who had once expressed the conviction that a yellow fever epidemic in Charleston was God's punishment for that city's "sins and debaucheries." His wife, Floride, was a well-born southerner who adamantly refused to have anything to do with Peggy. That was the beginning of Calhoun's break with Jackson and the end of his own presidential hopes. His admirers have argued that if Calhoun had been kept in the mainstream of the Democratic party, he could have helped avert war until the South agreed to give up the uneconomical institution of slavery on its own. (One monograph proposing this theory was called "Peggy O'Neale, or the Doom of the Republic.") It's an analysis that ignores the far more substantial issues that created a wedge between the two men. But one person who seemed to see a straight line from the Ladies War to the War Between the States was Calhoun himself. Years later, he recalled the fatal day when Mrs. Calhoun announced she would "not return Mrs. Eaton's visit" in terms of doom more appropriately reserved for the burning of Atlanta or the assassination of Abraham Lincoln. "I have heard that a drowning man will sometimes see, at a glance, his whole past life and at these words it seemed to me as though the future was shown to me in as sudden and vivid a manner," he wrote. Envisioning the panorama of events that led to the great conflict, Calhoun apparently did not consider telling his wife that a brief visit to the Eatons might be better than a civil war. He believed in suffering for your standards.

Life After Gossip

In the spring of 1831, Eaton and Van Buren resigned in order to end the Peggy crisis and allow the president to get rid of his pro-Calhoun appointees by dissolving the whole Cabinet. Eaton became a diplomat and took Peggy off to Spain, where they apparently lived happily for years until his death. As an aging widow, Peggy married her daughter's dancing teacher, forty years her junior. He stole all her money and ran off with her granddaughter.

To almost everyone's shock, John Quincy Adams accepted a nomination to the House of Representatives and served there until his death eighteen years later. It was considered a demeaning comedown by his family. But Adams, an instinctive senior citizen, finally hit his stride as an elderly congressman, arguing bravely and crankily for the abolition of slavery for seventeen years, before he collapsed on the floor of the House and died.

Chapter 3

Gossip and Mutating Morals

1830–1880

1. Politics as Entertainment

"It engrosses every conversation"

In the years that followed Andrew Jackson's first election, people became absolutely crazy about politics. "It engrosses every conversation," complained a visiting Englishwoman. At a time when the vast majority of Americans were living lives of endless drudgery, politics—along with religion—was the national pastime. The parties were like fraternal lodges, and the faithful rooted for their candidates as if they were a local baseball team. There were, of course, no real baseball teams in the middle of the nineteenth century. There were virtually no entertainments at all. It was an era when most people were isolated on farms, or in small towns where even simple pleasures like card-playing and dancing were considered immoral. It didn't take the political parties long to figure out that the best way to win the loyalty of voters was to amuse them. People could watch fireworks or attend barbecues in honor of a candidate with the pleasant feeling that they were performing their patriotic duty while having a good time. In small towns, they expressed their support for the Democrats or Whigs or Republicans by trying to raise the highest pole, or by rolling a huge, canvas-covered ball decorated with slogans from one town to the next. In the cities, the parties sponsored marching bands with gorgeous uniforms and parades with floats and caged eagles and trained bears.

The candidates who prospered in these times tended to be military heroes, well-suited for posters and parades, if not necessarily to running the country. (General Zachary Taylor, "Old Rough and Ready," had never even *voted* before he was nominated for president.) They were media creations before there was even much of a media, and since very few of the voters would ever really see them, they could be far more mythic than any modern politician. William Henry Harrison, the son of a Virginia governor, was repackaged in 1840 as a grizzled veteran of simple virtues, the "log cabin and hard cider" candidate. (Harrison defensively claimed a part of his sixteen-room Ohio house *had* been a cabin once.) In 1852, when the new craze of photography allowed pictures of the candidates to circulate for the first time, the handsome Franklin Pierce, a recovering alcoholic with a rather dismal record of fainting spells during the Mexican-American conflict, was presented as a glamorous war hero.

In the pre–Civil War era, when politicians tried to adopt the aura of a cartoon action figure, some of the gossip naturally was aimed at undermining their heroic appeal. Harrison was rumored to have been a coward—"Granny Harrison, the petticoat general"—and Pierce was derided as "victor of many a hard-fought bottle." There was also a great deal of talk about illegitimacy, which may have had a double meaning at a time when many of the candidates could reasonably have been called phonies. Virtually every presidential contender was rumored to be either a bastard or the father of a second secret family—sometimes both. Martin Van Buren was said to be the illegitimate son of Jefferson's vice president Aaron Burr. Abraham Lincoln and Andrew Johnson both tried to clear their dead mothers' reputations by documenting their legitimacy, but to no effect. John Frémont, the dashing young explorer whom the Republicans nominated for president in 1856, really was born on the wrong side of the blanket—his mother had run away from her harsh husband with Frémont's father, a French dance teacher. But the candidate was tortured by the way the story was twisted during his campaign. "His mother was a strumpet of a Richmond brothel," orated Henry Wise, the governor of Virginia.

"Designed to resemble an Amazon's bosom"

The gossip of every election is very much a product of the issues and anxieties of the moment. When a terrible recession hit at the beginning of Martin Van Buren's presidency, hard times made the country very sensitive to rumors that politicians were living high on the hog. Van Buren, who really did enjoy the good life, was absolutely deluged by gossip about conspicuous consumption. (A set of golden spoons, which had been purchased by a White House predecessor, figured prominently in the stories.) Congressman Charles Ogle of Pennsylvania made a sensation with his charge that Van Buren had landscaped the White House lawn with mounds, "every pair of which . . . was designed to resemble AN AMAZON'S BOSOM with a miniature knoll or hillock at its apex to denote the nipple."

Harrison, who defeated Van Buren in 1840, was a well-bred underachiever, whose last military victory lay thirty years in the past. But the Whigs marketed him as the plain-living, cider-drinking Indian fighter who had saved the western settlers at the battle of the Tippecanoe River. The idea was for Harrison to stay home and keep quiet while his supporters bought "Tippecanoe Shaving Soap" and danced the "Hard Cider Quick Step" and "Log Cabin Waltz." But Harrison had feelings. He did not seem disturbed by the rumors that he had lived with an Indian woman and sired a second family, but he was tormented by gossip that he was feeble, senile, or perhaps even dead. ("A living mass of ruined matter," claimed one editorial.) To prove he was not "a very decrepit old man, obliged to hobble about on crutches," he became the first presidential candidate to go out on the campaign trail himself, giving very loud and long speeches to prove his virility. He gave the longest one of all on Inauguration Day in a cold rain, and died a month later of pneumonia. It set a record for the impact of gossip on a presidency.

The stories people passed around about their highest officials in the pre–Civil War decades were not subtle, and generally aimed at the lowest common denominator. It was not a genteel age, and newspapers were still very much into the "Important If True" mode. Perhaps people also felt free to belittle politicians who were presented very much like performers in a circus. Congressman Davy Crockett described President Van Buren as "laced up in corsets such as women in town wear . . . it would be difficult to say from his personal appearance whether he was a man or a woman, but for the large red and gray whiskers." Frémont, who had been caught in a blizzard during one of his expeditions, was rumored to have eaten some of the other members of his party. Congressman Thaddeus Stevens of Pennsylvania, an acid-tongued cynic with a clubfoot, was said to have committed blasphemy by administering communion to a dog. Representative Stevens had gotten his own start in politics by claiming the Masonic order, to which Henry Clay belonged, was a "prostituted harlot" whose members drank wine out of human skulls.

The suspicion that politicians were not really what they seemed interacted with a national xenophobia that surged in the 1850s. The immigration rate quadrupled in those years, and the latest generation of arrivals, particularly the Catholic Irish, were blamed for crime, unemployment, and other assorted social ills. The public was susceptible to rumors that candidates were secret Catholics or Catholic fellow travelers. Frémont, the son of a French émigré, naturally was a particular target. "Scarcely any [field report] omits a reference to the fact that the Catholic story injures us materially," wrote one of his lieutenants from the Northwest. The stories about Frémont, who was actually an Episcopalian, had the tenor of the old Salem witch trials— that he had been overheard at a restaurant declaring his belief in the doctrine of transubstantiation, or that "when offered a book by a friend, he refused to read it on the ground of his being a papist."

A Brief Diversion—the Trial of Daniel Sickles

In 1859, one of Buchanan's close political allies, Representative Daniel Sickles of New York shot and killed the local district attorney, Phillip Barton Key, who had been having an affair with Sickles's young wife. The congressman became the first American to win an acquittal from murder charges by pleading temporary insanity. It's worth stopping to take a look at what happened, both for what it shows us about the attitudes toward sex and marriage in the mid-1800s and because the Sickles case was a forerunner of the gossipy trials-of-the-century that would soon begin occurring every decade or so.

Daniel Sickles was a New York lawyer, "one of the bigger bubbles in the scum of the profession, swollen and windy and puffed out with fetid gas," wrote diarist George Templeton Strong, a contemporary. He was a small, handsome man of stupendous daring, energy, and dissipation. He was rumored to have seduced his own mother-in-law. As a state legislator, he was censured for bringing his prostitute-mistress Fanny White onto the floor of the Assembly. When he was thirty-three, he married the beautiful sixteen-year-old Teresa Bagioli, and then left her in New York while he took Fanny White with him to England as part of the American delegation.

New York's Tammany Hall machine sent Sickles to Congress in 1856. There, the long-neglected Teresa fell in love with Phillip Key, the handsome nephew of the author of "The Star Spangled Banner." Everyone in Washington except Sickles seemed to know about the affair. "She was so young and fair, at most not more than 22 years old, and so naive that none of the party of which I was one was willing to harbor a belief in the rumors which were then in circulation," wrote a senator's wife who attended a dinner at the congressman's house. Teresa and Key had regular trysts in an apartment in a working-class neighborhood on Fifteenth Street that, the local residents noticed, was furnished with little more than a bed. The Sickleses' own neighbors off Lafayette Square talked about the way Key walked by Teresa's window and signaled her by waving a handkerchief in a "rotary motion."

When Sickles discovered he was being cuckolded, he confiscated

49

his sobbing, repentant wife's wedding ring and forced her to write an account of her Fifteenth Street assignations. ("There was a bed in the second story. I did what is usual for a wicked woman to do.") The next morning, when Key walked by, waving the handkerchief, Sickles grabbed his gun and shot Key several times as the writhing victim screamed for mercy. "Is the damned scoundrel dead yet?" the congressman demanded as he was led away.

What happened next was an excellent example of how judicial proceedings can create a form of hyper-gossip. There was no question about the basic facts—Teresa Sickles and Key had been lovers, and Daniel Sickles shot Key. But the side issues kept Washington and New York talking for months. As the trial approached, people passed along the old story about Sickles having seduced his mother-in-law, and a new one that he had forced his wife to sleep with his close friend, President James Buchanan. Teresa was also rumored to be pregnant by Key.

The nation's establishment lined up behind the congressman. President Buchanan himself convinced a critical witness to the shooting to leave town, and the prosecution, which had evidence of Sickles's own infidelities, chose not to mention them. "We may somewhat account for the seeming tenderness and extreme delicacy of the prosecution on remembering that the accused was a fast friend of the highest officer in the nation," wrote the *Baltimore Patriot*. While the defendant sat in the prisoner's cage in the courtroom, sobbing loudly, his lawyers referred to Teresa as a "prostitute" and argued that their client, maddened by grief, had been following the "unwritten law" that justifies a husband for avenging his defiled marriage bed. When the jury brought back a verdict of not guilty, the courtroom erupted into cheers.

Once he was free, Sickles offered to take his wife back, and Teresa, who was being shunned by everyone from old friends to the corner grocer, responded enthusiastically. But when the reconciliation was announced, all society shrank back in horror. "His warmest personal and political friends bitterly denounce this course," wrote the *New York Dispatch*. Almost every New York newspaper felt compelled to editorialize on the subject, and only Horace Greeley in the *Tribune* applauded the idea of forgiving the fallen woman. When Sickles returned to Congress the next term, he was a pariah—not because he had killed the district attorney, but because he had supported his wife's sin by resuming the marriage. "He was as left to himself as if he had the smallpox," wrote a woman visiting Washington. The Civil War saved Sickles's reputation. He became general of a Union battalion raised by his friends, and was hailed as a hero of the Battle of Gettysburg—where he lost both a leg and four thousand men under his command. He was rewarded with an appointment as ambassador to Spain. Teresa remained in New York, a virtual prisoner in their home. She died at the age of thirty-one.

2. The Gossip That Dare Not Speak Its Name

"If Old Buck loves anybody in the world . . ."

Despite the bitterness of the times, there was at least one politician whose personal life did not get bandied about in campaigns. Schoolchildren with a taste for trivia know that Democrat James Buchanan, who defeated Frémont in 1856, was the only bachelor president. From our vantage point, it also seems pretty obvious that he was a homosexual. But Washington's inner circle, which had been so eager to believe the most outrageous gossip about Peggy Eaton, John Frémont, and other politicians of the era, never spoke directly about Buchanan's sexual preferences.

As a senator, Buchanan shared lodgings with Senator William King of Alabama, another middle-aged bachelor. Hostesses invited King and Buchanan to parties as a couple, and all of Washington referred to them as "the Siamese twins" because they were so inseparable. Some people had snider terms. When Buchanan was sent to Europe as an ambassador, a Tennessee congressman wrote a gossipy letter to James Polk's widow, Sarah, in which he referred to King as Buchanan's "better half" and reported that the two were apparently seeking "a divorce." Andrew Jackson, who thought Buchanan was a meddlesome busybody, called King "Miss Nancy."

As president, Buchanan became intensely attached to his secretary of the treasury, Howell Cobb, the former governor of Georgia. "If Old Buck loves anybody in the world, that man is Gov. Cobb," wrote a friend. When Cobb's latest child was born in Georgia, the treasury secretary tried unsuccessfully for three months to go home and retrieve his wife. But Buchanan resisted letting him out of his sight. Cobb finally wrote his wife promising to come to get her "whether the President will permit me or not." But he wound up sending an assistant instead. Kate Thompson, another Cabinet wife, confided that she felt there was "something unhealthy" in the president's attitude.

That was about as far as the gossip went. No newspaper or political pamphleteer or stump speaker ever seems to have charged that Buchanan was what people then called a sodomist. Even the voluble Kate Thompson never came right out and questioned the president's sexuality. Compare this to Washington's reception of Peggy Eaton—its readiness to accept the adultery rumors as fact and then expand upon the story, adding shocking fictions about Peggy and her mother laughing over the miscarried fetus of her illegitimate child. The capital did not regard homosexuality as a lesser crime than adultery. Just the opposite—Buchanan was protected by the fact that society thought homosexuality was so awful that it could only be committed by the dregs of society. Prison reports lumped it under "crimes against nature," along with having sex with animals.

All the normal pleasures of spreading gossip—the sense of importance it gives the teller, the bonding effect between confidants—are lost if the story being spread is so disgraceful it degrades both teller and listener. Homosexuality was so off the screen for respectable Americans in the mid-nineteenth century that it was easy to practice. It was, as one historian noted "viewed as so terrible and so unnatural that it was not considered as having any connection with tender, affectionate [and sometimes erotic] relations between men." Civil War–era males treasured intense friendships that modern Americans might regard as drenched with sexual overtones. They also slept together as a practical necessity. (An early American etiquette book solemnly warned its readers that it was impolite to press up against a stranger with whom one was sharing a bed.) Andrew Jackson slept with his closest friend, John Overton, when the two men were bachelors in Tennessee. Overton, an attorney and later judge, devoted most of his life to promoting Jackson's career. Abraham Lincoln shared a bed for three years with Joshua Speed, a storekeeper who became a close friend (and charged him rent for the use of half the mattress). Women also slept together as a matter of course—chilly houses made any sort of warmth welcome once the sun went down and the fires were banked. Anxiety over homosexuality was so low that no one ever questioned what went on during those long-standing sleeping arrangements.

3. The Obsessive Underlying Anxiety

"His mistresses are generally colored women"

One of the reasons elections in the pre–Civil War era were being fought over golden spoons and Henry Clay's gambling debts was because no one knew how to deal with the overriding issue of slavery. The national leaders tried to distract people with barbecues and debates over foreign policy while they papered over the problem with one compromise after another. The mixture of economics and race that slavery embodied was poisonous, and the voters' own attitudes were utterly conflicted. Like homosexuality, the matter of miscegenation produced peculiar reactions, which were simultaneously explosive and muted.

Richard Johnson, Van Buren's vice president (1837–1841), was widely known to have lived for years with Julia Chinn, a slave he inherited from his father. Chinn ran his house and bore him two daughters. Yet he was one of Kentucky's most beloved politicians. Most people in Johnson's time didn't seem to regard a southern gentleman's sexual relations with his slaves as a damning fault, as long as the people involved didn't acknowledge it was happening. (Mary Boy-

kin Chesnut, a plantation owner's wife, noted wryly that every southern lady "tells you who is the father of all the Mulatto children in
everybody's household, but those in her own she seems to think drop
from the clouds—or pretends so to think.") In Johnson's home state,
the aspect of his private life that seemed to trouble people most was
whether he treated Chinn and their daughters as if they were white.
The most damning gossip was stories that he had placed his daughters
at the same table as white guests, and that he demanded they be seated
on the pavilion when he gave speeches. In 1836, *The United States
Telegraph* assailed Johnson's "connection with a jet-black thick-lipped
odiferous Negro wench, by whom he has reared a family of children
whom he had endeavored to force upon society as equals." In response, *The Washington Globe* printed a testimonial from the girls'
tutor attesting that while Imogene and Adaline were intelligent, attractive women of high character, "no attempt was made to impose
them on society; and although they are well-educated, they never entered a schoolhouse for that purpose."

The closer the nation came to the Civil War, the more bitter political gossip became. The northern abolitionists and southern slave-
holders both regarded their opponents as utterly deficient in sense
and morality, and they were ready to believe them capable of anything
bad. Jane Swisshelm, one of the first female journalists in Washington,
was a passionate abolitionist who arrived in the nation's capital in
1850 eager to learn (and write) the worst about southern politicians
who defended slavery and the northern lawmakers who advocated
compromise on the issue. It made for some creative reporting. She
told her readers, for instance, that one of former president John Tyler's daughters had been caught trying to run away from home and
was sold into slavery at her angry father's orders. Most famously, she
wrote that Senator Daniel Webster was an alcoholic who had a second
family of eight children by a black woman. "His mistresses are generally, if not always, colored women—some of them big black
wenches as ugly and vulgar as himself," she wrote in a dispatch to her
Pittsburgh newspaper that did not do much credit to her egalitarian
politics. Later, when asked for proof, Swisshelm said she had heard

stories that Webster paid the rent and grocery bills of a mulatto woman and her children. (The grocery bills may have referred to food ordered for the senator by his black housekeeper.) Since Webster's "whole life was full of rottenness," Swisshelm decided the woman and children must be his secret second family.

Not surprisingly, the rumors about Abraham Lincoln among southerners and southern sympathizers were exceptionally vicious. He was described as an idiot, a gorilla, and a monster. On a more down-to-earth level, Lincoln, a lemonade drinker, was repeatedly portrayed as an alcoholic. After South Carolina attacked Fort Sumter, southerners assured each other, the president was "so drunk he could hardly maintain his seat in the chair." Lincoln's enemies frequently claimed the man who freed the slaves was black himself. Gossip about "Negro blood" was common in political campaigns of the period. Martin Van Buren, John Tyler, and Andrew Johnson were all rumored to be part black. Charles Sumner, the abolitionist senator, had been subject to those rumors for years. "Who is Sumner? A free American of African descent," said a racist publication called "The Lincoln Catechism." The catechism, which was widely distributed during the Civil War, called the president "Abraham Africanus the First." But Lincoln, who received letters every day threatening him with flogging, burning at the stake, hanging, and more exquisite forms of torture, could not have spent much time worrying about talk that his blood was "tainted."

One of the most damaging and persistent stories circulating during the war was that Lincoln had taken a tour of the battlefield at Antietam and gaily called for the singing of a comic Negro song while his carriage drove past the thirty thousand corpses. The real incident had occurred sixteen days after the battle, several miles away from the scene of the fighting, and Lincoln pointed out that the Negro tune he requested was actually a "sad little song." Stories like this, that suggested Lincoln was not really sharing the suffering of the average citizens in the North, were most intense in 1864, when the president was running for reelection against General George McClellan, a man who knew what war was like (if not necessarily how to win one). Other gossip along the same line included a story that Lincoln had demanded his salary in gold rather than Union currency, and that his son Robert had made a fortune on government contracts.

Mary Lincoln, with her southern roots, compulsive spending, and hysterical temperament, was a natural target. In one of the most dramatic moments in the history of White House marriages, the president unexpectedly walked into the room where a congressional committee was discussing the possibility of indicting Mary for treason and somberly told the members, "I, of my own knowledge, know that it is untrue that any of my family hold treasonable communication with the enemy." While the congressmen stared speechless, the president finished his brief statement, got up, and left the room. The committee, one member said, was "so greatly affected" it dropped the inquiry and adjourned. Modern students of congressional investigations can judge how well that tactic would work today.

4. The Fickleness of Drinking Gossip

"Andy ain't a drunkard"

Politicians of the Civil War era were routinely talked about as possible alcoholics, as they had been ever since George Washington's day. The rumors, like stories about illegitimacy, generally had little effect on the voters. The main exception was Andrew Johnson, who was ruined by gossip about his drinking. An enthusiastic but not destructive imbiber in his early days, Johnson as president was apparently very temperate. But much of the nation was certain that he was a problem drinker—or, as the *New York World* put it more forcefully, "an insolent drunken brute in comparison with whom Caligula's horse was respectable."

Johnson, a Democratic senator from Tennessee, had stuck with the Constitution and the Union during the war. Lincoln chose him as vice president for his second term as a healing gesture. But after the assassination, Johnson was a fish out of water, a southern president who believed in states' rights and white supremacy, trying to lead a Congress full of northern Republicans who had just endured a long and brutal war to end slavery. The voters had no clear idea about his character. He had all the qualities that make a politician vulnerable to gossip. Worst, Johnson *acted* drunk much of the time. On the stump he compared himself to Christ, accused members of Congress of plotting to assassinate him, and in general behaved less like a president than an overwrought paranoid on a bender. He wasn't always more controlled in private. During a heated discussion with Senator Charles Sumner, the president became so overwrought he started using Sumner's hat as a spittoon.

Johnson had also given gossips a single hard fact on which to hang all the damaging legends: He had been drunk for his inauguration as vice president. A Tennessean from humble roots, Johnson was sullen and ill at ease among people he thought might be looking down on him. His inauguration before a large crowd of not necessarily supportive Washington potentates must have made him terribly nervous. He was also feeling ill, and he made the fatal mistake of seeking a boost by drinking at least three glasses of whiskey right before the ceremony. The vice president–elect walked into the Senate chambers feeling no pain. "I kiss this book in the face of my nation of the United States," he cried grandly as he took the oath. He spoke incoherently, rambling on until Hannibal Hamlin, his predecessor, nudged him to stop.

"I was never so mortified in my life," said one observer. "Had I been able to find a hole I would have dropped through it out of sight." The *New York World* noted, prophetically, that the nation would cherish Lincoln all the more now that he was the only person standing between the presidency and "the person who defiled our chief council-chamber on Saturday with the spewings of a drunken boor." After his humiliation Johnson went into seclusion—giving rise to new stories that he was off on a binge. Lincoln calmed his worried supporters. "I have known Andy Johnson for many years. He made a bad slip the other day, but you need not be scared. Andy ain't a drunkard," he told them.

After Lincoln was killed a few months later, Johnson's enemies were happy to have the drinking rumors to beat him with. One senator who particularly hated the new president told his friends that he had gone to look for Johnson on the night of the assassination and found him hungover, dirty, half-dressed. The story seems unlikely, but it stuck. Time and again, his opponents began by attacking Johnson's policies and wound up by repeating the drinking stories. "I don't want to hurt the man's feelings by telling him he is a rascal," said Thaddeus Stevens. "I'd rather put it mildly and say he hasn't got over that inauguration drunk yet, and just let him retire to get sobered."

In 1866, Johnson attempted to rally the country behind his policies with a national tour before the congressional elections. His opponents discovered that if they heckled the president at every stop, his speeches would degenerate into wild harangues that fueled rumors he was always drunk. In fact, people in a position to observe Johnson's conduct said that except for wine at White House dinners, he seemed to have stopped drinking entirely after the inauguration fiasco. The person who was drunk during the Johnson tour was actually Ulysses Grant. The general was traveling with the president in a show of support, but he had to be taken secretly aboard a steamer in Detroit and whisked away in order to keep his condition quiet. "It's very strange that some men will be abused like the devil for drinking a glass of whiskey and water while others in equally important situations may almost roll in the gutters and not a word is said about it," Johnson muttered.

A Gossip-Proof President

Ulysses Grant really did have a drinking problem. But unlike Andrew Johnson, he always seemed extremely sober—except when he was off on one of his periodic binges. Grant was a reticent man, who never seemed to smile, much less get overwhelmed by excitement or anger. "He is never in a hurry and never behind. Pain and beauty affect him alike," wrote a journalist who compared the president to a mastiff. "There he walks or sits, substantial, slow, in everlasting equipoise of countenance." Grant was also able to go long periods without touching alcohol. But loneliness or boredom left him depressed, and prey to drinking bouts. The worst came during his early military career when he plunged into despair during a series of dead-end assignments on the West Coast. He was forced to resign, and returned to work at a family store in Galena, Illinois. When the Civil War broke out and the Union was desperate for trained officers, Grant had more trouble getting a good commission than men with far fewer qualifications because the stories about his drinking had followed him east.

Contrary to popular opinion, President Lincoln never responded to complaints about Grant's alcoholism by saying he'd like to send his other generals bottles of whatever Grant was drinking. But that legend encapsulates public attitudes in the North toward the man credited with winning the war. While newspapers complained about his drinking early in the conflict, they became less interested in exposés as Grant became successful. Even reporters who were in his company during a drinking spree covered up for him. None of them wanted to destroy the savior of the Union. (And all of them wanted to be on the good side of the man who controlled access to the front lines.) "To the question they all ask, 'Does he drink?' I have been able, from my own knowledge, to give a decided negative," attested the future *New York Sun* editor Charles Dana. As an official in the Lincoln administration, Dana had helped drag a drunken Grant into his bed during a wartime bender, and diverted other officers from the general's room by announcing he was "sick."

Grant drank during the difficult period after Lincoln's assassination, when he was uncomfortably allied with Andrew Johnson. But the public targeted Johnson as the souse and ignored the talk about Grant. The general also seems to have gotten intoxicated on a world tour he and his wife undertook when he was at loose ends after his second term. But he received a hero's welcome when he returned— a fact made much more remarkable by the dismal record of corruption he left behind in the White House. There is no evidence that Grant actually drank during his presidency, although the pace of his administration could have accommodated quite a few binges without disruption. (Grant's normal routine involved a five-hour workday from ten to three, followed by a stroll, dinner, and visits with friends.) The drinking stories inevitably cropped up during his presidential campaigns, especially in 1872, when four years of scandals and corruption had turned Dana and many of Grant's other old newspaper supporters against him. *Sunday Capital* editor Donn Piatt referred to the president as "His Inebriated Excellency." When the administration got into trouble, Piatt would "defend" the president tongue in cheek, claiming he was not responsible for his actions due to a severe drinking problem. Grant complained of being the "subject of abuse and slander scarcely ever equaled in political history." But in truth, Grant was virtually gossip-proof, just as Andrew Jackson had been. His stature as a war hero inoculated him against any talk about his personal sins. His administration and Andrew Johnson's were both unsuccessful. But Grant would live out his days as the nation's most beloved citizen. Johnson would be known as the man who came within one vote of being tossed out of the White House via impeachment. In America, the best defense against unfriendly gossip is always a good war record.

5. The Postwar Era and the Defining Public Event

"The Pet of the Petticoats"

The Civil War was the first time Americans came to depend on newspapers for real news. "I'd give a quarter for a paper just now," cried an Ohio soldier serving in the South. (Papers cost a few pennies at the time.) The sudden demand for accurate information created the first generation of professional reporters. After the war the Washington press corps was no longer composed entirely of semi-derelict freelancers or political hired hands. As journalists became more respectable, they became less willing to make up stories, more worried about libel, and less enthusiastic about prying into the private lives of politicians. So the newspapers developed a rough—and frequently ignored—rule. Private activity remained behind closed doors until some event like a lawsuit, an arrest, or a brawl pushed it into the public sphere. These defining public events forced the more strait-laced media to take notice of things they preferred to ignore, and gave the friskier papers an excuse to delve into matters they were dying to print all along.

Senator Roscoe Conkling was an early victim of the new standard. As head of the Republican party in New York State, he was one of the most powerful politicians in the country and a man with presidential ambitions. Conkling was an arresting specimen, with reddish-gold hair, an impressive mustache, and a liking for fancy waistcoats. He strode through life with his head above the crowd—both physically (he was well over six feet tall) and emotionally. Aloof, arrogant, egotistical, he was withering in Senate debate and unforgiving in political battle. Conkling had a wife tucked away in Utica, New York, where he saw her whenever he came home to vote. Otherwise, he enjoyed his freedom—the disapproving Horace Greeley called him "The Pet of the Petticoats." Throughout the 1870s, Conkling had a long-running affair with Kate Chase Sprague, the beautiful and brilliant daughter of the late Supreme Court chief justice Salmon Chase. Her husband, William Sprague, was a wealthy war hero who had served as a U.S. senator and governor of Rhode Island. But he was an alcoholic who proved incapable of pursuing a political career and of handling his own finances. When Kate began to have money problems, Conkling got her Washington home declared tax-exempt in honor of the chief justice's public service.

One of the most famous men in Washington was sleeping with one of the most famous women, and neither made much attempt to hide the fact. Kate Sprague sent flowers to Conkling's Senate desk, watched his speeches from the ladies' gallery, and exchanged notes with him throughout the day. They were invited to parties as a pair. The affair was close enough to being an official relationship that reporters felt free to tease Conkling about it. But they never published a word until a defining public event occurred in 1879 at Narragansett, Rhode Island. The senator was staying with Kate at the Sprague oceanfront estate when her husband returned unexpectedly and ordered him out of the house at the point of a shotgun. Conkling walked into town, where the aggrieved Sprague tracked him down and created a scene in full view of the interested townspeople. "The usual peaceful routine of life at this charming resort has been thoroughly disturbed and the good people here, who dread even the appearances of scandal in their midst, are still a good deal agitated about the unfortunate occurrence in the streets of the place and at the home of ex-Senator Sprague," said *The New York Times*, shaking its journalistic head but devoting more than half the front page to the story.

All the gossip that had been kept pent up for more than five years came pouring out in papers all across the country. Kate Sprague finally gave an interview to the *New York Sun*, which made Conkling the innocent hero and her husband the bullying villain. She wrote a "private" letter to the *Providence Journal* that was reprinted across the country. She devoted all her efforts to clearing her lover's name, and in response, Conkling dropped her cold. The depths of his sensitivity might be measured by a letter he wrote his long-suffering wife, chiding her for confiding to a friend about her misery over the scandal. "Do you not think it better to abstain with acquaintances from discussing family matters of a private nature?" he demanded coldly.

"Indiana's Favorite Stud-Horse"

The rule about waiting for the defining public event to print gossip about a politician was far from inviolable. Donn Piatt of the Washington *Capital* had the very modern knack of using irony and snide asides to drive home his points about the great men of the Grant era. The drinking habits of the president's crowd was a favorite topic and Senator Zack Chandler of Michigan a particular target. Chandler, who had been attacked by Democrats for his imbibing for years, lost his seat after Piatt wrote that he had gotten tipsily aboard a streetcar and sat on a sleeping baby. (Chandler was resurrected by President Grant, who named him secretary of the interior.) But the sort of game Piatt was playing had its dangers, especially for reporters who were less skilled in wording their dispatches. Chandler sued another journalist who wrote that the Michigan Republican was so drunk he had to be carried off the Senate floor by his colleagues. The reporter was forced to admit he had made the story up.

Newspapers outside of Washington tended to be less cautious in the way they wrote about their elected officials. The *Chicago Times*, comparing the presidential ambitions of two Indiana politicians, quoted what it claimed was a much-repeated story about former governor Oliver Morton: A small boy on the losing end of a wrestling match cried out vengefully, "I can't lick you, but Governor Morton sleeps with your ma!"

"That's nothing," responded the second. "Governor Morton sleeps with *everybody*'s ma!"

The story became part of political folklore. But the *Chicago Times* was not exactly an objective source. It may have given away its preference for another candidate, Governor Thomas Hendricks, with its headlines:

HENDRICKS A MAN OF THE PUREST SOCIAL RELATIONS,
BUT MORTON A FOE TO SOCIETY, A SEDUCER AND A
LIBERTINE . . .
THE FORMER'S NAME UNTRAMMELED BY LUST; THE
LATTER'S REEKING WITH FILTH AND SLIME.
A FEW OF THE HELLISH LIAISONS OF, AND ATTEMPTED
SEDUCTIONS BY, INDIANA'S FAVORITE STUD-HORSE.

Neither man won the nomination.

The most egregious breach of the unwritten law on private behavior involved Senate President Pro Tem Matthew Carpenter, a Wisconsin Republican who was hated by reporters for his war on congressional leaks to the press. In 1873, Carpenter escorted the ailing wife of a friend to a resort hotel while he was en route to visit Grant at the president's summer home. When the woman discovered there were no rooms available, Carpenter took her to another establishment, then proceeded on to his appointment. But a Washington reporter had spotted Carpenter and his companion leaving the first hotel, and wrote an item suggesting the senator had been ejected for trying to register with a prostitute. Other papers picked up the tidbit and expanded on it. "It was a pitiful sight . . . a Senator refused quarters at a Long Beach hotel because he was not in a fit condition to associate with the people who are guests there," wrote one New York paper. The *New York Tribune* claimed that the senator's behavior en route to the resort had been so outrageous that "honest women turned away from the exhibition with a blush and prurient boys went round it with a chuckle and a leer." Carpenter failed to take any action to clear his name. "He could scarcely bring a libel suit in which the only issue would be in regard to the character of a lady," raged *The New York Times* in his defense. He was defeated for renomination.

"But his heart it was right I am sure"

The era following the war and Reconstruction was an overripe period—sentimental, greedy, and insecure. Postwar morals were loose, but morality was still rigid—a phenomenon that created not only a bonanza of gossip but a positive fad for blackmail. Mark Twain called it the "Gilded Age," an apt suggestion of both wealth and tawdry ostentation. The economic winners were making unprecedented amounts of money, and they felt compelled to spend it as publicly as possible. Everyone knew about Cornelius Vanderbilt II's new Fifth Avenue mansion, with its forty-five-foot-long dining room with jewel-studded ceiling and oak beams inlaid with mother-of-pearl. In San Francisco, James Flood built a forty-two-room house on Nob Hill, surrounded by a block-long bronze fence that required a full-time servant to keep it polished. Newspaper readers gobbled up stories about dinner parties in which every guest received an oyster containing a black pearl, or cigars wrapped in hundred-dollar bills. The new generation of speculators and entrepreneurs wanted their conspicuous consumption to be noticed. It proved that they had really arrived on top, even if they came from rootless, impoverished backgrounds. Big Jim Fisk, the son of an itinerant peddler, made several fortunes manipulating the stock of the beleaguered Erie Railroad. To remind the world of his success, he traveled in a coach pulled by six horses, one black and one white in each pair. Two black footmen dressed in white livery rode in the front, and two white men in black livery were positioned in the back. When Fisk arrived at a home to pay a call, they unrolled a purple and gold carpet to the door. "Erie-pressible," said the newspapers.

The voters seemed temporarily to give up the hope that they could find public men with public honor, and sometimes settled for public men who were at least fun to be around. Although Jim Fisk's major connection to politics involved paying off state legislators, he was a harbinger of a future generation of elected officials who would win immunity from their sins with their charm. Fisk bled the Erie for his own gain while the ill-maintained railroad was killing its passengers in crashes and fires, and failing to pay the workers' wages. But he mixed public graft with private charity—the residents of the tenements in the neighborhood around his gaudy marble opera house always got free coal in the winter. "We always knew he loved both women and wine," went a ballad written after Fisk's death.

> But his heart it was right I am sure.
> He lived like a prince in his palace so fine
> Yet he never went back on the poor.

Almost inevitably, Fisk's life ended in chaos and scandal. But it was scandal with a distinctly modern beat. When Fisk's ex-mistress, Josie Mansfield, attempted to blackmail him with some old love letters, Fisk had the letters suppressed rather than allow the public to make fun of his goopy notes to a woman who had spurned him for another man. The business community assumed the letters must have proof of some financial swindle that could bring Fisk's empire down, along with that of his partner, the financier Jay Gould. But Fisk was happy to let the world believe in his sins as a public man, rather than let them have a look at his private foibles.

When he was murdered by his mistress's new lover, even the *Times* decided that Fisk's misspent life contained "a grandeur of conception" that lifted him "above the vulgar herd of scoundrels." More than twenty-five thousand people showed up for the wake. The funeral procession passed through a city crowded with respectful mourners. "Never since the martyred Lincoln was borne through New York's streets was so impressive a spectacle witnessed," wrote one paper.

6. Henry Ward Beecher—Gossip and the Forces of Reform

"The scandal summer"

The Reverend Henry Ward Beecher had a particular gift for speaking to the growing middle class of the Gilded Age, which was obsessed with success and terrified of failure. It had never been easier to move up the social ladder. But the swings in the economy were extreme. In 1873, the stock market crashed and half a million men lost their jobs. Two years later, the New York jails housed a quarter-million homeless indigents. As often happens in America, the sight of appalling displays of wealth amid terrible poverty convinced most people they wanted to wind up on the side of appalling wealth. Radiating energy, optimism, and virility, Beecher assured his audience that God was a loving father who *wanted* them to succeed, and understood they might have to play by the gritty rules of Gilded Age commerce to do so. (While Beecher was pastor of Plymouth Congregational Church, in Brooklyn, the head of the Sunday school was Thomas Shearman, Jim Fisk's lawyer.)

Beecher straddled the worlds of politics and entertainment as much as those cartoon presidential candidates of the 1840s and 1850s had. He was the most famous public speaker of an era when public speakers were among the nation's chief celebrities. He was part of a community of social reformers who had learned during the abolition movement that publicity was an important tool for mobilizing political opinion. Beecher's own genius for self-promotion had inspired him to "auction" a beautiful young female slave, driving his congregation into emotional hysterics as they threw their jewels and money in the collection plate to pay for her freedom. After the war, Beecher drew thousands to his Sunday services. The crowded ferries that carried them over to Brooklyn were called "Beecher boats." Those who couldn't come could read his sermons, which were reprinted in newspapers all around the country. He was so famous, and so in tune with the times, that he also appeared in the papers' advertisements, endorsing everything from a piano manufacturer to a brand of trusses.

Beecher was at the center of the intellectual, religious, and political movement that would soon become the Republican Mugwump reformers. His sister Harriet was the author of *Uncle Tom's Cabin*. Two other Beecher sisters, Catherine and Isabella, were vocal advocates of women's rights. He was friends with the great suffragists Elizabeth Cady Stanton and Susan B. Anthony, the editor Horace Greeley, the poet John Greenleaf Whittier. His protégé, the handsome, brooding, ambitious Theodore Tilton, was a well-known lecturer and editor. Imagine the shock when Beecher was accused of having an affair with one of his parishioners, and that parishioner turned out to be Tilton's wife, Elizabeth. If the rest of the nation felt that they were looking in on a domestic crisis involving their own friends and neighbors it was no wonder. Virtually everyone involved in the case seemed to be a famous name.

The summer of 1875 was called "the scandal summer" in honor of the Beecher adultery trial. The public devoured every detail, trading the newest bits of evidence, rumors, and theories about which witnesses were telling the truth. (Mrs. Tilton eventually made six written statements, each, after the first, taking back everything she said in the one before.) They attempted to sort out the great social issues of the day in the context of testimony about the petty, sordid behavior of celebrated people. Like the Sickles trial and similar proceedings that were to follow, the Beecher trial often seemed to be only peripherally about the law, but it was most definitely all about gossip.

"The indomitable urgency of his great nature"

Even during Beecher's early days as a humble minister in Indiana, there had been gossip about his sex life. People whispered that the frosty Eunice Beecher, who was popularly known as "The Griffin," had been so shocked to discover her husband's affairs that her hair had turned prematurely gray. He became more skilled as both a preacher and a seducer, and came to use the same techniques in both endeavors. When Beecher wooed Elizabeth Tilton, he assured her that their "pure affection and high religious love" would not damage her virtue as long as she kept it secret from outsiders who were not spiritually evolved enough to understand their relationship. That kept the affair quiet for more than a year. But once the guilt-ridden Elizabeth confessed to her husband, the story spread rather quickly through Beecher's circle. Elizabeth told her mother, a distinctly unevolved woman who told everybody she knew. Theodore confided in his employer, publisher Henry Bowen—who told him that Mrs. Bowen had confessed on her deathbed that *she* had had an affair with Beecher. Tilton was devastated. His friendship with the pastor had been intense in that peculiar, nineteenth-century manner. "Your private letters are like so many kisses, send some more!" Tilton had written to Beecher in 1863. Mrs. Tilton had once walked into a room and found Beecher sitting in her husband's lap, discussing the Sermon on the Mount.

Tilton told the story about his wife's affair with Beecher to Elizabeth Cady Stanton over dinner. Later, in Washington, Stanton shared the gossip with Victoria Woodhull, the "Bewitching Broker" who had captivated Wall Street as its first female trader. Woodhull was then in her moment of glory as a heroine of the suffrage movement. Soon, she would metamorphose into an advocate of free love, and women's rights leaders would find their charismatic new spokeswoman to be an exceedingly loose cannon. Stanton learned that lesson when Woodhull published the Beecher adultery story in her newspaper, *Woodhull and Claflin's Weekly*, with additional details of her own invention. "Offended Susan, come right down and pull my ears. I shall not attempt a defense," Stanton wrote Susan B. Anthony shamefacedly.

Woodhull published the story because she was angry at one of Beecher's sisters, who opposed including her in the suffrage leadership. But like almost every writer who makes private gossip public, she felt compelled to come up with an excuse, and she cited one of the most popular—the need to expose hypocrisy. Beecher, she said, had denounced her dogma of free love in public, but practiced it privately. The minister, Woodhull told her readers, had personally informed her that he believed marriage was the "grave of love." (Anyone who got a look at Eunice Beecher's dour gray eminence at Plymouth Church might suspect that the minister had firsthand experience burying domestic affection.) Attempting to soften her attack, Woodhull added that she felt Beecher's "immense physical potency and the indomitable urgency of his great nature" were among his best traits.

Everyone in the Plymouth congregation assumed Tilton had been the one who told Woodhull about the affair. The cuckolded intellectual and the Bewitching Broker had become friends, and possibly lovers. In an attempt to distract her from the Beecher story, Tilton had also been writing Woodhull's biography, a glowing account that included her claim that she had raised her idiot son from the dead when he fell on his head. In truth, both Tilton and Beecher had been behaving very peculiarly. But the congregation knew which one had to be protected. If the great minister fell, it would be a blow to the whole movement for political reform, equal rights, and civic stability with which he was identified. Tilton had to be sacrificed to the greater good. He was expelled from the church and denounced by the other members. Tilton, in response, filed criminal charges against Beecher for seducing his wife.

The ensuing trial would have looked very familiar to modern Americans. Each side had a squad of high-profile lawyers, who took two months just to make their opening and closing statements. Beecher alone called ninety-five witnesses, and his legal fees were so enormous Plymouth Church had to quadruple his salary to one hundred thousand dollars to keep him solvent. Tickets to the trial were scalped for the then-enormous sum of five dollars. (Old copies of the fatal issue of Woodhull's magazine were selling for forty dollars.) As many as three thousand people a day were turned away from the courthouse. Beecher and Tilton were both pelted with flowers from their admirers, and peddlers sold opera glasses in the courtroom. Every newspaper in the country followed the story in exhaustive detail, and people debated Beecher's guilt or innocence at every dinner table in America.

It seemed clear that Beecher was guilty. But the minister's lawyer, in his closing argument, ignored the unhelpful evidence and focused on what it would mean about America if Tilton's accusations were true. A guilty verdict, he told the jury, would bring joy to "every quarter where the wicked classes make their meetings, and hold their gossips with a sneer and a smile." To side with the prosecution was the same as siding with free love cultists. The jurors debated for eight days through the sweltering summer, while reporters hung from lamp-posts to watch their shadows in the window. In the end, the jury deadlocked nine to three for acquittal and the trial ended without a verdict. Beecher retained his pulpit and much, if not all, of his old fame. When he died in 1887, Brooklyn held a day of mourning and the state legislature adjourned in his honor. About fifty thousand people lined the streets to see the funeral procession. Tilton drifted off to France, where he became a familiar figure in the cafés and chess clubs. The hapless Elizabeth Tilton remained as a sort of ward of Plymouth Church until she changed her story once again and publicly accused Beecher of having indeed seduced her. Victoria Woodhull recanted, too. She moved to England, and gave lectures on the sanctity of monogamy while her daughter, Zulu Maude, read a little Shake-speare to the audiences. She eventually married a wealthy London banker.

Chapter 4

The Birth of the Celebrity

Class

1880–1900

1. Grover Cleveland's Terrible Tale

> *"A vigorous, uncompromising man without any plans"*

The nineteenth century ended on a wave of confusion and irritation that people today might find familiar. There was no political ideology that attracted general enthusiasm, and the voters were sure all politicians were crooked anyway. "What the public desired just then with a furious passion was a vigorous, uncompromising man without any plans," wrote William Allen White. Into this great, angry void lumbered Grover Cleveland. The public knew little about him except that he was extremely honest. He had been honest in Buffalo, New York, where he was plucked out of obscurity to run as the reform candidate for mayor. After six months of vetoing every piece of pork the dim-witted city legislators could throw at him, he was selected to run for governor, and won by a landslide. In Albany, he sat at his desk writing veto messages for two years until July of 1884, when a cannon shot reverberated outside the capitol. An excited aide told Cleveland it was the sign that he had just been nominated for president by the Democratic convention in Chicago.

"Do you think so? Well, anyhow, we'll finish this work," said Cleveland, digging back into his papers.

Like John Quincy Adams, Cleveland seemed like an unlikely candidate for a gossip-driven presidential campaign. He was terribly shy of women in his own class, though as a young man he had enjoyed joking with the less threatening females at Buffalo's German beer gardens, where he spent his evenings drinking and singing. But by the time he became a national figure, the only evidence that the fun-loving Grover ever existed was his girth—as a presidential candidate he weighed more than three hundred pounds. Even his fabled honesty seemed presented in the most pompous way possible. "It is no credit to me to do right. I am never under any temptation to do wrong," he explained. His worldview was conservative in every sense of the word. (He deplored historians' attempts to debunk the story of George Washington and the cherry tree.) As president, he would veto a ten-thousand-dollar appropriation to send seed grain to drought-stricken farmers in Texas, saying a government giveaway "weakens the sturdiness of our national character."

The story of the election of 1884 lingers in the nation's collective consciousness as a cartoon—a picture of a fat man with a walrus mustache being pursued by a woman carrying a wailing baby yelling, "Ma, Ma, Where's My Pa?" Cleveland turned out to have a bastard child, the legend goes, but a tolerant public elected him president anyway. The real story is more interesting. Cleveland, who should have won easily, came within a hair of losing because of the stories about his private life. Although he probably could have convinced the public that the bastard child under contention wasn't his, Cleveland chose not to do so. He had his reasons, and they were far too romantic for anyone to connect with the stiff, tongue-tied, self-made man who spent most of his life hiding behind a desk full of papers.

"A coarse debauchee who would bring harlots to Washington"

Cleveland and his Republican opponent, Senator James Blaine of Maine, couldn't have been more different. Blaine, a former secretary of state, was the consummate Washington insider. Cleveland had never even been to Washington—in fact, he had hardly traveled at all. (During the presidential campaign, his advisers begged him to stop referring to his youthful transplantation from New York City to Buffalo as "moving west.") Cleveland was such a self-conscious speaker that when he was a lawyer he memorized every word of his arguments before he went into court. Blaine was a brilliant orator, an imaginative politician, and a man of enormous charm. "Had he been a woman, people would have rushed off to send flowers," a friend once said. To his admirers, who called themselves "Blaniacs," he was the beloved "Plumed Knight." But the senator was also a man who lived high without explaining how he paid his bills, who had a habit of ending his correspondence with "Burn this letter." He had profited from questionable railroad deals, and had avoided congressional censure only by absconding with the letters that were the major evidence against him. When reporters asked Blaine's old adversary Roscoe Conkling whether he would work for the party nominee, Conkling sneered: "I have given up criminal law."

The GOP reform wing, popularly known as the Mugwumps, was increasingly restive. The Democrats knew they could pick up their support with the right nominee. They cast their eyes on the New Yorker called "Grover the Good"—an utterly clean, utterly blank slate. The Mugwumps responded enthusiastically. But less than two weeks after Cleveland's nomination, the Buffalo *Evening Telegraph* arrived on the streets with:

A TERRIBLE TALE
A Dark Chapter in a Public Man's History
The Pitiful Story of Maria Halpin and Governor Cleveland's Son

The story, dragged out over column after column of type, announced that Halpin, a widow who worked in a Buffalo dry-goods store and "a beautiful, virtuous and intelligent young lady," had been seduced by Cleveland, who refused to make an honest woman of her when she became pregnant. When the fallen angel began to make a pest of herself, her heartless ex-lover "resolved to abate the annoyance and had her committed to an asylum." The end of the story saw Maria leaving town "broken-hearted, disgraced, an outcast, while her seducer continued to revel in the realm of the just, and pretend before the great American public that he is a model of virtue." If that were not enough, the paper published a statement from "one of the most discreet, honored and trusted" (but unnamed) of Buffalo's citizens, attesting that Cleveland was a drunk, a barroom brawler, and a lecher. Two "respectable citizens," also unnamed, claimed they had found Cleveland and another lawyer fighting "over a lewd woman" in a saloon, "both drunk . . . nearly naked and covered with blood."

The *Evening Telegraph* was not exactly a paper of record. "A poverty-stricken Buffalo paper of ill repute," sniffed Joseph Pulitzer's *New York World*. But the outline of the story was true. Halpin had given birth to a baby boy she named Oscar Folsom Cleveland, and although Cleveland had not acknowledged the child as his, he had accepted responsibility for its welfare. When Halpin developed a drinking problem, he sent her away for treatment, and had the boy adopted by one of his own friends. When the widow came back and tried to reclaim the child, Cleveland paid her off with five hundred dollars. After the *Evening Telegraph* published its exclusive, Cleveland declined to say anything except to deny all the "respectable citizens' " charges that went beyond little Oscar.

Over the next three months the plain-living bachelor's sex life would be discussed endlessly in newspaper editorials, thundered about from pulpits, and expanded upon in drawing rooms from sea to shining sea. "We do not believe the American people will knowingly elect to the Presidency a coarse debauchee who would bring harlots to Washington and hire lodgings for them convenient to the White House," said the *New York Sun*, withdrawing its endorsement. The Reverend Henry Ward Beecher, who had been preparing to

74

throw his support behind Cleveland's campaign, ducked out of sight. New York reform assemblyman Teddy Roosevelt surprised many people by endorsing Blaine, citing Cleveland's "public career in the first place, and then private reasons as well." Newspapers with Republican sympathies spread the story across the country, making the "Terrible Tale" more outrageous with every reprinting. In Cincinnati, the *Penny Post* bannered:

MORAL MONSTER

GROVER CLEVELAND'S TRUE CHARACTER LAID BARE

A BOON COMPANION TO BUFFALO HARLOTS

A DRUNKEN, FIGHTING, ROISTERING ROUÉ

The Democrats who engineered Cleveland's nomination had known at least something about Cleveland's "woman scrape" before the convention, but ignored it. They assumed that among all the changes and traumas of the Gilded Age, it was public dishonesty that bothered people most. They were not entirely right. People were upset about politicians who stole money, but many were even more disturbed about the breakup of family life in their own neighborhoods. Their children had left their rural homes for the cities, and they knew from reading the papers that the cities were full of crime, divorce, alcoholism, and a general flaunting of the old moral standards. Even a Henry Ward Beecher could not be trusted to be faithful to home and hearth. Public corruption, everyone agreed, *was* a disgrace. But it was a disgrace they could live with. Immorality in the private sphere was what worried people more. If Alexander Hamilton had been around in 1884, he might have hidden the adultery and let people think he was just another embezzler.

> *"Is this man crazy or does he want to ruin any-*
> *body?"*

The Maria Halpin story couldn't have been news to Buffalo's political inner circle. A judge and several detectives had helped Cleveland institutionalize Maria; a local orphanage took in the baby, who was then adopted by a prominent physician. Nevertheless, Cleveland remained a respected attorney, and several years after Maria left town, he had the mayoralty practically dumped in his lap. It may be that the ruling class of Buffalo held to the old Alexander Hamilton standards of public morality, or at least the double standard that held a male bachelor had the right to seduce any working-class woman who offered up her favors. But the inner rings of Buffalo society probably also felt that the baby's parentage was more questionable than the *Evening Telegraph* would later admit. Maria named her baby Oscar Folsom Cleveland, and everyone in Buffalo would have known that Oscar Folsom was the name of Cleveland's late law partner and dear friend, a wealthy, charming (and married) man who died a few months before Maria's baby was born. Cleveland and Folsom had been men-about-town together. They were members of a social club of professional men called the Jolly Reefers. They had once entertained the Prince of Wales on a boat trip to Niagara Falls. When they practiced law together, Oscar had served as the firm's rainmaker while Grover was the workhorse. Once, when Folsom asked his friend about a legal issue, Cleveland told him to look it up "and then you'll remember what you learn."

"I want you to know," said Folsom scornfully, "that I practice law by ear, not by note."

The two were Buffalo's version of the grasshopper and the ant, and like all careless grasshoppers, Folsom came to grief. Racing back from a social gathering on July 23, 1875, he was thrown from his buggy and killed instantly. Cleveland remained close to his widow and daughter. They were his honored guests at the governor's mansion, and at the celebration in Albany when Cleveland was officially notified he was the Democratic presidential nominee.

Maria Halpin would claim later that she had barely known Oscar Folsom. That was clearly untrue, since she named her baby after him. (Cleveland would certainly not have urged such a potentially embarrassing honor.) It seems likely that she was either Folsom's mistress or that she slept with several members of the Jolly Reefers. Either way, Cleveland must have taken responsibility for handling the problem because, unlike the other men in his circle, he was a bachelor.

When Cleveland was serving his second term as president, a badly written novel named *The Honorable Peter Stirling* was published. It told the story of an awkward but very honest young politician who takes responsibility for the bastard child of his married friend. The book became a bestseller because everyone assumed it was the true story of the Oscar Folsom Cleveland scandal.

The Cleveland forces never challenged Maria Halpin's version of the story, however. Their candidate wouldn't let them. "I learned last night that [*Buffalo Courier* owner Charles] McCune had started the story . . . that I had nothing to do really with the subject of the *Telegraph* story—that is, that I am innocent—and that my silence was to shield my friend Oscar Folsom," wrote Cleveland on July 31 to his secretary, Daniel Lockwood. "Now is this man crazy or does he want to ruin anybody? Is he fool enough to suppose for a moment that if such was the truth (which it is not, so far as the motive for silence is concerned) that I would permit my dead friend's memory to suffer for my sake? And Mrs. Folsom and her daughter at my house at this very time!" He concluded by decreeing that "this story of McCune's of course must be stopped. I have prevented its publication in one paper at least. Let me hear from you."

Cleveland was deadly serious about shielding Folsom, and for a reason that not even the most eager gossips in Buffalo had guessed. The fat, awkward, middle-aged presidential candidate was madly in love with Folsom's daughter, Frances, then a beautiful college student. Everyone thought of her as his ward. He bought her first baby carriage, and took her for walks during Jolly Reefer picnics when she was a toddler. At the time of the election, Cleveland had yet to declare his feelings, but he sent Frances flowers from the governor's greenhouse every week. All in all, as one modern commentator noted, it was a situation that belonged in a Thomas Hardy novel rather than an American presidential campaign.

Neither Cleveland nor Frances nor the widowed Mrs. Folsom would ever make a public comment about the scandal, or the parentage of little Oscar Folsom Cleveland. "Whatever you do, tell the truth," Cleveland wired his campaign. But he did not explain what the truth was. (His sense of delicacy did not go so far as keeping the telegraph private. The Democrats shared it with every reporter in sight.) Cleveland retreated to the governor's mansion and took virtually no part in the campaign that followed. While Blaine toured the country, speaking every day, Cleveland emerged only twice to deliver very brief and very flat speeches on civil service reform. Inwardly, of course, he writhed with humiliation and worry about the scandal's effect on Frances. "How often I wish that I was free and that some good friend of mine was running instead of myself," he wrote to a friend.

"I have heard a rumor . . ."

All of Cleveland's supporters, of course, could not be kept from speculating, or making up their own scenarios. The *New York World* told its readers that while Cleveland was "sowing his wild oats he met this woman . . . and became intimate with her. She was a widow and not a good woman by any means. Mr. Cleveland, learning this, began to make inquiries about her and discovered that two of his friends were intimate with her at the same time as himself. When a child was born, Cleveland, in order to shield his two friends who were both married men, assumed the responsibility of it." Notice that Cleveland, who was older than Maria Halpin, was "sowing his wild oats" while his sexual partner was simply "not a good woman by any means." That was just the sort of double standard that drove women's advocates crazy, and it was one reason Lucy Stone's *Women's Journal* crusaded against Cleveland's candidacy. The tale, Stone wrote, "fills half the newspapers in the United States with apologies for a degrading vice— apologies which every profligate man and fast youth will appropriate to his own justification."

Still, the most damaging part of the talk about Cleveland were the rumors that Maria Halpin was only one of a long string of victims of the governor's lust. Every one of those stories seemed to trace back to the same man, the Reverend George Ball, pastor of Hudson Street Baptist Church, in Buffalo. "Investigations disclose still more proof of debaucheries too horrible to relate and too vile to be readily believed," he thundered from the pulpit. ". . . The Halpin case was not solitary. Women now married and anxious to cover the sins of their youth have been his victims, and are now alarmed lest their relations with him shall be exposed. Some degraded and broken-hearted victims of his lust now slumber in the grave. Since he has become governor of this great state, he has not abated his lecheries. Abundant rumors implicate him at Albany, and well-authenticated facts convict him at Buffalo."

Behind almost every gossip-driven campaign there lies a figure like Ball, someone who is willing to work full-time spreading and improving upon the scandal. Ball was the only Buffalonian to publicly claim he had direct evidence (which he never revealed) that Cleveland's sins extended beyond Maria Halpin. A respected minister, he never gave any clear motive for his crusade to save the world from Grover Cleveland. But Ball was so central to the scandalmongering that E. L. Godkin, the editor of *The Nation* and the *New York Evening Post*, undertook to investigate the private life of the minister himself. Unfortunately for Godkin, there turned out to be two clergymen named George Ball, one a ne'er-do-well who had been run out of Indiana "due to an insult to a Christian lady" and one upright if over-judgmental Buffalonian. Godkin's exposé mixed them up. The Buffalo Reverend George Ball sued, and Grover Cleveland paid half of Godkin's legal fees.

Ball may have been the only person pushing the Cleveland-as-sex-addict story in public, but plenty of other people were spreading the gossip in the old-fashioned way—over dinner, in parlors, clubs and workmen's taverns. Cleveland's campaign chairman, trying to track down the source of a rumor that Cleveland regularly associated with prostitutes, got the following response from one Rufus Green:

Dear Sir,

In answer to your inquiry if I ever said that 'a prominent man in Buffalo, had visited Albany & there met Gov. Cleveland, who insisted upon his going out to dine & . . . when he got there he found a notorious courtesan.' I would say that I never made such a statement. I have heard the rumor that a prominent man in Buffalo had the above experience. No

name, however, was mentioned. Two or three times in private
conversation I have repeated the story, but each time as a
rumor.

If Cleveland had been married—if he had had a nineteenth-century
version of Hillary Clinton to defend him—the wilder rumors would
probably have died away quickly. But his bachelor state fueled talk
that there was something perverse going on. "... It proves nothing," admitted *The Evangelist*, a Massachusetts religious newspaper.
"But it creates a suspicion of many things we would rather not have
to think about." Even Cleveland's supporters seemed to be uncomfortable with the fact that he apparently had never even had a date
with a respectable woman. A campaign biography written by Benjamin LeFevre blithely solved the problem by inventing a dead fiancée. Unable to leave it at that, LeFevre also confided to his
readers that the candidate, having gradually recovered from his
grief, was in correspondence with "a charming brunette about 35
years old with pleasing manners and considerable property" who
would probably become Mrs. Cleveland after the election. (Like most
campaign biographers, Mr. LeFevre insisted on finding a positive
side to every failing he couldn't deny. "There is a decided tendency
toward corpulence—as is usually the case in vital temperaments," he
wrote.)

Given a choice between an honest public man with a questionable private life and a corrupt politician with an admirable family
life, the country seemed to be leaning toward the family man. In
an attempt to bring Henry Ward Beecher back to his corner, Cleveland wrote to the daunting Mrs. Beecher, denying all of Reverend
Ball's charges and giving her a pathetically short list of every social
outing he had taken while he was governor. Beecher eventually
came around, and in an unfortunate burst of enthusiasm, announced that if Cleveland drew the support of every man who had
ever cheated on his wife, he would win New York by two hundred
thousand votes. It sounded, the *Sun* sniped, like a call to arms for
adulterers.

*"The mother of the son of our bachelor gover-
nor"*

It was a bad time for a politician to be fighting a sex scandal. Not
only was the public sensitive to what we would call family values
issues, but there was an unprecedented amount of media to cater to
their concerns. The big-city papers were engaged in brutal circulation
wars, competing wildly for exciting news. The cost of producing a
newspaper was still relatively low, and even a town of ten thousand
had at least one daily. Medium-sized cities often had half a dozen—
many of them small, underfinanced, fly-by-night organs like the *Evening Telegraph*. They got their news mainly by reprinting what the
larger papers said. Investigative reporting was still in its infancy, and
few of the papers actually tried to check out the baby Oscar story
beyond a cursory interview with a friend or critic of the candidate.
But when it became known that Maria Halpin—the woman the newspapers liked to call "the mother of the son of our bachelor governor"—was living in New Rochelle, the small New York town became
as crowded with visitors as Miami Beach in high season. The *New
York Star*, which seemed to be keeping a careful eye on the New
Rochelle train station, reported that "strangers of free and easy manner with sharp good looks" were loitering around. The fabled Rev.
Ball arrived, and was refused admission into Maria's house. He left
town, the *Star* reported, "in disgust and more convinced of the truth
of the story now than ever."

At about the time New Rochelle started attracting so much traffic,
local Democratic leaders contacted James Seacord, Maria's uncle, and
offered him money to make sure his niece was kept in strict seclusion.
Seacord, who evidently shared a family inclination to take cash whenever it was being handed around, agreed. But in August, the *New
Rochelle Pioneer* reported breathlessly that Maria appeared to have
been abducted. "The public can easily imagine who was most interested in getting control of Maria Halpin," the paper added darkly.

The saga of Maria's kidnapping was reprinted in an anti-Cleveland
booklet, *Tell the Truth, or the Story of a Working Woman's Wrongs*.
It contained, according to the cover, "the History of the Recent Ab-

duction of Maria Halpin from Her Home in New Rochelle together with the Buffalo Evening Telegraph's 'Terrible Tale.' " The booklet was copiously illustrated with scenes from Maria's mundane life, including a picture of the Flint & Kents store in Buffalo, where Maria had worked as a clerk before getting pregnant, and a reproduction of the note she allegedly left behind when she was abducted: "New Rochelle, N.Y. Uncle Albert, Don't worry I am going away." Maria was apparently a woman who believed in putting a dateline in every communication, including kidnap letters left on the living room table.

Obviously, she had not really been abducted. Maria had left under her own power, probably with friends of Cleveland who were hoping to get her to agree to let the Democratic candidate off the hook. But she returned without comment and dodged the flock of reporters trying to beat in her door. On August 14, the ever-active *Evening Telegraph* published an interview it had allegedly gotten from Maria via an "intermediary." When asked if she intended to sign any statement vindicating Cleveland, the paper claimed, "Maria Halpin drew herself up as preparing for a supreme effort and replied in the most impressive and earnest manner: 'Me, make a statement exonerating Grover Cleveland? Never! I would rather put a bullet through my heart!' "

"Full of the milk of human kindness"

The pro-Cleveland press spared no effort to refurbish the reputation of the man who was being called "the Beast of Buffalo" in some quarters. The *World* promised a feature on "Cleveland's Inside Life" that ignored Maria Halpin and instead revealed that the candidate was "full of the milk of human kindness and his heart is big enough to take in all mankind." Like so much of the coverage, it focused on personality rather than platform. Cleveland's opinions on the great issues of the day were murky. He had intended to run a character campaign, and he had gotten caught in the backlash.

The Democrats dug through Blaine's past and discovered a story that the senator had been forced to marry his wife when she became pregnant. It was an old rumor that had popped up almost every time

Blaine ran for office, and a rather piddling excuse for a sex scandal, made even less promising by Grover Cleveland's refusal to get involved. When the governor's aides presented him with a packet of allegedly compromising letters, Cleveland tore them up, saying: "The other side can have the monopoly of all the dirt in this campaign." As with the "tell the truth" telegram, the story of the governor's principled stand was quietly conveyed to all the interested media.

Blaine had been campaigning hard, making four hundred speeches in six weeks while Cleveland stayed home. He ended the race with what may have been the most disastrous day in the history of American elections. On October 29 (his "Black Wednesday," said the *World*), Blaine spoke to a group of Protestant ministers who had been gathered by his staff to emphasize which candidate was really on the side of the angels. The Reverend Samuel Burchard delivered the welcoming address. "We are Republicans and don't propose to leave our party and identify ourselves with the party whose antecedents have been rum, Romanism and rebellion," he said—referring to anti-temperance, Catholic, and southern Democrats. Blaine certainly was not sympathetic to anti-Catholic talk—his mother was Catholic and his sister was a nun. But he was either too exhausted to hear the remark or unwilling to pick a fight with Burchard in public. It was a critical mistake, since the Irish vote was crucial to his chances of carrying New York. Blaine's handlers then bundled him off to a restaurant, Delmonico's, for a dinner given by financier Jay Gould and some of the city's other famous money men. The idea was to underscore Blaine's soundness on economic matters. But the next day, along with the stories about the "Romanism" speech, the *World* published a devastating front-page cartoon titled "The Royal Feast of Belshazzar Blaine and the Money Kings," which showed Blaine dining with his fat-cat friends on "Lobby Pudding" and "Patronage Cake" while a starving family begged at the foot of the table.

If Blaine had been confined to bed with a cold on October 29, the Republicans would almost certainly have won the election. New York turned out to be the key—the two parties split the other state electoral votes almost evenly. After a long delay and days of suspense, Cleveland was declared the winner in New York by 1,149 votes. "I should have carried New York by 10,000 votes if the weather had been clear on election day and Dr. Burchard had been doing missionary work in Asia Minor or Cochin China," said Blaine. In fact, he ought to have lost the election by far more than he did. The country was in a severe recession, and the Republican party's record for graft had alienated even a large chunk of its own members. Many of the country's most prestigious Republican papers had endorsed Cleveland. The real story was that the Democrats came within twelve hundred votes of losing their candidate's own state, and the election.

Life After Gossip

The president-elect was not in a particularly triumphant mood. "I intend to cultivate the Christian virtue of charity toward all men except the dirty class that defiled themselves with filthy scandal and Ballism," Cleveland wrote a friend. "I don't believe that God will ever forgive them and I am determined not to do so. I look upon the four years next to come as a dreadful self-inflicted penance for the good of my country." The realization that thousands of strangers, as well as many of his former friends, were gossiping about his sex life made Cleveland more starchy and repressed than ever.

Maria Halpin dropped out of sight completely. Cleveland would hear from her just once more—in a letter asking for money in 1895. He didn't answer. Little Oscar was adopted by a Buffalo physician, and took the name of James King. He grew up to be a doctor himself. Most of his colleagues had heard the story of his parentage through the grapevine, but Dr. King never referred to it. He never married, lived in a large house in Buffalo with one (the gossips said perhaps two) of the nurses who assisted him in his work. He became one of the most prominent gynecologists in the country, sought out for his ability to perform hysterectomies quickly in an age when anesthetics were still dangerous. He died in 1947.

A year and a half after his election, Grover Cleveland married Frances Folsom, then twenty-one.

2. The New Celebrity

"Shake the hand that shook the hand . . ."

In Grover Cleveland's time, presidents still carried on the old White House tradition of holding regular receptions where any citizen could come to meet the chief executive. So Cleveland dutifully presented himself every Monday, Wednesday, and Friday evening to let hundreds of total strangers give him the once-over. It was probably not his favorite part of the job. "I've voted for lots of presidents in my time," an elderly man once told him enthusiastically. "But I ain't never seen one before. Well, you're a whopper!" The visitors might not have found the receptions all that exciting either. Cleveland's sister Rose, his first White House hostess, summarized the general ambience when she told a reporter that she kept alert on the receiving line by mentally conjugating Greek verbs.

But when Cleveland arrived for his duties on April 4, 1887, the crowd was not in its normal subdued mood. They hardly seemed to notice when the president entered the room. Their attention was directed at a tall and remarkably brawny young man in an elegant black suit who was standing with a couple of older associates, looking oblivious to the fuss. John L. Sullivan, the world's bare-knuckle boxing champion, was, in some ways, more famous than the president. His picture was everywhere—in magazine ads, on the cigarette cards that little boys collected and traded, behind the mirrors of half the saloons in the United States. The newspapers were full of his triumphs in the ring and his debacles in bars and bedrooms. His posters were plastered on the walls of every city where he fought—and Sullivan fought absolutely everywhere. Papers published poems about him, and the music business produced endless tunes in his honor, including "Throw Him Down McCloskey," one of the hits of the era.

Sullivan was also a self-destructive drunk, a wife-beater, and a brawler who had once knocked out a horse that offended him. None of that affected his status. Indeed, it helped maintain it. His athletic achievements and his messy personal life were part of the same package. Legends about his strength (he was supposed to have blackened an aunt's eye when he was still in the cradle) were mixed in with legends about his dissipation. (He drank sixty-seven gin fizzes at one sitting, the story ran. Another version had him downing fifty-six in an hour.) He was the first American entertainment celebrity. The people who stood behind him in the White House reception line undoubtedly went home and bragged to their neighbors, in the catchphrase of the day, that when they met President Cleveland, they "shook the hand of the man that shook the hand of John L. Sullivan."

"I remain your warm, personal friend, John L. Sullivan"

Sullivan was the harbinger of a new era for the nation, and for gossip. Until the end of the nineteenth century, American heroes had been generals, politicians, and the occasional intrepid explorer. The post–Civil War era also worshiped wealth and progress, so inventors and business tycoons were added to the list—even though the saga of Andrew Carnegie's gold plumbing would never strike exactly the same chord as that of George Washington and the cherry tree. But these heroes and heroines had always been admired for what they *did*. Sullivan's fame transcended function. He could fill theaters as a "model statuary," posing in a series of tableaus depicting what one paper called "the biggest undressed heroes of antiquity." Fans had to be turned away at the door even though the undressed hero was sixty pounds overweight at the time. They paid to watch him pitch badly in exhibition baseball games, then waited for hours to see him drive away at the gate. Despite a total lack of theatrical skills, he drew audiences when he starred in plays like *A True American*, in which his only lines were "I am a true American!" and "I will fly to your assistance!" Like every "actor" of his generation, he made money by appearing in *Uncle Tom's Cabin*. (Sullivan, a terrible racist, made Simon Legree the hero.) When he opened a bar in Boston in 1883, it required sixty patrolmen and six mounted police to keep the crowd under control.

The miracle of celebrity raised Sullivan into a new transcendent class. He had a good sense of public relations when he was sober, and always ended his performances with a good-bye speech in his sonorous, pleasant voice, assuring the audience, "I remain your warm, personal friend, John L. Sullivan." Touring the South and Midwest with exhibition fights, he was cheered by fans who would normally have driven a big-city Irish Catholic out of town on a rail. Sullivan met not only the president but Europe's all-purpose celebrity, the Prince of Wales. ("I shook his flipper and wished him well," the fighter reported.) At a time when the president earned twenty-five thousand a year, and a college professor twenty-five hundred, Sullivan made close to a million dollars—and blew all of it.

Sullivan was a crowd pleaser, but he would never have become a legend if he had not come along just when the newly urbanized nation had acquired both more money and more leisure. The average work week for non-farmworkers dropped from sixty-six hours at the time of the Civil War to fifty-six by 1900. It would decline to forty-five hours by 1920. To occupy that spare time, and separate the people from their spare dollars, the mass-entertainment industry was born. Around the time John L. shook hands with the president, Buffalo Bill Cody was organizing his Wild West show, resurrecting the recently vanished frontier as a pageant starring the real Annie Oakley and Chief Sitting Bull along with re-creations of stagecoach robberies and Indian raids. The first professional baseball series was held in 1884, the same year moving pictures made their first appearance as kinetoscopes—short, jerky films of anonymous actresses and actors dancing, fighting, or staging pratfalls.

The newspapers became a mass-entertainment industry, too. Now that people were crowded conveniently together in large cities, a paper could aspire to hundreds of thousands of readers and the advertising that went with them. Editors struggled to print stories the masses wanted to read. Sports pages made their debut in the 1880s. Joseph Pulitzer's *New York World* set the model for a mix of sensational crime reports, heartrending human interest stories, and dramatic exposés. The public also loved gossip, but it was hard to print interesting gossip when your readers were uprooted farmers or European immigrants with no common friends or neighbors. So the papers created a new kind of celebrity community—a collection of shared human references. Men working next to each other in a factory or sitting side by side in a tavern might have no mutual acquaintances, but they both "knew" John L. Sullivan and could talk about him endlessly. A century before the Internet, the papers created a virtual neighborhood, populated by the new national celebrities.

Professional Beauties and Public Pets

Thanks to new technology, newspapers and magazines had started to reproduce pictures in a way that really showed the public what people looked like, and a new class of heroines emerged out of London known as Professional Beauties. The PBs were famous just for being photogenic. The public could buy copies of their pale brown portraits and paste them in albums that were left in the parlor for visitors to peruse. It was the ultimate proof that the album's owner had joined the global neighborhood, and the most telling sign that the nation was moving from an age that worshiped the spoken word into one that obsessed on physical appearance. The most famous PB was Lillie Langtry, and she came to define the new celebrity class. Like Sullivan, she understood what the public wanted from her. Unlike the fighter, she knew how to control it for her own advantage, and that was the reason Sullivan would burn out in his thirties and die a pauper while Mrs. Langtry could continue displaying herself into her fifties and die a wealthy old woman on the French Riviera.

Lillie had arrived in London from the Isle of Jersey in 1875, a complete unknown, and appeared at her first society party wearing a simple black dress that showed up dramatically against the ornate gowns of the other women. (She wore it so often people debated whether it was a fashion statement or simply the only gown she owned.) Within months, people were leaping on chairs to get a glimpse of her when she entered a room. She became mistress to the Prince of Wales while her husband, a bland but socially useful shield of respectability, seemed perpetually dispatched on fishing vacations. The prince, who generally kept his lovers behind closed doors, proudly took Lillie around in public, and even Queen Victoria was curious enough to receive the woman the world called "the Jersey Lily." When a girl who resembled Langtry had the bad judgment to sit down in a London park to rest, the police had to extricate the unfortunate woman from a crush of admirers and rush her off to the hospital, unconscious.

Lillie achieved all this fame without "doing" anything. But when she became pregnant with a daughter who could not have belonged to her long-absent husband, her relationship with the prince ended. Short on money and snubbed by society, she decided to translate her celebrity into a moneymaking career onstage. Unlike Sullivan, she made an effort to learn her new craft, and by the time she arrived for her first American tour in 1882, she was able to make a respectable showing. But she could probably have filled the theaters just by being a model statue. Reporters flocked to meet her boat in New York harbor, demanding to know what the Jersey Lily thought of the United States before she had ever set foot on shore. (Having spent nine days on board an American ship, Lillie responded sweetly, "I already know your kindness and your hospitality. I am enchanted.") On Langtry's first drive through New York, her coach was so beset by admirers she had to be rescued by the police. The papers were full of stories about her long-running romance with Frederick Gebhard, Jr., a dry-goods heir.

Langtry, who toured the United States regularly for a quarter of a century, developed a persona that wore well in the small town of celebrity gossip—the outrageous belle of the ball or the perhaps too-popular best friend. People knew all about her wardrobe, her houses, the seventy-five-foot-long railroad car with brass lilies on the roof that she rode in while touring the country. They knew about her boyfriends and her beauty secrets, down to her exact weight and secrets for maintaining her complexion. (She recommended Pear's soap in the first celebrity endorsement.) "Public pets might be objectionable, but few could so well have survived the ordeal of public admiration and preserved so much of the natural good-hearted woman as Mrs. Langtry," concluded *The New York Times*.

3. Celebrity Moves to the White House

"The poor, defenseless girl"

Grover Cleveland's young wife, Frances, was the first person from the political world who was regarded by the public as if she had come from the world of entertainment. The First Lady certainly did nothing to encourage her celebrity. She never gave an interview while she was in the White House. She seldom appeared in public at all. When she tried, people stampeded and smashed furniture and threw themselves off dangerous heights just to get a glimpse of her. Americans hung pictures of her in their homes, or pasted them in those celebrity albums in the parlor. Advertisers used her shamelessly to sell soap, cigars, perfume, ashtrays, underwear. A candy-bar manufacturer named a new confection after her daughter, Ruth. Women all over the country copied her hairstyle.

The president always called her "Frank," her real name, after a favorite uncle. When she became an adult, she adopted the more feminine "Frances," but the popular press, to her great disgust, called her "Frankie." Everyone agreed she was lovely—slender, with pale skin, rosy cheeks, and thick lashes. (Beauty had married the Beast!) A young and attractive First Lady was a novelty, since presidents' wives tend to be like presidents—middle-aged or older, emanating an aura of rather dispiriting respectability. There would not be another until Jacqueline Kennedy caused the same sort of hysterical reaction in 1961.

Cleveland had wooed Frances when she and her mother visited the White House, taking his beloved on two-mile walks up and down the East Room. He apparently proposed, and was accepted, by mail. They intended to keep their engagement secret until she finished a post-graduation tour of Europe. But Cleveland's affectionate good-bye telegraph fell into the hands of a reporter who presumed, not unreasonably, that it was Frances's mother, Emma, whom the president was courting. The rumors he was going to marry his intended's parent must have been humiliating for Cleveland, who was already self-conscious about the nearly thirty-year difference in age. The public, having been alerted that something was up, wanted every detail. But Cleveland refused even to admit that he was getting married, let alone to name the lady. When the *Cincinnati Enquirer* correspondent asked him if he was engaged, the president reacted as though he had been accused of a foul perversion. "I am not going to say a word in the matter, but let you go on in your own way until you get tired of dragging the name of the poor, defenseless girl into cruel publicity," he said.

The president, who finally announced his engagement only a week before the June 2 ceremony, banned all reporters from the small family wedding. The White House promised an account of "everything that any one ought to want to know about a wedding"—small comfort to reporters who had plenty of experience with Cleveland's ideas of how much the public ought to want to know. The bride and groom went off to their honeymoon in Deer Park, Maryland, undoubtedly very much in need of a little time to themselves. "When President Cleveland rose at ten o'clock this morning and looked from the front windows of his cheerful little domicile . . . among the objects which met his astounded gaze was a small pavilion standing in the midst of a handsome cluster of tall trees, and in and around this pavilion lounged the flower of Washington journalism . . . ," one of the papers wrote proudly.

The Cleveland wedding was the first instance of a collision between the press and the president in which the media dug in its heels to defend its right to know something personal and utterly trivial. The First Family would be forevermore a topic of avid interest to the public at large, and the reporters would generally press for every possible homely detail. "It is foolish to pretend not to know that the facts relating to the wedding have been the most interesting news to the millions for the last three or four weeks," said the *New York World*. There is a straight line from the pavilion full of reporters in Deer Park to the night that a UPI reporter woke up presidential press secretary Pierre Salinger to ask if it was true that Caroline Kennedy's hamster had died.

". . . the papers do say I beat and abuse her"

The "Frankie" fervor never really abated. At Mrs. Cleveland's first White House reception, the crowd pressing to meet her was so dense that several women fell into the Marine band. When Frances appeared in St. Louis, the crowd stormed the stairs where she was preparing to descend, smashed through barricades, climbed the walls, and hung on to the ornamental carvings. In 1887, when the Clevelands undertook a five-thousand-mile tour of the South and West, the streets were so packed with Frankie fans that the carriages were unable to proceed. Among the hordes of young farm girls who traveled to Kansas City to catch a glimpse of Frances was Mattie Young. Her son, Harry Truman, would remember seeing the yellowed newspaper clippings about Mrs. Cleveland in his mother's scrapbook.

Frances was lively, good-natured, and seemed to take her remarkable situation as much in stride as might be humanly possible. The president bought a country house to keep her away from her throngs of admirers in Washington, and characteristically urged his wife not to "try anything new" as First Lady. But Frances did institute a Saturday afternoon reception in which women who wanted to meet the president's wife could come to the White House and shake her hand. White House advisers were horrified by the mixes of class that marked the lines of visitors and urged her to move the receptions to a weekday, when shopgirls would not be free to pollute the White House with their presence. Frances ignored them, and went on ahead with her Saturday at-homes.

The newspapers wrote about the First Lady all the time, even if the stories had to be created out of whole cloth. (When one reporter made up a story that Mrs. Cleveland had given up wearing a bustle, the bustle went out of fashion.) But the media understood that some topics were out of bounds. The editors who were so wildly interested in little Oscar Folsom Cleveland during the campaign never mentioned him in connection with Frances. While the mystery of the illegitimate child must have given an overlay of sexual melodrama to the White House marriage, it was not one that came out in the print. The world had not changed so much that newspapers would have considered pointing out that the new First Lady might be the half sister of the "Ma, Ma, Where's My Pa?" baby.

But while Frances was never attacked in the press, Cleveland was the target of continual rumors that he was a bad husband. Perhaps the stories rose up to meet the nation's yearning for Frankie gossip. Or perhaps they reflected her fans' resentment at having Cleveland come between them and their idol. They did seem to reflect a public conviction that he wasn't good enough for her. The cruelest story, which popped up in several different forms, was that the First Lady was a battered woman. "My wife sits by me and bids me to send you her affectionate regards," Cleveland wrote to his friend Wilson Bissell during the 1888 campaign. "I tell you, Bissell, I am sure of one thing. I have in her something better than the presidency for life—though the Republican parties and the papers do say I beat and abuse her."

The wife-beating rumors eventually made their way to the floor of a Worcester, Massachusetts, valentine factory. Margaret Nicodemus heard her co-workers discussing a story in the paper, which quoted a local minister as saying that Cleveland's violence had driven Frances's mother out of the country. Nicodemus, a Frankie fan, wrote directly to the White House, asking the First Lady if the stories were true. Mrs. Cleveland took the opportunity to try to stamp out the whispering. "I can wish the women of our country no greater blessings than that their homes and lives may be as happy and their husbands may be as kind, considerate and affectionate as mine," she said in a response that was released to the press.

Cleveland lost his reelection bid to Benjamin Harrison, then won a rematch in 1892. When the family returned to the White House bearing the fabled Baby Ruth, the nation really did react as if the nice young woman next door (with the grouchy husband) had given birth. Frances, looking out the White House window, saw a tourist snatch Ruth from her nurse and pass her around the crowd. The lawn was declared off-limits to visitors, and Ruth and her little sister, Esther, were kept so far away from the public there were rumors one of them was retarded as the result of the beatings Frances suffered when she was pregnant. During one of Frances's final White House receptions, the First Lady told Ruth's nanny to bring Ruth in so the visitors could confirm that she "was not minus legs, arms or fingers."

Not long after Cleveland's second term ended, Lyman Gage, a longtime admirer, visited the ex-president at his summer home in Buzzards Bay, Massachusetts. As the two men shared a glass of whiskey and soda, Cleveland remarked bitterly about the widespread gossip that he had been a heavy drinker, and the stories about Ruth's deformity. "It was broadly reported that she was feeble minded and one account detailed how I had placed her in the keeping of an institution for the feeble minded in St. Louis." Gage could see that Ruth, who was playing on the front porch, was obviously not deformed or retarded. But Cleveland's literal-minded sense of injustice caused him to add that Ruth had never even *been* to St. Louis.

Chapter 5

The Anxiety of the Moment
1890–1920

1. The New Women and the New Gossip

The American public has never been shy about passing around outrageous gossip about its presidents. But wife-beating had not really
come up until Grover Cleveland's day, when it suddenly became a
rather common rumor. Cleveland's successor, William McKinley, was
also the target of spousal-abuse stories during his first presidential
campaign. People actually said Woodrow Wilson *murdered* his first
wife. There was nothing in the presidents' own behavior that was
sparking this kind of talk. Cleveland and Wilson were devoted husbands, and McKinley was an absolute paragon. The gossip said less
about them than about the public's new awareness of women's help-
lessness at the hands of their husbands.

Women could not vote in the decades that flanked the turn of the
century, but they were beginning to define the nation's social agenda.
Many of them were being well educated—30 percent of the college

students in 1880 were female. They were also shunning marriage in record numbers, and the proportion of women who stayed single for life has never been as high before or since. Many of them gravitated toward places like Hull House in Chicago or the Henry Street Settlement in New York, where they could live communally in poor neighborhoods and work together for social change. The six settlement houses that existed in 1891 grew to four hundred in two decades. All sorts of organizations that channeled women's energies toward social betterment were booming. The Women's Christian Temperance Association became a major national political force, and the drive for women's suffrage picked up steam. In a society where male efforts were obsessively directed toward the cause of personal economic advancement, a sizable number of well-educated, well-focused, idealistic women had the power to make an enormous impact on the social attitudes.

Their influence tended to legitimize some forms of political gossip, because their concerns centered on the family, and they saw the problems of the family mainly in terms of bad behavior by men—drinking, gambling, spousal abuse, and the ills that centered around prostitution. A nation that worried about these issues was going to pay attention to the private lives of politicians. People may have whispered about wife-beating that never took place. But they also noticed, and reacted strongly, to real instances of congressmen behaving badly.

"No man under any circumstances can be
expected to marry a woman who is not
chaste"

The most talked-about political morality tale began on July 21, 1893, when *The New York Times* printed a short but rather tantalizing report from Richmond, Virginia:

> The marriage a few days ago of Congressman W.C.P. Breckinridge and Mrs. Louise Scott Wing of Louisville has caused considerable surprise here. It was understood among the congressman's friends that he was engaged to Miss Madeline

Breckinridge Pollard of Lexington, Ky. The engagement was publicly announced here and there.

Readers who suspected that the little item was the tip of the iceberg were right. Only a few weeks after the *Times* story appeared, Madeline Pollard sued Breckinridge for breach of promise. It was one of those defining public moments that puts private gossip into the newspapers. The response by Breckinridge's jurors, and later by his own constituents, showed he had picked the wrong point in history to be accused of seducing and abandoning a woman.

William Breckinridge was a prominent Democrat, sometimes mentioned—at least by his friends—as possible presidential material. Known as the "silver tongued orator," the gray-maned, gray-bearded Kentuckian specialized in those gorgeous, highfalutin disquisitions on grand moral themes that had been popular throughout the nineteenth century. Faced with a roomful of veterans, he would, one newspaper sniped, "bare his white head . . . and talk of the bright and beautiful moon, the men that fought for the 'lost cause,' the green sward that separates the beloved dead in our own beautiful country, your fathers and my fa-a-a-a-thers. . . ." When he lectured at women's schools in his district, he focused on a different theme: "chastity as the cornerstone of human society." In an address he would live to regret, Breckinridge urged the young women at Sayre Institute, in Lexington, to protect themselves against the males of the species by avoiding "useless handshaking, promiscuous kissing, needless touches and all exposures."

Madeline Pollard was a student at Wesleyan Female Seminary, in Cincinnati, when she met Breckinridge on a train trip in 1884. He was forty-nine. Madeline later claimed she was only seventeen. The congressman said she begged him to come to visit her at school, and then made it clear that she was available for a long-term relationship. Madeline's lawyers said Breckinridge had dropped in unexpectedly, convinced the awestruck dean to allow her to join him on a buggy ride, and "by wiles and artifice and protestations of affection subsequently took advantage of her youth and inexperience." At the congressman's urging, she transferred to Sayre Institute, in Kentucky, the

97

site of that famous chastity speech. Later she followed him to Washington. Along the way she gave birth to two children and miscarried a third.

At his breach-of-promise trial, Breckinridge portrayed Madeline Pollard as a knowing hussy, and she was certainly a less innocent and more interesting woman than her own court papers suggested. She got her education courtesy of James Rodes, an elderly Kentucky gentleman who had agreed to pay her tuition in return for her promise to marry him. "She had an ambition for learning," the smitten Rodes explained to a friend. The defense presented Madeline's letters, in which she alternated pleas for money with invitations that Rodes visit her. "Come early, and we will go see mama," she suggested repeatedly. It was clearly a code for something more exciting than a trip to her parent.

Madeline was the star essayist at her school, and she had a dream of becoming a great novelist like Mary Ann Evans (George Eliot). On her fatal buggy ride with Breckinridge she told him Eliot was her role model—the great artist who dared flout convention by living publicly with her devoted, but married, lover. "She . . . said she would rather live the life George Eliot did than grow up an ignorant Kentucky country woman, raising a houseful of children, churning milk and all that sort of thing," Breckinridge said at the trial. He mentioned the conversation, he told the jury, "merely to give . . . an idea of the mawkish sentiment of this plaintiff's mind."

The principals in the Breckinridge case weren't as famous as the stars of the Beecher trial, but the breach-of-promise suit engrossed the nation in the same way. The judge, Andrew Bradley, was outraged at the number of respectable people who flocked into his courtroom to hear testimony about adultery, illegitimate babies, and teenage girls who invited old men to "go see mama." He shooed away young ladies he found waiting for seats when the courtroom opened, and tried to shame the rest of the crowd into leaving. "Judge Bradley's remarks yesterday at adjournment about 'human buzzards' watching the 'carrion' of sensationalism had their effect on attendance, for not one-third of the seats in the courtroom were occupied," the *Times* reported one day. But the crowd, laced with high-profile spectators ranging from the governor of Indiana to the Princeton baseball team, always crept back.

The congressman initially denied he had ever had sex with Madeline. But when that story fell apart, he changed his tactics and simply claimed that as a fallen woman she did not deserve the law's protection. "No man under any circumstances can be expected or required to marry a woman who is not chaste," said one of Breckinridge's friends, outlining the trial strategy. His lawyers argued that even if Pollard *had* been his mistress, her character would have been improved, not lowered, by association with such a distinguished man. As in the Beecher case, the lawyers urged the jurors to vote based on their view of the moral universe. "I stand here for womanhood," announced one of Madeline's attorneys. ". . . I stand here to protest against allowing this man to enter my parlor and your parlor, while the basement door and the gate of the back alley are bolted against this woman." The defense warned the all-male jury that awarding money to Madeline would "encourage her kind to bring suits in court."

In another era—say, the one in which Daniel Sickles had flourished—Breckinridge's strategy of dismissing Pollard as a woman of ill repute who deserved whatever befell her might have worked. But fin de siècle America was getting tired of the Sickleses and Roscoe Conklings who took their pleasure where they liked, while somewhere in the background a woman suffered. And not even Sickles or Conkling had ever dared to give chastity lectures to a school for young women and then enroll his mistress as a student. Reporters discovered that Breckinridge, who had been widowed twice, had secretly married Louisa Wing months before the ceremony was performed publicly, in what had all the appearances of a shotgun wedding. "He has become entangled, as many another man has before him, and he was so perplexed he hardly knew which way to turn," explained a friend. The jury awarded Madeline fifteen thousand dollars—the equivalent of three years' salary for the congressman—and many of the men on the panel said later they had argued for a much higher sum. The sister of one of the congressman's deceased wives presented flowers to Madeline's attorney after the verdict.

*"Strong-minded women are doing their utmost
to defeat you"*

Breckinridge ran for reelection in 1894 anyway, counting on his silver
tongue and the tolerance of the twenty thousand or so male voters
who would decide the critical Democratic primary. The media found
the election even more fascinating than the trial. *The Washington Post*
claimed the campaign was unprecedented in American history. "In
intensity and feeling it was like civil war. It divided neighborhood,
churches and families." Breckinridge opened the campaign with a
bang. In a speech at the Louisville Opera House, he tearily asked his
constituents' forgiveness for having been "entangled by weakness, by
passion, by sin, in coils which it was almost impossible to break." The
previously skeptical all-male crowd wound up cheering with wild enthusiasm.

A race that started out on such a note could not help being larded
with new layers of gossip. William Owens, Breckinridge's strongest
opponent, was rumored to have made money by plying young men
with drink, and then inducing them to gamble. More believably, the
Breckinridge forces claimed that Owens had helped pay for Madeline
Pollard's lawsuit. The congressman, inevitably, was rumored to have
other lovers, and to be entertaining prostitutes on his campaign train.
During the trial, Madeline had helped those stories along by claiming
she had received anonymous letters informing her that Breckinridge
had a black mistress.

Even though Kentucky women were unable to vote, they were a
critical factor. Some threatened to boycott stores that supported
Breckinridge, and at least a few issued public warnings that young
men courting their daughters had better abandon the Breckinridge
cause or find another love object. "Strong-minded women are doing
their utmost to defeat you," a friend warned Breckinridge. The congressman's reaction was not much different from that of Senator Robert Packwood when that longtime supporter of women's rights
legislation got caught up in a sexual harassment scandal. "I have been
and am a consistent friend of the advanced notions of permitting
women to win their bread," Breckinridge protested. ". . . It seems a

travesty of justice that I should be the victim of unscrupulous women who have taken advantage of these benefits."

The turnout for the Democratic primary was the highest in the district's history. Owens defeated Breckinridge 8,074 to 7,819, with a third candidate receiving another 3,406 votes. DECENCY WINS IN KENTUCKY, headlined *The New York Times*. Other papers were even less restrained. THE SILVER-TONGUED AND MORAL LEPER DEFEATED, one announced. Despite continuous tries, Breckinridge never regained office. He became a local newspaper editor and lawyer, while his wife degenerated into an abusive hysteric whose nervous attacks were rumored to be drug-induced. Madeline, meanwhile, took to the lecture circuit, then attempted a career onstage.

Congressmen Behaving Badly

The activist women of the turn of the century had interests and world-views as varied as any large section of American citizenry. But there was a shared concern for the plight of poor women that united religious conservatives with agnostic socialists. They fought for the temperance movement because the violence engendered by drink was usually taken out on a helpless woman at home, and the jobs lost from absenteeism meant the breakup of impoverished families. They opposed gambling because men who gambled lost money their wives and children needed for food and clothing. Houses of prostitution spread sexual diseases (which men brought home to their wives) and lured young girls into hopeless lives of degradation. On primary day in Breckinridge's district, women passed out cards addressed to the male voters on behalf of their "wives, mothers and sisters." Once the battle over Breckinridge is over, the leaflets said, "we pledge ourselves to go on from this to other equally useful victories, and in a short time will free our lovely city from the curses that now endanger our beloved ones, the saloons, the houses of the scarlet women, the gambling halls, the race track. . . ."

As the twentieth century progressed, more women began to realize that banning alcohol and outlawing sin would not solve the problems of the poor while housing was inadequate and factories failed to pay a living wage. The remarkable Frances Perkins, who became Franklin Roosevelt's Secretary of Labor, recalled that as a college student, she visited a Massachusetts mill town and was stunned to discover that the workers' poverty and misery "was not due solely to the fact that they drank." But the turn-of-the-century women's movement was still heavily moralistic and focused on issues of private behavior. Because of that, activist women encouraged the voting public to consider candidates' activities behind closed doors as important. If members of the U.S. Congress felt free to seduce and abandon helpless women, drink too much, and gamble away their family's assets, there would not be much hope for the rest of the country.

The politicians were not doing much to calm the public's anxiety about the kind of examples their elected representatives were setting in their treatment of women. The run that had begun with Roscoe Conkling continued with Senator William Sharon of California, who was sued by one of his former lovers, Althea Hill. Sharon had bribed Hill to become his mistress, and then tried to get rid of her by having the door taken off her San Francisco hotel suite. Next came Florida senator Charles Jones, who vanished in 1885, missing the entire year's legislative session. Newspaper reporters finally located him in Detroit, where he had been harassing a wealthy spinster with "passionate notes and bouquets." In 1889, a Kentucky paper revealed that a married congressman had been having a lunchtime dalliance with a clerk at the Washington patent office. The reporter who wrote the story later killed the disgraced legislator, and was acquitted on the grounds of self-defense.

In 1906, Senator Arthur Brown was killed by his mistress after an affair that was even messier than Breckinridge's. A Utah Republican, Brown had a long-running relationship with Anna Bradley, a married employee of his local Republican ward committee. After his wife, Isabel, twice had him arrested for adultery, Brown made a stab at reformation and actually hired a guardian to make sure he kept away from Mrs. Bradley. The watchdog proved useless, and Brown ran off to meet his lover in Idaho, with Mrs. Brown hard on his heels. The marital drama continued until Isabel died in 1905. But once he and Anna Bradley were free to marry, Brown began to dither. He left her at the altar once, and was still stalling when Anna took a train to Washington, broke into the senator's hotel room, and discovered evidence that he was having an affair with a prominent actress named Annie Adams. When Brown returned, Bradley shot and killed him. "I am the mother of his two children," she told the police. Newspapers soon discovered that Brown had been married to another woman before Isabel, and that she, too, had tried to shoot him because of his infidelity. Searching for something positive to say about the dying man, the *Times* noted that he was "known to be intensely loyal to his male friends."

It did not take long to determine where public sympathy was going. As the senator lay expiring from his wounds, local restaurants were besieging the House of Detention with offers to cater Anna Bradley's meals. A number of Brown's western political colleagues offered to help underwrite her defense. When Anna did go on trial, she was acquitted due to temporary insanity—just as Congressman Sickles had been a half-century before.

A Brief Diversion—the Patent Office Sex Scandal

One of the congressmen whose sexual sins were exposed during the era was William Preston Taulbee, a Kentucky minister's son whose only crime was a series of lunchtime trysts with one Miss Dodge, a Patent Office worker who was said to be "plump as a partridge" as well as "bright as a sunbeam and saucy as a bowl of jelly." The story of Taulbee's backstairs dalliance was well known in Washington, and it had been reported in a blind item in one of the local papers. But his constituents back home apparently did not get wind of it until reporter Charles Kincaid wrote the story up for the *Louisville Times*. Unlike the Washington paper, Kincaid named names. It was one of the most dramatic instances before the Gary Hart era when a reporter would go out of his way to turn private gossip into public scandal without any provocation from the erring politician.

Taulbee's political influence in his eastern Kentucky district was so strong that people said "as goes Pres Taulbee so go the mountains."

But he was apparently made of more sensitive material than many of his political colleagues. When he was depicted in the newspapers as a lecher, Taulbee could not bear to face his constituents. His fellow congressmen urged him simply to ignore the whole business. But Taulbee dropped out of politics, abandoned life in East Kentucky, and became a Washington lobbyist—unsurprisingly, one with a stiff grudge against the reporter who had exposed him.

Kincaid was politically well connected in Kentucky and personally popular with the Washington press corps. Frail and in poor health, he was terrified of the big, rawboned ex-congressman. In February of 1890, the two ran into each other outside the House of Representatives and Taulbee angrily demanded they have a talk. "I am a small man and unarmed!" Kincaid cried. Before bystanders could separate them, Taulbee pulled Kincaid's ear, and that was the end of the incident. But two hours later, as Taulbee was talking with another man on the Capitol steps, Kincaid walked up and fired a bullet into his head.

"He pulled my ear," the reporter said later to a friend. "Oh, if only he had killed me." It was, the *Journal-Courier* reported, "the last gross affront, the taunting provocation that could not be borne." Kincaid was taken off to jail. The bleeding Taulbee was removed to the Committee on Public Buildings and Grounds, and later home to his hotel, where he died a few days later.

The newspaper reports on the shooting, all written by Kincaid's friends, were not particularly objective. (One reported that the dying congressman said he did not hold the shooting against his assassin.) It's hard to tell whether Kincaid really had any reason to fear Taulbee might hurt him. But the humiliation of being branded an ear-pull victim in the papers seemed to take on immense significance. "When he pulled my ear today and I knew that the boys on the [newspaper] row had it, I was crazed," Kincaid said in a jailhouse interview after the shooting. During his subsequent trial, the prosecutor urged the jury to find the reporter guilty of murder. But they could settle for manslaughter, he admitted, if they felt that "he had not had time to cool off after the ear-pulling episode." The jury did neither, and acquitted Kincaid on the grounds of self-defense. To this day, tourists visiting the Capitol are shown the steps where Taulbee died, and a discolored patch of marble that legend says is a stain from the congressman's blood.

2. First Family Gossip

*"Women came in carriages, on horseback
    and on foot"*

It would be a long while before the public became as wild about another First Lady as they were when Frances Cleveland was in the White House. But the nation remained interested in the president's family life, even when the families in question were not really all that compelling. Benjamin Harrison, who was the president in between Cleveland's two terms, was an icy man and his wife, Caroline, was a quiet homebody with a passion for painted china. By default, the administration celebrity became grandson "Baby McKee," whose family shared the White House with the Harrisons. The papers regaled the nation with amusing stories about the president cavorting with his dictatorial little descendant. They must have been the product of desperate reporters' imagination, since relatives said Harrison never gave any sign he was particularly interested in the child.

When Theodore Roosevelt succeeded the assassinated William McKinley in 1901, however, the nation finally had a First Family that was both compelling and accessible. This president and First Lady presided over a brood of youngsters—five children ages five to eighteen—instead of the usual grown-up offspring. Even more important, Roosevelt was happy to allow the media to write about them. T.R. had spent most of his life creating the persona that was Teddy Roosevelt—dynamic, heroic, living every moment to the hilt, ready for anything. He did not distinguish between the private and public self, and he did not see anything strange in the fact that all America wanted to know about young Kermit's dog or Alice's boyfriends or Theodore Jr.'s progress in school. It was an important moment for the new industry of newspaper gossip. Roosevelt legitimized the public's curiosity about what went on in the family quarters of the White House. Once newspapers were given tacit permission to look behind those doors, the president and his family officially became part of that great celebrity neighborhood about which the public gossiped so eagerly.

Over Roosevelt's seven and a half years in office, the nation developed a proprietary interest in his children: Alice the fearless debutante, Theodore Jr. the hard-fighting football player, thoughtful Kermit, tomboy Ethel, good-natured Archie, and outrageous Quentin. People particularly wanted to know everything about Alice, and Alice seemed to glory in the attention, stalking around the White House with a blue macaw on her shoulder and a green garter snake wound around her arm. Her marriage to Congressman Nicholas Longworth obsessed the nation. In Pittsburgh, two thousand working-class girls stopped traffic when they gathered in front of a newspaper office to wait for word that Alice was Mrs. Longworth. When the bulletin was posted, "they all seemed as thoroughly happy as though they had been personally concerned," the *Times* reported. And of course they were. Alice received so many wedding gifts that when she died seventy-five years later, a pile of them were found in her house, still unopened.

When the newlyweds returned to Nick Longworth's home in Cincinnati, more than fifty thousand people showed up to see Alice unveil a statue of William McKinley. "Nothing like the wild rush that the people made was ever seen in Ohio before," wrote the *Times*. Dramatic as Alice's day was, however, she had to share the front page of the nation's newspapers with her sister, Ethel, who was tossed from her buggy by a runaway horse, and then stunned the admiring crowd by getting up and insisting on driving the beast home. There were often two or more headlines about the Roosevelts on the front page during that era. Even Pete the Roosevelt bulldog starred in several stories when he bit a clerk and later ran away from the White House.

The constant surveillance could not have been as easy for the children, but they learned to accept the fact that their every activity was going to be shared with the entire country. When Theodore Jr. got dangerously ill at Groton, *The New York Times* followed his progress from DOUBLE PNEUMONIA! to BETTER! to SAVED! (A few years later, when Archie got diphtheria, a similar set of stories were accompanied by the observation that the flood of get-well telegrams to the White House were due in part to the fact that "Archie is one of the most popular of the president's children.") While attempting to hike across the Midwest with a military troop in 1907, eighteen-year-old Kermit was finally forced to flee the hordes of women who followed the soldiers, demanding to see the president's son. "Women came in carriages, on horseback and on foot," reported the *Times*. ". . . The last straw came at Joslyn, when an elderly woman opened the tent flaps while young Roosevelt was asleep, and lifting a hat with which he had covered his face, petted him, saying 'You are a dear boy.' " On Ted Jr.'s honeymoon, reporters banged on the newlyweds' hotel door, demanding an interview.

Everything the Roosevelt children did, from their pranks (Archie carves his initials in a church pew) to their heroics (Kermit saves a woman on a runaway horse) was of enormous public interest. Like the Kennedy children decades later, they continued to be regarded with fascination long after they reached adulthood. When the four Roosevelt boys went off to serve in World War I they were the "Fighting Roosevelts," doing their duty for the nation. The family baby, Quentin, was shot down over enemy lines and killed. In one of the most grisly examples of the price of fame, the Germans manufactured a postcard with a picture of the boy with a bullet through his forehead.

During the early months of Woodrow Wilson's presidency the press attempted to turn the three Wilson girls into new versions of Alice Roosevelt. But their father, who had spent most of his life in academia, never accepted the idea that the nation had any right to pry into his family's business. The girls arrived in Washington just when they entered the delicate mating stage, and none of them were able to swagger their way through it as Alice had. Wilson and his wife were upset that Margaret, their oldest and least socially adept daughter, was continually reported as being on the brink of an engagement. It was particularly embarrassing because one of the men Margaret was linked with, a dashing lumberman named Ben King, was actually secretly engaged to her younger sister Nell. Meanwhile Nell was falling in love with Wilson's secretary of the treasury, William McAdoo, the widowed father of six children who was twenty-six years her senior.

Wilson, who still expected reporters to behave like respectful junior faculty in the presence of the dean, finally held a press conference and announced that reporters who continued to write about his family might be barred from access to the White House. The papers backed down—a sign of the media's shift away from the impudent and sassy spirit of the 1880s and 1890s. The wheel had turned since the Grover Cleveland honeymoon.

3. Theodore Roosevelt's Drinking Problem

*"The addition of the morphine habit to my
insanity and drunkenness gives the story
new flavor"*

The Lake Shore Limited rolled across Wisconsin in May of 1913, carrying ex-president Roosevelt and his friends to the shores of Lake Superior. Jacob Riis, the eminent muckraker, was there, along with James Garfield, the son of the assassinated president. There were Frank Tyree and James Sloan, T.R.'s old Secret Service bodyguards, and a goodly chunk of his former Cabinet. As the train ran along they reminisced, rehashing old campaigns, old White House battles won and lost during the eventful Roosevelt era that had ended four years before. The ex-president generally stayed in his compartment, visiting privately with one old pal after another.

An aide walked in at one point, bearing a chapter of Roosevelt's about-to-be-published autobiography. He pointed out a slight mistake on one page.

"I suppose I was intoxicated when I wrote it," Roosevelt said dryly.

The train was en route to Marquette, Michigan, where Roosevelt would try to get a jury of his peers to declare, once and for all, that he was not a drunk.

"The ex-President is determined to bring out in public, where it can be attacked and destroyed, a story which has been whispered and even openly insinuated all over the United States," wrote *The New York Times* correspondent from the train. "He does not wish it to be spread into popular legend about him, as it has about other Presidents and public men who let it go uncorrected. Probably in no previous case has the story assumed such mammoth proportions and been spread so widely."

The story that Teddy Roosevelt was an alcoholic was one of the most purebred pieces of gossip ever passed around about an American president. It was not a fiction created by his political enemies, although they enjoyed repeating it. The story seemed to have spread across the country on its own power. Reporters covering Roosevelt's last presidential campaign were stunned by its pervasiveness. "The farther West they went, the more men they met who asked: 'Is he really drunk all the time?' " reported the *Times*.

Chances are, the story was inadvertently started by Roosevelt himself. The president had an unusual presence—he walked with a rolling gait, he clenched his teeth again and again when he spoke, in a peculiar chopping manner. When he became excited, his voice grew higher and higher, until it was an absolute falsetto. "His spirits ran to such a high pitch that he appeared to be bereft, in some measure, of the normal restraints," said James Faulkner, the political reporter for the *Cincinnati Enquirer*. The *Times* put it less delicately: "These stories gain currency because the Colonel's habitual deportment is that of a raving alcoholic." In an age without television or radio, when most people never had a chance to hear a president speak, Roosevelt's demeanor could be startling. The crowds who gathered to listen as he campaigned, or sat near him at political dinners, could not have known that he always sounded like that. Many must have left shaking their heads, convinced they had seen him drunk. Roosevelt's friends did him the dubious favor of recounting every new permutation of the rumors—possibly so they could also report their own loyal denials. "The addition of the morphine habit to my insanity and drunkenness gives the story new flavor," Roosevelt wryly wrote a friend in 1907.

He tried issuing public denials. His friend, Dr. Lyman Abbott, told reporters that "the only thing Col. Roosevelt drinks to excess is milk.

He sometimes takes as many as four or five glasses at a single meal." The statement was less successful in quenching the rumors than in making Roosevelt the subject of the same sorts of jokes Bill Clinton would later call up when he swore he never inhaled. ROOSEVELT DRINKS TOO MUCH MILK, said one newspaper headline after another. Letter writers speculated wittily about whether all that lactose could be healthy, expressing concerns about "fermenting fumes." Newspaper cartoonists had a field day.

If only some editor would say he was a drunkard flat out, Roosevelt told reporters during his final presidential campaign in 1912, he could sue for libel and prove his sobriety in court. Not long after, someone did. George Newett, the publisher of *The Iron Ore,* an obscure weekly in the mining town of Ishpenning, Michigan, went to listen to Roosevelt speak and was outraged when the candidate attacked a local congressman who was Newett's friend. Stalking back to the paper, Newett ordered up an anti-Roosevelt editorial that concluded: "Roosevelt lies and curses in a most disgusting way. He gets drunk, too, and not infrequently, and all his intimates know about it." It was the chance Roosevelt had been waiting for. He filed criminal and civil charges against Newett.

Testifying on his own behalf during the trial, the ex-president gave a painfully detailed recitation of his alcohol consumption. "I have never drunk a cocktail or highball in my life," he swore. "I don't smoke and I don't drink beer, because I dislike smoking and I dislike the taste of beer." Whiskey and brandy only when a doctor prescribed it "or possibly on some occasion after great exposure (in the weather)." At public dinners, a glass of champagne or two. At home a glass or two of white wine. "At the White House we had a mint bed, and I should think that on average I may have drunk half a dozen mint juleps a year." In the four years since he left office, Roosevelt added carefully, he had consumed two more.

Then came the parade of witnesses—reporters who had covered his campaigns, a valet who had packed all his bags and never saw a whiskey flask, college classmates, family friends, aides, bodyguards, Cabinet members. But the defendant, George Newett, stole the show. Taking the stand, the publisher admitted that he had been unable to find a single witness who could personally testify to seeing Roosevelt drunk, although he found hundreds who were willing to swear they had heard the stories. Even his friend the congressman, on whose behalf Newett had started the whole business, had skipped town. He was convinced, Newett told the jury, that Roosevelt was a sober man indeed.

"In short, he proved to be the best witness for Col. Roosevelt that had been produced in the whole trial," wrote the *Times*. "He pleaded only that he had acted in good faith, having been made a victim of that hole-and-corner gossip that had been smirching the Colonel's reputation in many other places than Ishpenning."

When Newett left the witness stand, Roosevelt leaped to his feet and asked that the jury be instructed to award only nominal damages. "I did not go into this suit for money," he declaimed, his voice ringing through the hushed courtroom. Pointing a finger at the judge, he continued: "I went into it, and made my reputation an issue, because I wish, once and for all during my lifetime, to deal with these slanders fully and comprehensively, so that never again will it be possible for any man in good faith to repeat them." Lifting his hand above his head, clenching his fist, he concluded, "I have achieved my purpose, and I am content."

It was a patented Roosevelt performance. In a different context, some of the onlookers might have wondered whether all that intensity of emotion was artificially stimulated.

Scientific Drinking

Gossip about politicians and alcohol has always been very much affected by the era's level of alcohol consumption. Roosevelt was living in a backlash period, when the ranks of nondrinkers were increasing, and very suspicious of those who still imbibed. The nondrinkers were also inflexible. Earlier temperance movements had been aimed mainly at ridding the country of hard liquor and encouraging moderation in the drinking of beer and wine. But the new abstainers were made of sterner stuff. Many regarded even coffee or red meat as a road to stimulant addiction. The nation was well on the way to Prohibition.

111

Large chunks of the country had already banned the sale of all alcoholic products, and nearly 40 percent of adult Americans classified themselves as nondrinkers.

But alcohol was still the nation's biggest consumer industry. The country had more bars than schools, hospitals, parks, or churches. Americans spent $1.8 billion a year on alcohol—just short of their $2 billion budget for food and nonalcoholic drinks. Everybody who was not abstaining seemed to be drinking constantly. For the working class, that meant sitting in a saloon with friends and "treating" each other until everyone passed out. The professional classes were far more discreet, but not necessarily all that much more sober. In 1908, a writer in *The Independent* magazine gave a perfectly sincere explanation of the more wholesome habits of the white-collar drinking classes:

> Such a man will commonly take a whiskey and soda at ten in the morning and another before luncheon. During dinner he will take a cocktail. With dinner he will drink wines and during the evening he will take perhaps a couple of whiskeys with seltzer. . . . He has drunk scientifically, so to speak. . . . Such men work at high pressure, hard and fast, in business hours and they drink in order to work harder and faster and get the pressure higher. They drink for stimulus. This is the difference, as I have seen it, between club men's drinking and workingmen's drinking. . . ."

Naturally, there was hostility between the temperance movement and "club men" who regarded any attempt to dictate their drinking habits as unwarranted meddling. While he was president, Roosevelt attended a businessmen's lunch in St. Louis at which champagne was served, and the guests were avid to see whether the president would dare public censure by drinking his. Responding to the first toast by touching the glass to his lip, Roosevelt then jumped up, grinned, and gulped down the whole glass to enormous applause. His defiant response to the temperance movement's absolutism (which Alice mimicked at her wedding) helped give Roosevelt his unwelcome reputation. During the White House days, guides in Washington sight-seeing cars would tell their customers that when they passed the White House tennis courts, if they looked carefully, they might see "Mr. Roosevelt reaching for a highball."

4. The President's Second Wife

"Just about the most exciting topic we had ever had"

Woodrow Wilson was a peculiar politician to suffer from rumors of womanizing. "You can't cast a man as Romeo who looks and acts so much like an apothecary's clerk," sneered Theodore Roosevelt. But despite his prim appearance, Wilson was a passionate man who adored the opposite sex. Almost all his closest friends were women— devoted, intelligent and eager to sit at his metaphorical feet and listen to him hold forth on the issues of the day. But he was also almost obsessively moralistic about his own behavior—a sort of polar opposite of the Congressmen Breckinridges of this world. (Alice Roosevelt, who hated the Democratic president, joked that Wilson always said his prayers before he jumped into bed with anyone.)

Wilson did have a sexual skeleton in his closet. In 1907, while he was president of Princeton University, he had vacationed alone in Bermuda and embarked on a romantic flirtation with a woman named Mary Allen Peck. Mrs. Peck was cheerful, charming, rather flighty, and very lonely. Separated from her husband, she lived in a lovely white villa and ran a sort of salon for the more interesting American visitors to the islands, like Mark Twain. Wilson, who was having trouble with both his job and his own marriage, was clearly attracted. They were together almost all the time. He sent her some of his essays "that you may know me a little better" and Walter Bagehot's writing on the English constitution. She introduced him to her circle of friends. He returned to visit her in Bermuda again the next year, and

113

in 1909, after she returned to America and broke permanently with her husband, they met in her apartment in New York. Wilson would later refer to it as a period of "folly and gross impertinence."

Whether Wilson and Mrs. Peck ever had a physical relationship is one of the many sexual mysteries of American politics, like Jefferson and Sally Hemings or the parentage of Maria Halpin's baby (or, in later years, exactly what it was that Eleanor Roosevelt did with her friend Lorena Hickok). Over the years, Wilson and Mrs. Peck would exchange hundreds of letters and he would "lend" her considerable sums of money. The letters that have survived show an intense friendship, but if any of them contained evidence of something more erotic, they were destroyed.

At the time, many people certainly believed Wilson and Mrs. Peck had done more than read Walter Bagehot together. But whatever romantic notions Wilson nurtured had clearly faded by the time he became president, and Mrs. Peck had turned into a harried divorcée with constant money troubles. Still, rumors about their relationship dogged him throughout his presidency. When Wilson first ran for the Democratic nomination in 1912, the undercurrent of gossip was particularly hurtful to his wife, Ellen, who once told a confidante that her husband's relationship with Mrs. Peck was the only great sorrow in her marriage. The story of the Peck affair was "whispered about the corridors of the Democratic National Convention at Baltimore," and cropped up intermittently throughout the campaign, said journalist David Lawrence.

Seventeen months after Wilson's inauguration, Ellen Wilson died of kidney disease, leaving the president achingly lonely. With his daughters off on their own and no admiring wife to shore up his self-esteem, he withered. "If he does not marry and marry quickly, I believe he will go into a decline," Wilson's close adviser Edward House wrote in his diary. But the president did find a replacement in Edith Bolling Galt, the forty-three-year-old widow of a Washington jeweler. Gossip about the romance would entertain Washington for the last half of Wilson's first term, and its aftermath would have a far more serious effect on his second.

The president had been a widower less than eight months when he met Mrs. Galt at a White House tea in March of 1915. They hit it off so well that by May, Wilson was declaring his love. They became secretly engaged in June, and probably consummated their relationship around the same time. The president never appeared in public with Mrs. Galt unless a third person was present, but she was a constant presence at the White House. Ike Hoover, the White House usher, noted that after dinner Wilson and his flame "would often retire to the President's study and the rest of the company would find amusement in other parts of the house." Edith was so entrenched in the household, Hoover added, that "every activity now revolved around the lady, every plan included her. . . . At every place where the President was to be, provision must be made for her to be there also."

Having retreated in the battle over the Wilson girls' engagements, the press corps was not going to drop hints about the president's own love life. But everyone in Washington was aware of the romance and everyone was riveted. "Few of my friends knew Mrs. Galt, but all were frantic to know more about her," wrote Evalyn Walsh McLean, the wife of *Washington Post* publisher Ned McLean. "They used to chide me because I did not know, right off, the inside story of the White House love affair." The most hotly desired dinner guest of the period, McLean said, was anyone who had the least bit of gossip about the president's courtship. Hostesses' friends would plead: "Get someone who knows this Mrs. Galt to come. I'm wild for information."

The fact that all Washington was talking upset Edith. She was the product of an old, if impoverished, Virginia family, and very much part of the tradition of southern womanhood. A woman's reputation was her main treasure, and the idea of being gossiped about was appalling to her, especially given the kind of stories that were making the rounds. One rumor alleged that she had been the mistress of German ambassador Johann von Bernstorff. The capital was also endlessly amused by the fact that Wilson—the apothecary's clerk—was apparently having an intense and satisfying sexual relationship with his middle-aged lover. Later, after the engagement became public, *The Washington Post* ran a social item with an infamous typo: "The president spent much of the evening entering Mrs. Galt." The inner circles of Washington believed it had to be the work of the publisher's wife, the irrepressible Mrs. McLean.

But the general public was out of the gossip loop, and under the impression that Wilson was still mourning his late wife, struggling under the combined gloom of his personal loss and the war in Europe. The president's advisers were understandably worried about what would happen if he announced his engagement before the 1916 election. They were particularly concerned about the mysterious "women's vote." (Although the Nineteenth Amendment would not become law until 1920, women were already allowed to vote in a number of states, including most of the West.) Hoping to get rid of Edith Galt, or at least keep her under wraps until after the election, Wilson's advisers summoned up the specter of Mrs. Peck. Treasury Secretary McAdoo made up a story about receiving an anonymous letter that reported Mrs. Peck—now Mary Allen Hulbert—was allowing other people to read Wilson's letters, and threatening to publish them if the president married anyone but her.

McAdoo's warnings frightened Wilson. Besides his letters, he had sent fifteen thousand dollars to the beleaguered Mrs. Hulbert, who was under constant financial strain due to the misadventures of her only son. He confessed to his fiancée about his old flame, and begged her forgiveness. (Hoping to have it both ways, Wilson denied there had ever been a sexual relationship but asked for absolution anyway.) After a few rather hysterical days, the engagement was cemented rather than broken off. Edith, who had a gift for self-dramatization, later claimed that the president's personal physician appeared at her door to beg her to take Wilson back, saying: "The president is very ill. I can do nothing. You are the only person who can help. . . . If you could see him you would not hesitate. He does not sleep or eat."

Poor Mary Hulbert (who always remained "Mrs. Peck" to the world of gossip) was an innocent victim in all this. Her relationship with Wilson was the high point of a life troubled by financial and family woes. When the president became a widower, she really had hoped he would turn to her, and she still treasured a piece of lace that she dreamed of wearing to her own White House wedding. Now she received nothing but a brief note from Wilson announcing his engagement, and signed, "your devoted friend." She had never tried to sell the letters, but she was still being pursued by reporters, and was once again the center of the Washington rumor mill. "Her mysterious friendship with the President was just about the most exciting topic we had ever had," wrote Evalyn McLean. "Who is Mrs. Peck? Reporters scampered here and there to propound that question in a whisper." Whatever the reporters learned must have been confined to confidential memos to their editors. But the rumors included stories that Wilson had bribed Mrs. Peck into silence, and that Louis Brandeis, who served as intermediary, was rewarded with a Supreme Court appointment. Another story had her on salary as a Treasury Department employee. No one could resist referring to the popular turn-of-the-century comedy, and calling Wilson "Peck's Bad Boy."

"He had not imagined that his enemies could be so unjust"

The rumors about Mrs. Peck were exciting, but Washington had even more to whisper about when the White House announced the engagement of Woodrow Wilson and Edith Galt in a press release written by the happy couple themselves: "In the circle of cultivated and interesting people who have had the privilege of knowing her, Mrs. Galt has enjoyed an enviable distinction, not only because of unusual beauty and charm, but also because of her unusual character and gifts. She has always been sought out as a delightful friend, and her thoughtfulness and quick capacity for anything she chose to undertake have made her friendship invaluable to those who were fortunate enough to win it." Most newspapers mercifully refrained from printing the announcement in full, but it quickly made the rounds in the capital.

Once again, the nation was fascinated by the idea of a presidential marriage—the public fixated particularly on Mrs. Galt's claim to be a direct descendant of Pocahontas. But this time the interest was mixed with what began as wry skepticism and developed, in some places, into outward hostility. The Wilsons were married in December of 1915, in the bride's house "under circumstances of extreme simplicity," noted *The New York Times*. The press was able to recount every detail of what went on in the private ceremony, from the exact moment when Mrs. Galt's mother placed her daughter's hand in Wilson's to the gifts (including fourteen vases, one Navajo blanket, a "huge silver loving cup" from the Virginia congressional delegation, and a statue of Pocahontas). The newlyweds managed to avoid the press after the wedding and left for their honeymoon in Hot Springs by train. The next morning an aide entered the president's private car and saw the fifty-nine-year-old Wilson, with his hands in his pockets, clicking his heels and singing "Oh You Beautiful Doll."

The president was smitten, but his critics responded to the marriage in just the way Wilson's advisers had feared. The Republican Hearst papers visited Ellen Wilson's grave and noted pointedly that a tombstone had not yet been erected. But newspaper comment paled next to the private whispers. Average citizens wondered whether a man who got over a wife's death so quickly could have really been a good husband. Before the wedding, a railroad executive wrote to presidential adviser Colonel Edward House, warning that Wilson's plans for remarriage were "extremely unpopular" in the West, particularly among women. "It seems to have been something of a shock to the people to suddenly realize that, instead of this weight of sorrow, he was falling in love so soon after the death of his wife; and it apparently is regarded as an evidence of selfishness and a certain lack of propriety on the part of the president." David Lawrence, sent out to tap public sentiment across the country, said that wherever he went he "invariably was asked what effect the widespread discussion of Mr. Wilson's personal life was having. . . ." People passed around the story that Wilson and Mrs. Galt had been having an affair while he was still married, and even that they had plotted together to kill Ellen. "The most exaggerated stories are being told of him, none of them having the slightest foundation," wrote Colonel House. Someone left anonymous messages at Washington newspaper bureaus claiming that— shades of William Breckinridge—Mary Peck had just filed a breach-of-promise suit.

Wilson, who had not realized what the public was saying about his marriage, was stunned when Frank Glass, an old college friend who had become publisher of the *Birmingham News*, told him about the gossip. "Before he got all of my story, tears came into his eyes," Glass wrote later. ". . . He had not imagined that his enemies could be so unjust, so cruel." Short of calling a press conference to announce he was neither an adulterer nor a wife-murderer, there was little Wilson could do to counteract the rumors. However, one of Ellen Wilson's relatives was recruited to write an article praising the happiness of the president's first marriage.

Wilson eventually won a narrow victory against Charles Evans Hughes. But the whole country told variations of the joke Murray Kempton remembered hearing as a child: that when the president proposed, Mrs. Galt was so excited she fell out of bed. Edith heard the joke too, and she was not the sort of woman who would be amused at the idea of people laughing about her sex life. She had no political background, and very little education of any kind. She was not equipped by either training or temperament for life at the epicenter of American politics.

Charles Crauford-Stuart, an attaché to the British ambassador, told the Edith joke at a dinner party, and made some other rather loud and undiplomatic comments on the relationship. The story got back to Mrs. Wilson, and soon the White House demanded that Crauford-Stuart be sent back to Europe. The disgraced aide begged the State Department not to destroy his career, and the matter stayed in limbo until the ambassador himself returned to England, bringing his staff with him. Edith blamed Secretary of State Robert Lansing for failing to take more decisive action, and Lansing went down permanently on her enemies list.

"Suppose Wilson was running around naked?"

After World War I, Wilson became ill while hammering out a peace treaty in Paris, and suffered a stroke while campaigning to win support for the treaty at home. For more than six months, he was unable to function as chief executive and Edith became something very close to a surrogate president. Her powers were mainly negative—she did not make policy so much as stop policy from being made, in an effort to keep Wilson from being stressed. But she walked into her extraordinary position still a creature of the private, wifely world of southern womanhood. The resentment she felt about Washington's jokes and gossip became, on some issues, the most important factor in administrative decision making.

The critical problem facing the Wilson government was ratification of the peace treaty that would bring the United States into the League of Nations. Virtually everyone except the president believed it was necessary to compromise with the Republican majority in Congress in order to accomplish that goal. Former British foreign secretary Edward Grey, now Viscount Grey of Falloden, came out of retirement in order to return to the United States as British ambassador and help arrange a compromise. Grey had had a good relationship with the president, and the League's supporters in Europe believed he could convince Wilson that the changes demanded by Congress were far less significant than getting the United States into the League. Unfortunately Grey, old, sick, and half blind, brought Major Crauford-Stuart along as an attaché. The State Department, acting on instructions from the White House, demanded Crauford-Stuart be sent home for having slandered the First Lady. The astonished old viscount demurred. After four months, Grey went home without ever having seen Wilson. The compromises were rejected at the ailing, isolated president's insistence, and the treaty was never ratified.

Speculation about the president's physical condition, meanwhile, sparked what the *New York World* estimated were "1,000 rumors." In October, someone on Wall Street noticed the flags were at half-mast (the Manhattan borough president had passed away) and spread the story that the president had died. Stocks plunged. The White House windows that Teddy Roosevelt had barred to protect the glass from baseballs were noticed for the first time, and people pointed to them as proof the president was insane—from syphilis contracted during a sex spree while he was in Paris working on the peace accord. (It was the beginning of a spurt in syphilis rumors about prominent politicians. The public had begun to refocus on venereal disease as young people's interest in maintaining their virginity dropped, and their parents looked for other arguments against premarital sex.)

Mrs. Wilson and Cary Grayson, the president's personal physician, conspired to keep the country in the dark because the truth about his condition would certainly have led to calls for his resignation. Virtually no one had access to Wilson's bedroom but Edith and Dr. Grayson. Washington's inner loop was as mystified as the average voter. Late in 1919, a worried wire-service official asked his Washington bureau chief: "Suppose Wilson was running around naked on the second floor of the White House and nobody could catch him. How would you find out about it?"

For all they knew, the bureau chief responded grimly, Wilson was doing exactly that right now.

Even when it did have information, the press had never been very good at letting the public in on the true state of an important politician's health. Back in 1824, William Crawford's backers managed to make him a serious candidate for the presidency despite the fact that a mysterious illness had left him almost completely blind and paralyzed. Grover Cleveland, whose private life was publicized endlessly, still managed to have himself operated on for cancer of the jaw in secret. (The one reporter who did find out about the surgery was scoffed at by the rest of the media for his wild flights of fancy.) But as the country was becoming more complicated, it could less and less afford to have an invalid in the White House. While Wilson was lying virtually incommunicado, the United States was plunged into a murky and dangerous crisis with Mexico involving seized American oil wells and a kidnapped American official. Attorney General A. Mitchell Palmer was arresting four thousand people in raids on alleged Communist meeting places in thirty-three cities, violating civil rights at will. The coal miners went on strike, and of course the League of Nations went down to defeat. Hundreds of less important matters, like the appointment of ambassadors, filling of vacant administration posts, and treaty negotiations, simply fell by the wayside.

Everyone acknowledged in theory that the health of a president was a matter of public concern, yet illness still seemed to fall into that bin of private matters that could not be pried into without embarrassment. Over the decades to come, as the nation continued to retreat from the idea that politicians' private lives were legitimate topics for discussion, the problem of how to react when a president was not able-bodied would come up again and again.

Chapter 6

Political Gossip Goes
Underground
1920–1945

1. The Campaign of 1920: Negro Blood and Hints of Homosexuality

"One of my ancestors may have jumped the fence"

The story that Warren Harding was part Negro was purebred small-town gossip. Marion, Ohio, had whispered that the Harding family was not really white long before the future president was born. His parents claimed that the rumor had been begun out of revenge, by a man some long-dead ancestor had accused of theft. Much later, Harding's admirers would theorize that the story sprang out of the family's abolitionist sympathies before the Civil War. Possibly it started simply because it was true. In the eighteenth and nineteenth centuries, Ohio had been a favored destination for free blacks and runaway slaves looking for a place to settle in the North. Some of the state's longtime citizens must have been descended from those old émigrés.

The only reporter who ever asked Harding himself was James Faulkner, the revered political writer for the *Cincinnati Enquirer*.

"Do you have any Negro blood?" Faulkner once blurted out in a private conversation.

"How do I know, Jim?" Harding said easily. "One of my ancestors may have jumped the fence." He was utterly unqualified to be president of the United States, but no one who ever met Warren Harding denied that he was a likable man.

Rumors that someone in a small town had "Negro blood" were not uncommon earlier in this century. Whites passed them around partly to reassure themselves that blacks were really different. Identifying a family as mulatto gave people a comforting feeling that they really could differentiate between the races, and pick out one light-skinned Negro in a town full of various shades of white residents. The fact that their targets were usually poor and unsuccessful reinforced the whites' feelings of racial superiority. The Hardings had almost always been poor and unsuccessful. But young Warren was ambitious, and people who resented his upward mobility regularly brought up the "Negro blood" rumor. When Harding took over the faltering *Marion Star*, a competitor ran a snide editorial announcing he had "no desire to draw the COLOR line on the kink-haired youth. . . ." When he became engaged to be married, his future father-in-law, the wealthy and awful Amos Kling, cursed at him in public and called him "nigger."

The rumors resurfaced every time Harding ran for office in Ohio, but the reporters ignored them. When he was nominated for president in 1920, Harding personally called Robert Scripps, the head of a large newspaper chain, seeking—and getting—assurances that the Scripps people would not print anything about his hometown's gossip. The Democrats in the Wilson administration had also decided to steer clear of the subject. In her memoirs, Edith Wilson remembered Joseph Tumulty, the president's private secretary, joyously bringing the ailing president a flyer delineating Harding's mixed-race "family tree," and predicting the information could destroy the Republicans. "Even if that is so, it will never be used with my consent," Mrs. Wilson remembered her husband saying. "We cannot go into a man's genealogy; we must base our campaigns on principles, not backstairs gossip." Poor Tumulty never came out looking like the hero in Mrs. Wilson's anecdotes. (The president's wife had quite a few prejudices of her own, one involving big-city Irish Catholics.) Not surprisingly, Tumulty recalled the incident differently: *He* was the one who decided the Wilson administration would not tolerate such slander, and ordered the suppression of literature about Harding's racial background. Federal authorities had been given a great deal of censorship power during the war, and the reflex to outlaw disruptive writings continued into peacetime. When 250,000 copies of a "Negro blood" leaflet were discovered at a San Francisco post office, ready for mailing, the federal government had them destroyed.

"It is affecting the woman vote!"

The fact that the old gossip about Harding's ancestors did get into national circulation was due to a single small-town college professor with an obsession. William Estabrook Chancellor was to Warren Harding what the Reverend Ball had been to Grover Cleveland. A popular professor at the College of Wooster, in Ohio, Chancellor was the author of a number of books on education, and an utter loony on the matter of race. Somewhere along the line, he had heard the story about Harding, and Chancellor became a missionary, bent on telling the world that the candidate was part of a conspiracy to establish Negro domination of the nation. He passed out his "research" at the Republican convention, and gave it to nearly every journalist who came near Ohio. (He complained bitterly about a *New York Times* reporter covering Harding who had been "educated and trained in Norway," and therefore lacked a proper American attitude toward racial issues.) The 250,000 mailings destroyed by the government were also his product.

It's hard to tell how many of Chancellor's pamphlets, leaflets, and family-tree diagrams actually got distributed, given the rather spectacular willingness of both political parties to ignore the First Amendment when it came to questions of the racial identity of a potential president. Besides the leaflets destroyed in California, the literature seems to have shown up mainly in Ohio, the home of Harding, his Democratic opponent, Governor James Cox, and Professor Chancellor. But the Harding campaign also received reports from southern and border states that the story was being spread around. A North Carolina man wrote demanding to know if people circulating it could be arrested. A traveling salesman warned Harding that customers along his route said they could not vote Republican "BECAUSE YOU HAVE NIGGER BLOOD IN YOU." A report about the whispering campaign claimed "women who answered rings of the doorbell late at night were told hastily and emphatically by persons who seemed respectable enough that Senator Harding's blood was not pure white." Women, who were voting across the nation for the first time, were a particular concern for the Republicans, who wondered if these wildcard voters might be particularly concerned about racial issues. "You have no conception of how the thing is flying over the state. . . . It is affecting the woman vote!" wrote one worried campaign worker.

The Republicans chose not to attack the rumors, at least in part because Harding did not want to alienate the traditionally Republican black voters. But in Ohio, where Chancellor's flyers and pamphlets flooded parts of the state just before the election, the pro-Harding newspapers couldn't resist leaping in with a denial. On October 29, the *Dayton Journal* ran a hard-to-ignore headline across its front page:

THE VILE SLANDERERS OF SENATOR HARDING
AND HIS FAMILY WILL SEEK THEIR SKUNK
HOLES 'ERE TODAY'S SUN SHALL HAVE SET.
THE MOST DAMNABLE CONSPIRACY IN HISTORY
OF AMERICAN POLITICS

The larger papers picked up the theme the next day, but many of them could not bring themselves actually to tell their readers what the "vile slanderers" were saying. They ran mysterious attacks on an unknown person named Chancellor and his alleged Democratic underwriters, coupled with stories on the Harding family's "blue-eyed stock from New England and Pennsylvania, the finest pioneer blood,

Anglo-Saxon, German, Scotch-Irish and Dutch." Some papers, in an excess of zeal, traced the hitherto ne'er-do-well Hardings of Marion, Ohio, to the Domesday Book of 1066 and Lord Hardinge, British Viceroy of India. *The New York Times* denounced a "whispering campaign" about a shocking and untrue rumor that it declined to identify further.

Chancellor was fired from his job at Wooster, and on election night his home was set upon by a mob bearing tar and feathers. (He was rescued by a handful of his ex-students.) Unemployed but undeterred, he went on to publish a book on his favorite subject. It claimed that the leaflets circulated during the campaign, while based on the research of the white Professor Chancellor, had really been written by another William Chancellor "who is black and 65 years old, born and raised among the Hardings." The whole episode, the book theorized, was really a plot to aid Harding's candidacy, promoted by a conspiracy of Irish Catholics, Jews, Standard Oil, income-tax supporters, Germans, and opponents of Prohibition.

The federal government responded to these incoherent ramblings of deranged paranoia by actually organizing a plot against the author. Secret Service agents raided Chancellor's home and forced him to burn his papers. He fled to Canada with a copy of the manuscript, which he printed and sold door-to-door. FBI agents seized copies of the book from libraries, stores, and traveling salesmen, confiscating and destroying the publisher's plates. It may be the only book in American history to have been suppressed by the government without any legal authorization whatsoever. Chancellor himself eventually gave up the fight, returned to Ohio, and became a professor at Xavier University in Cincinnati. He denied he was any relation to the man who called Warren Harding part-Negro. "As a matter of a fact, I despise all race hatreds and all such political treacheries," he told a reporter in 1939.

"Details are unprintable"

The "Negro blood" stories had no impact on the outcome of an election that was always expected to be a Republican rout. The sunny, good-natured Harding with his promise of "normalcy" was exactly what the nation wanted after the war and the weird last years of the Wilson presidency. But the hysteria of the campaign's final days did produce a peculiar by-product. Convinced that the Democrats were behind the race rumors, the Republicans tried to counterattack. They didn't go after Governor Cox, even though Cox was the first divorced presidential candidate in American history and was rumored to have been involved in some shady financial dealings. The GOP didn't seem to regard either of these failings as comparable to having a black ancestor. Instead, they went after the vice-presidential nominee, and tried to suggest that Franklin Roosevelt was a homosexual.

John Rathom, the editor of the *Providence Journal,* was an eccentric crusader whose obsessions were Roosevelt and gays. Rathom had covered Roosevelt's attempts, as assistant secretary of the navy, to prosecute homosexuals who were seducing young sailors in Newport. The navy investigators used forty-one enlisted men as decoys, and Rathom was outraged at the idea that the federal government was encouraging young sailors to get involved in homosexual activity in order to make cases against gay civilians. (Roosevelt claimed, somewhat improbably, that he thought the evidence was collected by "someone under the bed or looking over the transom.")

At the instigation of the Republicans, Rathom pounced on Roosevelt while he was visiting Newburgh, New York, toward the end of the campaign. He handed the candidate a long letter full of personal denunciations, which broadly hinted that Roosevelt was himself a homosexual, "utterly lacking . . . in frankness and manliness." The Republicans mailed the letter to selected papers around the country and waited to see what would happen. The newspapers handled the charges much like they handled the "Negro blood" pamphlets. Many printed the story, but in language that was oblique enough to guarantee that readers who were unfamiliar with the concept of same-sex relationships would be no wiser after finishing the paper. Later, when a Republican-dominated Senate subcommittee issued a report concluding that Roosevelt did know sailors were being recruited to serve as homosexual decoys, *The New York Times* headline began, LAY

NAVY SCANDAL TO F.D. ROOSEVELT and concluded, DETAILS ARE UN-PRINTABLE.

2. The New Discretion

"He always stays here when Mrs. Harding goes away"

Like the Negro blood story, gossip about Harding's roving eye was current in Marion, Ohio, well before he became a presidential candidate. When the town welcomed its local hero home from the Republican convention in 1920, the reporters couldn't help noticing that every storefront was decorated in red, white, and blue for the occasion except one. "When the reporters asked about it, they heard one of those stories about a primrose detour from Main Street," wrote William Allen White five years after Harding's death. What White meant was that the reporters learned the undecorated department store belonged to Jim Phillips, who had been a close friend of Harding's until Phillips discovered that his wife, Carrie, had been Harding's mistress for fifteen years. It was one of a number of stories about Marion's favorite son that the press corps discussed endlessly over the next few months, sitting under an apple tree on the Harding lawn while the candidate conducted a low-key, well-controlled, news-free "front porch campaign." One night, an attractive Marion widow took pity on a few of the bored newsmen and invited them to dinner. Returning to the apple tree, the lucky guests reported that they were taken on a tour of the house by a child who pointed out Harding's toothbrush in the bathroom. "He always stays here when Mrs. Harding goes away," she explained innocently.

Harding and Mrs. Phillips did keep their affair secret even from their neighbors for years. But by 1920, the walls of discretion had started to collapse. A history professor from Ohio Wesleyan who was visiting Marion during the campaign saw Carrie Phillips approaching Harding while he was sitting on his famous front porch. Suddenly Florence Harding, who was grimly named "The Duchess," appeared and threw a feather duster in her former friend's direction. Next came a wastebasket, then a piano stool. On another occasion when Mrs. Harding was seated onstage for one of her husband's speeches, she spied Carrie in the audience. Jumping up, she walked to the edge of the stage and shook her fist at her rival. During the campaign, the Republican National Committee shipped Mrs. Phillips and her cuckolded husband off to the Far East for an all-expenses-paid trip to "investigate the silk trade" until the election was over. The RNC also promised them two thousand dollars a month in hush money for as long as Harding was in office.

If the press corps had not found out about the payments on their own, they could have read about them in Professor Chancellor's pamphlets, which were a bizarre amalgam of racist meanderings and local gossip. But there was no real appetite for that kind of story on the part of the newspapers anymore. The country had moved into an era when people seemed to prefer regarding their political leaders as virtuous, and rather distant.

But there was still word-of-mouth talk that whirred through Washington. The people on the inside knew that the new president liked bootleg liquor and women. Some of the stories were actually more sensational than the facts. There was a frequently repeated tale about a stag party Harding was supposed to have attended which became so wild that one of the girls present was hit on the head with a liquor bottle, and died after being taken to the hospital. There is no evidence any of this really happened, but the inside gossip loop believed it. "It got all around Washington," Evalyn McLean told an interviewer years later. McLean not only insisted that the story was true but claimed that when the girl's brother tried to blackmail Harding, someone from the Justice Department had the man incarcerated in a mental hospital. "A pure frame-up job," she said.

People seemed to talk much more about the mythical bludgeoned party girl than Harding's real mistress, Nan Britton, whose small daughter was probably Harding's illegitimate child. Like the much older Carrie Phillips, Nan was a product of Harding's hometown. For some reason, as a teenager she fixated on the middle-aged state senator, covering her high school notebooks with "Warren Harding, he's a darling." Their affair began in 1917 when she graduated from secretarial school in New York, and Harding, then a United States senator, invited her to a meeting at the bridal suite of his hotel to discuss her employment prospects. "I shall never, never forget how Mr. Harding kept saying after each kiss: 'God! God Nan!' in high diminuendo," she wrote later. Their daughter, she claimed, was conceived in the Senate office building. Later, after Harding became president, Nan visited him in the Oval Office. "He introduced me to the one place where, he said, he thought we might share kisses in safety. This was a small closet in the anteroom, evidently a place for hats and coats, but entirely empty most of the time we used it, for we repaired there many times in the course of my visits to the White House, and in the darkness of a space not more than five feet square, the President of the United States and his adoring sweetheart made love."

Nan claimed that Florence Harding knew about the affair, and once almost caught them in flagrante in the presidential cloakroom. Certainly Mrs. Harding kept a keen eye on her husband's activities. It may have been Nan and baby Elizabeth she was talking about when the First Lady assured Evalyn McLean that she could keep Harding in line because "I have something on him." (It's less likely that she tried to hire someone to kidnap the baby, as the deeply unreliable Justice Department detective Gaston Means claimed later.) But some people in Washington definitely knew about the affair. Secret Service agents carried letters and money from the president to Nan, and the McLeans allowed Harding to use their yacht and their home for his trysts. "He would just walk in, and go right upstairs. Evalyn completely ignored him. I was appalled the first day I saw him there," said the widow of A. Mitchell Palmer, Woodrow Wilson's attorney general.

After Harding's death, *Kansas City Star* reporter Roy Roberts asked Majority Leader Charles Curtis if he knew anything about some mysterious bank records that Harding's friend Attorney General Harry Daugherty was reported to have destroyed. "My God, Roy," said the distressed Curtis. "It has to do with an illegitimate baby." In another tribute to the times, Roberts didn't follow up. The rest of the country didn't hear a hint of Harding's philandering until 1927, when Nan published an under-the-counter bestseller called *A President's Daughter.*

"Hey, Jimmy, have you made her yet?"

It was easier for the general public to be part of the gossip loop when the politicians were closer to home. New York mayor Jimmy Walker's sexual habits were a very open secret in the city, even though the newspapers didn't report on them. When the mayor rode through Manhattan with the city's honored guest, Queen Marie of Rumania, a bystander on the sidewalk yelled: "Hey, Jimmy, have you made her yet?" to general laughter. (The queen said she found Americans "quite droll.")

Like Harding, Walker was known for his winning ways, a wandering eye, and protective press coverage. His affinity for women other than Mrs. Walker was a legend in Albany when he was a state legislator, but New York politicians observed a rule that sins committed in the state capital did not count in the home district. Still, Walker's philandering was so energetic that Al Smith, the famously monogamous party leader, warned him that one of the worst things a public man could do was "chase women if he's married." When Walker ran for mayor in 1925, he spent his evenings entertaining girlfriends in the privacy of a friend's penthouse, giving the pleased Smith the impression that he had given up nightlife.

During his seven years in office, Walker, forty-five, carried on a very public affair with Betty Compton, a twenty-two-year-old British showgirl. Even New York cardinal Patrick Hayes called Walker on the carpet to warn him he was causing scandal. But until the final days of his administration, Walker's name was never linked with Compton's in the papers. "The reporters tried to protect Jim from himself, for he took almost no precautions to conceal his way of living," wrote Gene Fowler, a *New York Telegraph* reporter. The press, Fowler contended, "did not wish to penalize the man for his lack of hypocrisy when all around him there were public figures who posed in piety and righteousness but cavorted behind the doors of their secret harems." A half-century or so later this standard would flip, and political commentators observing Gary Hart's campaign would suggest that a failure to cover one's tracks when committing adultery was a serious character flaw, and perhaps even a sign of mental imbalance.

> *"Is it true that you had an affair with Senator Borah?"*

While Walker was running—or pretending to run—New York, another famous womanizer was running the United States House of Representatives. Nick Longworth, hitherto known mainly as Alice Roosevelt's husband, was elected Speaker in 1925. At about the same time, forty-year-old Alice gave birth to her only child, a daughter. Since all Washington believed the Longworths were no longer functioning as husband and wife, the inner loop of gossip was wild with speculation about who the father really was. Most of the bets were on Senator William Borah of Idaho, a powerful Republican who headed the Foreign Relations Committee. One of Alice's relatives said much later that she had been at a tea at Alice's home when a Roosevelt cousin suddenly asked Mrs. Longworth: "Is it true that you had an affair with Senator Borah?" Alice simply giggled in response.

Alice, who was one of President Calvin Coolidge's confidantes and always an important woman on the Washington social scene, was rumored to be planning to name her baby Deborah in honor of her liaison. But the infant was mercifully christened Paulina, and Longworth accepted her as his own. (He turned out to be a doting father, while his wife was at best an indifferent mother.) Alice was somewhat unfortunate in having a rival for Borah's affections in the form of publishing heiress Cissy Patterson, who always had a newspaper available when she wanted to get even with her enemies. When Cissy and the senator disappeared during a party at Alice's house, a maid later found some of Cissy's hairpins in the library. According to Cissy's biographer, Alice sent them to her former friend with a note: "I believe they are yours." Cissy responded with a note of her own: "And if you look up in the chandelier, you might find my panties."

Since Alice had previously found her friend and her husband making love on a bathroom floor during a party, she would seem to have some claim on the moral high ground. But Cissy never forgave her for stealing Borah away. She published a novel in which the heroine, a thinly disguised version of the author, vied with a thinly disguised version of Alice over a man who was even more transparently the senator from Idaho. Later, when Alice helped her friend Ruth McCormick run for a House seat, Cissy used her position as editor of the *Washington Herald* to produce a series of editorials assaulting Alice, fascinating Washington gossips, and referring to Senator Borah's *"close"* friendship with Mrs. Longworth. Meanwhile Nick was livening up his service as Speaker with his own series of affairs and a drinking problem so serious that many of his friends wondered if he was actually capable of carrying through any of his romances.

Hints of the Washington gossip made their way into the national loop, thanks to Cissy's book and editorials, and the 1931 bestseller *Washington Merry-Go-Round*, in which the anonymous authors (Drew Pearson and Robert Allen) suggested that Nick and Alice each went "his or her own way" and dropped suggestions about the Speaker coming home unexpectedly and finding the door locked against him. But even that book, which was regarded as a sensation in its time, did little more than make discreet hints. The authors tidied up the anecdote about the exchange of notes between Alice and Cissy, quoting Patterson as writing: "If you look up in the chandelier, you may find my shoes and chewing gum."

The rumors about sexual misbehavior and the certain evidence of Nick's drinking never harmed either Longworth. When Alice returned home with her baby of doubtful parentage, the crowds who jammed the streets to welcome the new mother were so huge that mounted police had to be called out to keep them under control. Alice remained a pillar of Washington society and a force in Republican politics for nearly another half-century. Nick was an enormously popular Speaker, despite (or perhaps because of) his unbreakable habit of marching out of the House at 5 P.M. every day to begin drinking in his private Capitol hideaway. When he adjourned Congress in 1931, the House gave him a wildly emotional tribute expressing real affection from both sides of the aisle. Longworth died unexpectedly of pneumonia before Congress reconvened, and most of the country's political leaders, including President Hoover, traveled to Ohio for the funeral. One of Nick's most devoted mistresses, Alice Dows, created a sensation when she walked down the aisle past all the dignitaries at the end of the service and laid a bunch of violets on the coffin.

3. Celebrities Up Close

"There is radio music in the air"

The newspapers did not lose interest in political gossip during the 1920s just because reporters were charmed by men like Warren Harding and Jimmy Walker and shared their affinity for the more expensive variations on the theme of bathtub gin. Everything from the state of feminism to the economics of the media was changing in ways that discouraged reporters from poking into officials' private lives. Women had encouraged the media to focus on the personal affairs of public men because a man's bad behavior in private was a threat to his wife and children. But in the twenties, women had won the right to vote, and many of them were focused on issues like sexual liberation, the elimination of restrictions on women's dress and freedom of movement. To them, mixing government with private life meant Prohibition, censorship, the ban on dissemination of birth-control information, and regulations that prohibited women from doing everything from dining alone to swimming in one-piece suits. Congressmen who committed adultery and presidents who drank were not a concern, as long as they kept their nose out of the younger generation's affairs.

Newspapers, meanwhile, were becoming more conservative in what they printed because they were becoming big businesses. The technology for creating and distributing newspapers was getting much more sophisticated and expensive. Shoestring operations like the *Buffalo Telegraph* that tortured Grover Cleveland were disappearing. The worst of the newspaper wars were dying out. The survivors were generally larger, more homogeneous, less lively, often part of a national chain. Everything from the reporters' increasing tendency to identify themselves with the establishment to publishers' desire to avoid offending advertisers argued for a more polite kind of political coverage.

Even the sensational papers that remained in the big cities preferred other kinds of gossip, because readers seemed to have lost their taste for politics. The marching clubs, the torchlight parades, the mass barbecues that had made campaigns so much fun in the nineteenth century had dwindled away. In the North, where competitive two-party politics was strongest, turnout in presidential elections had run above 80 percent in the late 1800s, but by the 1920s the number had dropped to less than 60 percent. Political scientists have come up with lots of good explanations for this surge of apathy. Women's suffrage had expanded the base of potential voters, making it harder to get huge proportions out to the polls. The turn of the century good-government movement had the dispiriting by-product of making election campaigns more of a civic duty than a welcome social activity. But certainly the main reason politics and politicians lost their appeal was that there was suddenly so much competition for people's attention. In the post–World War I period, movies, motor cars, phonographs, and radios became available in rapid succession. "There is radio music in the air every night, everywhere," reported a San Francisco paper in 1922. "Anybody can hear it at home on a receiving set, which any boy can put up in an hour." It's hard to imagine how profound the change must have been for a nation that was used to a home life in which silence was broken only by the sound of the family's own voices. A political rally might have been thrilling when compared to alternatives like playing checkers, or going to bed early. But it paled against broadcasts of baseball games, famous bands playing the latest popular tunes, or—soon—a comedy, melodrama, or detective serial.

Naturally, politicians began dwindling as celebrities when the average person's circle of "acquaintances" exploded to include the actors, musicians, and athletes who seemed to be visiting right in the living room. (Presidents were on the radio, too, beginning with a speech by Harding in 1922. But the rhetoric of Calvin Coolidge or

Herbert Hoover was poor competition for Rudy Vallee's singing.) Those who mourned the new apolitical mood of the nation tortured themselves with surveys that claimed to show more Americans could identify the coach of the Notre Dame football team than the vice president.

"Come home, all is forgiven"

None of these new topics of gossip, however, was as powerful as the lure of movie stars. During World War I motion pictures moved out of the working-class nickelodeon parlors and into grand theaters where the middle class could feel comfortable. The films got longer, developed real plots and characters. The men and women who appeared in them quickly became the most popular members of the artificial community that newspapers had built up around celebrities like John L. Sullivan and Theodore Roosevelt's children. The fans knew what the movie stars looked like, and they imagined that by watching their travails on the screen they had come to know what they *were* like. Information about their homes, their favorite foods or hobbies, their clothes, their families, and their romances was much more readily available than it had ever been for any First Family, even the Theodore Roosevelts. As representatives of a make-believe industry, the movie stars were also free to embellish the details. When the movie magazine *Photoplay* appeared in 1910, it featured a column called "Facts and Near-Facts About the Great and Near-Great of Filmland." It was reminiscent of the old "Important If True" headlines in early newspapers.

Magazines and movie newsreels created the first really national media, most of it heavily weighted toward visual appeal. The age of words to which politicians were so well suited had been replaced by a picture-dominated culture. Attention turned to the people who, through their physical attractiveness or athletic skills, were the most interesting to watch. (When Douglas Fairbanks met the assistant secretary of the navy during World War I, he could condescendingly assure Franklin Roosevelt that he was good-looking enough to make it in Hollywood.) Except in times of national crisis, the nation would never again be as interested in politicians as in movie stars. The only exception would be the Kennedy family, whose genius was to appear to be movie stars impersonating politicians.

From the first, the public identified movie actors as people they wanted to know in a personal way, much as if they had noticed an interesting-looking new family in church on Sunday and resolved to get acquainted. The early movie producers did not encourage the relationship. It did not occur to the studios that the "talent" could be used as drawing cards, but it did occur to them that if the actors thought they had a following they would demand more money. The first motion pictures did not even identify the stars by name. Still, letters poured in, addressed to "the girl with curls" or "the fat guy" or "the Biograph Girl." The public soon found out that "the girl with curls" was Mary Pickford. By 1915, the blond actress who specialized in playing spunky child-heroines was receiving five hundred letters a day. In 1920, she would look out her London hotel window and see "thousands and thousands of people" who had been waiting all night in the street just to get a glimpse of her.

The phenomenon of movies, movie stars, and movie-star gossip was so new that it would require a shakedown period before everyone figured out what the real rules should be. The early actors and actresses were taught to believe that the public would not tolerate the least slip in their image. "If fans came to see me on the set and I wasn't dressed for a role, I'd run into my dressing room, let down my curls, and put on the little-girl dresses they expected me to be wearing," said Mary Pickford. When Pickford, who was secretly married to an actor named Owen Moore, fell in love with the already-married Douglas Fairbanks, the studio heads assured her that the romance would bury their careers "under an avalanche of malignant gossip and denunciation." Fairbanks was so terrified that he denounced stories about their affair as "German propaganda" during World War I. But when the two stars did divorce their mates and marry, their fans found the coupling too delicious to object to its moral implications. The nation would demonstrate—as it did with Andrew Jackson and his illegal marriage, or Ulysses Grant and his corrupt presidency—that it had an extremely selective memory when it comes to people it wants to admire.

"Come Home—All Is Forgiven," *Photoplay* begged the honeymooners.

> *"He staggered about, raving, drooling, laughing, crying . . ."*

The media did not have to worry about whether to wait for defining public events before writing about the movie colony's private lives, because the public events came so fast and furious. The first generation of film stars was disaster-prone. It included many veterans of the roustabout life of vaudeville or cheap theater tours, as well as younger men and women who were plucked off the street or recruited via the casting couch. They were much like the congressmen of the Gilded Age, accustomed to heavy drinking, disorganized romantic lives, and little scrutiny. And just like those politicians, they tumbled into a rapid-fire series of scandals.

These began in 1920, when actress Olive Thomas, star of *The Flapper,* was found dead in a Paris hotel. Only twenty, she had recently married Mary Pickford's brother, Jack, in a union that fan magazines decreed created "the Ideal Couple." Pickford claimed that he and his wife had returned from a long night out in which they had been "drinking a little," and that Olive had accidentally swallowed a "hygienic toilet solution" that contained bichloride of mercury. "She screamed 'Oh my God, I'm poisoned,'" he told reporters. Hollywood's inside gossip loop theorized that Olive had died of a drug overdose, or committed suicide after discovering that Jack had given her syphilis. The newspapers never mentioned venereal disease. But they did let their readers in on "sinister rumors of cocaine orgies, intermingled with champagne dinners which lasted into the early hours of the morning." They also revealed that Jack had almost been dishonorably discharged from the navy during World War I after serving as a go-between for rich young men trying to bribe their way out of dangerous duty.

The media response to Olive Thomas's death followed the pattern it set for misbehaving politicians a couple of decades earlier. Once a public event moved private behavior into the headlines, the papers tended to quickly print all the gossip that had accumulated along the way. Because movie stars sold papers, and because the stars—at that point—were less powerful than politicians, the papers had a tendency to add on unproven rumors, slurs from enemies, and the occasional pure fiction to keep the story going.

In 1921, Roscoe "Fatty" Arbuckle, a much-loved comedian, wound up in the most public event possible when he stood trial for killing a starlet named Virginia Rappe. She died of peritonitis from a burst bladder after attending a party Arbuckle threw in a San Francisco hotel. The newspapers never got too explicit about how Rappe was supposed to have been fatally injured, but word spread around the country that Arbuckle had raped her with a bottle, or a large piece of ice, or that the 260-pound comedian had somehow ruptured her with his weight.

It seems pretty obvious in retrospect that Arbuckle was innocent. But the papers whipped up sentiment against the actor by dredging up other gossip, including an overblown story that Arbuckle's studio had previously paid to hush up another rowdy party in Massachusetts. Director Henry Lehrman, Rappe's boyfriend, was quoted as claiming Arbuckle was a former "bar boy" who hung around "women's dressing rooms" and ran around with a crowd "who resort to cocaine and opium and who participate in orgies that are of the lowest character." Rappe's lively personal history was plowed through, too. Although the papers never mentioned the word "syphilis" they did quote a nurse who said that Rappe's "relations with a sweetheart were responsible for the ailment from which she had been suffering."

Arbuckle's trials—he had three—were less about gossip than was the furor that led up to them. But they did have some awfully familiar aspects. The parade of witnesses made it clear to the nation that the California celebrity community was a species apart. (One prosecution witness brightly assured the grand jury that she was feeling fine because "I had a hypodermic this morning.") The first jury stalemated at ten to two for acquittal, and a retrial ended with a ten-to-one vote for conviction. Arbuckle was found innocent by a third jury after only six minutes of deliberation, sending the media into a fit of soul-searching about what was wrong with the system of justice and whether it was possible for a celebrity to get a fair trial in America.

Next Wallace Reid, one of the most popular leading men, collapsed and was reported to have "suffered a stroke of paralysis," possibly due to overwork. Both the studio and Reid's family claimed he was suffering from "klieg eye," a reaction to the strong lights used in making pictures. (The media expressed a sudden concern about the effect of klieg lights on vision. It foreshadowed the TV news features decades later about the dangers of cheap cigarette lighters after comedian Richard Pryor was severely burned while freebasing cocaine, and tried to cover the story by blaming his injuries on an exploding disposable lighter.) The inner gossip loop knew that Reid was suffering from a narcotics addiction, but the actor's wife convinced the *Los Angeles Times* to put the best spin possible on the story. "For four hours in that hot, noisy city room, Dorothy Reid, tears streaming down her face, told newsmen the truth and convinced them she was thinking of all the kids whose idol Wally was," wrote Adela Rogers St. Johns. The paper eventually reported that Reid was committing himself for treatment, and quoted Mrs. Reid as saying her husband had become addicted to morphine after he was injured on location and given the drug to ease his pain.

The California media had a local industry to consider, and continued taking a rather positive view even after the head of Reid's sanitarium was arrested for selling cocaine to his patients. But papers in other parts of the country were more interested in keeping a sensational story going as long as possible. MOVIE IDOL A "DOPE" announced the New York *Daily News*. Reid's mother-in-law, Alice Davenport, was quoted as saying that Reid was a longtime alcoholic who frequented "orgies" and "dope parties." (Mrs. Davenport later denied the story, claiming Reid disapproved of orgies and regarded dope parties as "false and artificial.")

With Reid locked away and unavailable for comment, the papers had to roam farther afield to come up with new angles. "Dope, in one of its many forms—heroin, morphine, cocaine—has entered into the daily life of many of the noted movie folks," announced the *Daily News*. The paper dug up Evelyn Nesbit, the famous "girl in the red swing" who had been the central figure in the murder of architect Stanford White. Nesbit, then dancing in Atlantic City cabarets, volunteered that she was a recovering addict, and obligingly recalled "one party in Hollywood where cocaine was served in a big sugar bowl." The paper also quoted the less famous—in fact utterly anonymous—Ralph Obenehain, who reported that when he "announced he was going into the movies, a kind friend remarked: 'Well, I suppose you'll be carrying a hypodermic needle soon. They all do.'" A week into the new cycle of Reid stories, the collapse that had originally been referred to so discreetly had taken on more interesting dimensions. Blackmail threats, the *News* said, were probably "directly responsible for his dramatic collapse on the Lasky lot, when he staggered about, raving, drooling, laughing, crying until he fell insensible after a frenzied outburst of rage." When the star died in the nursing home, the *News* trumpeted, DEATH'S FILM DROPS ON DOPE FIEND, and regretfully informed its readers that "Wally Reid went out on location across the Great Divide." Mrs. Reid, a former actress, did get a second shot at stardom as the heroine of a series of antidrug movies.

Unlike politics, where one man's disaster is another man's career opportunity, Hollywood quickly figured out that scandal about any movie star was bad for business. Reid's tragedy had blossomed into stories about the whole industry's narcotics problem, just as Arbuckle's trial had caused fans to wonder how many other lovable stars were secretly having around-the-clock parties with syphilitic starlets. That perception would define the way gossip about entertainers was controlled until the studio system fell apart in the 1950s. Hollywood settled down into a discreet, if not utterly correct, existence. The studios controlled the actors' careers, covering up for stars who misbehaved and getting rid of any less famous miscreants. "The studios did nothing but damage control," said gossip columnist Liz Smith. "People would get arrested for drunk driving, for homosexuality, and the guy from the studio would be down before the actor could be fingerprinted, and get it covered up." Movie reporters, like the capital press corps, never looked behind closed doors unless they were forced to, since they were dependent on "access" to get the interviews and information they needed to survive. Soon, the movie gossip industry would be dominated by Louella Parsons and Hedda Hopper, columnists who were basically spokeswomen for the studios themselves rather than the nosy public.

3. Eleanor and Franklin

"He is not one of us!"

The Great Depression and World War II temporarily made Washington the focus of attention again. The crises, and the sudden accumulation of power by the executive branch, turned even Cabinet officials and presidential advisers into minor celebrities. Most dramatically, Franklin Roosevelt and his wife, Eleanor, became a part of the fabric of American life in the way no other White House residents ever had—partly because the government they represented had such a profound impact on people's lives, and partly just because they lived there for so long.

Unlike his cousin Theodore, or Washington or Lincoln, Franklin Roosevelt led a country that knew exactly what he looked like and how he sounded. The people watched Eleanor tour work camps and housing projects on movie newsreels and listened while Franklin seemed to talk directly to them on the radio. The intimacy of the Roosevelts' relationship with the American public has never been equaled. Nevertheless, a great deal about their private lives managed to escape notice. Their lifestyle was unconventional, even by present-day standards. During the thirties and forties, the Roosevelt White House was more like a sixties commune than a traditional American nuclear family. People came to visit and stayed for months or even years. Eleanor and Franklin lived separate lives, and saw each other infrequently.

The woman who actually presided over the president's afternoon cocktail hour and served as the mistress of his vacation home at the

Warm Springs rehabilitation center was his devoted secretary, Missy LeHand. Missy lived in the White House, too, and wandered in and out of the president's quarters at all hours of the day and night, often clad in a nightgown or bathrobe. Another resident whose tax forms showed her official address as 1600 Pennsylvania Avenue was Lorena Hickok, a former reporter who was in love with Eleanor, and whose affections Eleanor on some level returned. Later on Joseph Lash, a young radical who was listed in J. Edgar Hoover's files as Eleanor's lover, stayed in the White House as a regular guest. Mrs. Roosevelt walked into Lash's room one evening without knocking and came face-to-face with a naked stranger. It was an aide to Crown Princess Martha of Norway, one of Franklin's particular friends, who had been moved in while Mrs. Roosevelt was traveling.

The gossip about the Roosevelts that was passed around the country seemed to be more unpleasant, and less interesting, than reality. Some of the most vicious rumors were spread through privately published propaganda that focused on the Roosevelts' alleged Jewish ancestry. Like the "Negro blood" rumors, and the talk that John Frémont was a Catholic, the stories that Roosevelt was a Jew were aimed at separating him from the general population, defining him as an Other. HE IS NOT ONE OF US! cried one of the pamphleteers on the eve of the 1936 election. Like Warren Harding, Roosevelt was careful not to offend potential voters by denying the stories. He told a Jewish newspaper that his family was descended from Claes Martenssen van Rosenvelt who settled in New Amsterdam in 1649. Beyond that, he said, he knew little about his ancestors: "In the distant past, they may have been Jews."

The more informal whispering, which flourished at Republican dinners and country-club cocktail parties, revived the ever-popular speculation about presidential drinking habits. Although Prohibition was ended in 1933, the Roosevelts were targeted with far more rumors about alcohol abuse than the Hardings, who imbibed when buying alcohol was illegal. Marquis Childs complained in 1936 that he was told "across a well-appointed dinner table that 'everybody in Washington knows that the whole Roosevelt family is drunk most of the time.'" The president did enjoy the ritual of evening cocktails, but

Eleanor, whose father and brother were alcoholics, was violently averse to drinking.

The bars that Theodore Roosevelt had put up to protect the White House windows from baseballs were brought to the fore again. They had just been installed, people insisted, to keep the president from flinging himself out one of the White House windows. People claimed to have heard manic laughter in the middle of the night. The president was deranged from the effect of syphilis, they whispered. Or people told each other that the effects of his polio had spread upward "toward the head," paralyzing his brain. The stories did not die out after Roosevelt had been in office awhile. They multiplied. He was said to have broken down in the middle of a press conference, laughing hysterically for fifteen minutes until his aides took him away. Senator Borah (starring, this time, on the other end of a Washington rumor) was supposed to have dropped in on the president to find him cutting out paper dolls in his study. Or a captain of industry was unable to hold a conversation with Roosevelt because he kept babbling incoherently.

The White House encouraged reporters to attack the rumors head-on. *Newsweek* reported that people were saying Roosevelt had become addicted to drugs he used to relieve pain from his disability. "All over the country tongues waggled about the President's physical and mental condition," the magazine added disapprovingly. An Associated Press reporter finally asked the president about his mental state at a press conference. "The President toyed with his long cigarette holder . . . leaned back . . . laughed," reported *Newsweek*. "Back to the roomful of correspondents he tossed the question. How did they think he looked? 'Okay from here.' " Roosevelt was unusually thick-skinned about these sorts of attacks, which he claimed actually helped him politically by keeping his name fresh in the voters' minds.

The venomous gossip directed at the Roosevelts had a great deal to do with the perception by the ruling classes that they were being undermined by a traitor from within their own ranks. But the persistence of the stories about Franklin's health may also have been due to the public's intuition that the president was not as healthy as the national press claimed.

"I didn't realize he was a paraplegic"

The magazine and newspaper stories that denounced rumors about presidential drug addiction or insanity also expressed horror that rumormongers were spreading stories that (as *Newsweek* decried) "the President was a hopeless, helpless invalid!" Yet Roosevelt was, throughout his presidency, utterly helpless when it came to getting out of bed, moving across a room under his own power, or doing anything that required the unassisted use of his legs. And it was a secret as well kept as any paranoid critic might have imagined. J. B. West, the White House usher, said that before meeting Roosevelt he imagined like most Americans "that he walked with a limp or something," and was stunned when he first saw the president wheeled off the White House elevator. "Everybody knew that the President had been stricken with infantile paralysis and his recovery was legend, but few people were aware how completely the disease had handicapped him," West said.

The idea that Roosevelt had won a heroic battle against polio was a key part of his image. In reality, he had fought the disease to a standstill—he was back in an active political life, but he couldn't really walk at all. The president was so successful at concealing the fact that he was crippled that even inside Washingtonians were stunned when they first saw him in person. "I was shocked," Representative Tip O'Neill, the future House Speaker, told a friend. "I didn't realize he was a paraplegic. I don't think anybody in America had known it." Roosevelt staged his public appearances carefully to give the impression he had the use of his limbs. On the campaign trail he sat in cars or stood at the back of campaign trains, his legs enclosed in braces, leaning on the railing and waving to the crowd. At formal receptions, workers set up a device like a bicycle seat, obscured by ferns and protruding slightly at just the level that the president could balance on it and look as if he were standing under his own power. He concealed his disability with the active cooperation of the press corps. White House reporters never revealed the extent of the president's handicap and White House photographers never took pictures of him in his wheelchair. They also helped censor outsiders, snatching the camera of anyone who broke the rule, and exposing the film.

Roosevelt believed, as did his advisers, that the American public would not elect a handicapped man president, so he was determined to hide his condition. Certainly his first terms as president demonstrated that his inability to walk had no bearing on his ability to do his job. But it's possible that Roosevelt's success at concealing his irrelevant but real handicap empowered him to deny the symptoms of heart disease when they appeared during the war. By 1944, almost everyone but the voting public doubted the president would live out another term. The *Atlanta Journal* ran a front-page interview with New Dealer Aubrey Williams in March of 1944, saying that he had dined recently with the president and was "shocked" by his appearance. *Time*'s correspondent must have been a bit shocked, too, when Roosevelt held his first press conference in May after a long vacation. "Suddenly, seeing him after a month's absence, newsmen who have been seeing him once or twice a week for eleven years were struck by the realization that Franklin Roosevelt at sixty-two is an old man," the magazine reported. But Roosevelt's personal physician, Admiral Ross McIntire, called him "perfectly okay." *Time*, noting that McIntire was an ophthalmologist whose specialty was sinus, told its readers that sinus infections were the president's "most nagging health problem."

One of columnist Drew Pearson's editors asked him to investigate the gossip about the president's health. Pearson was a rather spectacular exception to the rule about not discussing politicians' private lives in print. "I've always tried to emphasize the personal side of journalism," he once wrote. "It makes my point . . . more effective and it does not put people to sleep the way some of my thumb-sucking colleagues do." If Pearson discovered that a politician of whom he disapproved was having an affair with his secretary, or was supporting an illegitimate child, or drinking too much, he put it in his column. But he was less forthcoming about officials he supported. Pearson's sources told him FDR had been scheduled for surgery, but that the operation had been put off because the president's heart was too weak to stand it. The columnist never ran the story.

Roosevelt died of a stroke only a few months into his fourth term. Riding back to Washington with Roosevelt's body after his death in Warm Springs, the press corps debated whether they had done enough to let the public in on the state of the president's health. Veteran UPI reporter Merriman Smith remembered that some felt "the president's death was as unexpected to his doctors as it was to the public at large." We know now that a cardiologist had diagnosed Roosevelt as having congestive heart failure in 1944 and that he was suffering from angina attacks and being given digitalis. The information may have been kept even from Roosevelt himself, who never inquired what the doctors thought about his condition. But everyone around the president knew that he had lost weight, that his color was bad, and that he was repeatedly laid up with ailments described as "grippe," "bronchitis," or "a head cold." He tired easily, and during the 1944 campaign, he began giving speeches from his wheelchair for the first time. "It seemed to me in retrospect," wrote Smith in 1972, "that the older Mr. Roosevelt got, the less his staff tried to say about his health."

The death itself sparked a new series of rumors—that Roosevelt had committed suicide, been shot by Eleanor, been murdered by Nazis or Communists, or had not really died at all but been spirited away to disguise his increasing insanity.

"He was so salacious about Eleanor"

The state of the Roosevelt marriage was another area where Eleanor and Franklin tried, understandably, to conceal the true nature of their private lives. They were working partners who had, over the years, found in other people the companionship, support, and intimacy they could not find in each other. No one, including their children, knew whether Franklin was actually capable of having sexual relations after he contracted polio, or whether Eleanor ever found a sexual connection outside marriage. But the president and his wife each had intense relationships that many of the people closest to them believed were romantic. Naturally the traditional media shied away from any speculation about the First Lady's sexuality or the president's intimacy with his secretary, and the vast public that revered the Roosevelts wouldn't have wanted to hear the stories anyway. But there were plenty of people who hated Franklin and enjoyed hearing bad things about him. "I still meet people who now say their parents threw the radio out of the room when Roosevelt came on," says biographer Doris Kearns Goodwin. It's puzzling that the people who happily spread stories about venereal disease and drug addiction in the White House seemed to have ignored much more realistic rumors.

Actually, if the people closest to the Roosevelts are reliable sources, there was plenty of gossip in Washington about Franklin and Eleanor's personal lives, and speculation about their possible affairs. Lucy Mercer Rutherford, who had been Franklin's lover before he contracted polio, had resumed her friendship with the president during his third term. Reporters covering the White House traded jokes about Lucy, and took note of the fact that when the president's special train went from Washington to Hyde Park, it often made an unscheduled stop in New Jersey, where she lived. Everyone knows now that Lucy, not Eleanor, was at Warm Springs with the president on the day he died. The story was not reported at the time, but Donald Ritchie, associate historian for the U.S. Senate, says he remembers hearing his anti-FDR relatives explain after the president's death that the coffin had been closed to cover up the fact that Eleanor had shot her husband after finding him with another woman.

There were rumors about the president and his secretary, too. A story going around Washington in the prewar years had Roosevelt warning ambassador Joseph Kennedy to end his affair with actress Gloria Swanson, and Kennedy snapping back: "Not until you get rid of Missy LeHand." The exchange might not actually have taken place, but the fact that the story was so frequently repeated suggests there was speculation about the relationship. Many of Roosevelt's enemies must have taken note of Eleanor's perpetual traveling and compared her apparent inattention to Missy LeHand's devotion as described in glowing magazine accounts. "Her time is the President's time," wrote *The Saturday Evening Post.* "If there is no formal entertaining to be done . . . she and FDR will spend the evening at work in his upstairs study. Or he will work at his collections, while she sits nearby and reads, ready to lend a hand if need be." How could people not have put two and two together, even if the truth really didn't add up to four? The answer is that they undoubtedly did. The reason we don't have more specifics is that this sort of gossip wasn't written about at the time it was being passed along.

The mainstream newspapers and magazines that recorded the anti-Roosevelt gossip stuck to the most outrageous and improbable rumors—the insanity reports, and the bizarre stories about Roosevelt being involved in the Lindbergh baby kidnapping. But no one ever decried gossip that the president was romantically involved with his secretary, or that Eleanor was having a relationship with her former chauffeur and good friend, Earl Miller. It cut too close to the bone. A few decades later, reporters would write stories denouncing political gossip in order to get the juiciest stories into print via the back door. But writing about the Roosevelts that way would have violated the journalistic culture of the Depression and war years.

The media decried the "intimate," "shocking," and "cruel" comments it said people were making about Eleanor, but it did not define them. "Most of what we know is from oral history—people just remember what their mothers said," notes Goodwin. Mainly, Americans who lived in the Roosevelt era recall mean joking about Eleanor's looks—the large teeth and recessive chin—and racist sneers about her relationship with the black community. There were also "dirty" stories, the details of which many of Eleanor's lifelong fans have suppressed. "I remember on a troopship in Normandy, there was a big kid from Texas who blamed everything on Eleanor Roosevelt. He was so salacious about Eleanor," says retired journalist Bob Donovan. But Donovan claims he can't put his finger on exactly what those salacious remarks were. Margaret Marquez, the Hyde Park town historian, was born on the Roosevelt estate and lived in Roosevelt's hometown, which is a very Republican enclave, throughout his presidency. "There was gossip," said the eighty-year-old Mrs. Marquez. "But I don't want to express it because I don't believe most of it."

"... so nice it was a colored man"

One of the most important pieces of gossip during Roosevelt's era was about Assistant Secretary of State Sumner Welles's drunken attempts to proposition several railroad porters on a train full of Washington dignitaries in 1940. Welles, a haughty, married alcoholic, was a graduate of Groton and Harvard who traveled in the same social circles as the Roosevelt family. The president, who got confirmation of the story from J. Edgar Hoover, tried to keep the incident quiet. But his efforts were doomed. The State Department was divided into opposing camps, one centering around the elderly Secretary Cordell Hull, and the other around the more energetic Welles, a favorite of the liberal New Dealers. The Hull faction eagerly passed on negative rumors about Welles, including the one about his sexuality.

William Bullitt, the ambitious former ambassador to Russia, was particularly diligent in spreading the story. Bullitt was a peculiar person to be attempting to ruin someone's reputation with a charge of unconventional sexual practices. He was perpetually unfaithful in his own marriages, and his most trusted aide, Carmel Offie, was a homosexual. But with his own career stalled and Welles occupying the place he coveted, Bullitt confronted Roosevelt with the stories about Welles's encounter with the Pullman porters. "I know all about this already," the president said. "I have a full report on it. There is truth in the allegations." Roosevelt claimed he had assigned a bodyguard to follow Welles and prevent the incident from being repeated. When Bullitt argued that the story could ruin wartime morale if it got out, Roosevelt assured him that no newspaper would ever publish anything about it.

(The president had reason to be confident. Even in 1951, an under-the-counter sleazy bestseller called *Washington Confidential* that reported the incident did not dare name names. "One high State Department official was a notorious homosexual who preferred young Negro boys," wrote the authors in a chapter called "The Garden of Pansies." The unnamed official, they continued "was detected in a Pullman car of the Southern Railroad—on the funeral train to bury Speaker Bankhead, father of Tallulah—making immoral advances to a porter. The story reached newspaper offices, but before it could be printed the State Department sent out an urgent appeal to editors to 'kill' because it might impact the war effort.")

The president attempted to distract Bullitt with a series of fact-finding assignments, but Secretary Hull picked up the crusade. Hull told J. Edgar Hoover that Welles's homosexuality was being discussed at tea parties for senators' wives, and warned the president that the tale was the talk of Embassy Row. A rumor spread that Bullitt had given documents about the episode to the dreaded Cissy Patterson, who was then publisher of the *Washington Herald*. Unable to contain the gossip, Roosevelt finally let Welles go in 1942. Columnist Drew Pearson, Welles's longtime supporter, wrote that "stories of divorce, domestic infelicity and sex rumors have spread regarding certain progressive members of the State Department whom it is out to purge. Once these stories circulate to enough people through the gossip underground, the target of the gossip is told by his superiors that his usefulness is over and he must resign." Pearson was the only reporter who came close to explaining what had precipitated Welles's departure. Most of the newspapers gave their readers the impression that he had been sacked due to anti-Russian attitudes in the State Department. Meanwhile, the department was thrown into disarray, since Welles had done most of the day-to-day management and had refused to share information with his underlings.

Welles's homosexuality was not fatal to his career, but the gossip about it was. Although it never made print, it spread throughout the enormous loop of people with connections to the Roosevelt administration. "That was the most famous story of the time," Murray Kempton recalled. "I remember a liberal friend writing me: 'It's so nice it was a colored man.' "

Addendum: Gossip on File

Gossip is meant to be transitory, to die away almost as soon as it's whispered. But FBI head J. Edgar Hoover kept it on neatly typed reports, locked in a file cabinet. The story of Eleanor Roosevelt and

Joseph Lash is a good example of Hoover's pioneering work in insti-
tutionalizing Washington gossip.

Lash was a leader of left-wing youth groups who became Eleanor's
protégé in the period when Franklin was focusing on the coming war,
and cooling to the social concerns he and his wife had shared during
the New Deal. When the war began, military intelligence maintained
a remarkable interest in Lash, who was an unimportant air force
weather-forecasting trainee. He was followed, his conversations were
taped, and his mail was opened. When Lash was on leave in Chicago,
military intelligence officers bugged both his meetings with Eleanor
and his assignations with his fiancée, Trude Pratt. The First Lady was
alerted by a sympathetic hotel employee that her conversations had
been recorded, and she complained to General George Marshall. Disturbed at the clumsy overreaching of the military surveillance, Marshall disbanded the Army Counter-Intelligence Corps and ordered its
files destroyed. But the files were offered instead to the FBI, and
Lash's was kept in a special collection of particularly sensitive cases
in J. Edgar Hoover's office.

A rumor persisted well into the 1950s that the FBI files contained
a tape of Lash and Mrs. Roosevelt making love. But no such recording
ever existed. The army had taped a sexual encounter between Lash
and his fiancée, which it intended to use as evidence to bring morals
charges against him. Eleanor's complaints to Marshall apparently
thwarted that plan. But Hoover kept building his file on Eleanor and
her young leftist friend. Meanwhile, the myth of the Lash-Roosevelt
sex tapes mutated into a legend that the cuckolded Franklin Roosevelt
conspired to have Lash and other soldiers who knew about Eleanor's
affair killed.

An FBI liaison agent sent Hoover a thirdhand account of the story,
based on what he said were sources in the disbanded and disgruntled
Counter-Intelligence Corps. FDR had ordered the head of the Military Intelligence Division to the White House with all the tapes of
Eleanor and Lash making love, he reported. After hearing them, an
enraged Roosevelt called his wife into the room and confronted her.
"This resulted in a terrific fight between the President and Mrs. R,"

wrote the liaison agent in a 1943 memo that remained in the Bureau files for years. "At approximately 5 A.M. the next morning, the president called General [Hap] Arnold, chief of the Army Air Corps, and . . . ordered him to have Lash . . . on his way to a combat post within ten hours." The president, the memo continued, also demanded that anyone else who knew about the tapes should also be sent to the South Pacific and kept in combat "until they were killed."

It was a fantasy. There was no such tape. Lash, who did go into combat but emerged intact, pointed out later that even if there *had* been, the Roosevelts were so intensely private about their relationship that it was inconceivable they would air their sexual differences in front of strangers from military intelligence. But the file, and the story, lived on. People who had read the file told other people, who told FBI informants, who wrote it down and sent the report in as fresh evidence that the affair and murder plot really did occur. In 1954, an FBI official wrote to Hoover suggesting that President Eisenhower be informed about the Eleanor documents. "The attached memorandum details Lash's connections with Mrs. R. . . . the subsequent confrontation with Mrs. R. and the order issued by FDR that everyone knowing of this action should be sent to the South Pacific until they were killed," it read.

Chapter 7

The Quiet Years

1945–1964

1. Politics in the TV Age

The TV President

In January of 1953, forty-four million Americans—about a third of all the people over infancy—watched the birth of Little Ricky on *I Love Lucy.* It was a conclusive answer for anyone still wondering whether television was going to become a central part of the national culture. It also gave commentators who worried about the citizenry's lack of interest in the political process a new statistic: Fifteen million more people gathered around their sets to watch Lucy go into labor than tuned in for Dwight Eisenhower's inauguration the following day.

Once politicians understood TV's power, they naturally wanted to be on the air themselves. People like House Speaker Sam Rayburn, Senator John Kennedy, and ex-presidential candidate Tom Dewey took Edward R. Murrow on tours of their dens and kitchens on *Person to Person,* just as Marilyn Monroe and the Duke of Windsor did. In a 1956 election-year coup, actor-turned-presidential consultant Robert Montgomery convinced CBS to air a birthday tribute to Mamie Eisenhower as a news special in March—even though Mrs. Eisenhower was actually born in late November.

Television created a transformation in political marketing much like the one in 1840, when the Whigs figured out how to turn election campaigns into entertainment. The Republicans were first to grasp the potential of the new medium, airing sixty-second commercials in 1952 that showed Dwight Eisenhower answering questions from "ordinary citizens." Two years later, GOP strategists noticed that crowds for their congressional rallies were dwindling, even with Eisenhower as a drawing card, and they concluded that the campaigns of the future would have to be beamed into the voter's home. The president showed a surprising affinity for the new medium. He recruited his friend Robert Montgomery to produce his television appearances and advise him on makeup and wardrobe. When Richard Nixon went down to defeat in the 1960 election, Eisenhower shook his head and muttered: "Montgomery would never have let him look like he did in that first television debate."

Adlai Stevenson, Eisenhower's Democratic opponent in both his presidential races, couldn't adjust to the artificiality of TV politics. In 1956, Stevenson was still campaigning the old-fashioned way. He traveled seventy-five thousand miles, making up to six speeches a day, while Eisenhower left Washington only ten times, and concentrated on the small screen. The Democrats mulled, then rejected, the idea of having Elvis Presley appear in a commercial for Stevenson. The candidate himself turned down an invitation to appear as a mystery guest on the popular quiz show *I've Got a Secret*. Instead, Stevenson's handlers spent large sums on poorly staged televised events, which the candidate muffed because nobody could convince him to practice working with a TelePrompTer. Bobby Kennedy, who traveled with Stevenson as a campaign observer, admitted years later that he voted for Eisenhower.

"The Dollies That John Foster Dulles Couldn't Handle"

Over on the wild side of the publishing business, Robert Harrison realized that TV was going to swallow up the mass-market middle-brow periodicals like *The Saturday Evening Post*, and concluded that the future for magazines would be in sensational fare that the networks wouldn't dare broadcast into American living rooms. He created *Confidential*, the first and most successful of what would soon be about forty publications with names like *Hush-Hush* and *On the Q.T.* By the middle of the prototypical white-bread decade, the scandal magazines were selling fifteen million copies a month, with *Confidential* accounting for 4.2 million. They specialized in stories about topics the regular media didn't dare handle, like abortion and venereal disease; shocking "confessions" (I JOINED AN ORGY OF SEX AND PERVERSION); and gossip about celebrities that revealed more interesting information than James Dean's notion of the ideal girl or Lana Turner's preferences in furniture.

Confidential's staff originally included several conservatives who believed they were going to be putting out a magazine about political scandals that would further the causes of law, order, and anticommunism. LOVE IN THE U.N. announced the banner headline of the first issue in 1952, which also included a story on a former New York mayor turned ambassador (O'DWYER: SAINT OR SINNER?), an exposé on prison violence (I WAS TORTURED BY A CHAIN GANG), and the requisite mob feature, which promised to show how gangsters were living it up in Hot Springs, Arkansas (HOODLUMS IN PARADISE). But publisher Harrison soon discovered what those hand-wringing commentators on dwindling voter participation already knew—politics and social issues were not enough to draw a mass audience, even if they were being covered from the most sensational angle possible. Movie stars soon began to creep onto *Confidential*'s cover, and despite bitter protests from some of the staff, the magazine quickly became a celebrity gossip sheet. (Howard Rusher, the right-wing editor, said later that he quit when Harrison refused to let him run an article about Eleanor Roosevelt that *Confidential*'s lawyers felt was "in bad taste.") Political figures still did make their way into the table of contents on occasion, but the features generally had an air of desperate stretching. In 1956, *Confidential* managed to come up with a pseudo-exposé about Eisenhower's extremely unsensational secretary of state: "The Dollies That John Foster Dulles Couldn't Handle." (American clerical workers seduced by spies at overseas embassies.) It printed the story of Sumner Welles, who was by then long retired and half-dead. *Uncensored* ventured overseas, revealing "The Lusty Lovelife of Marshal Tito." ("If you think headlines are all he makes, you haven't heard the whispers making the rounds of those Belgrade boudoirs!")

The political world was fortunate to be such a poor attraction for readers. *Confidential* went where no American periodical had ever gone before, paying off private detectives and ex-spouses for information and outfitting its photographers with telephoto lenses. A prostitute named Ronnie Quillan got fifteen hundred dollars for the story of an affair she had with Desi Arnaz, the TV and real-life husband of Lucille Ball. In a feature called "Does Desi Really Love Lucy?" *Confidential* recounted how Arnaz and a friend had checked into the Beverly Hills Hotel and ordered up a pair of "cuddle-for-cash babes." The magazines printed stories about stars who got in drunken brawls, about baseball hero Joe DiMaggio's bungled attempt to catch his estranged wife, Marilyn Monroe, with another man. (DiMaggio and companion Frank Sinatra, according to *Confidential*, went to the wrong floor in the apartment building and broke into the bedroom of a strange woman.) The scandal magazines' favorite topic, *The New York Times* noted disapprovingly, "is adultery, detailed in breezy but unmistakable euphemisms." But homosexuality and interracial dating came in a close second.

The Hollywood celebrities were horrified. Although the American public has always envisioned entertainers as living at the mercy of gossip columnists, their private lives were generally as well protected as politicians'—perhaps even more so considering the stars' far more lively social calendars. But the studio system that had both restricted and protected the stars was starting to dissolve, and the entertainers knew what could happen when the walls of discretion crumbled. In 1950, when Ingrid Bergman had left her husband and daughter to live with director Roberto Rossellini and bear his child, she had become a pariah. Bergman, formerly one of Hollywood's biggest stars, was denounced in the U.S. Senate as "a free-love cultist and apostle of degradation," assailed by virtually every religious group in the nation, and boycotted by her former fans. Even after she reestablished her career and won an Academy Award for *Anastasia,* TV variety host Ed Sullivan cautiously asked his audience to send in their opinions on whether Bergman should be permitted to appear on his show.

Hollywood struck back at the scandal magazines with a cannonade of litigation. Stars like Errol Flynn, Maureen O'Hara, and Liberace filed forty million dollars' worth of lawsuits against *Confidential* and its distributors. The Motion Pictures Industries Council, which handled public relations for the studios, formed a special committee to "combat attacks by scandal magazines." The council chairman, dancer (and future U.S. senator) George Murphy, announced that actor Ronald Reagan would be among the committee members. The state of California threw its weight behind the stars, charging the magazine's operators with conspiracy to commit criminal libel and publish obscene material, in the form of a story on abortion. *Confidential* retaliated by subpoenaing a raft of Hollywood celebrities with the clear intent of questioning them about their private lives on the stand. But the raunchy scandal magazines were only stalling for time. Eventually, publisher Harrison surrendered. He promised, the *Times* reported, "to run no more exposés about the private lives of movie stars and other celebrities" in return for the state dropping its suit.

2. The Private Life of Ike and Mamie

"It was a very, very shocking thing to have done"

Meanwhile, gossip about political figures was confined mainly to word of mouth, or in at least one case, song. In Alabama, when Governor

"Kissin' Jim" Folsom got a clerk at Birmingham's Tutwiler Hotel pregnant, the story was passed around to the tune, more or less, of "You Are My Sunshine."

> *She was poor*
> *But she was honest*
> *Victim of a rich man's whim*
>
> *When she met that country guvner*
> *Big Jim Folsom*
> *And she had*
> *A child by him.*
>
> *Now he sits*
> *In the Legislature*
> *Making laws for all mankind*
>
> *While she walks the streets*
> *Of Cullman Alabama*
> *Selling grapes*
> *From her grape vine.*

During World War II, stories about Dwight Eisenhower and his female chauffeur, Kay Summersby, were passed around Washington and almost anywhere the military was stationed in Europe. Although newspapers never mentioned the gossip, readers in the remotest American prairie towns could draw their own conclusions from the repeated references to "Eisenhower's pretty Irish driver." A divorced ex-model whose soldier-fiancé was killed in Africa, Summersby was the only woman in Eisenhower's "family" of personal aides, all of whom were regularly profiled by reporters eager to relay every possible bit of color about the man who controlled the fate of the Allied liberation of Europe. "When it came to the great love stories of World War II, the romance between Ike Eisenhower and Kay Summersby was right up there with the infatuations of MacArthur, Montgomery, and Patton with themselves. That, at least, was what everyone from the humblest G.I. in the European Theater of Operations to Red Cross ladies in Tacoma believed," wrote a *New York Times* reviewer when Summersby's revisionist autobiography came out in 1977.

Eisenhower was protected from any negative effects by that blanket absolution that Americans give military heroes. The last thing anyone cared about as the world war reached its crisis point was the marital fidelity of the supreme Allied commander. But the gossip must have tortured Mamie Eisenhower, who was stuck in Washington while her husband metamorphosed from a successful but unknown soldier into the nation's most beloved hero. Physically rather fragile, with few interests outside her family and card-playing friends, Mamie seems to have spent much of the war as a semi-invalid. The memories of that traumatic time remained so fresh that decades later she would urge her granddaughter-in-law, Julie Nixon Eisenhower, to accompany her husband, David, whenever he traveled.

After the war, Summersby wrote a popular account of her wartime experiences in which she extolled Eisenhower and dismissed the rumors of a romance between them. But the story of a love affair between the general and his female aide became one of those pieces of accepted wisdom in Washington that were never shared with the nation at large. "He'd had an affair. People obviously knew about it. They talked about those things at parties, but it was like a tree falling into the woods. It didn't get into the press," said Steven Hess, who was a young speechwriter during the Eisenhower administration. "Back then, it wasn't even considered appropriate to write memoirs."

But Murray Kempton remembered having dinner on the last night of Eisenhower's administration with a group of journalists and administration insiders and debating whether the Summersby story was true. One of his fellow diners, a man who knew the president rather well, argued no. "He said at receptions during the war she'd have two drinks and start denouncing Eisenhower for assigning her fiancé to North Africa and getting him killed," Kempton remembered. But then someone else at the table retorted that the story proved Kay and Ike *were* lovers: "No woman would treat a man like that unless he was sleeping with her."

The legend of the Summersby affair was half-forgotten until 1973, when Merle Miller published *Plain Speaking,* the oral autobiography of the recently deceased Harry Truman. The ex-president, who made no secret of his contempt for Eisenhower, was asked about an old story that he had once promised the general his support for the presidency. That would never have happened, Truman avowed, "even if I didn't . . . hadn't known about his personal life."

Miller perked right up.

"I'm sorry, sir," he said, as Truman must have hoped he would. "What do you mean about his personal life?"

"Why," the old man said, "right after the war was over he wrote a letter to General Marshall saying that he wanted to be relieved of duty, saying that he wanted to come back to the United States and divorce Mrs. Eisenhower so that he could marry this Englishwoman."

It was a new twist in the history of political gossip. Truman was going public, in an interview he knew would be part of a book, with a sex story about another president. "It was a very, very shocking thing to have done, for a man who was a general in the Army of the United States," said Truman, in phrases that could only be used by a man who knew that there were no sex stories about *him* for anyone to repeat. Marshall, Truman said, warned Eisenhower that if he "even came close to doing such a thing" he would drive him out of the army.

When Truman's allegations became public, Summersby was in a New York hospital, where she had just been diagnosed with incurable liver cancer. Her response was to agree to write a second version of her wartime experience, *Past Forgetting*. In it, Summersby said that her friendship with Eisenhower became romantic after her fiancé was killed by a land mind in North Africa. After months of necking in the back of airplanes and a disastrous visit home by Eisenhower (during which, Summersby claimed, he called his wife "Kay" several times), they went to bed. But Eisenhower was unable to consummate the relationship. She wrote that he told her: "For years I never thought of making love. And then when I did . . . when it had been on my mind for weeks, I failed." As the war was coming to an end they tried again, but the results were no more satisfactory. Summersby said Eisenhower promised to bring her back to the Pentagon as his secretary. But after he left Europe she received an army telex informing her she had been dropped from the roster of personnel scheduled to leave for Washington. A letter followed, dictated by the general to a secretary, telling her he couldn't keep her on his staff since her citizenship had not yet been approved. On the bottom, he penned a note: "Take care of yourself and retain your optimism."

No one may ever know for sure how accurate Summersby's story was, or even how much of the detail was really hers—she died well before the book was published. Even if it was all true, many Americans felt it was a story the public didn't need to know. It certainly had nothing to do with Eisenhower's qualifications to be president, and nobody went to the polls in 1952 less well informed because the rumors had been contained. But its political irrelevance did not necessarily make it trivial. One of the reasons people gossip is to learn about life—what their culture demands of them, how others have behaved in different circumstances, and what to expect from their own friends, family, and mates. Kay Summersby's version of what happened during World War II must reverberate for anyone who has been casually betrayed in a romance, or failed to live up to a passionate lover's expectations. There's something about it that's both mundane and extraordinarily sad.

"We hear she's a drunk"

Before the 1952 Republican convention, Eisenhower's handlers had him out touring the country, meeting and greeting the party members who would vote for the presidential nominee. The delegates breathed out a combination of awe and entitlement. Ike was a war hero, but *they* were the kingmakers. Some major politicians have enjoyed exercises like these. But Eisenhower probably thought he was in the seventh circle of hell.

"General, we're not worried about what you stand for. We think we understand that pretty well. But we're worried about your wife. We hear she's a drunk," a man from Nebraska told him.

"Well I know that story has gone around, but the truth of the matter is I don't think Mamie's had a drink for something like eighteen months," the candidate replied, smoothly and blandly.

He had obviously been briefed to expect the question. The rumor about Mamie's drinking was the most widely circulated bit of gossip about the Eisenhowers, and was better known in the country at large than the Summersby story. Betty Beale, an Eisenhower-era society reporter, recounted receiving "countless phone calls from magazine writers and out-of-town reporters asking if Mamie overindulged in the sauce." The Associated Press assigned Ruth Cowan Nash to look into the rumors, and after a long investigation Nash told her editors the stories were false. Watching Mrs. Eisenhower making a grand entrance one evening, Nash worriedly told reporter Maxine Cheshire, "If Mamie ever falls on her ass, I'm out on mine."

The rumors probably started during World War II. "It was tied to a whirl which led many officers' wives during that period of stress and loneliness to drink too much," said Texas editor Henry Jameson, who described himself as a family friend. "For a year or two, Mamie was part of that whirl, worrying too much, drinking a little too much." Concerned family members talked to her about her drinking, he added, and "she stopped at once." (Susan Eisenhower, in her biography of her grandmother, denied that Jameson was enough of a "family friend" to know such a personal story. The Eisenhowers have always said that the Mamie-drinks legend rose out of an inner-ear problem that sometimes made the First Lady unsteady on her feet.)

The gossip had no effect on Mrs. Eisenhower's considerable popularity, but it made the Republicans extremely nervous. In 1955, newspaper readers might have noticed how hysterical Republican congressmen got when Paul Butler, the Democratic national chairman, predicted the president would not run for reelection "because of a personal situation in the Eisenhower household." Pressed for an explanation later, Butler said he was talking about rumors that "Mrs. Eisenhower's health is not too good." It was a clumsy statement. But the Republican reaction was absolutely over the top—particularly for a party that had only recently finished a twelve-year stretch of attacks on Eleanor Roosevelt. "Why does Mr. Butler do this inhuman thing?" demanded the normally mild-mannered Senator George Aiken of Vermont. The Democratic chairman, Aiken said, sounded like he *hoped* Mamie was ill. "I don't know what goes on in the mind of a man who uses such tactics. Just how low and loathsome can an animal in human form get?" Political insiders believed the party was trying to make sure Butler—a novice politician—understood that Mamie's alleged drinking was not to be mentioned.

The First Lady claimed not to be disturbed by rumors that all her friends knew to be untrue, but she was careful never to allow herself to be photographed drinking anything, even water. Much later, when Barbara Walters asked her during an interview about something that had been "a rumor for years," Mamie quickly responded "Oh yes—that I'm a dipsomaniac."

3. TV Creates a Candidate

"You mean he's a square?"

The gossip about Mrs. Eisenhower may have grown out of a reaction against drinking, just as the talk about Teddy Roosevelt did. The nation was heading toward one of the highest rates of alcohol consumption in its history, and many teetotalers were upset that the ranks of the cocktail drinkers had grown to include even aging matrons. The Eisenhowers were part of the World War I generation that had learned a new way of approaching liquor. The men of their parents' era had huddled together in saloons or clubs, drinking themselves into insensibility. The women stayed home and consumed copious doses of alcohol-enhanced "tonics" like Lydia Pinkham's Compound. But ever since the 1920s, drinking had become coed and social, part of the rhythm of everyday life. By the time the sixties arrived, alcohol had become such a part of normal existence that abstainers were suspect. Margaret Truman's husband, Clifton Daniel, recalled that when he met his future father-in-law for a get-acquainted drink and ordered a glass of milk, Harry Truman was traumatized. The ex-president was fearful, Daniel said, that "he was to get a milksop for a son-in-law" until Margaret assured her parents that her fiancé was a scotch drinker who was temporarily on the wagon while being treated for a possible ulcer.

The late John Tower claimed that Mark Hatfield of Oregon was taken off the list of Richard Nixon's possible running mates because he wasn't a drinker. When Hatfield's name was mentioned at a strategy session with Nixon and top Republican leaders, Tower said, Senate Republican leader Everett Dirksen "turned to Nixon and said: 'Mark's a nice boy. However one is not even served a soupçon of wine when invited to his house for dinner.' Senator Thurston Morton of Kentucky cut through Ev's baroque style in his own unique way by asking: 'You mean he's a square?' To which Ev replied: 'Yes, he's a square.' And that ended the discussion of Mark Hatfield for vice president."

If Mamie Eisenhower was a case of much ado about very little drinking, Congress in the 1950s was the other way around. "There was an awful lot of drinking," recalled Murray Kempton. "Warren Magnuson, Dennis Chavez—he made some of the greatest speeches Congress ever heard, denouncing McCarthy, when he was drunk." Russell Baker remembers seeing a member of the Senate "open the cloakroom door, hit the first step, fall flat on his face and never wake up." The stories about the legislators' inebriated performances were passed casually around the press corps. But they seldom reached deep into the home districts.

The lifestyle of Congress has always been a recipe for alcohol abuse: a pack of men, most of them separated from their families, taking part in a legislative ritual that involves a great deal of waiting around for something to happen. There had always been too much alcohol and boorish behavior in the Capitol. But by the 1950s it had been a very long time since any legislator had been embarrassed by newspaper reports of his drinking. "There was so much we didn't write," says Warren Rogers, who covered the Capitol for several major publications in the fifties and sixties. "A guy like Russell Long would be staggering around the floor and you couldn't understand a thing he said. But the rule was that we respected people's privacy unless the behavior affected policy." Somehow, policy was never judged to have been affected. A young reporter from New Jersey once saw an obviously inebriated Senator Harrison Williams attempting to speak in support of a bill that was of interest to her paper. When she filed a story describing Williams's performance, she received a chilly note back from her editor: "I don't care if he was drunk. I just want to know if he passed the bill."

"He never did fool around in Tennessee"

One of Washington's most legendary drinkers and womanizers in the 1950s was Senator Estes Kefauver of Tennessee. In his prime, Kefauver could drink a quart of scotch in an evening without losing control. Murray Kempton claimed one of Kefauver's most famous acts of political courage—casting the lone Senate vote against a bill making it a crime to be a member of the Communist party—occurred when the senator was drunk. "He lurched on the floor, said 'What's this all about?' Then someone told him and he said: 'Well I can't vote for *that*," Kempton said. "He was a very special case. I happened to like him enormously."

Kefauver is an important figure in the drama of gossip and American politics. He was the first politician whose national image was created by television, and in 1952 he used that TV fame to try to impose himself on his party's leaders as presidential nominee. It was a preview of a time when voters would replace party insiders in picking the candidates. When that happened, the media would have to decide whether to let the voters into the insiders' gossip loop, too.

A lanky Yale graduate, Kefauver had succeeded in Tennessee politics by presenting himself as a sort of brainy populist who wore a trademark coonskin cap on the campaign trail. Thanks to the discretion of the Washington press and his own talents at sneaking liquor into dry parts of the state, he was generally able to conceal the unhousebroken side of his character from his constituents. "A lot of people knew of his propensity for women, but he was clean as a whistle in Tennessee," says Charles Fontenay, who covered Kefauver for the *Nashville Tennesseean*. "He never did fool around in Tennessee."

Kefauver probably would never have made a dent on the national consciousness if he had not wrangled the chairmanship of a Senate investigation of organized crime. He held hearings across the country in 1951, subpoenaing each city's neighborhood mobsters as witnesses. The infant television industry was always searching for local programming, and stations in the cities where Kefauver had his hearings started broadcasting them. An estimated twenty to thirty million viewers watched at one point or another. It was the country's first great communal TV experience. The hearings made the Mafia a national watchword and taught the country a great deal about bagmen and "Murder, Inc."

The soft-spoken Kefauver had the kind of cool demeanor television likes. His prey came off sweaty and sinister. (Mobster Frank Costello protested against having his face shown on TV, so the camera dwelt solely on his nervously tapping fingers.) Before the hearings were over, Kefauver had changed from a vague face in the pack of U.S. senators to an American hero—a little like the fifties' other coonskin-cap-wearing sensation, Davy Crockett. A ghostwritten book bearing Kefauver's name was quickly produced after the hearings ended, and *Crime in America* led the bestseller list for twelve weeks.

Kefauver, still a freshman senator, decided to run for president. He entered sixteen primaries in 1952, coonskin cap aloft, and to the shock of the party leaders, he won fourteen. His supporters assumed that a demonstration of his appeal would force the party to pick him as the nominee, but they had guessed wrong. The primary results did not yet dominate the selection process. After a long, bitter roll call, the convention nominated Adlai Stevenson.

The Democrats who crushed Kefauver were expressing the natural aversion of establishment politicians to crowd-pleasing mavericks who come galloping in from left field. But they also had a right to feel that they knew the senator from Tennessee better than the voters who had only seen him on TV. The party insiders knew that the private Kefauver was a problem drinker and an adulterer who could be offensively crude in pursuit of women. He once seduced a woman in Paris who did not realize he was married, and then shocked the respectable lady by "recommending" her to a friend who was passing through town. Fontenay, in his generally admiring Kefauver biography, says the senator once showed up at a society dance in Europe escorting a well-known local prostitute, and that he made his secretary answer the love letters from his old conquests.

The public had no way of knowing these stories, and the newspapers would certainly not have printed such gossipy fare. Most of what they heard about Kefauver's private life was, after all, just rumor. But over the next four years, the frustrated senator demonstrated these particular rumors were significant. His drinking grew more out of control, and his private behavior grew more extreme. When the party gave him the consolation prize of the vice-presidential nomination in 1956, some Democrats wondered whether his behavior on the campaign trail would explode into a world-class embarrassment. Word got around that Kefauver was sending his minions out to find women for him during overnight stops on the campaign trail. Russell Baker remembers being with Kefauver "in the middle of the night in the upper Midwest somewhere" on a bus carrying the candidate and reporters. When they pulled into town, Baker said, the senator turned to an aide and said: "I gotta fuck!"

Kefauver's national career ended with Eisenhower's second victory and he died a few years later. He was a disappointed man. But from our perspective, it's easy to imagine far worse fates for a politician with a flawed private life and presidential ambitions. Kefauver died with his reputation and family intact. He was never humiliated by having his secrets broadcast around the nation. His friends mourned him in peace, and even *National Review*'s grumpy obituary referred only to Kefauver's "incredibly hedonistic habits."

4. Adlai Stevenson's Identity Crisis

"You can't hardly separate homosexuals from subversives"

Thanks to soldiers' experiences in two world wars, Freudianism, and gay-themed novels like *The Well of Loneliness,* by the 1950s the nation had learned that homosexuality was not confined to a few degenerates

169

along the waterfront. This was not a case in which knowledge bred wisdom. Everyone from the scandal magazines to the U.S. Senate was warning that homosexuals were everywhere, and that they were dangerous. The Washington police told a Senate subcommittee that thirty-five hundred "sex perverts" were employed by the federal government. The sensational bestseller *Washington Confidential* announced there were "at least 6,000 homosexuals on the government payroll" as well as tens of thousands of others who hung around the nation's capital after failing to make it onto the civil service lists. (The book had a theory that the really talented homosexuals always moved to New York.) Congressional committees debated the number of homosexuals in the State Department.

Senator Joseph McCarthy's Communist witch-hunts were tied in with a search for "deviates," and the consequences of passing on gossip about someone's sexuality suddenly became grave. During the first sixteen months of the Eisenhower administration, 655 federal employees were fired for "sex perversion." Senator Kenneth Wherry, a Republican from Nebraska who was leading the charge to drive every last homosexual from government, told an interviewer that "you can't hardly separate homosexuals from subversives. Mind you, I don't say every homosexual is a subversive, and I don't say every subversive is a homosexual. But a man of low morality is a menace to the government whatever he is, and they are all tied up together."

The scandal magazines specialized in identifying homosexual celebrities, in part because they often had minor police records that made the stories libel-proof. "The fans who mob this six-footer want to know all about their idol . . ." announced a 1955 *Confidential* feature on Tab Hunter. "Well, this reporter remembers the night a cop moved in on that limp-wristed pajama party." In the same year, *Lowdown* attempted to "help" the popular singer Johnny Ray by demanding that the governor of Michigan pardon him for a long-buried homosexual solicitation charge. "If we wished, we could take Johnny Ray, put him on the block of public opinion and chip him to bits. We could pulverize him, mascerate him so badly that never again could he lift his voice in song—only in sob. If we wished, we could strip him right down to his bare psychology and leave him trembling and naked before the world," the magazine announced benevolently, as it called for the erasure of Ray's conviction. Even the actors who were not officially exposed were pretty well defined by their story titles ("Montgomery Clift's Odd Sex Secret . . . Are Girls Too Swift for Montgomery Clift . . . Montgomery Clift's Strange Obsession . . . Montgomery Clift's Weird Compulsion . . . The Strange Love Life Montgomery Clift Hides . . . The Strange Love Life of Montgomery Clift"). Universal Studios convinced *Confidential* not to out one of its biggest stars, Rock Hudson, and in return slipped the scandal magazine information on another actor's arrest record.

In Washington, Senator McCarthy himself was the subject of gossip alleging that he was either a homosexual or an alcoholic or both. McCarthy, who died in 1957 of cirrhosis of the liver, was very definitely a problem drinker. But he broadcast his contempt for homosexuals, even though most of Capitol Hill believed some of his top aides, including counsel Roy Cohn, were gay. (Cohn, who always claimed to be heterosexual, died of AIDs in 1986.) To be on his enemies list, the senator once told reporters, "you've got to be a communist or a cock sucker." Given the way in which McCarthy was cheerfully ruining careers with utterly unsubstantiated allegations, it's not surprising that the homophobic Drew Pearson tried to be just as nasty in return. "Sen. McCarthy's outcry against sexual unfortunates in the State Department is about to backfire against him," Pearson wrote. "While he has been calling the roll on these persons he has overlooked a member of his own staff who is on the Washington police department's secret list."

"Adelaide"

Adlai Stevenson, twice Dwight Eisenhower's Democratic opponent in the presidential campaigns, was dogged by rumors that he was a homosexual. The New York *Daily News* enjoyed referring to him as "Adelaide." *Confidential* did an anthropological investigation of the gossip in 1953, and tracked it back to Stevenson's ex-wife, Ellen. In a not-for-attribution interview with a reporter for the *Chicago Daily News*, the magazine said, Mrs. Stevenson had "confided in him the 'real reason' for her divorce, thereby initiating one of the vilest slanders ever distributed about a man destined for high office." The "reason," *Confidential* continued in its usual libel-resistant prose, "reflected on the manhood of the father of her three sons. In addition, Ellen named a lifelong friend of Adlai whose character and happy relations with his wife are above reproach." The magazine's tone of high dudgeon ("an act of treachery to rank with the vicious scandal circulated about the wife of Andrew Jackson") was one the scandal press (and later the establishment media) learned to use when they wanted to pass on gossip without taking responsibility for it.

Confidential's right-wing political loyalties would not have allowed the magazine to name a more likely source of the gossip. J. Edgar Hoover had a file referring to Stevenson as one of the "best-known homosexuals" in Illinois, which his aides leaked to reporters covering the presidential campaign. The file was based on information provided by a college basketball player under indictment for game-fixing who knew the story only as a rumor. Hoover had other material on Stevenson as well, containing similar charges that seemed to have come from people who had read the original file, and passed the gossip along to a new FBI informant. But that didn't stop Hoover from treating the file as if it had been carefully vetted by crack investigators. When Stevenson was appointed United Nations ambassador by John Kennedy, Hoover warned the attorney general's office that he was a "notorious homosexual."

During Stevenson's presidential races, the gossip kept the already-overstressed candidate even more on edge. In 1952, the Democrats kept hearing that Joseph McCarthy was going to add "pansies" to the "punks and pinks" he already claimed were supporting the Democrats. According to columnist Marquis Childs, the Stevenson campaign delivered a retaliatory threat to the Republicans. If McCarthy mentioned "pansies," the Democrats would release a copy of the letter General Marshall had sent Eisenhower, forbidding him to leave Mamie for Kay Summersby. No one ever confirmed Childs's story, and no one else ever referred to a Marshall letter about Eisenhower's marriage until *Plain Speaking,* Merle Miller's Truman autobiography, was published two decades later. But if Childs was right, the 1952 campaign was an early example of the kind of gossip cold war that characterizes most current presidential campaigns—both sides armed with so much ammunition that neither dares fire the first strike.

Stevenson was the first divorced presidential candidate since James Cox in 1920, and like Cox he began the campaign so far behind that it was hard to tell whether his marital status had any impact on the outcome. But certainly it helped to keep alive the rumors that he was homosexual. Divorce was not all that common in the early 1950s, and the idea of a single man in the White House had unnerved people even in the far less sexually imaginative 1880s. A single man who had failed at being married must have given a good many voters pause, even if they claimed not to care when pollsters asked them about the divorce issue. Eisenhower's handlers starred Mamie in a TV ad of her own in order to remind the voters that only one candidate could provide them with a First Lady. "Women will decide the election and they like Ike—and here's something else they like, Ike's beloved wife, Mamie," said the announcer.

There were all sorts of explanations for the staying power of the rumor that Stevenson was gay, from the fifties political ideology (homosexual = subversive = liberal Democrat) to his reputation as something of an intellectual egghead. The irony was that while the readers of the *Daily News* were picking up the hints that Stevenson was sexually suspect, the inner Washington gossip loops were humming with stories about his incredible success with women. In her autobiography, publisher Katherine Graham said that President Kennedy once jealously demanded to know what women found so attractive in the balding, paunchy, badly dressed United Nations ambassador. The friend explained that Stevenson actually listened to what women were saying, and was interested in what they had done. "The president's response," Mrs. Graham wrote, "was: 'Well, I don't say you're wrong, but I'm not sure I can go to those lengths.' "

When Stevenson collapsed and died in 1965 on a London sidewalk, he was with his longtime lover, United Nations Representative on Human Rights Marietta Tree. On the night before, Graham reported to her readers obliquely, Stevenson had spent some time with her in her bedroom and "left behind his tie and glasses." Society columnist

Betty Beale said in her memoirs that she, too, was having a long-running affair with Stevenson at the time. When their romance began in 1962, Beale said, Stevenson warned her that he was "already committed" to another woman, but she wasn't sure which of his many admirers he was referring to. She thought his true love might be Tree, or perhaps Alicia Patterson Guggenheim, the owner of *Newsday,* who was rumored to have been willing to leave her husband if Stevenson wanted.

One night shortly after Stevenson's death, Beale said she sat down with Nan Tucker McEvoy, whose family owned the *San Francisco Chronicle,* and counted ten women, including themselves, who were in love with him at the time. Later, she said, "I learned that two English women he saw regularly in London were equally stuck on him."

5. The Era of Rising Recollections

"The jumpers and the screamers"

R. W. Apple, Jr., of *The New York Times* was a new reporter on the city desk when he was assigned to help cover President Kennedy's visit to New York in October of 1963. Given the deeply undesirable job of staking out the lobby of Kennedy's hotel overnight, Apple saw "a young woman of a Hollywood nature" en route to the presidential suite. When he informed his editor that the president appeared to be having an assignation, Apple was thoroughly rebuffed. "I was told I was there to report the comings and goings of statesmen, not starlets," he recalled. Even today, Apple says, he's not sure if the *Times,* which is conservative about printing political gossip, would pursue a simple story of consensual presidential sex. "But I do know the reaction in the city room would not be boredom."

John and Jacqueline Kennedy were the first attractive presidential couple since the arrival of motion pictures, and their celebrity was very much a mixture of the Hollywood and Washington versions of fame. Jackie was featured on movie magazine covers as well as the usual women's magazines. Jack was made into a movie hero (*PT 109*) and a fashion leader whose preference for going outside bareheaded single-handedly ruined the men's hat industry. Nothing the Kennedys did was too trivial for transmission through the media or discussion in American homes. Yet like the Roosevelts, they managed to keep a great deal private. Mrs. Kennedy might complain about living in a goldfish bowl, but the fact that so few of the family's real secrets seeped out is a tribute to both the power of the Kennedy myth and the degree of protection American politicians received in their era.

Despite nearly two hundred years of gossip about presidential sex lives, Kennedy was perhaps the first president who actually had sex *appeal*. "The TV debate with Nixon was the turning point," said Warren Rogers, who covered the campaign for the *New York Herald Tribune*. "After that, whenever he came to a new town, all the young girls would come out. They'd act as if he was a rock star. We called them the jumpers and the screamers." The president and his entourage knew how useful his magnetism had been during the campaign, and they were proud of his effect on women. "We're going to do for sex what Eisenhower did for golf," a euphoric Press Secretary Pierre Salinger told people at the inauguration.

The picture we have now of what the Kennedy administration did for sex is less playful, more pathological. Yet many people who were Washington insiders during Kennedy's brief term of office, like *Washington Post* editor Ben Bradlee, claimed later that they had no idea the president was seducing women with the sort of almost mindless compulsion that recent biographies suggest. Most reporters who covered the administration have random anecdotes like Apple's, or stories about "Fiddle" and "Faddle," the White House secretaries whose actual duties were the subject of endless speculation. "I've always been suspicious of people who tell you: 'I knew this, I knew that,' " said Kennedy biographer Richard Reeves, who feels the security systems of the White House would have shielded the president from observation.

Any history of gossip is vulnerable to what historian Ronald Steel calls "rising recollections." As we move through life our minds improve memory with information we pick up long after the fact. There was virtually no talk outside Washington about Warren Harding's womanizing until after he died. But people who lived in the 1920s looked back on that era when they were very old and believed they recalled how everyone used to gossip about the president's illegitimate child. Americans in their eighties think about the Depression years and remember very distinctly that the whole world suspected Eleanor Roosevelt was a lesbian. The people who remember Washington as humming with talk about Kennedy's sex life in the early 1960s may be looking back with memories that have been seasoned by the revelations of the 1980s and 1990s.

Still, some people who were very well positioned to hear Kennedy gossip claim the stories really were all around. "Oh, I heard things all the time," says Liz Smith. "I knew all about how disgraceful the Kennedys were. Oleg Cassini used to get him girls." Cassini, Jacqueline Kennedy's dress designer, was the brother of Smith's boss Igor Cassini, who wrote the "Cholly Knickerbocker" society column for the Hearst syndicate. Smith, a native Texan, was also tied into the gossip of the Texas mafia that worked for Vice President Lyndon Johnson. "One of Johnson's assistants and I went all through high school and college together," Smith says. "He told me the most incredible stories. Johnson's people kept dossiers on Kennedy. They'd interview the hotel maids. The maid would be there making the bed, and Kennedy would come in and give her a boff." One of Smith's friends told her that the president had taken her up to his office during a White House dinner dance, and quickly seduced her while she was still wearing her elaborate ball gown. "She was lying there with her dress over her head," Smith recounted. "She looked up and he was standing there at his desk, reading some papers and zipping his fly. He just left her lying there."

Perhaps Smith's memory has been improved with the years, too. However, it may be that unlike most of the journalists and political insiders of the era, she could put the different gossip loops together. The Washington political inner circles knew that Kennedy had been what the 1950s called a "playboy" when he was in the Senate. They had speculated about "Fiddle" and "Faddle." (One reporter who had covered the president's Palm Beach vacations told his colleagues he saw Kennedy disporting with the two women in his beachfront hotel room, with the blinds open.) Washington and New York society passed around rumors that Jacqueline was unhappy in the marriage. The Hollywood gossip loop knew a number of rumors connecting the president to Angie Dickinson or Marilyn Monroe or Kim Novak. The Mafia's loop knew about Judith Campbell who, mob groupie Frank Sinatra told his friends, was "shacking up with Jack Kennedy."

If most people never wound all these different threads into a full pattern, it may simply be because it never occurred to them to look for that kind of promiscuity in the White House. Like James Buchanan, Kennedy might have been protected by the very fact that his sexual behavior was so far removed from what the nation of his era expected in a president.

"Something of a medical marvel"

Shortly after John Kennedy's death, reporter Warren Rogers went with an artist friend to show Robert Kennedy a bust of his brother that was to be placed at the Special Forces Center in Fort Bragg, North Carolina. Kennedy, who was still attorney general, said the head looked a little too jowly. "That's from the cortisone," he added. Although the president had denied it during his life, he suffered from Addison's disease, a failure of the adrenal glands that had to be treated with regular doses of cortisone and other drugs that left his face looking puffy and reddish. The sculptor promised to make the face a little thinner. Robert Kennedy stared at it thoughtfully.

"You know, he never had a day without pain," he said.

Like Franklin Roosevelt, John Kennedy went to great lengths to conceal his physical disabilities. He had always been frail, prone to near-fatal infections, fevers, and mysterious weaknesses that apparently stemmed from the Addison's disease, which was not diagnosed until he was thirty. His back had been unstable since he was a child, and it betrayed him over and over as he grew up. He underwent multiple operations, which became progressively more dangerous as the Addison's compromised his immune system. He received the last rites of the Catholic church at least five times. "He was something of

177

a medical marvel, kept alive by complicated daily combinations of pills and injections," Richard Reeves wrote in a devastating summary of Kennedy's physical problems in his 1993 biography. Besides Addison's and the faltering immune system that gave him sudden, wildly spiking fevers, Reeves listed "persistent venereal disease" problems, stomach disorders, asthma, allergies, and deafness in the right ear.

People who knew Kennedy during his congressional years recalled open sores oozing pieces of bone from the back surgery, calluses under his armpits from crutches, and pain so incapacitating that he needed two men to help him maneuver down only a few steps. But Kennedy always fought against showing weakness in public. He would hand his crutches to aides before he walked into a room full of people, climb the capitol steps briskly in front of his colleagues, and lay on his stomach talking unconcernedly on the telephone while doctors performed all sorts of gruesome procedures on his spine. He managed to convince even some of his closest friends that his excruciatingly painful conditions did not really leave him in any great discomfort. It was a perpetual act of heroism and denial.

The Kennedy legend was built to a great degree on an image of youth and physical vitality—"vigah," in the president's much-imitated Boston accent. In the White House, he conveyed the impression of athleticism and energy even though he was operating under handicaps that would have leveled most other men. "Boy, he looked great," said Bob Donovan, who wrote a book about Kennedy's PT-boat adventure. Helen Thomas of UPI, who saw the Kennedys constantly during their White House years, knew he was unable to pick up his son, John, because of his back. "But he swam, he sailed, he played golf. He was very active," she said.

The Kennedys stored supplies of his medication in safe-deposit boxes around the globe so the president would be able to get at it while he was traveling. For years, Kennedy's doctor, Janet Travell, injected novocaine directly into his back muscles—sometimes several times a day. "He had to address a meeting at the Mayflower Hotel, and riding over from the White House in his limo, his back went out," said Warren Rogers. "He couldn't move. So [his aides] formed a crowd around him, and the Secret Service guys picked him up and carried him downstairs to a men's room. Dr. Travell came and gave him an injection, straightened him up. He walked out, went down the hall, gave the speech, came back, and nobody knew anything was wrong. There were a lot of stories like that."

During the presidential campaign, the gossip about Kennedy's health spread around, with a great deal of encouragement from supporters of his chief competitor for the nomination, Lyndon Johnson. But the clumsiness of the Johnson camp tainted the issue and discouraged reporters from pursuing it. Nobody felt much inspired to follow up charges framed in terms like: "He looks like a spavined hunchback." At the Democratic convention India Edwards, a Johnson organizer from Texas, brought up the rumors about Addison's disease and told a press conference that Kennedy "would not be alive if it were not for cortisone." Robert Kennedy denied his brother had Addison's, resurrecting an old story that a mild adrenal problem had been caused by the malaria he contracted fighting in the Pacific but had long since been completely cured. The Johnson people had no evidence, and reporters dismissed the story as more spavined-hunchback talk.

"It was very quickly hushed up. There wasn't the same skepticism there is today," said Helen Thomas. Ben Bradlee said in his memoirs that he realizes in retrospect the president he saw frequently and regarded as a friend was "sicker with various stomach and back ailments than I had ever imagined."

Anyone who has traveled with a candidate on a major national campaign knows how debilitating the experience is even for someone in perfect physical shape. When Kennedy was running for president he began receiving injections several times a week from Dr. Max Jacobson, a New York physician who would later be dubbed "Dr. Feelgood." The injections were a combination of amphetamines and steroids that had the capacity to give the recipient an almost euphoric sense of energy, power, and well-being. In 1961, just before his critical first meeting with Nikita Khrushchev, in Vienna, Kennedy injured his back while planting a tree during a ceremony in Canada. He refused to show any weakness by using crutches on his way to meet the Soviet leader. The president opted instead, his aides said later, for "excruciating pain." He also took along Dr. Jacobson.

The press continued to regard a politician's health as more or less a private matter. Unless a defining public event occurred—like Eisenhower's heart attack—reporters accepted assurances by presidential physicians that everything was fine. (During his hospitalization, Eisenhower was diligent in allowing the public access to all information possible about his condition. He was understandably taken aback, however, when the doctors happily reported that he was having normal bowel movements.) One of the interesting things about Kennedy's health problems is that although the nation was generally informed about the president's bad back and his frequent problems with ailments described as flu, cold, or grippe, there was really not all that much gossip about his physical condition. There were no stories that JFK, who *did* have venereal disease, was laughing maniacally or cutting out paper dolls in his office. Television, which brought the Kennedys into American living rooms, also transformed them into their TV images, just as Mary Pickford had been turned into a perpetual thirteen-year-old with golden curls.

Chapter 8

The Deluge of
Defining Events
1964–1980

1. The Election of 1964

"An appalling shock to the moral sensibilities"

On the final days before the New Hampshire Republican primary in 1964, Nelson Rockefeller was on the stage of the Hollis High School auditorium, talking about defense policy. But Theodore White, the chronicler of presidential campaigns, noticed that no one in the audience was looking at the New York governor. They were staring at his pregnant wife, Happy, who was sitting near him on the stage, her head lowered. "They might have been a gathering of Puritans come to examine the accused," wrote White.

The election of 1964 occupies a kind of no-man's-land in American memory, between the prosperous, discreet, credulous postwar era and the rebellious, cynical, exhibitionist days of Vietnam and Watergate. The Republican presidential primary in New Hampshire was perhaps a preview of things to come. Rockefeller had been the early favorite for the GOP presidential nomination. But his standing became shaky when he announced in 1961 that he and his wife, Mary, were ending their thirty-one-year marriage. In 1963, when he married the newly divorced Margaret "Happy" Murphy, who was twenty years his junior, it prompted the most comment on a politician's romantic life since Grover Cleveland's day. "Questions and eyebrows are bound to be raised," editorialized Long Island's *Newsday*. Reporters scrambled for details about the new Mrs. Rockefeller, her former husband, and the whereabouts of their children. "Good God, what is wrong with you people? Leave me alone," cried Dr. Murphy as he tried to get into his front door through a press stakeout. Religious leaders weighed in, but if there were any who thought that true love should triumph over all, they kept it to themselves. Philadelphia's Methodist bishop declared the union "an appalling shock to the moral sensibilities and sense of fair play of the rank and file of Americans." Theologian Reinhold Niebuhr reported that his cleaning woman disapproved, "and I share her view." The minister who performed the wedding service was disciplined for violating a Presbyterian ban on marrying people who had been divorced less than a year.

Rockefeller was risking his career for the woman he loved. When Douglas Fairbanks did it, he swept the nation off its feet. But the public looked at Happy and saw not Mary Pickford but Ingrid Bergman. The voters seemed most upset that Happy's children, who ranged in age from three to twelve, were living with their father. Neither Dr. Murphy nor the new Mrs. Rockefeller ever explained their arrangement, and Rockefeller made it clear that he thought the details of his marriage were none of the public's business. But the public was free to speculate, and in New Hampshire, *Life* reported, "many persons remain morbidly curious and mistrustful." The gossip, Theodore White wrote disapprovingly, "was to echo and re-echo through every turning of the Republican struggle of 1964—from a supermarket rally of housewives to smoke-filled gatherings of politicians." White himself was very much in the same camp as those 1920s journalists who refused to punish Mayor Jimmy Walker for doing openly what other politicians did on the sly. Decrying the "henyard clucking" of disgruntled female voters, White romantically theorized that Rockefeller felt it was "the burden of his honor" to end "the public sham" that was his first marriage and openly unite with the woman he loved.

A voter in the Republican primaries, of course, might have re-garded Rockefeller's "public sham" as a thirty-one-year commitment and seen his "burden of honor" as an excuse to dump a middle-aged wife for a younger model. After campaigning energetically with her husband, the second Mrs. Rockefeller had to watch on primary night while the voters—in a preview of the alienation to come—repudiated all the names on the ballot and chose a write-in candidate who wasn't even in the country, Vietnam ambassador Henry Cabot Lodge.

"It would never have been known if the Republicans hadn't pushed it"

Barry Goldwater, who eventually won the Republican nomination, was far behind from the day he left his party's rancorous convention, and President Lyndon Johnson, successor to the assassinated John Kennedy, appeared to be on his way to a stunning victory. Then in October of 1964, rumors started circulating that Walter Jenkins, Johnson's friend and longtime aide, had been arrested at a local YMCA bathroom during a homosexual encounter. The Goldwater campaign had known about the arrest since a day or two after it occurred, thanks to a police source. But despite the Republicans' prodding, the story moved through Wash-ington's gossip routes remarkably slowly. The White House was appar-ently among the last to know, via a call from the *Washington Star* to Lady Bird Johnson's press secretary, a week after the arrest.

Jenkins was a pudgy, middle-aged man, a Catholic with six chil-dren. He had been the president's confidential assistant for more than a quarter of a century. He was not a policy maker, but he handled everything from the Johnson family finances to overseeing the White House staff. On the night he was arrested, he had worked late as usual, and dropped in briefly at a cocktail party. He then walked over to the YMCA's basement men's room, a homosexual pickup place so well established that the district police had their own permanent sur-veillance peephole. Jenkins and a sixty-year-old resident of a nearby Soldiers' Home for Disabled Veterans were arrested there, taken into custody, and booked for "disorderly conduct (indecent gestures)."

The Washington police were not known for their aggressive prosecution of cases like these. Congressmen picked up for such offenses, in fact, were automatically released. Less prominent suspects were usually permitted to leave after paying the equivalent of a fine. Jenkins paid fifty dollars and went home. He probably assumed that would be the end of the incident. He had been arrested at the same Y under almost identical circumstances in 1959, and it hadn't drawn any attention. But this time, Jenkins's employer was no longer Senate Majority Leader Lyndon Johnson but the president of the United States and a candidate in an election that was only a few weeks away. After failing in more discreet efforts to nudge the story into the open, Dean Burch, the chairman of the Republican National Committee, issued a press release directing attention to "a report sweeping Washington that the White House is desperately trying to suppress a major news story affecting national security."

Rumors that someone in the government might be homosexual were still regarded as policy matters in the 1960s. "We all thought that homosexuals did not belong in sensitive jobs, because they could be subject to extortion and forced to betray their government," recalled Max Frankel, who would later be credited with opening up *The New York Times* to serious coverage of gay issues. "Back then it was common wisdom. Nobody questioned the idea." Shortly after Burch's statement, Merriman Smith of United Press International went down to the police station and checked the arrest records. "It would never have been known if the Republicans hadn't pushed it," said Helen Thomas. "It was very painful, very tough. But we felt it was legitimate once we knew it was on the police books."

Some of the top officials in the Johnson administration went to the Washington bureaus of one newspaper after another, begging editors to kill the report for the sake of Jenkins's family. But it was too late. UPI, a national wire service, had already sent the story to half the newspapers and radio and TV stations in the country. "We were writing the story, and in walked Clark Clifford and Abe Fortas to see [James] Reston, our bureau chief," recalled Frankel. "Their request was to suppress the story. Reston said that was totally unrealistic. It was all over town, and on the wires. They tried very hard, but it came to nothing."

If there's any place in America that savors the story of a powerful man's fall it's Washington. But there wasn't much appetite for this one. The reporters went out of their way to point out in their stories that Jenkins was a decent man, devoted to his employer and his wife and children. It was the first time that the huge small town of America's media consumers would be introduced to a man who committed homosexual acts but was neither the dregs of society nor a sinister subversive.

Still, the mainly male press corps' discomfort was obvious. One story after another explained that Jenkins's homosexual impulses were due to overwork. "Gentle Walter Jenkins, closest of all to the president and his family, had collapsed in a psychiatric breakdown under the strain, a strain to which the President, his master, had been blindly insensitive," Theodore White decided. Attributing Jenkins's actions to the stress of working for an impossible taskmaster like Lyndon Johnson made homosexuality seem both controllable and less threatening to the vast majority of Americans who were employed by someone else. The FBI's sympathetic report attributed Jenkins's trip to the Y washroom to the fact that "his mind was befuddled by fatigue, alcohol, physical illness and lack of food." Jenkins himself told investigators that he did not recall any other homosexual episodes besides the two that had already been identified. "If he had been involved in any such acts, he would have been under the influence of alcohol and in a state of fatigue and would not remember them," the FBI report added, in a preemptive strike against any disclosures that might arise in the future.

Once the rumors about Jenkins had been confirmed, the story stopped being gossip and became a campaign issue. Goldwater's aides, in the ever-familiar guise of unidentified sources, assured reporters that the scandal would have "a terrific impact." Jenkins, who was hospitalized for nervous collapse, tendered his resignation and the Johnson campaign ordered an instant public-opinion poll. The results showed that the public did not care about Walter Jenkins one way or the other. The president ignored the issue, attention shifted, and Lyndon Johnson won the election with 43.1 million votes to Goldwater's 27.2 million.

2. All-Purpose Celebrity and the New Journalism

"Almost everybody at the party was a celebrity"

The merger of political and entertainment celebrities in the public mind peaked in the late 1960s and early 1970s. Adlai Stevenson might have turned down the chance to be a mystery guest on *I've Got a Secret,* as unseemly, but even Richard Nixon was willing to show up on *Laugh-In* in 1968, between comedy skits and gyrating go-go dancers, and mutter the program's trademark "Sock it to me." Entertainers, meanwhile, were embracing the pop-protest culture spawned by the war in Vietnam. Movie stars and politicians found they could work together for their mutual advantage, with actors contributing their money-raising abilities in return for the power—or at least the image—of being political movers and shakers. "I got to know them quite well," said George McGovern, of the stars who flocked to support his antiwar presidential campaign. "Shirley MacLaine traveled with me for many weeks. I don't think there was ever anything like it in presidential politics."

Looking back on that campaign, which began with such excitement and ended so dismally, McGovern has glowing memories of the huge fund-raising concerts packed with his celebrity supporters. Barbra Streisand and Carol King singing at the Los Angeles Forum. Simon and Garfunkel at Madison Square Garden. Gary Hart, McGovern's campaign organizer, and Hart's friend actor/director Warren Beatty, became costars of the amorphous lump of fame that was the Hollywood antiwar movement. A few years later, when would-be actress Donna Rice met then-Senator Hart at a New Year's Eve gala thrown by a member of the rock-and-roll band the Eagles, she recalled proudly: "almost everybody at the party was a celebrity."

The entertainers couldn't help noticing that the public was more interested in them than the politicians they were supporting. Unsurprisingly, some of the older actors and actresses whose stars were fading began thinking of taking up a career in politics themselves. George Murphy became a U.S. senator in 1964. Shirley Temple Black lost a bid for Congress but was appointed ambassador to Ghana. Ronald Reagan became governor of California. Most of the morphed celebrity/politicians were not from Hart's crowd but conservative Republicans. Perhaps that was because the states where the celebrities dwelled were already stuffed with incumbent Democratic congressmen and governors and younger Democratic mayors and state legislators waiting in line for their jobs.

Whatever entertainer/politicians like Ronald Reagan, Warren Beatty, and the Kennedy family (not to mention counterculture political stars like Abbie Hoffman and Eldridge Cleaver) were, there was an enormous appetite for information about them. But the print media couldn't serve up the kind of fifties-era personality profiles that burbled about Mamie's pretty pink dresses and Ike's passion for golf. People could get that and more from television. Something fresher and juicier was needed, and it was being pioneered in places like *Esquire*, where writers like Gay Talese and Norman Mailer and Rex Reed were producing carefully observed, detail-laden portraits that were perhaps less than art but more than traditional journalism. Their stories, often written in the first person, showed what it was like to be in Frank Sinatra's entourage, to work for Lyndon Johnson, or to try to conduct an interview with the desperately self-absorbed Warren Beatty. The stories were in many ways the equivalent of a long gossip session with a friend who let you in on the fact that Sinatra was trailed everywhere by a gray-haired lady who toted a tiny satchel full of his sixty hairpieces, or that Beatty had tortured the actress Jean Seberg when they worked together by picking his nose and "flinging the contents at her when it was her turn to face the camera."

Like all the best gossip, the stories went well beyond anecdote, providing a view into a kind of existence most people never experienced for themselves. The middle-aged Ava Gardner, alternately sipping champagne and cognac through a straw, confided to Rex Reed that "the only time I'm happy is when I'm doing absolutely nothing. When I work I vomit all the time." A witness described Lyndon Johnson chewing out his press secretary "using language I never heard one human being use to another." The media had not yet entered the world of full disclosure—Johnson's congressional romances were never hinted at while he was in office, and Reed's interview with Ava Gardner said only that she made an "unprintable" remark when asked about her ex-husband Frank Sinatra's romance with the coltish twenty-year-old Mia Farrow. (When Reed's articles were republished as a book, it was revealed that Gardner had said: "I always knew Frank would end up in bed with a boy.") But the old restraints were gone, and the celebrity-profilers of the era treated politicians and entertainers with the same combination of cynicism, concern, and a dollop of awe.

3. Out with the Old

1972: "Strong rumors of alcoholism or mental illness or both"

Senator George McGovern had not given much thought to the vice-presidential slot when he arrived at the 1972 Democratic convention, victorious after a year and a half of struggle to impose his candidacy for president on the party regulars. He nurtured the dream of getting Ted Kennedy. The Massachusetts senator had been political damaged goods since 1969, when he had driven off a bridge and left his passenger, Mary Jo Kopechne, trapped in a car lying upside down in six feet of water. But McGovern regarded that as a minor drawback compared to the legend of the family name. Kennedy, he thought, might be convinced to take second place "as a kind of penance" for Chappaquiddick, that would allow him to put the issue to rest. But Kennedy was not interested in cleansing his soul via the vice presidency, and most of the other names on McGovern's wish list also refused to make what looked like an almost impossible race against incumbent Richard Nixon. Thomas Eagleton, an attractive and energetic senator from Missouri, emerged as the favorite by default.

Someone needed to check into Eagleton's background. Vetting a vice-presidential possibility is basically a matter of collecting gossip, and the McGovern campaign was operating at a disadvantage. They were outsiders, who had done an end run around the Democratic establishment, appealing directly to the voters in the primaries. Given the mood of the country in 1972, outside was not a bad place to be. But the McGovern team did not have the dense network of personal relationships that come from a lifetime of back-scratching and glad-handing. They were cut out of a lot of the party's gossip loops.

Eagleton and McGovern were both senators, but they hardly knew each other. The Senate had become a collection of one hundred fiefdoms, and the two men had really spoken only twice—at a crowded dinner party and once when they both happened to be taking a steam bath in the Senate gym. McGovern, obviously, was not going to be able to provide much help. As his staff tossed Eagleton's name around, press aide Gordon Weil remembered someone mentioning that "around Missouri there were strong rumors of alcoholism or mental illness or both." There was also some vague talk about past hospitalizations. Dispatched to investigate, Weil learned that Eagleton had been diagnosed with a physiological difficulty that gave him a very low tolerance for alcohol. But he was definitely not an alcoholic. The rumor was wrong. Case closed. Satisfied, McGovern picked up the phone. Eagleton, who had been eagerly waiting for an invitation to join the ticket, was asked if he had any "skeletons in the closet." Unlike Warren Harding, he did not need ten minutes to say that there were no problems.

The McGovern camp had dismissed the rumors too soon. There were two different strains of gossip. Eagleton was not an alcoholic. But he *had* been hospitalized three times for mental illness and depression during the 1960s, and received electroshock treatments twice. The story had never been printed, and his opponents had never mentioned it in his campaigns. But there were plenty of politicians who knew about it, both in Missouri and in the Senate. The McGovern team had not asked enough people, or the people in the right gossip loops.

Eagleton would say later that he had not mentioned his history to McGovern because he regarded the problem as no different from "a broken leg that had healed." That was sheer evasion, and the senator would later admit that he just didn't like discussing it. But Eagleton had barely accepted the nomination before the story of the shock treatments came out. "Apparently it was leaked by the son of one of his psychiatrists," says McGovern.

The presidential candidate had to make a very quick decision about the mental health of a man he didn't know, who had deliberately misled him once. Was Eagleton psychologically fragile, or simply a human being who knew how to get help when he had a problem? Cornered, McGovern told reporters he was behind his running mate "one thousand percent." But his supporters were unhappy. Did they fight for all those months to nominate an antiwar, antiestablishment candidate only to waste the campaign arguing about electroshock therapy? "I have nine kids. I don't want to see them destroyed because some unstable person might become President," said Matthew Troy of Queens, one of the few regular Democrats among McGovern's backers. New allegations popped up—columnist Jack Anderson reported that the senator had a raft of traffic citations for drunken or reckless driving. That would later turn out to be untrue, but no one on the McGovern team knew Eagleton well enough to be sure of that right away. Only eighteen days after the convention, McGovern agreed that Eagleton had to go. He arranged to meet with his running mate in private to break the news. It was, Eagleton noted bitterly, the first time they had actually been alone together since their forty-five minutes in the Senate steam bath in 1969.

Looking back on the whole episode a quarter-century later, McGovern saw it as a turning point that "broke our momentum" and sent the campaign spiraling downward. McGovern may have been overestimating the long-shot campaign's chances. But he never believed his staff could have avoided the Eagleton disaster by being more thorough in checking the right gossip loops. (Insider Richard Nixon had, after all, picked Spiro Agnew, the soon-to-be-indicted former governor of Maryland.) Still, after his overwhelming loss in November, McGovern sought out Senator John Sparkman, a former vice-presidential candidate, and asked him whether it was true that Adlai Stevenson had invited Sparkman to be his running mate without a single question about his background.

Of course it was, Sparkman said. If they had tried asking him any personal questions "I'd have told them where to go. I'm a U.S. senator."

"We were waiting on the cops"

Political gossip went into the 1960s as a background noise, an undercurrent that flavored and occasionally informed the insiders' lives but that reached the public only in occasional snatches. But by the end of the 1980s it would be a quasi-official part of the political process: The very fact that a rumor was in circulation became something that could be reported by the media, investigated, and weighed by the voters just like a candidate's health-care program or tax policy.

All sorts of social and economic changes were responsible for gossip's new role in the political process, from the public's increasing perception of candidates as just another kind of celebrity to the breakdown of the party system to the explosion of cable television. But nothing could happen until journalists decided to share the gossip they knew with the entire nation. For generations, the Washington press corps had believed that virtually nothing about politicians' private lives was the public's business. The personal might be relevant to movie stars because they were *personalities*. Cary Grant could stop making movies and twenty years later people would still line up for his autograph. But a politician was wedded to his function. Out of office, he was a nonentity. Anything besides the way he did his job was irrelevent.

A series of events occurred in the 1970s that would change those feelings and open the doors to the explosion of printed political gossip. The most important, of course, was Watergate. The voters, already alienated by the government's inability either to chart a straight course or tell a straight story about the war in Vietnam, saw their most cynical ideas about politics confirmed in 1973 by the tapes of Richard Nixon swearing, bullying, and conspiring to obstruct justice. Watergate itself was not a matter of political gossip by the definition we're using here. It was about public behavior, involving the most profound issues about the powers of the presidency and the Constitution. Still, it left the public ready to hear and believe the more tawdry and trivial stories about politicians' personal lives.

For journalists, Watergate was, at least professionally, a self-affirming experience. Public power had been misused, and the media had exposed it through hard work and courageous persistence. It was exactly what their business was supposed to do. But at the same time, over in Congress, things were happening that undermined the rules under which many journalists had been operating for decades. The men whose private behavior they had overlooked until an arrest warrant was issued were acting out in ways that made the media think their discretion had been misplaced. "Suddenly there was this notion—maybe we should peek into their lives," said Robert Semple of the *Times*. "Until then, we were waiting on the cops, basically."

The transformation came incredibly fast. The mainline media could hardly bring itself to hint that the Speaker of the House had a drinking problem in 1972. Four years later, it was casually printing rumors that his office was the scene of regular "orgies."

4. Congress out of Control

"You can't touch me . . . I just got you your raise"

In 1972, Speaker of the House Carl Albert got into a minor traffic accident outside a Washington bar called the Zebra Room. Police, who were called to the scene, drove the congressional leader home but did not file a report on the incident. *The Washington Post*, however, found witnesses who said the Speaker appeared to have been driving while drunk. "Albert was plastered. He was belligerent, he kept speaking loudly, his speech was slurred and he was unsteady," said a law student who ran across the scene while en route to a local pizza parlor. "I've seen a lot of drunks and he was drunk, period. It was so obvious." Other witnesses told the *Post* that Albert had pushed two policemen who were called to the scene and yelled: "Leave me alone. I'm Carl Albert, Speaker of the House. . . . You can't touch me . . . I just got you your raise." Whether the veteran Oklahoma Democrat had actually been that blunt or not, his alleged comments did point to an important reason why there had historically been so few defining public events that highlighted the private misbehavior of American congressmen. The money used to run the Washington police department and other city services came from Congress. Shortly

192

before Carl Albert's white Thunderbird hit a Pontiac Grand Prix in the Zebra Room parking lot, Congress had, indeed, voted a 17.5 percent pay raise for entry-level D.C. police officers. The D.C. police actually had a century-old *rule* about not arresting members of Congress for anything short of a felony, like armed robbery or murder. The rule was based on a section of the Constitution that prohibited arresting members of Congress while they were attending to their legislative duties. You could never really be sure, the police department felt, that a congressman whose car was weaving erratically down the sidewalk wasn't racing to pick up an important amendment he'd left in his desk.

Capitol Hill gossip had long since pegged Carl Albert as a heavy drinker, and since the Speaker of the House is second in line for succession to the presidency, that was the kind of rumor inquiring minds might want to know. But the journalistic standards of the day made it impossible to write about the drinking rumors directly. "It was just not something a family newspaper printed," said Max Frankel of the *Times*. In 1966, Drew Pearson had flouted the unwritten laws of discretion and wrote that Mendel Rivers of Mississippi, the powerful head of the House Armed Services Committee, sometimes was discovered in his office Monday mornings "surrounded by empty bottles after a drinking weekend." But no one else followed suit. The whole idea seemed somehow offensive, more the province of a scandal magazine writer than a serious reporter.

But Albert's central role in the House and proximity to the presidency made the media think twice. "Everybody was talking about it, and it was getting to be a serious problem," recalled Frankel. "We felt it was time to let the country know—but the indirect way we went about it!" The *Times* prepared an analysis of Albert's performance as Speaker, trying to hint at the private problem while sticking to the public evidence. "I don't think the word drink was actually mentioned at all," Frankel said. A year later, Albert became first in line of succession when a kickback scandal forced Vice President Spiro Agnew to resign. The Speaker, who appeared as eager as anyone else to wipe out the possibility of an Albert administration, helped engineer the quick confirmation of Gerald Ford as the new vice president.

"Everybody knew he drank too much"

On an October night in 1974, U.S. Park Police officer Larry Brent and his partner saw a car speeding with its lights off near the Jefferson Memorial in Washington. Inside, they found several people, including a hysterical striptease dancer named Annabella Battistella and a drunken Wilbur Mills, the chairman of the House of Representative's Ways and Means Committee. Mills had a scratched face and bloody nose. Battistella had two black eyes. While the other occupants were getting out of the car, the stripper ran off and leaped into the Washington Tidal Basin. Showing a keen understanding that the U.S. Park Police get their salaries from the same Congress as the District of Columbia force, Officer Brent dragged Battistella out of the water, had a colleague drive Mills home, and filed a police report describing the incident as an "attempted suicide" without mentioning any of the car occupants' names. A cameraman from a local TV station, who happened to be on the scene, said one of the officers told Mills, "Congressman, come on. You don't need this kind of publicity."

Mills, a sixty-five-year-old Arkansas Democrat, was one of the most powerful members of the House, head of the committee that sets tax policy. But he had also become one of the congressmen who had been gossiped about as a problem drinker. "Everybody knew he drank too much," said Warren Rogers, the former *Herald Tribune* reporter. "You could see him at two-thirty in the afternoon finishing a lunch he began at noon. Later he started going to the clip joints on Fourteenth Street, where they charge you twenty dollars for champagne and a woman who'll come and sit with you and make promises that are never kept. He liked that, spent money like crazy. But even through his ordeal I respected him. He was the best financial mind on the Hill, and a very courteous man."

In one of those details that make an embarrassing incident live on into history, reporters soon learned that Annabella Battistella had met Mills at the Silver Slipper nightclub, where she worked under the name of "Fanne Foxe, the Argentine Firecracker." Other strippers at the club provided interviewers with a wealth of colorful information. Foxe, they said, had stopped dancing when she met Mills, who later moved with his wife into an apartment in the building where the dancer lived. The Ways and Means chairman continued to escort Foxe to the Silver Slipper, they said, and recently had brought TV reporter Nancy Dickerson and her husband along for an evening in which Foxe became angry at Mills's attention to another dancer and knocked the glasses off the table. When asked about the story, Dickerson declined to comment. As a reporter, she said, "I never work after six o'clock."

After a short period in seclusion, Mills went home to Arkansas to campaign for his nineteenth term in Congress. He jokingly advised his constituents never to "drink champagne with foreigners." When a class of high school students gave him a hard time, he claimed a newsman had bribed them with five-dollar bills. On election day, the district voted to send back the representative whose seniority and position had provided so many advantages over the last thirty-six years. But Mills's fellow members of Congress felt less need for his services than the voters in Arkansas. The post-Watergate generation of reformers, emboldened by signs of weakness, began whittling away at his authority. The Ways and Means chairman was in no condition to defend himself. Shortly after his reelection, the formerly frugal Mills chartered a private jet, flew to Boston, and appeared onstage with Foxe, who was dancing for three thousand dollars a week as "The Tidal Basin Bombshell." Sitting in her dressing room, he told reporters he had written a script for the stripper, whom he planned to turn into a movie star, and called her "my little old Argentine hillbilly." Asked if his antics might hurt his career, Mills announced, "It won't ruin me. . . . Nothing can ruin me."

There was a time, perhaps, when Mills's behavior might have qualified him as a colorful congressman. But post-Watergate, the public had too close a view of Washington not to understand that he was a sick man. When he next walked into the Capitol, looking ill-at-ease, hands trembling, his fellow House Democrats were planning to strip him of his chairmanship. Heeding his friends' pleas, Mills resigned from his committee and checked into a hospital. On New Year's Day he issued a statement that he had realized he was an alcoholic. After a long recuperation he finished out his term and then retired from Congress. Many people were appalled by the media's role in Mills's demise. "Shall we have a rule that any member of Congress seen in the company of a member of the opposite sex to whom he or she isn't married will be put in the stocks by the media and snickered to death by his confreres?" demanded columnist Nicholas Von Hoffman.

When Mills returned to Washington as a teetotaling tax lawyer, he revealed that he had suffered from a dual addiction to prescription drugs and alcohol. Mills said he had often drunk a half a gallon of bourbon or vodka a night, had hallucinations that buzzards were chasing him, and suffered from blackouts that lasted for up to two weeks at a time. During that same period, he had regularly visited the White House and had responsibility for shaping the national tax policy. In an interview with *The New York Times* in 1978, Mills blamed his alcoholism for the fact that the United States did not have a comprehensive medical health-insurance plan. "I had President Ford convinced on national health," he said. "I could have passed it on the floor. But hell, I couldn't get the damn committee to go with me. They had never failed to do that before, and I know now it was because of my drinking that they didn't."

"Closed Session Romance on the Hill"

In 1976, when Representative Wayne Hays of Ohio divorced his wife of thirty-eight years and married his district office secretary, the last person to hear the news was Hays's Washington mistress, thirty-three-year-old Elizabeth Ray. Not only had the veteran congressman failed even to pretend that Ray was herself a possible candidate to be the next Mrs. Hays, she was the only member of his congressional staff not invited to the wedding. It looked on the surface like the Representative Breckinridge affair all over again. But Hays and Ray, a failed actress–model–rental car agent, had a more pragmatic relationship. When making love, Ray claimed, the congressman kept his eye on her digital clock to make sure he was out the door by 9:30. "If I could have, I'd have put on a blindfold, worn earplugs and taken a shot of Novocain," she declared. The worst thing about the new marriage, Ray said, was that Hays had started coming around four nights a week instead of his usual two.

Still, Ray picked up the phone and called a *Washington Post* reporter she'd met on a train a few years earlier. She allowed the reporter to listen on the extension while Hays assured her that his new marriage would not interfere with their arrangement. CLOSED SESSION ROMANCE ON THE HILL, read the *Post* headline, over a story that detailed Ray's assertion that she was paid the then-respectable salary of fourteen thousand dollars a year in taxpayer money as a committee clerk, while her only real job was having sex with the committee chairman. "I can't type, I can't file, I can't even answer the phone," Ray said, summarizing her claim to fame. While it was the sex that made the story sensational, it was the fact that Ray was being supported on the congressional payroll that gave the media a sense of security about making a big fuss.

Ray was the first in a new breed of defining public events—the political sex partner who, out of exhibitionism, a lust for a sort of sleazy immortality, or a desire to get even for real or imagined wrongs, calls a press conference to expose the affair. Ray was already set, when the scandal erupted, to be a topless feature in *Playboy's* "The Girls of Washington" display. She had also written, with the help of a ghostwriter, a novel called *The Washington Fringe Benefit.* Later it would turn out that Ray's sudden urge to come clean about her no-show job was timed to coincide with the release of the book. She had flitted around the edges of the Washington political/social scene for a long time. Senator Hubert Humphrey admitted to at least vague memories of having met her, and Representative Barry Goldwater, Jr., acknowledged he had tried to help her find a movie job. She had worked for a while as a secretary for former Illinois congressman Kenneth Gray, who lived, as *Newsweek* said, on "a swinging houseboat on the Potomac." (Gray claimed that when he had employed her, Ray knew how to type, albeit very slowly.) The houseboat would take on a fame all its own when a second congressional pink-collar worker would report having witnessed Ray and Senator Mike Gravel of Alaska having sex there, and the National Park Service would admit it had been supplying the boat with free electricity for five years.

As with the Wilbur Mills story, it was the details that gave the Hays imbroglio resonance. Ray was officially a clerk on the Oversight Subcommittee of the House Administration Committee that Hays chaired. But the committee staff director told reporters he had never laid eyes on her, and it turned out that the Oversight Subcommittee had never had a meeting since Hays had created it. Ray, who was happily taking every reporter in town on a tour of her apartment, with its red carpets, velvet chairs, and blue plastic fern in the bedroom, produced a secretarial school teacher who attested that the Oversight Subcommittee's typist was a dropout in serious need of "remedial work."

The Ray affair was distinguished by the fact that everyone in a position to mitigate its effects loathed the man under fire. No reporters wrote sadly about the tragedy that had befallen gentle Wayne Hays. None of his colleagues stood up to say they couldn't believe such a thing was true. Hays was a sixty-five-year-old, heavyset House veteran with cold, hooded eyes and a habit of calling his fellow legislators "pipsqueak" or "potato head." Hays's power derived in part from his position as chairman of the Administration Committee, which controlled mundane matters close to legislators' hearts, like parking spaces, travel allowances, and office equipment. The word in the House of Representatives was that Hays was fully capable of taking away a duplicating machine from a congressman who defied him on a vote. When Hays finally rose in the House to defend himself, and said he had been called "arrogant, ruthless, cold-blooded temperamental, and mean," no one complained about being misquoted. Indeed, Hays's fellow Democrats practically stood in line to demand an Ethics Committee investigation.

A famous junketeer, Hays had to cancel a trip to London in order to consult with a lawyer after Ray's press conference. (The other twenty-four members of the congressional delegation managed to pick up a copy of the Magna Carta without him.) He initially denied Ray's charges. ("Hell's fire! I'm a happily married man.") Later, he claimed she was a suicidal basket case who would say anything to get attention. ("This is the reward I get for trying to help somebody who's sick.") Finally, he admitted Ray had been his mistress, but claimed the part about not doing any work for her salary was untrue, and part of an elaborate blackmail plot.

Back home, Hays's new wife, Pat, was recoiling at the news that their long-standing relationship in Ohio had been the flip side of his capital romance with the worst clerical worker in the postindustrial era. (As Hays's district secretary, the former Pat Peake had made the news herself when reporters noticed how frequently she accompanied the congressman on his fact-finding journeys abroad.) "Only time will tell if Miss Ray has been successful in destroying my career. I pray to God she has not destroyed my marriage," Hays said on the House floor. But within a few days columnist Jack Anderson was telling the nation that Hays's new wife refused to speak to him. A week after his primary victory over token opposition, Hays was rushed to the hospital after taking an overdose of sleeping pills. The House insurgents postponed their attempts to strip him of his chairmanship until he recovered.

Predictions that Elizabeth Ray's assorted black books, diaries, and tape recordings would ruin the careers of dozens of congressmen turned out to be either scare stories or wishful thinking, depending on your point of view. *The New York Times* discovered another former congressional secretary who claimed to have received taxpayer money for sex. Colleen Gardner said Representative John Young, a ten-term Texas Democrat, had raised her salary from eighty-five hundred to twenty-six thousand dollars a year once she agreed to sleep with him. (The Dallas *Times Herald* noted that was eight thousand a year more than the congressman's administrative assistant was paid.) "It wouldn't have been so bad going to bed with him if he'd at least have let me work, but he wouldn't," said Gardner, who estimated she had met Young for sex more than thirty times over a two-year period. The congressman, who admitted having booked motel rooms under a false name, said he used them for secret meetings with Pentagon employees who were helping him save a military base in Corpus Christi from closing.

Anyone hoping for some clean resolution of the scandals was doomed to disappointment. The Justice Department found it could not prosecute Hays for giving Elizabeth Ray no-work employment, since there were no official job descriptions for congressional staff, or even a definition of what "work" was. Colleen Gardner's accusations were dismissed for lack of supporting evidence, even though she had actually reported Young for sexual harassment long before the Ray scandal occurred. But the one-two punch from the Hays and Mills debacles had an enormous and almost instantaneous effect on what newspapers and magazines were willing to print about politicians' private habits. When Carl Albert temporized about stripping Hays's committee assignment, James Reston wrote that it was "not surprising, since he [Albert] is not widely admired here as a model of temperance or Congressional probity." *Time* passed along rumors that "orgies were reported to have taken place in a Capitol Hill office assigned to Albert." It was the beginning of a whole new era.

"I feel such super love for you"

By 1976, Robert Redford and Dustin Hoffman were breaking the Watergate story on movie screens, playing *The Washington Post*'s Woodward and Bernstein, and investigative reporting was a glamour career. (The *Columbia Journalism Review* nervously noted that there were enough college students majoring in journalism at that very minute to completely staff every single newspaper in the country.) Everybody wanted to be part of the heady world of exposing rogue politicians. There were plenty of reporters outside of Washington who knew gossip about their governors, mayors, and members of Congress, too. The desire to get it into the paper occasionally proved irresistible.

In 1976, the *Detroit News* printed parts of a transcript of conversations between the married Representative Donald Riegle, Jr., and his former girlfriend. Riegle was, at that time, running for the U.S. Senate, and the paper claimed it was just letting Michigan in on what already *was* gossip in Washington, where the tapes had "been played for a select few in Washington social circles." Anyway, the paper pointed out, there were issues involved: Voters might want to note that their senatorial candidate had been recorded telling his lover that their affair was more interesting than "a lousy subcommittee hearing."

The tape was seven years old, and Riegle naturally cried foul. "My personal life in the distant past is my personal life," said the thirty-eight-year-old Democrat, who had not only changed wives, but also political parties since the conversation was recorded. Republican politicians (who counted the paper as a firm ally) came to the *News*'s defense. The head of the state party claimed Riegle's marital infidelity demonstrated he was "a hypocrite because he's been going around talking about ethics . . . things like opening up the political process and morality in government." Many of the *News*'s supporters pointed out that Riegle had encouraged his ex-girlfriend to tape their conversations so she could replay them whenever he was away. Voters, they said, had a right to know when a candidate was that dumb.

Riegle won the election anyway, and the *News* was generally judged to have gone too far. But the transcripts did give a memorable insight into the heart and mind of the modern American politician. Ending his conversation with his lover, who was also working as a campaign volunteer, Riegle said: "I—I—God, I feel such super love for you. By the way, the newsletter should start arriving."

"A woman tried to entice me"

In the same election year, Representative Joe Waggoner, a powerful Louisiana Democrat, got picked up in Washington for soliciting a policewoman posing as a prostitute. "A woman tried to entice me. She failed," claimed Waggoner, who had led police on a high-speed chase before he was picked up. The matter never would have seen the light of day, he insisted, were it not for the publicity over the Hays affair "and the attitude of the times we live in." He was right about that. Once the police realized he was a member of Congress, the tearful Waggoner was allowed to leave the booking station without being charged. The incident became public only when the *New York Post* included it in a post–Wayne Hays roundup of congressmen run amok.

Meanwhile, in Salt Lake City, a freshman Democrat named Allan Howe was arrested for the same offense in his home district. Howe also assured his constituents he was entrapped. ("I was lured to the scene of the incident under false pretenses of an invitation to a political gathering.") But unlike Waggoner he was quickly booked, scheduled for trial, and eventually convicted. The difference in treatment the two men got attracted a certain amount of attention, and the District of Columbia police chief finally announced, somewhat sadly, that he was changing the policy that had "served us well for over one hundred years." Members of Congress were no longer above the law (except perhaps the ones regarding parking).

That little-noticed change in procedure may have accounted for a sudden spurt of arrests of congressmen for homosexual activity. In 1978, Representative Fred Richmond of Brooklyn announced—one step ahead of a Jack Anderson exposé—that he had been charged with soliciting a young male undercover police officer. In 1980, Representative Robert Bauman of Maryland pleaded guilty to a sex-solicitation charge involving a sixteen-year-old boy. In the same year, Representative Jon Hinson of Mississippi acknowledged he had been arrested—four years earlier—for committing an obscene act at the Iwo Jima Memorial.

The voters may have been appalled by the scandals in Washington in general, but they seemed willing to ignore misbehavior by their own congressmen. Bauman, a political conservative who ran on an anti–homosexual rights platform, was defeated for reelection, as was Representative Howe. But Waggoner won another term easily. Richmond, who admitted he was gay, was quickly forgiven by his liberal constituents, and Hinson, who denied it, was reelected by conservative Mississippians who found it hard to imagine their representative had done the things he was accused of.

Representative Robert Leggett, a California Democrat, was reelected after confessing to financial and personal entanglements *The Washington Post* could only summarize in the headline LIFE OF IMMENSE COMPLICATIONS. The married seven-term congressman had for thirteen years been secretly supporting a former Capitol Hill secretary with whom he had two children, and had forged his wife's name on the deed to a house he bought for his second family. "I've been very strapped," he admitted. Leggett also had been having a long-running affair with Suzi Thomson, an aide to Speaker Albert. The Korean-born Thomson had just been granted immunity by a federal grand jury probing allegations that some House members had accepted bribes from the Korean government.

The public was once again demonstrating its pragmatic attitude toward private sinning in Washington. As the 20th century wore on, what had earlier been a willingness to disregard inconvenient rumors for the sake of party loyalty was turning into a transactional attitude toward elected officials. The voters seemed to see their representatives less like heroes and more like the sanitation men or the bus drivers—they were hired to do a job, and what they did in their off-duty hours was of little matter. Wilbur Mills's ability to bring money home to Arkansas meant far more than his drinking habits or sexual fidelity. Legislators with substantial seniority were valuable commodities, and people seemed loathe to get rid of them even after they became embarrassments.

But the emotional effect of having one's personal secrets plastered across the nation's newspapers is more lasting than the political damage. The fact that most of the congressmen caught in the scandal season of the 1970s got reelected did not mean their lives went on as before. Leggett resigned, saying he was tired of "the gossip and garbage," and separated from his wife, who had stuck by him during his reelection campaign. Richmond and Hinson resigned after getting in further trouble with the law. Hays dropped out of his reelection campaign shortly after winning the Democratic primary. Mills retired after finishing out his term. Young's wife was found dead of a gunshot wound in 1977, an apparent suicide.

5. Kennedy Redux

"A close friend of President Kennedy"

Gossip about John Kennedy's womanizing had been dribbling out ever since his assassination. By the mid-seventies, anyone with a library card could have collected quite a bit of detail from the memoirs of Broadway columnist Earl Wilson, or the White House kennel-keeper, who had a lot to say about the semiclothed women who kept turning up while he was going about his doggie duties.

In 1975, Judith Campbell turned into the defining public event that pushed the Kennedy gossip into public consciousness. The Senate Intelligence Agency was investigating the CIA's bizarre attempt to use American mobsters to assassinate Fidel Castro during the Kennedy administration. The committee wanted to know, among other things, whether the president had been aware of what the agency had been plotting. Examining the White House visitor and telephone logs, staff members came across Campbell's name repeatedly. She was a woman who traveled in mob social circles, who had a relationship with Chicago mob boss Sam Giancana at about the same time she was talking to and visiting the president. Meeting with investigators in a closed session, with what she thought was a promise her name would be concealed, Campbell stressed she was afraid for her life. (Sam Giancana had been shot to death. Another mob friend, Johnny Rosselli, who appeared before the Senate committee himself, soon popped up off the Florida coast, stuffed inside an oil drum.)

The Senate committee's final report said that there was no evidence Kennedy knew about the CIA-mob plot—a conclusion that would be undermined dramatically in later years. But it added, in a peculiarly worded section, that "a close friend of President Kennedy" during the period when the Castro assassination was being planned was also "a close friend" of Giancana and Rosselli. That was supposed to be Campbell's protective cover. But a Senate committee is not generally good at keeping this sort of juicy secret, particularly when the Republican staff members are irritated at the Democratic chairman's insistence on focusing only on misuse of the CIA by Richard Nixon. The story leaked out.

Campbell (who was then married and known as Judith Exner) called a press conference and became the first woman to publicly discuss sex in the Kennedy White House. "My relationship with Jack Kennedy was of a close personal nature and did not involve conspiratorial shenanigans of any kind," she told the reporters. Giancana and Rosselli knew about her affair with the president but never tried to take advantage of it, she claimed. The press conference had barely ended before she had a literary agent and was peddling a more explicit version of her story. It was a signal for the media to dump all the gossip they had been storing up in a barrage of Kennedy girlfriend roundups. "She was only confirming what had long been a matter of open and widespread speculation," said *Time*, which went on to name Jayne Mansfield, Marilyn Monroe, "Fiddle" and "Faddle," and a list of movie stars who were "linked" to Kennedy, including Angie Dickinson, Kim Novak, and Janet Leigh. *Newsweek* announced that Campbell had broken "a gentleman's code of silence" that kept the media from reporting "backstairs whispers of supposed Kennedy amours—with stenographers and stewardesses, an off-Broadway star, and a Hollywood star-in-the-making, a syndicated reporter and an ambassador's wife." *Time* also decided, in retrospect, that the night during the Democratic convention when reporters caught Kennedy climbing over a fence near the house where he was staying in Los Angeles, he had probably not really been going to see his father as he'd claimed.

A few weeks later the *National Enquirer* reported that Kennedy had had a two-year affair with Mary Pinchot Meyer, a divorced Washington artist who had been murdered in an apparent mugging about a year after the president was assassinated. The *Enquirer*'s favorite detail was a claim by Meyer's friends that she had smoked marijuana with the president in a White House bedroom. The gloves were officially off when it came to Kennedy's sex life, a fact that was reinforced when the dying scandal-magazine industry quickly produced *JFK's Love Affairs,* a collection of alleged first-person accounts ("I Bore JFK's Illegitimate Baby") and features written in prose that sounded like a very senior citizen's idea of how cynical big-city journalists write. ("Jack, the little old lamplighter, lit her fire and rang her chimes.") It included a story about a German woman who said her three-year affair with the president led to pregnancy and abortion, and a rehash of the Mary Meyer story titled, "They Balled and Blew Grass in a White House Bedroom."

These revelations eventually began to chip away at the national vision of a long-lost Camelot. But the effect was more a slow erosion than a sudden loss of faith. A *Newsweek* poll on the twentieth anniversary of Kennedy's assassination in 1983 showed 75 percent of respondents rated his presidency as "good" to "great" and 30 percent wished he were still president. (The runner-up in the latter category was Franklin Roosevelt with 10 percent.) "Kennedy," the magazine concluded, "has become our favorite president of all time." Asked what qualities they associated with Kennedy's presidency, 79 percent said "concern for working people" and more than two-thirds picked qualities like a commitment to racial justice, government activism, and the ability to inspire young people to work for social progress. Only 24 percent said they thought of "sexual misconduct in the White House."

Like Kay Summersby, Judith Campbell never seemed to get her life past her affair with an American president. She had a child out of wedlock and gave it up for adoption, married golf pro Dan Exner, who became incapacitated from a brain tumor. Her marriage fell apart and in 1988 she revealed that she had terminal cancer. Like Summersby, she announced that she wanted to clear the air before her death by revising her memoirs. "I lied when I said I was not a conduit between President Kennedy and the Mafia," she announced in a *People* magazine interview written by Kitty Kelley. Campbell claimed she had carried envelopes back and forth between Giancana and Kennedy and arranged for ten meetings between them. Liz Smith, who became her champion, published an interview with Campbell in 1997, in which she upped the ante again, claiming she had become pregnant by the president and gotten an abortion at his request. "I believe every word she said," Smith said later. Campbell's first attempt at a tell-all autobiography had been ruined, according to Smith, when she panicked at the prospect of winding up like the slain Giancana and Rosselli, and allowed her ghost writer to "just make up stuff."

Later in 1997, investigative reporter Seymour Hersh produced an analysis of the links between Kennedy's sex life and his presidency that suggested a hard-pressed weapons manufacturer might have spied on Campbell and used evidence of her affair with the president to win a big government contract. But in the 1980s, Campbell's revelation that John Kennedy's White House lovers had included a woman with Mafia connections was already enough to undermine whatever faith official Washington still had in the irrelevance of a presidential candidate's private sex life.

Chapter 9

The Institutionalization
of Gossip
1980–1990

1. Gary Hart

"We'd like to ask you about the young woman"

The front-running candidate for the Democratic presidential nomination entered a dark alley behind his Washington town house on Saturday evening, May 2, 1987. Close behind came a reporter and editor from *The Miami Herald.* "We'd like to ask you about the young woman staying in your house," one of them said. Reporter Jim McGee and investigations editor James Savage had been staking out Gary Hart's home to see if he was committing adultery. They had flown to Washington on the same plane as a stunning blonde who they believed was on her way to sleep with the married senator from Colorado.

"No one is staying in my house," said Hart, leaning against a brick fence, his arms folded protectively around his middle. As he stood nervously in the alley, doing himself no good whatsoever—admitting he telephoned the mystery woman frequently while he was campaigning, denying he knew what she did for a living, claiming he didn't remember if they had taken a weekend yacht trip together—he was creating a landmark in the history of political gossip. He was also, of course, destroying his own political career.

The small but influential segment of the American population that is truly interested in politics remembers the fall of Gary Hart with the same clarity as the Nixon resignation, the 1968 Democratic convention, and other dramatic turning points in modern political history. Hart, who had burst on the scene as the manager of George McGovern's antiwar presidential candidacy in 1972, had gone on to become a U.S. senator from Colorado and a surprisingly strong candidate for the 1984 presidential nomination. He was far and away the Democratic front-runner for the nomination four years later, against a field that would later come to be known as the "seven dwarfs."

The candidate had insisted he was running on issues, not fuzzy personality politics. He resisted talking about his personal life. His twenty-eight-year marriage was well known to be rocky, but his campaign biography tried to present that as a plus: "We were able to resolve those temporary stresses where others had not." Still, when Hart officially announced he was running for president in the spring of 1987, *Newsweek* greeted the event with a profile that claimed he was "haunted by rumors of womanizing" and quoted John McEvoy, a former adviser, as saying: "He's always in jeopardy of having the sex issue raised if he can't keep his pants on." McEvoy disassociated himself from the comment without actually denying he said it. But it created the sort of furor other stories could build on ("Gary: I'm Not a Womanizer").

Tom Fiedler, a *Miami Herald* reporter, wrote a rather disapproving analysis of the way vague rumors of Hart's infidelity were being treated as news. Then he received an anonymous call from a woman who said: "Gary Hart is having an affair with a friend of mine." The caller's professed motives seemed to ricochet from principled anger over hypocrisy in politics to a desire to sell pictures of Hart disporting with women other than his wife. But she provided some convincing details. She also described her friend, and told Fiedler the woman would be flying to Washington that evening for an assignation with the candidate. Fiedler and other *Herald* staff members got on the same plane. Two days later, the *Herald* printed a front-page story that began: "Gary Hart, the Democratic presidential candidate who has dismissed allegations of womanizing, spent Friday night and most of Saturday in his Capitol Hill townhouse with a young woman who flew from Miami and met him. Hart denied any impropriety."

The question of what went on behind closed doors stopped being a metaphor and became the only story in the Hart campaign. Suddenly, the cream of the national press corps was asking a major presidential candidate about his sex life, and interviewing his reputed girlfriend with questions that might have been asked in 1956 by a priest preparing to forgive sins against chastity. ("Did Gary Hart ever touch you? Did he talk about his wife? Do you think he was attracted to you? What were the sleeping arrangements last weekend in Washington?") The media was taking an interest in the private lives of politicians at a level that had not been seen since the turn of the century. And it was doing it with the professionalism, investigative tools, and moral cachet of modern journalism.

The young woman the *Herald* trailed would turn out to be Donna Rice, a former model turned baby formula saleswoman. Before her visit to Washington, reporters discovered, Rice and Hart had taken an overnight trip to Bimini with another couple on a yacht named *Monkey Business*. Although Hart denied anything sexual had happened on the cruise, the name of the boat alone would have been enough to seal his fate. So were the résumés of his companions. Rice's friend Lynn Armandt was the owner of the Too Hot Bikini Shop, and William Broadhurst was a lobbyist-lawyer from Louisiana with a less-than-elevating reputation as a party maker. ("Billy was more careful when he was pimping for me," sniped Edward Edwards, the former Louisiana governor.) During the excursion, Hart played the maracas while the women sang "Twist and Shout," and he allowed himself to be photographed wearing a "Monkey Business" T-shirt with Rice on his knee. ("She dropped into my lap," Hart later told Ted Koppel on *Nightline,* much in the same way teenage delinquents tell police "the gun went off.")

Monkey Business became the most infamous pleasure boat since the *Titanic.* While David Letterman unveiled his "Top Ten Gary Hart Pickup Lines" on late-night TV, Hart himself insisted he had done nothing wrong, attested to the "high standard" he had always maintained in his private life, blamed sloppy journalism and a political establishment that feared his "crusade to move the nation forward." His adamant denials merely forced the reporters to keep pressing. Asked if he had ever committed adultery, the floundering Hart said: "You can get into some very fine distinctions." Paul Taylor of *The Washington Post*, who asked the question, remembered seeing in his eyes a "wild look of hurt, bewilderment and god-awful betrayal."

"Put a tail on me, go ahead"

When you gossip about your neighbors' overactive sex lives, you don't generally expect to see them run out of town as a result. The reporters who covered Hart's campaign had not dropped hints about "womanizing rumors" with the idea that he would be immediately forced from the race in disgrace. The media looked upon the ruined candidacy like an overeager gardener who has been pruning so enthusiastically that he suddenly realizes he's lopped off the entire bush.

Time compared Hart to the *Scarlet Letter* heroine Hester Prynne, and called the episode "the most harrowing public ordeal ever endured by a modern presidential contender." In *The New Republic* Hendrik Hertzberg wrote angrily that Hart was the first "presidential candidate, president, prime minister, Cabinet member, congressional committee chairman, party leader or television evangelist, American or foreign" ever to be destroyed simply for "screwing." Hertzberg had to stretch a bit to explain the "additional factors" that had made other lethal sex stories different. ("In the Jeremy Thorpe scandal, an innocent dog was cold-bloodedly murdered.") But he became one of the most influential spokesmen for the school of journalism that found the entire Hart episode appalling.

Nicholas Von Hoffman raged in *The Nation* that Hart was playing the Grover Cleveland part in the old fight over the importance of private versus public character. "But there was no *Washington Post* to come to Cleveland . . . and say that it would publish the name of another of his mistresses unless he got out of the race," Von Hoffman fumed. Cleveland, of course, *had* no other mistress, a fact that did not keep some newspapers from insisting that he had harlots stashed all over Buffalo and Albany. Gary Hart's experience wasn't unique. Representative Taulbee had been trailed, spied on, ruined, and then assassinated by a reporter because of a lunchtime affair in a patent office. President Grant's friend Senator Carpenter had been destroyed for an offense not unlike Hart's—and had the additional complaint of knowing that he was being wrongly accused. Only a few years before, Congressman Riegle had been exposed as an adulterer on the basis of an affair that had been over for seven years.

Still, the Hart case was different. Those old instances in which political gossip got into print were random events. Subtract a couple of characters—a vengeful reporter, a crusading minister, a girlfriend with a tape recorder—and most of them would never have occurred. But if there had been no *Miami Herald* or Paul Taylor, or even Donna Rice, Hart's active extramarital sex life would still eventually have been reported on. The system for electing public officials, particularly presidents, had changed. Before the 1970s, there had been an assumption (sometimes misplaced) that the parties would weed out anyone they knew was morally, psychologically, or physically not up to the job. But by 1988 the candidates were being created by media consultants, professional fund-raisers, and organizers-for-hire. The field was narrowed in open primaries uncontrolled by the parties. The party leaders and grass-roots party workers could throw their support here or there, but they had no veto. The power all lay with voters who did not have access to any of the gossip about the candidates' private lives or character.

Gary Hart's insistence that the campaign stick to the higher ground and write only about "issues" made the reporters feel guilty. But it was out of date. The 1970s had shown how hard it was to separate private and public behavior. The Wilbur Mills who hung around stripper joints was also the Wilbur Mills who discussed tax policy with the president while having alcoholic hallucinations about buzzard attacks. The revelations about John Kennedy had caused many people to question whether the same recklessness that produced such promiscuous behavior might also have produced the Bay of Pigs invasion. If any of these concerns were the least bit valid, what sort of trouble could the country expect from a candidate who would cruise to a "Hot Bod" contest in Fort Lauderdale with a Louisiana lobbyist at the same time he was urging reporters to follow him around and see how mundane his personal life really was? ("If anybody wants to put a tail on me, go ahead. They'd be very bored," Hart told *The New York Times Magazine*.)

The American public was about to return to the debate about private vs. public character that it had been revisiting since the age of Alexander Hamilton. This time, the argument would have a slightly different cast. When the public worried about Grover Cleveland's sex life, the main concern was that a sinful man in the Oval Office might infect the nation's morality. The worries about Hart seemed more pragmatic, fears that a man whose womanizing seemed to court disaster would bring the same bad judgment into his decision making as president.

As usual, the debate ended inconclusively. The voters would have to decide for themselves how important marital fidelity was for a candidate, just as they would have to decide how much weight to place on his position on abortion or gun control. But there was still the question of how much information it was appropriate for the media to share. Did the public's right to know extend to vetting the sex life of every single candidate?

The Hart case was a textbook example of the quandary journalists were in, and how difficult it was to find a comfortable stance that was fair to both the candidate and the public. The gossip about Gary Hart and women had begun almost as soon as he appeared on the national political scene as George McGovern's campaign organizer in 1971. At the end of the 1972 campaign, some of the reporters said they were stunned to learn Hart was married, since he had always behaved like a very available bachelor. "There were a lot of movie stars and starlets hanging around the McGovern campaign," remembered *The Boston Globe*'s Curtis Wilkie, who worked then for the *Wilmington News Journal*. "Warren Beatty was around. I bet that's where the gossip started, whether fairly or not. There was a lot of screwing around in that campaign for *everybody*, from the press corps to the steward-esses."

When Hart ran for president in 1984, reporters knew that he had officially separated from his wife, Lee, while he was in the Senate, and that he palled around with high-libido Washingtonians like Senator Chris Dodd of Connecticut. Anonymous sources offered the reporters information on unnamed girlfriends. There was nothing anybody could put on the record, but the gossip was strong enough to require that almost every profile of the candidate include a reference to the rumors. "We had a little debate in the Style section about whether you said 'ladies' man' or 'womanizer,' recalled Elizabeth Bumiller, who profiled both Hart and his wife for *The Washington Post*.

The rumors escalated in 1987 because they were being fed by the candidate's own staff. A lot of the top people in the campaign were relative strangers, who barely knew the candidate they'd been hired to promote. Many had asked about the womanizing rumors before they came on board and been assured that the gossip was wildly over-blown. They were quickly disillusioned. One of the new hires at-tempted to recruit an old contact in Iowa to help with Hart's primary effort there, and got a quick refusal. "Everybody here knows that he's fooling around with a woman in Florida and that he came out of a bar a few nights ago with some other guy and two college women," she said before hanging up. When the staff members needed Hart to spend time on the phone raising money to retire his 1984 debts, he wandered off for weekends with Broadhurst. Anxious and angry, they shared their woes with the reporters who were covering Hart. "It was *the* topic," recalled Tom Oliphant of *The Boston Globe*. "It was noth-ing unusual to find yourself in a long conversation late at night with a staff member or campaign worker who thought they'd been be-trayed." The irony, Oliphant thought, was that John McEvoy, the brain-truster who became a pariah to the campaign when he got himself quoted in *Newsweek*, was one of the relatively few people around the Hart headquarters who were personally close to the can-didate.

In days of yore, people like that angry Democrat from Iowa who had heard about Hart's barhopping would have gone to the convention and chosen the candidate. They might have ignored the gossip and nominated Hart anyway. But they would have known the stories the reporters knew from their long barroom conversations with his staff. Shouldn't the voters who were now doing the selecting have the same option? The reporters tried to hint, with all those references to "rumors of womanizing." But they were criticized for writing about things they couldn't prove. Then *The Miami Herald* tried to prove it and was depicted as sending reporters to skulk in the bushes and spy through keyholes.

2. The Gossip Standard of Probable Cause

"We can't get around printing gossip"

Gary Hart's political career may have been killed by stories about his private life, but not at the American public's hand. Hart dropped out of the presidential race in May of 1987, long before the primaries began, driven by the wrath of the media, his own staff and other political insiders, as well as his own fears about what further allegations might follow if he stayed in to fight. He attempted to resurrect his candidacy in early 1988, and the first polls taken among New Hampshire's potential primary voters showed him the favorite candidate. But Hart was running a shell of a campaign, without staff or money or even any real core of supporters. The voters perceived that fairly quickly, and he fell off the radar screen. It was a pattern much like the one those misbehaving congressmen of the 1970s experienced, when they were punished not by the voters but by their peers in Washington—or in this case, the political insiders who withheld their backing and their money. It also suggested a coda to the rule that the public does not vote on private behavior. If the official loses his public effectiveness as a consequence of his sins, his constituents will desert him, too.

Hart always comforted himself with the idea that he had been picked upon because his new ideas were a threat to the political establishment. In 1984, just before losing the Democratic nomination to Walter Mondale, he had complained to *The Washington Post* that only *his* personal life had been a constant focus of attention. "You can't find one article that did that to Walter Mondale," he said bitterly. The real difference, of course, was that Mondale had never been gossiped about as a habitual adulterer.

It was what Hendrik Hertzberg of *The New Republic* unenthusiastically called "The Gossip Standard of Probable Cause." Gossip had become institutionalized. It was no longer just word-of-mouth detraction or a source of information for inside-the-loop Washingtonians. It was a shifting, amorphous standard that, once met, allowed reporters to go off investigating the private life of political candidates. "No one would have noticed or cared (about Donna Rice) if the rumors about Hart's womanizing were not so persistent," said *People*.

After Hart left the race, the first question was whether the new standard would be applied to the rest of the presidential field. The national press corps had lost whatever small appetite it ever had for questions about the candidates' marital fidelity. But those reporters were far from the only journalists watching the contest. Once Hart was out of the race, many Democratic officeholders on the local level looked at what was left of the field and concluded there was nothing out there that looked more impressive than they did. One of those new hopefuls was Richard Celeste, the forty-nine-year-old former Peace Corps director who was serving his second term as governor of Ohio. No sooner had Celeste admitted at a Columbus press conference that he was sniffing the air than a reporter raised his hand and asked if he had what had already come to be known as "Gary Hart–type problems." Celeste said no. The next day, the Cleveland *Plain Dealer* produced a front-page story headlined CELESTE WOMANIZING WORRIES AIDES. The paper claimed the governor's answer to the "Gary Hart–type problems" query called into question his "truthfulness and integrity." Citing unnamed sources, it said that Celeste, the father of six, had been "romantically linked to at least three women other than his wife in the past decade."

The presumption that Celeste had not always been faithful to his wife of twenty-five years had long been part of the accepted wisdom in Ohio political circles. His opponent in the last election had occasionally made not terribly subtle references to the talk. ("Nobody is going to have to stand on a street corner and defend *my* morals.") But the gossip had never been directly reported. The *Plain Dealer*, which had endorsed Celeste when he ran for governor without raising any reservations about his private life, claimed presidential candidates were subject to a different standard. "Those who seek the highest office ought to be role models for the rest of society," publisher Tom Vail told a meeting of newspaper executives. As a result, he said, newspapers that cover presidential politics "can't get around printing gossip." Vail also told his fellow publishers that the three Celeste girlfriends were just the minimum, and there might have been as many as eight.

Celeste dropped out of the race before he was ever really in it, but there were other Democratic canidates in 1988 who had been long rumored to have "Gary Hart–type problems." One was the Reverend Jesse Jackson. Godfrey Sperling, Jr., of *The Christian Science Monitor*, whose on-the-record breakfasts for politicians and the press were a Washington tradition, complained that when Jackson was his guest, "the press pounced on him like a wolf pack," asking one variation after another of the adultery question. Several newspapers investigated Jackson's private life during the primary campaign, but none published much more than general references to rumors about womanizing.

That may have been because Jackson never specifically denied the rumors, as Hart had. His wife, Jackie, had also made it clear whom she would blame if a scandal erupted. "If my husband has committed adultery he better not tell me, and you better not go digging into it. . . . I won't let you be the one to destroy my family," she warned a *Life* interviewer. Some of the other candidates felt the media was going easy on Jackson because he was black, but the biggest reason was probably the near-universal conviction that Jackson had no real chance of becoming the Democratic nominee. Massachusetts governor Michael Dukakis, who did win the nomination, was not a likely target for womanizing gossip. But he was subject of a rumor that he had been treated for psychiatric problems. The story began in a classic way, with pamphlets distributed at the party's nominating convention by an off-the-wall political extremist. In Dukakis's case, literature claiming he had suffered from depression was passed around by followers of Lyndon LaRouche, Jr., whose political theories included a conviction that the queen of England was part of a worldwide drug-selling conspiracy. Officials from the Bush campaign helped keep the talk going by suggesting that reporters investigate the matter. The conservative *Washington Times* chimed in with a story reporting the fact that there were rumors, and a representative of a LaRouche publication showed up at a White House press conference to ask whether Dukakis shouldn't make his medical records public. "Look, I'm not going to pick on an invalid," said President Ronald Reagan, in what he later told reporters was a joke.

"A persistent rumor, for which no evidence has ever surfaced . . ."

Reporting the *fact that there are rumors* became a standard practice in the 1980s. Gossip that had circulated for years without ever being proven or printed became significant, simply because it was being repeated. There had, for instance, been rumors for years that former congressman Jack Kemp was gay. They started in the 1960s, when Kemp was a quarterback for the Buffalo Bills with an off-season job working for then–California governor Ronald Reagan. Early in Reagan's first term, two of the governor's aides were fired because of suspicion they were homosexual. When Drew Pearson—still naming names, still homophobic—printed a column about what he called a "homosexual ring" in Reagan's administration, he claimed "an athlete" was also involved. Kemp turned out to have owned a cabin on Lake Tahoe with one of the dismissed aides.

When asked about the rumors, Kemp always said that he had purchased his share of the cabin as an investment and had never visited it. Arthur Van Court, the investigator Reagan's staff hired to uncover gays in the administration, said later that Kemp had not been a suspect. But the gossip was incredibly durable. Most of the printed references to it were veiled: "The persistent rumor that one of the potential 1988 presidential candidates has a homosexual past is testing the unacknowledged code of silence among reporters," said a 1985 item in *Esquire*'s Washington column. But a few months later, *Newsweek* took notice of Kemp's interest in the nomination and mentioned "a persistent rumor, for which no evidence has ever surfaced, that Kemp is or was a homosexual." Then in 1986, during an at-home interview on NBC's *Today* show that his aides had presumed would be upbeat and folksy, interviewer Nancy Collins brought up the stories, and asked Kemp to "categorically" deny he had ever been involved in a homosexual encounter. Kemp complied, but later made it clear he regarded being quizzed on television about his sexuality—in an interview conducted in his home, with his wife and children present—as going too far. His spokesman accused the network of "irresponsible journalism" and claimed Kemp would be far more combative if anyone ever raised the issue again.

Post-Hart, the rumor seemed to show up in Kemp profiles almost as a matter of course. Running for the Republican presidential nomination, Kemp traveled to California for a fund-raising tour, and was greeted by a *Los Angeles Times* story saying that Kemp hoped to exploit his connections to the state, which included a stint as quarterback for the San Diego Chargers. "But Kemp, who also served as an aide to then-Gov. Ronald Reagan in 1967, would prefer one old rumor about his past remain forgotten by the voters," added the *Times*, which then proceeded to remind them.

Meanwhile, a new strain of womanizing gossip cropped up around Kemp, making him perhaps the first politician since Adlai Stevenson to be widely gossiped about as a philanderer with both sexes. When Bob Dole chose Kemp as his vice-presidential nominee, the expected announcement was held up for hours while Dole's staff tried to vet one last late-breaking rumor about another woman. By the time the Dole campaign had been satisfied that there was no incipient Gennifer Flowers incident in the making, the reporters waiting to hear the big news had long since missed their deadlines. Consultant Ed Rollins joked that he didn't know whether "to line up fifteen airline stewardesses to deny one side or fifteen football players to deny the other side."

"The kind of pieces we used to do are impossible now"

The conservative columnists Rowland Evans and Robert Novak claimed one of the reasons Kemp was blindsided by the *Today* interview was because it was conducted by Nancy Collins, a freelancer who specialized in reporting show-business gossip. "Considering Collins' background . . . his aides had prepared him for a soft interview," they wrote. That was a strange turnabout, given the fact that commentators usually complained that writing about politicians' private vices meant treating them like movie stars. During the Hart furor, *Time* magazine had worried that "Americans now demand the same intimate knowledge about their leaders that was once reserved for the romantic entanglements of Clark Gable or Elizabeth Taylor."

At the time, entertainment celebrities were actually starting to get more control over what "intimate knowledge" the public got about them. Movie stars had been left somewhat adrift when the studio system collapsed, at the mercy of keen-eyed magazine profilers and confused by changes in public morality that made it unclear exactly what private activities they should be trying to keep out of print. But in the eighties mega–public relations firms replaced the studios as the protectors of celebrities' reputations. They quickly brought the lid down on the sort of arty, edgy reporting that marked profile writing in the seventies. "The kind of pieces we used to do are impossible now," said Rex Reed.

The publicists, like the old studios, could keep writers from getting access to their clients, and make it hard for magazine editors to get suitable photographs. "There are just so many celebrities whose picture on the cover can sell an issue," explained an editor at one of the nation's largest magazines, who spoke on the condition of anonymity. "Things started to change in the late eighties. The celebrities started wanting to know who would be doing the interview and what the questions would be. Their publicists wanted to be present, and they reacted very strongly to what they called 'negativity.' Compared to movie stars, politicians were like babes in the woods." While only a handful of the very top celebrities had the draw to make any magazine willing to meet their demands, the publicists they employed also had dozens of lesser clients they wanted to protect. "If you're mean to X, you'll never get Y," said Ed Kosner, former *Esquire* editor.

As the eighties ended, the entertainers returned to a status somewhat like the one they had enjoyed in the fifties. They were vulnerable to the exposés of the sensational tabloid press and the irritations of the paparazzi, but the mainstream media generally refrained from speculating about their secrets. Gay movie stars were able, in some cases, to negotiate with sympathetic writers on how the subject could be handled indirectly. In 1997, when *Esquire* broke the unspoken rules and ran a coy cover story on actor Kevin Spacey that suggested he was homosexual, an executive at the William Morris talent agency issued a press statement announcing he was advising all the William Morris agents to "dissuade their clients from doing interviews with *Esquire*.") The far more dangerous issue of drug use, which suggested unreliability on the stage or set, was generally avoided. "This may sound naive, but unless the stars are real asses, people want to like them and protect them a little bit," said Lisa Hintleman, a former publicist turned *Esquire* editor.

The politicians, meanwhile, were left with the downside of celebrity and none of the advantages. Like the movie stars, they had lost the big institutional umbrella that used to promote and protect them, and they had turned to publicists and consultants for help. But they lacked the critical armor of popularity that would allow their handlers to bargain for the best possible treatment. Stories about politicians did not sell magazine covers, or improve ratings. No reporter would have negotiated over what questions he or she could not ask a politician. It was unethical, and perhaps more important, it was unnecessary. The politicians simply had to live by the rules the media dictated. The stars didn't, and for that reason, Michael Jackson, accused of molesting children, got a more gentle treatment from TV interviews than Gary Hart got when he was accused of sleeping with an adult who was not his wife.

3. Gossip in the Eighties—Three Stories

"My name is Ronald Reagan. What's yours?"

Ronald Reagan was the ultimate mixture of celebrity and politics, the man who regularly pulled out anecdotes from old movies and cited them as proof of a point, apparently believing they had really happened. (His account of entering a concentration camp with the Signal Corps during World War II brought tears to the eyes of Israeli prime minister Yitzhak Shamir, who did not realize Reagan had spent the war in Hollywood. Reagan, who had seen the Signal Corps films of the camp liberations, came to believe that he was in them.) He was also almost gossip-proof, like the war heroes he had occasionally played on the screen. Although Reagan as a politician leaned heavily on memories of the old days, old mores, and family values, he was also the first president who had been divorced, and a man whose own performance as a father was far from inspiring. Reagan's daughter from his first marriage, Maureen, said that when she was nineteen she discovered that seven-year-old Patti Reagan had never been told Maureen was her half sister. "Well, we just haven't gotten that far yet," her father said. During his campaign for governor, he refused to intervene when his political consultants tried to conceal the existence of his first marriage, along with Maureen and her brother, Michael.

But as a seventy-year-old newly elected president, Reagan had left his parenting days long behind. There has been no serious gossip about sex in the Reagan White House, although reporters and staff did note that Mrs. Reagan seemed to have a girlish crush on Frank Sinatra. (Tell-all biographer Kitty Kelley claimed it was an affair.) The president's lifestyle did not leave much to whisper over. He was devoted to his wife, disciplined, abstemious, and possessed of almost invariable cheer and good manners both in public and private. Whatever flaws the voters picked up—the Reagans' attachment to a rich, superficial social set, a reliance on a pricey lifestyle the president took for granted, even the problems of his adult children—were all deposited on his wife.

What the people inside the Washington gossip loop did talk about was Reagan's extraordinarily disengaged character, his lack of any real ties to the people in his administration. The fact that he had greeted his Housing Secretary, Samuel Pierce, as "Mr. Mayor" at a gathering of urban leaders was well reported at the time. ("How are things in your city?" he asked solicitously.) But it was whispered that Reagan read from staff-prepared cue cards even when he made routine courtesy calls to people who thought of themselves as his friends. He did not even seem attached to his dog. Once, at the Reagans' Santa Barbara ranch, Steve Weisman of *The New York Times* pointed to the family's handsome collie and asked the president what he was called. Reagan paused. "Lassie," he said finally. Later, an aide explained that "Lassie" was not, in fact, the dog's name. It was just the only name for a collie the president could think of at the moment.

Future biographers may investigate whether the president's notoriously bad memory was an early sign of the Alzheimer's disease that was diagnosed after he left office. But his inability to remember names and faces was a lifelong characteristic. (In his autobiography, Reagan's son Michael said that when his father came to see him graduate from boarding school, Reagan stuck his hand out as the boy approached and said, "My name is Ronald Reagan. What's yours?") And Reagan's lack of connection to the individuals around him went beyond a bad memory. "He rarely inquired about those who went out of his life, even his grown children," wrote his biographer, Lou Cannon.

It was one of the most unusual lines of gossip about presidential personality. Ronald Reagan was just as sunny and charming in private as when the public saw him on TV. But he was also totally remote. He not only forgot his staff's names, he seemed uninterested in what their contributions were. That detached interior disillusioned many of his closest associates, who began to feel the president would not even notice if they disappeared from the White House forever. During his second term in particular, there was also incessant squabbling and bloodletting among top aides whom Reagan never bothered to oversee. As a result, he became the first president to be the subject of a raft of tell-all books before he even left the White House.

The tradition of waiting until a president is dead to tell behind-the-scenes tales was long gone. But never, until the Reagan era, had a president's top officials raced to get their memoirs in print while he was still in power. Ten books, by everyone from Chief of Staff Donald Regan to Secretary of State Alexander Haig, came out while Reagan was president. Most of them portrayed Reagan as a nice man who didn't pay attention to what was going on around him. In their detail, their attempts to show what life was really like behind the scenes at the White House, and their occasional rancor, some of them were like the old *Esquire* profiles, only without the stylish writing. It was through Reagan's top appointees' memoirs that the public learned the president's travel schedule was planned with the consultation of Nancy Reagan's astrologer, that the Reagans were often in their pajamas by 6 P.M., that the president preferred reading the comics to the newspaper front page and had difficulty in handling conversations in which people made "unscripted responses."

"Twenty-five hundred of his closest friends"

In 1987, while the Democrats' crop of presidential candidates was being sneered at as dwarfs, San Antonio mayor Henry Cisneros was golden. (A "blue chip" politician, cheered the *Los Angeles Times*, "a man of staggering promise.") He was smart, handsome (*Texas Magazine* once said he resembled an Aztec lord), a business-friendly progressive famed for his talents in coalition-building. In his third term as mayor, Cisneros was being talked about as Texas's next governor or senator, a potential vice president soon or a chief executive later.

Early that year, while his wife, Mary Alice, was confined to bed with a difficult pregnancy, Cisneros had begun an affair with Linda Medlar, a local jeweler's wife who had been working for him as a fund-raiser and consultant. Despite the fact that San Antonio was the nation's ninth-largest city, people did not need a newspaper report to find out about the romance. The gossip lines were extremely efficient. Linda Matys O'Connell, the editor of the local alternative weekly, was asked about the affair by the woman who stood next to her in church choir. Another reporter was quizzed by the checkout clerk at a grocery store.

Part of Cisneros's political success had been built on his identity as a family man. The mayor took TV crews on tours of his home to show off a remodeling job or the Christmas decorations. The city knew about the problems of Mary Alice's pregnancy, how much Cisneros had wanted a son (he and his wife had two daughters), and the details of young John Paul Cisneros's medical problems. "My life has been just about one hundred percent open," Cisneros said. It was part of his bond with the voters, and it almost guaranteed that the city would also be in on his adulterous relationship.

Cisneros himself confided in what local wags called "twenty-five hundred of his closest friends," including fellow politicians, newspaper columnists, and even editorial boards. He told them that his marriage had long been troubled, that Mary Alice's conversion to a fundamentalist religion had pulled it farther apart. He said he was in love with Linda Medlar, but he wanted to protect his children—especially John Paul, who was facing dangerous heart surgery. He was going to withdraw from politics so he could work things out, away from the hot light of his local fame. The affair did stay out of the newspapers for a remarkably long time, given the fact that San Antonio's two daily papers were involved in a bitter circulation war. Citing John Paul's illness, Cisneros surprised the state by announcing he would not run for senator or governor, then announced that he would not be a candidate for another term as mayor.

The dual effects of Cisneros's announcements and the whispers from the twenty-five hundred or so confidants were creating an absolute crescendo of gossip, and the local papers were printing more and more explicit hints. Finally, in October of 1988, Paul Thompson, the columnist for the San Antonio *News-Express*, unloaded all the off-the-record information he and other insiders had been receiving for months. "Mayor Henry Cisneros confesses that he is deeply in love with Linda Medlar, a 39-year-old political fundraiser here, and may marry her after serving out his term and entering private life next June," the front-page column began. Thompson said later that although Cisneros had not given him permission to use the confidences, "this thing was breaking all around me and we didn't want to be shut out."

Cisneros, who had declared 1987 San Antonio's Year of the Family, was called upon to choose between his wife and his mistress in an atmosphere that resembled the Elvis stamp selection. His mother referred to Medlar as "the other woman" and made it clear to interviewers she favored family unity. Mary Alice took the children to a public prayer meeting where the minister asked God to inspire the mayor to do the right thing. Cisneros's uncle compared the marriage to the space shuttle: "He had a bad booster ring that didn't work well. Now we're back in the space program again." The rest of the city called or wrote. Medlar's sixteen-year marriage broke up, and she moved back to her hometown of Lubbock, where the former mayor continued to visit her. It was not until 1991, when Mary Alice filed for divorce, that Cisneros finally chose. He dropped his mistress and reconciled with his wife. "I was planning my life with him. I didn't understand I was expendable," Medlar said later. She might have been better prepared if America had spent more time gossiping about the Kay Summersby affair.

In 1992, Cisneros joined Bill Clinton's Cabinet as secretary of housing and urban development. Medlar filed suit demanding $256,000 and sold a tabloid TV program transcripts of her telephone conversations with Cisneros. The tapes made it apparent that Cisneros had already given her much more money than he told the FBI when he was being investigated for the Cabinet post. Attorney General Janet Reno concluded the HUD secretary had lied during the background check and recommended an independent counsel look into the issue. Cisneros toughed it out through Clinton's first term, settling Medlar's suit out of court and compiling a strong record administering the federal government's most troubled agency. He resigned after the 1996 election, saying he couldn't afford to remain in public service with two daughters in college, a son with medical problems, and legal costs for the independent counsel's investigation—which was still dragging on well after he left office. Linda Medlar, meanwhile, had been more than punished for her attempt to make money and get revenge for her broken love affair. The special prosecutor, angry that Medlar had given investigators edited copies of her tapes, hit her with a 28-count indictment for bank fraud, based on the fact that Medlar had her sister and brother-in-law put their names on her mortgage. She wound up serving a three-and-a-half year jail sentence.

"It was almost inconceivable, so it was not conceived of"

Representative Stewart McKinney, a Connecticut Republican, died in 1987. He was fifty-six years old, and he was the first member of Congress known to have contracted AIDS. "It wasn't even really in the rumor mill," said Barney Frank, the openly gay congressman from Massachusetts. "I knew people who said it, but I had never discussed it with him."

McKinney was a married man with six children. Even in the 1980s, that inoculated him from gossip almost as completely as if he had lived in pre–Civil War America. "It was almost inconceivable, so it was not conceived of," said one of his aides, Jay Malcynsky. "Nobody ever asked me if he was gay." Malcynsky suspected his boss was having homosexual relationships, but he never discussed it with McKinney. "He'd make allusions to things that were clearly intended to let me know where he was coming from. But I don't think he was capable of having a direct conversation with me—or a lot of people. I think, because of the way gay people were regarded then, that he was afraid he'd let people down." When McKinney developed AIDS-related symptoms the same pattern continued. "He never told me, but he did things and said things in ways that let me know what was going on," said Malcynsky. Back in his district, people knew that the congressman was ill, and speculated about a recurrence of his old heart problems. But no one mentioned AIDS until the last few months of his life, when McKinney developed skin lesions his office claimed were psoriasis.

McKinney, who represented the Connecticut Gold Coast of suburbs near New York City, was working on issues that had little appeal to most Republicans, like homelessness, the problems of the cities, the fate of the illegitimate offspring of American servicemen in Vietnam. In March of 1987, when he was already ill, he joined other protesters and congressmen spending part of a cold night on a Capitol

Hill heating grate to call attention to the plight of the homeless. "After that he never really got back his health," said his press secretary later. When McKinney died, his personal physician, Cesar Caceres, confirmed that he had died of AIDS and said the congressman had wanted that fact made public. But the doctor claimed his patient had contracted the disease from transfusions he received during a 1979 heart bypass operation. Under questioning it became clear that Caceres had simply ruled out homosexuality and worked backward to the next most likely cause. *The Washington Post* reported in its story on McKinney's death that "knowledgeable sources on Capitol Hill and in the gay community said McKinney had had homosexual relations."

No one in McKinney's family ever commented on his sexuality. The congressman's widow, Lucie, issued a statement calling for his friends to "help in finding a cure for this disease, however we look at how people get it." She helped establish a foundation in his honor, which assists homeless AIDS patients. At the time of McKinney's death, Connecticut senator Christopher Dodd angrily claimed that because of the *Post,* McKinney would be remembered for his sexuality. Dodd turned out to be wrong. "I've been in office ten years now and except in the rarest of occasions, I only hear comments about his service," said Representative Christopher Shays, who succeeded him.

4. Drinking Gossip Mutates Again

"Talked about wine as if it was Diet Rite soda pop!"

When the 1988 campaign finally ended and George Bush was president, the confusion over what gossip meant, and where politicians' privacy ended, claimed its first Cabinet nominee, former senator John Tower of Texas. Tower, sixty-five, was Bush's choice for secretary of defense. He was a man who had been talked about—as a drinker, philanderer, and a pincher of women's behinds, no matter how prominent the posterior. In retrospect, it's clear that some of the talk was

227

false, some was true, and much was the product of the nation's perpetually shifting attitudes toward alcohol.

Tower, who died in a plane crash in 1991, was a product of the postwar drinking mores, in which teetotalers were regarded as rather suspect, businessmen made a stereotype of the two-martini lunch, and suburban couples sometimes stretched their before-dinner cocktail hours all the way through the evening. But by the time Tower's nomination came up for a Senate vote in 1989, the nation had switched attitudes again. At high-powered business lunches, people drank designer water, and consumption of martinis would have been regarded as adequate grounds for canceling the contract. A glass of wine at dinner every night counted as rather heavy drinking in much of the younger professional class. *Two* glasses every night was seen in some circles as a sign that it was time to seek help.

Tower was a social drinker of long standing who, by most accounts, had drunk more than was good for him at some points during the 1970s. The nominee, whose character was not of a confessional nature, admitted that his second wife had demanded he "choose between her and Johnnie Walker Black," and that "as a concession to good sense" he had given up scotch and whiskey. He also admitted having cheated on his first wife, Lou, with the woman who became the second Mrs. John Tower. But beyond that, Tower insisted, all the allegations about womanizing and drunkenness were false.

There were all sorts of reasons why different members of the Senate did not want to confirm Tower as secretary of defense. Some right-wing Republicans regarded him as "soft" on the Star Wars defense program. Reformers objected to the fact that after leaving the Senate, he had been a consultant to defense companies. Democrats secretly liked the idea of torpedoing one of George Bush's first important nominations. And although Tower served twenty-four years in the Senate, he had not left behind many credits in the friendship bank. "He didn't suffer fools gladly," admitted an aide, using the congressional euphemism for extreme unpopularity.

Throughout the long and grisly process that became the Tower nomination hearings, no one offered any first-person accounts of excessive drinking outside the period more than a decade earlier that

Tower had defined himself. But the gossip took on its own life. "The old saying that 'Where there is smoke there is fire' must give one pause in this case. The smoke surrounding the nominee's personal life seems rather intense," said Paul Weyrich, the chairman of the conservative Coalition for America. He was the first person to appear before Tower's confirmation hearings claiming to have "personal knowledge" of what Armed Services chairman Sam Nunn called "defects in personal behavior." Weyrich claimed that "over the course of many years" he had encountered Tower "in a condition—lack of sobriety—as well as with women to whom he was not married." That fact was especially notable, Weyrich added virtuously, because "I do not frequent the social activities of Washington. In fact, I avoid them because I find [they are not] good for family life." The hearing then went into a closed session to hear Weyrich's specifics. In his autobiography, Tower said that he was told Weyrich said he saw him "coming on" to a woman, but when pressed could only say he was holding her hand. If the testimony was any more interesting than that, it never leaked into the press during what proved to be an extremely leaky confirmation process.

Among the people spreading stories about Tower's drinking was his second ex-wife, Lilla. The Texan's friends had regarded his abandonment of Lou Tower for Lilla as a personal disaster. It was a conclusion that the nominee, who later dedicated his autobiography to Lou, came to agree with. Among Lilla Tower's confidantes were Sarah McClendon, the eccentric veteran reporter who wrote for her own small one-woman news service. "Why is it that the president will not take the word of a woman who was married to Tower for ten years and says he is an uncontrollable alcoholic?" demanded McClendon at a White House briefing. Representative Larry Combest, a former Tower aide, made things worse by trying to impress the committee with the scope of Tower's reformation. He assured Armed Services Committee chairman Nunn that the senator had come a long way since the days when he consumed up to a bottle of scotch a day. (Later, another former aide who was a recovering alcoholic came forward and took responsibility for most of the vanishing liquor.)

By the end, Tower was trudging from one TV interview to another, quantifying his liquor consumption just like Theodore Roosevelt had done at his libel trial. For years, Tower told the camera, he had drunk nothing but "wine, perhaps an occasional martini, occasionally a little vodka with smoked salmon or caviar or something like that." On another show, he added "champagne, maybe an occasional glass of sherry or port, and just occasionally a martini or a vodka." He concluded, rather proudly, that he sometimes went for "days without drinking anything, even wine." Tower was clearly a soul mate of the 1908 writer who praised the art of drinking "scientifically." But he was talking to a different era.

"The nominee has talked about wine as if it was Diet Rite soda pop!" cried former astronaut John Glenn on the Senate floor.

Tower was also beleaguered by a form of institutionalized gossip—his FBI investigation. The Bureau background reports on administration nominees are supposed to be kept secret, and for good reason. They're basically transcribed gossip. FBI agents begin with a list of acquaintances provided by the nominee and use them as a reference to branch out, interviewing people who know the potential Cabinet member, transcribing what they say. If someone tells an FBI agent that the nominee is a bottom-pincher, it gets written down. "They don't check anything," claims Morton Halperin, whose nomination to a top defense post by Bill Clinton was rejected by the Senate in what some Democrats claimed was revenge for the Tower defeat. "The FBI will tell you its business is simply gathering information. They talk to people. Whatever people say they write down—notoriously inaccurately. You could say this guy was divorced six times and three of his wives died mysteriously and they'd just put it in the pile of interviews. They wouldn't try to track it down. They're just collecting gossip, and collecting it badly." Tower at one point found himself being asked by a somber FBI agent whether he had ever taken off his clothes and danced on a piano.

The background report was leaked, bit by bit, from both sides of the aisle, and newspaper reporters were sent off chasing apparently nonexistent women whose breasts Tower was supposed to have drunkenly grabbed a dozen years earlier. The nomination was slipping away. Although the press kept noting that nobody would cite a specific incident in which Tower had been proved to have behaved improperly, the senators felt they *knew*. They were not going to go into details about a former colleague, but they were not going to make him secretary of defense, either. Senator Joseph Lieberman of Connecticut, who was a brand-new member and one of the critical undecided votes, remembers that the stories he heard privately about Tower's behavior mainly involved "college-fraternity–type stuff. But then again, this was a grown man who was being asked to be secretary of defense." In the end, Lieberman voted no. "I just thought there was too much of a history of personal instability, which had mostly to do with the drinking," he said.

In an increasingly pathetic series of defensive moves, Tower released a letter from his doctor saying that during a recent hospitalization to remove a colon polyp, he showed "no evidence of alcoholic withdrawal." He went on TV again, this time to announce that if confirmed he would promise to "not consume beverage alcohol of any type or form." (Reporter Sam Donaldson asked if he would take an oath not to date women, either.) Like Gary Hart, Tower couldn't or wouldn't give the responses necessary to shut the inquiries off. When Nunn first asked if he had an alcohol problem, Tower responded: "I have none, Senator. I am a man of some discipline." Given his history, it was regarded as something of an overstatement.

Tower, who came from a culture in which men never discussed their personal problems in public, was talking to a culture that presumed a tendency toward drinking too much could never be resolved by mere act of will. In the final Senate debate before the nomination went down, 53 to 47, Nunn did not argue that Tower had been overimbibing too much in recent years. He simply contended the nation could not be sure Tower wouldn't slide back into old habits. "The committee searched in vain for a point in time when the nominee himself acknowledged this problem and dealt with it decisively," he said. "The nominee made it very clear that he has never sought medical assistance for his drinking problem." The nation, Nunn argued successfully, could not trust a man who cut back without enrolling in a twelve-step program.

"The way to shut those people up was to deal by their rules," a disappointed Tower aide said much later. "Their rules were that you go to Betty Ford."

Chapter 10

Endless Exposure

1990–1999

1. The Election of 1992: An Affair to Remember

"Denying our love"

Reporters who went to Little Rock, Arkansas, in the early 1990s were delighted to find that the local culture was that of a very gossipy small town. "My daughter went to ballet class with Chelsea," said a well-to-do matron on Election Day, 1992. "Hillary is a good mother. And so attractive now that she's started washing her hair more."

"I see them in the supermarket and whatever he puts in the cart she puts right back on the shelf," said a man who had just voted at the polling place where Clinton himself had made an appearance a few hours before. In honor of the candidate's proximity, a black promoter known as the Sweet Potato Pie Man had parked his battered truck across the street. He was one of several Arkansans who had been vying for the role of Bill Clinton's Reverend Ball or Professor Chancellor. The Sweet Potato Pie Man's particular issue, proclaimed in paint all over the truck, was a claim that Clinton fathered an illegitimate child by a black woman.

"His pies are really *very* good," said the woman whose child went to ballet class with Chelsea, deflecting the conversation.

In Little Rock, Bill Clinton had long been talked about as a "womanizer"—a disgruntled state employee had even provided a list of alleged girlfriends in a civil suit. Everyone knew that the governor's brother had been jailed for drug dealing and that Clinton's mother was a colorful woman who had been married several times—twice to a man with a drinking problem. The talk in Little Rock about Bill and Hillary Clinton was much like the talk in Marion, Ohio, about Warren Harding—stories that had been spread for so long that the natives hardly bothered to repeat them anymore. But when a politician goes national, the old gossip takes on a new life. The nation pulls it out like another family's scrapbook and looks at it with fresh, outsider eyes.

Clinton had considered entering the 1988 Democratic primary after Gary Hart's candidacy collapsed. But his longtime aide Betsy Wright had forced him to sit down with her and analyze the chances of what she would later come to term "bimbo eruptions." It was reportedly a long and detailed assessment. Clinton was one of the few politicians—at that point in his career at least—with an adviser who was capable of forcing him to have such a discussion. As a result, Clinton sat out 1988, and waited for the next time around. But the womanizing rumors still preceded him, and they were numerous and specific enough to be regarded as ripe for investigation under the post-Hart rules of campaign conduct. As he geared up for 1992, Clinton and his advisers decided he should confront the issue head-on at the earliest opportunity. He chose an on-the-record breakfast with reporters hosted by Godfrey Sperling. It was the same forum at which, a few years before, Sperling had complained that his guests had gone after Jesse Jackson like a "wolf pack" on the adultery issue. But it was a new year, and there was little interest in bringing up "Gary Hart–type issues" with a candidate who was not really running for anything yet. When the question finally did come up, Clinton delivered what would become his patented response. Like all long-married couples, he and Hillary had a relationship that "has not been perfect." But it was good now, "and we intend to be together thirty or forty years from now whether I run for president or not."

The answer worked, more or less. By not denying the rumors, Clinton did not invite further investigations. By not attempting to frame himself as a perfect husband and head of an all-American family, as Henry Cisneros and any number of other come-to-grief candidates had done, he defused the inevitable irritation voters and reporters feel at a whiff of hypocrisy. Unlike Gary Hart, he did not leave his aides frustrated by a refusal to take the issue seriously.

However, the fact that Clinton had figured out how to answer the question did not stop the stories from spreading. In 1991, rumors about the Arkansas governor's sex life toured the country, reaching a new gossip loop whenever the presidential hopefuls—Clinton, Senator Tom Harkin, former governor Jerry Brown, Senator Bob Kerrey, former senator Paul Tsongas—began making forays into another state. "The womanizing stuff he's already dealt with," said Clinton's New York press person when the phalanx of Democratic contenders first marched into the city. "Everybody knows he's had affairs and nobody cares. Of course if the black baby the reporters keep asking about shows up, we go home tomorrow." No black babies showed up—except as a fictional character in the campaign novel *Primary Colors.* But Gennifer Flowers did. The spiritual sister of Elizabeth Ray held a press conference at the Waldorf hotel in New York on January 27, 1992—just before the New Hampshire primary—to publicize a story in the *Star,* a supermarket tabloid, about what she said was a twelve-year affair with Clinton. Flowers also played recordings of her conversations with the presidential candidate. The tapes, which Flowers would later try to market and which a right-wing conspiracy advocate would play on a 900 telephone number, made it clear that unlike Don Riegle, Bill Clinton was not the sort of man who would urge a woman to record their pillow talk so she could have something to play back on lonely nights. The closest he came to intimacy was calling Flowers "my friend." Her side of the conversation consisted mainly of a string of complaints about harassment by the media. The main lesson a listener could carry away from Clinton's responses was

235

the remarkable number of different ways it was possible to say "all you've gotta do is deny it."

The character of the aggrieved political mistress had changed from the days of Madeline Pollard or Maria Halpin, when women who admitted to an affair always claimed they expected the man to marry them. (Flowers' highest hopes seemed to be that Clinton might someday take her out in public.) But although a whole new generation of political mistresses had been mining the career opportunities of their situation, the reward for going public was not sensational—a few months of celebrity, a six-figure fee from a paper like the *Star,* a contract with No Excuses jeans and perhaps a year's worth of engagements at low-end nightclubs or dinner theaters. It was not a prospect to tempt a woman with a career or family and friends who would be embarrassed by the scandal. (Flowers's own post-Clintonian career included marrying a wealthy businessman, performing in *Boobs, the Musical*, and acquiring a piano bar in New Orleans where she could sing whenever the mood struck. Neither the marriage nor the bar survived into the post-Katrina era.)

When the Flowers story broke, among the people who didn't know whether it was true or not were the Clinton campaign team members. In his White House memoir, several years later—after the president had admitted to a single sexual encounter with Flowers—George Stephanopoulos would write that he still did not know whether Clinton and the former cabaret singer had ever been involved in a serious affair. When the *Star* exclusive ("They Made Love All Over Her Apartment") first came out, Stephanopoulos listened while Clinton pointed out errors and inconsistencies, but didn't press him to identify which parts were true. "I wanted to believe that it was all malicious fiction," he wrote. When their candidate wasn't around, Stephanopoulos and James Carville speculated about exactly what Clinton and Flowers might have shared—a one-night stand? Five minutes in the back seat of a car? Their conversations were apparently not all that much more informed than Democrats around the country who were reading quotes from the *Star* in their local papers and trying to decide if it made any difference.

Stephanopoulos was far from the first aide to a presidential candidate who did not pry when a sex scandal broke. Andrew Jackson's campaign handlers, after all, never asked him to explain how he had come to be living with Rachel when she was still married to someone else. When Grover Cleveland said "tell the truth," and stalked off to sulk in the governor's mansion, no one ran after him demanding to know what the truth was. In the modern era, campaign staff have tended to be more curious. But the candidate himself is often the last person they consult for information. In 1984, a Gary Hart aide, John Holum, wrote a memo to Hart's campaign manager proposing they forestall any nasty surprises by having someone on staff investigate their own candidate. ("This may sound indelicate," he admitted.)

It was hard to gauge what the voters' response to the Flowers story was, since her emergence coincided with revelations about Clinton's maneuvers to avoid being drafted for service in Vietnam that seemed to hit a much stronger chord. (It would be the prelude to many wrangles about candidates' war experience that erupted as the men who were draft age in the Vietnam era began running for president.) In retrospect, it appears that neither the affair nor the alleged draft-dodging had much effect on the election. Flowers' revelations certainly did not shock voters as much as the media expected, and the side issue of hypocrisy had been defused by the Clintons' careful preparations. The story was certainly embarrassing—Flowers claimed Clinton called her "Pookie" and that they once had sex in the bathroom of the governor's mansion. But over the long run, people who wanted to laugh at Clinton seemed to prefer focusing on stories about his weight problems and fondness for fast food. Perhaps in the 1990s, the public had more anxiety about overeating than illicit sex.

When she first appeared on the scene, however, Gennifer Flowers seemed as if she might be capable of derailing Clinton's campaign. Virtually every major newspaper and television news bureau sent reporters to her New York press conference. It was not exactly the kind of event most people go into political reporting to experience. Flowers, looking both tough and out of her depth, played her tapes and told the reporters she had gone public because she was angry at Clinton for "denying our love." Elaborating, she explained that "ninety percent of me wanted to believe he would stand by me, but ten percent of me said maybe my feelings wouldn't be as important to him as being president of the United States." (The *Star* article suggested that the most personal moment Clinton ever shared with Flowers was a trip to a drive-in hamburger stand. Flowers' revelations were convincing mainly because they made it so clear that Clinton's interest in her never went beyond casual sex.) During a question-and-answer period, an employee for radio disc jockey Howard Stern demanded to know whether Clinton used a condom.

"What are we doing here?" asked columnist Bob Herbert of no one in particular. It was pretty clear that the next self-proclaimed mistress was going to need a more profound excuse for telling her tale in order to lure the national media to another press conference. During the Democratic convention in New York that summer, another alleged Clinton girlfriend did show up. Sally Miller Perdue, a fifty-three-year-old former Miss Arkansas, said she had had a three- or four-month relationship with Clinton a decade earlier. Perdue gave the story a bit of a feminist twist, claiming the affair had ended because Clinton was threatened by the fact that she decided to run as a Republican for mayor of Pine Bluff, Arkansas. (She won 13 percent of the vote.) Perdue appeared on the Sally Jessy Raphaël syndicated TV talk show, where the hostile audience repeatedly demanded to know why she was exposing herself and the candidate. Perdue admitted she knew Clinton was married and that neither of them regarded their relationship as more than "an encounter." If there was such a thing as adultery without political implications, this seemed to be it. Perdue did not even claim that Clinton told her their affair was more interesting than a subcommittee hearing. (Unlike Congressman Riegle, Clinton actually found things like subcommittee hearings riveting.) Raphael never aired the program.

By the middle of the Democratic primary season, Clinton's personal life had become an obsession on right wing talk shows, but the vast majority of voters didn't seem to feel there was anything he was keeping secret that they wanted to hear more about. Clinton sensed his position was strong enough to appear on Phil Donahue's talk show and take a stand against any further vetting of the Flowers matter. When Donahue pressed him to confirm or deny he and Flowers had

had sex, Clinton easily turned the attack around. "We're gonna sit here a long time in silence, Phil. I'm not going to answer any more of these questions," he said. "I've answered them until I'm blue in the face. You are responsible for the cynicism in this country. You don't want to talk about real issues." The audience applauded.

The aspect of adultery the public was most sensitive to was the vision of the betrayed wife, left at home suffering. But despite whatever private pain she endured, Hillary Clinton came across as a woman more than capable of taking care of herself. Holding hands on their famous post–Super Bowl interview on *60 Minutes*, the Clintons were a team—Hillary and her husband allied against outsiders who wanted to threaten their marriage. ("This was no Nancy Reagan," wrote Gail Sheehy. "This was the look of the *consigliere* sitting vigil over a member of the family.") During the taping of the show, a piece of lighting equipment fell over, narrowly missing Mrs. Clinton's head. A technician noted admiringly that the future First Lady cried out: "Jesus, Mary and Joseph!" She was, he said, "still composed enough to keep her comment broadcast-worthy."

"A warm friendship with the vice president"

By 1992, the Republican and Democratic parties were devoting enormous effort to collecting every unfavorable piece of information they could find on the opposition, both in terms of public and private history. Each side had amassed so much stuff that it may have created a political version of the nuclear standoff—no one dared make the first strike, for fear of triggering some sort of Armageddon. George H. W. Bush, who never brought up either Clinton's sex life or his Whitewater financial deals, had sensitive issues of his own, some involving his youngest son's dealings with a failed savings and loan in Colorado.

The candidates' staffs and supporters did attempt to leak their tidbits, in hopes they might turn into more or less spontaneous campaign gossip. "Among the choicer items floating down this Washington sewer were ridiculous tales of Hillary Clinton's lesbian experiments, Clinton's role in covering up the use of a private airport at Mena in Arkansas for cocaine shipments, George Bush's romantic tryst with a New York socialite during the 1980 campaign and his alleged protection of another former mistress when U.S. Customs detained the British-born woman trying to smuggle in some expensive fur coats," wrote Martin Walker in his Clinton biography, *The President We Deserve.*

The story about George Bush's fur-smuggling mistress was a venerable rumor, like Mamie-drinks. It had been circulating for more than a decade in Washington gossip loops. Like most such stories, it generally lay dormant, just one of those things people thought they *knew.* But periodically, particularly when Bush was campaigning for office, it would explode into a flurry of public speculation. Jennifer Fitzgerald was a State Department official with the rather dismal title of deputy chief of protocol in 1992. She had been Bush's closest aide during much of his government career, running his office in China when he was ambassador, following him to the CIA, and serving as his executive assistant and gatekeeper during his first term as vice president. When a powerful man's closest assistant is a single woman, there is usually some speculation that their relationship is more than professional. (Despite the surge of powerful women with male aides, the gossip has yet to start working much in the other direction.) The intensity of the rumors vary, but they are almost always fanned when the aide in question is strict in denying other people access to her boss. Fitzgerald was a very determined gatekeeper.

In 1981, a story that then-vice president Bush had been shot and superficially wounded while leaving Fitzgerald's house in the middle of the night went raging around Washington, creating such a sensation that the *Washington Post* eventually published a story called "Anatomy of a Rumor" about the incident. The *Post* left out the part about Fitzgerald, and simply reported how "a rumor that George Bush had been nicked by a bullet in a predawn shooting outside a townhouse near the Capitol" became so overwhelming that the vice president demanded the FBI interview him so he could prove it wasn't true. The rumor began, the *Post* discovered, when a Washington artist heard—or thought she heard—a police officer say that Bush had been shot that day. She mentioned it to one friend, who told a legislative aide at a bar. The aide told his roommate and a friend who worked for columnist Jack Anderson. Several *Post* employees heard it at the next level, and all of them told the same editor, who assigned a reporter to check it out. So did dozens of other media outlets. Soon the beleaguered artist was driven from her home by reporters camped at her door. One of her neighbors demanded to know if this was going to hurt property values.

The Fitzgerald rumor—minus the gunplay—popped up repeatedly in the 1988 campaign, in which Bush defeated Bob Dole for the Republican nomination and Michael Dukakis for the presidency. Suspecting the Dole camp of passing the story around during the primaries, the Bush forces decided to stage a preemptive attack, offering up a snippet to *Newsweek*'s gossipy "Periscope" section in which son George W. said: "The answer to the Big A question is N.O." The first response, to Bush's dismay, was a series of headlines along the lines of BUSH SON DENIES DAD'S ADULTERY. But then the talk quickly died off.

Things stayed quiet until the end of the presidential campaign, when the Jennifer rumor seemed to re-emerge out of nowhere. Wall Street, which was banking on a Republican victory, buzzed with rumors that a national magazine or newspaper was about to publish a Bush adultery story. The market plunged. The story never appeared and the stocks recovered, leaving financial reporters to puzzle over how to explain the phenomenon to their readers. The next day, a midlevel Dukakis aide, Donna Brazile, brought the rumor up on the press bus, urging reporters to write about it, and saying the vice president should "fess up." Brazile was moderately successful—the story about her demand that the reporters write the story did make some papers. But it was at the price of her job. "We all liked Donna but we also knew she was setting herself on fire," said Adam Nagourney, who now covers politics for *The New York Times*. "Some of the reporters were goading her. She was pissed off. All in all it was an amazing moment." (Brazile recovered better than Dukakis did, and went on to manage Al Gore's presidential campaign in 2000.)

After Bush won the election, *The Washington Post* let slip an item noting that Fitzgerald "who has served President Bush in a number of positions" was expected to be named deputy chief of protocol. Then things quieted down until Fitzgerald started a minor defining public moment of her own. She was disciplined for trying to avoid paying customs on some furs she purchased while on State Department business in Argentina. Jack Anderson took full advantage, writing that "despite what sources describe as a 'natural surliness,' " Fitzgerald "enjoyed wide influence and warm friendship with the vice president."

There were several reasons the Fitzgerald story refused to die, even when Fitzgerald had been shipped off to the Siberia of the State Department's protocol section. Bush, like Jimmy Carter, did not create a large supply of interesting personal gossip, so people tended to hang onto what they had. And in 1992, the Fitzgerald rumors became powerful for their symmetry: Bill Clinton from Arkansas had an affair with a part-time nightclub singer named Gennifer, and preppie George Bush from Connecticut had an affair with a middle-aged State Department employee named Jennifer. "I don't understand why nothing's ever been said about George Bush's girlfriend—I understand he has a Jennifer too," newspaper heir Anne Cox Chambers told Hillary Clinton over tea in Atlanta. Mrs. Clinton promptly trotted out the tale of the tea in a *Vanity Fair* interview, claiming that Chambers had launched "into this long description of, you know, Bush and his carrying on, all of which is apparently well known in Washington." Unlike most other people whose private conversations wind up in the public media, Chambers did not try to claim she had been misquoted.

The Fitzgerald rumor was of great interest to the Clinton team, since it suggested that all politicians strayed from home, and the only difference was between those who admitted it and those who played hypocrite. Hillary theorized that the "establishment" was shielding Bush from the grilling her husband had gotten. "They're gonna circle the wagons on Jennifer—and all these other people," she complained to *Vanity Fair.* Mrs. Clinton was as self-deluded as Gary Hart had been when he theorized that the press asked him about womanizing because they were afraid of his "new ideas." In fact, many papers had put reporters on the Fitzgerald story but none had come up with any evidence to substantiate the gossip. When the campaign had its final, most public Jennifer eruption, *The Washington Post* would wonder in print whether it should have run a story about the fact that there were no facts.

Clinton partisans found what they thought was evidence that might nail down the gossip in a new book about lobbying called *The Power House*. The book contained a footnote quoting a by then deceased American diplomat as saying he had arranged for Bush and Fitzgerald to use a guest house together in Geneva in 1984, when Barbara Bush was on a book tour. It was perhaps the most discussed footnote since Isaac Hill wrote that one about John Quincy Adams pimping for the czar of Russia. But most papers to whom copies of the book were sent declined to revive the Fitzgerald story solely on the information of a dead man. "Obviously, you'd rather have a live guy," said Richard Gooding of the *New York Post,* who nevertheless went ahead and bannered the story on the front page: THE BUSH AFFAIR.

Bush's next press conference was tense, with correspondents wondering if someone would ask, wondering if *they* should ask, trying to imagine the scene that would follow. The fact that the president was sharing the microphone with Israeli Prime Minister Yitzhak Rabin made it even more difficult to bring up the question of adultery. CNN reporter Mary Tillitson took the leap, and the president reacted about as everyone had expected. "I'm not going to take any sleazy questions like that from CNN," said Bush. "I'm very much disappointed that you would ask such a question of me. . . . I'm outraged. . . . I'm not going to respond other than to say it's a lie." CNN, which was carrying the press conference live, broadcast Bush's response repeatedly. Later on the same day, during an interview on NBC, Stone Phillips asked Bush if he had ever had an affair and the president threatened to stop the interview. "You're perpetuating the sleaze by even asking the question, to say nothing of asking in the Oval Office," he said angrily.

2. The New Indiscretion

"He was so boyish and charming . . ."

Bill Clinton was the first president who had grown up in the TV age and his own experience taught him that the public liked a politician who could let his hair down in front of the cameras. In 1988, Clinton's first bid for public attention had ended in disaster when his nominating speech for Michael Dukakis went on for so long he was almost laughed off the stage. (The biggest applause line, Democrats joked, had been "In closing. . . .") He became the butt of late-night talk show monologues and worried that his career was over. But he saved himself by appearing on the Johnny Carson show, playing his saxophone and making fun of his own performance. "It wasn't my finest hour. It wasn't even my finest hour and a half," he told Carson genially. The appearance got rave reviews—CNN dubbed it the "fastest turnaround ever"—and a bigger audience than the convention drew. "He was so boyish and charming. I'm sure he won a lot of hearts," said TV critic Tom Shales.

The saving grace of a few self-deprecating minutes on the air was driven home again during the 1992 primaries, when what had seemed like Clinton's smooth march to the Democratic presidential nomination began to falter. He lost the Connecticut primary to the unelectable Jerry Brown. On TV in New York, he made the fatal "I didn't inhale" remark. Voters seemed to plunge into one of those fits of buyer's remorse that make them recoil from any front-runner. *Newsday* gave its primary endorsement to Paul Tsongas, who had already dropped out of the race.

To win over the cranky New Yorkers, Clinton turned to the entertainment media—*Donahue,* the Charlie Rose interview program (on which he did his Elvis Presley imitation) and most important, Don Imus' radio show. There, Clinton joked gently about the marijuana story and defused New Yorkers' natural suspicion of down-home accents, telling Imus that "Bubba" was southern for "mensch." It was an enormously successful experiment. Imus told his listeners he had to admit that "the redneck bozo" had a sense of humor. Clinton won the New York primary easily, and while Imus's claim that he had made the difference was an exaggeration, almost all political commentators agreed he had been a help. Clinton appeared twice more on the show during the campaign and Imus eventually told his listeners that he intended to vote for the man he called "Fatso."

Once in office, it was natural that Clinton would become a trailblazer in eliminating the public's sense that there were certain things you just didn't say about a president in public. His willingness to answer a question on an MTV forum about what kind of underwear he wore was the first stunning breach of the old propriety. All this had a liberating effect on the transmission of political gossip. If the president would talk about his briefs on air, surely no subject was too delicate for discussion.

"*I heard the First Lady say, 'Oh my God.' *"

Don Imus had begun incorporating political comment into his radio show even before he had his famous encounters with Bill Clinton. It was a move not unlike the one gossip columnist Walter Winchell had made decades earlier when he found the dwindling Broadway scene too feeble for a daily column and started cultivating Franklin Roosevelt and J. Edgar Hoover as subjects. Imus turned out to have a knack for forcing politicians to talk in ways that his politics-hating listeners found interesting. "You get an opportunity to see a different side of these people. It loosens them up when we get them to try to humiliate themselves and reveal some embarrassing aspect of their lives," he explained.

Elected officials lined up to be humiliated. Americans' dislike of politics, which was already founded on a too-intimate knowledge of their human frailties, forced the politicians to expose themselves more and more. They needed to make connection with the voters and they knew irreverent media stars like Imus could serve as intermediaries. Producers of David Letterman's late night show complained that after Vice President Al Gore was invited to come on and recite the top ten reasons why he liked his job, they were besieged with calls from senators and congressmen begging to appear on the program, too, promising to make themselves as ridiculous as necessary. (Gore's staff, in an effort to maintain dignity, did reject the suggestion that he say being vice president was fun because "chicks dig it when I break a tie vote in the Senate.")

In 1996, the Radio and Television Correspondents Association recognized Imus's new position in the world of politics by inviting him to be featured speaker at their annual dinner in Washington, where the

Clintons sat on the dais as guests of honor and most of the top politicians and television journalists in the country were part of the audience. The result was a really spectacular example of what happens when the barriers of decorum collapse. "You know, I think it would be fair to say that back when the Clintons took office, if we had placed them all in a lineup . . . ," Imus began, in a long joke about Hillary Clinton's recent appearance before a grand jury. There was nothing in his performance that was different from his normal radio patter. But this time, Imus was talking about important people's personal lives while they were sitting behind him, being watched by all the other most important people in Washington and being broadcast live on C-SPAN. Imus reminisced about a day when Clinton was watching a baseball game in Baltimore and being interviewed on the radio. "Bobby Bonilla hit a double and we all heard the president, in his obvious excitement, holler 'Go, baby.' And I remember commenting at the time: 'I bet that's not the first time he said that.' " Looking over at the Clintons' table, Imus realized things were not necessarily going well. "I can't even describe his face," he told Maureen Dowd. "If he'd had a gun, he'da shot me."

Imus then moved on to the media celebrities in the audience. ("Here's Peter Jennings, sitting there each evening, elegant, erudite, refined and I'm wondering what's under his desk. I mean besides an intern.") It was somewhere during this section, Imus said later, that "I heard the First Lady say 'Oh my God.' " He finished his monologue, joking about newsman Sam Donaldson and Senator Joseph Biden for their hair replacement techniques, claiming that when Tim Russert of NBC worked as an aide to New York politicians earlier in his career, his "duties included hiding the bottles for Pat (Moynihan) and the bodies for Mario (Cuomo)."

Official Washington was left reeling. Presidential spokesman Mike McCurry unsuccessfully tried to get C-SPAN to cancel the scheduled rebroadcast. The Correspondents Association sent the president an apology. The president ended all relations with Imus, and many of the radio personality's Washington guests backed away, at least temporarily. Bernard Kalb of CNN said he walked out of the dinner at the point where Imus "poked fun at marital problems of correspondents who

were there, by name." That was several minutes after Imus had poked
fun at the marital problems of the president of the United States, by
name.

3. The New Nastiness

"Coming out of the liberal closet"

The new indiscretion was combined with a new viciousness. Even before Bill Clinton became a serious factor on the national scene, the
tone of politics had become more personal, more strident, more
mean. After decades in which the Democrats appeared to have established a perpetual control of Congress, the balance of power was
changing. The Republican leaders who had risen to prominence on
their gentlemanly ability to cooperate with the ruling majority were on
the way out; the more aggressive conservatives led by Newt Gingrich
were on the offensive. True believers, they could be appallingly cruel
in what they said about their opponents, just as the left had been during the anti-war movement of the 1960s and 1970s. The Republicans
had been bitterly frustrated during decades in the minority, under a
Democratic leadership that ignored their wishes and refused to provide an even playing field for legislative decision-making. It was time
to prepare for the payback.

In 1989, Gingrich was pounding away at Speaker Jim Wright, over
fat payments Wright got for the sale of what was basically a very boring vanity press book. Wright appeared to be doomed, and suddenly
rumors began to crop up that his logical successor, House Majority
Leader Thomas Foley, was gay. A TV reporter supposedly had a tape
of a prison inmate making charges about Foley's sex life. The tape
never surfaced and the rumors about precisely what the prisoner had
said changed by the hour. *The New Republic* printed an oblique reference to rumors of "sexual improprieties" that were the only thing
standing between Foley and the speakership.

Joel Connelly, a reporter for the Washington bureau of Foley's
home-state newspaper, the *Seattle Post Intelligencer*, mentioned the

rumors to his editor back home. The editor told Connelly not to write anything, but to "keep on top of it just in case." One of the paper's columnists heard about the conversation and told his friends on the county Democratic committee. The people on the county committee nervously called the Democratic state chairwoman and told her: "We're hearing Foley's gay." The chairwoman reached out herself, and called: Joel Connelly. It had taken less than a day for the story to make its way through the state's political gossip loop and come winging back to its start.

Some of Foley's friends wondered if Jim Wright's supporters had started the rumor, in an effort to keep the Democrats from feeling they could easily replace the embattled House Speaker. But the Republicans were the ones fanning the story, keeping it going and adding new variations. "We hear it's little boys," Karen Van Brocklin, a Gingrich aide, told Lars-Erik Nelson of the New York *Daily News*. The Republican National Committee issued a memo to its state leaders that described Foley "coming out of the liberal closet" and comparing his voting record to that of Barney Frank, the openly gay Democrat from Massachusetts. Frank, in retaliation, threatened to start naming all the Republican Congressmen he knew were homosexual. "I won't tell what my evidence is, or how many people are on my list, or anything else," Frank said later. "It's not in my interest to discuss it at all. The threat is best used if you take it out every so often, aim it and fire."

Foley, who was in his sixties, was a reserved and cerebral man who could do little more than yell "I've been married twenty-one years!" His wife, Heather, who was one of her husband's closest political advisers, sat helplessly with her head in her hands saying, "We can't do anything about this." But as the 1990s wound along it would become apparent that rumors like the one torturing Foley withered rather quickly under public assault. Lars-Erik Nelson wrote about what Van Brocklin had said to him, causing Gingrich to simultaneously denounce Nelson and apologize to Foley. The media, in response to the RNC's "liberal closet" letter and Frank's outraged response, went on the attack. The party leaders backed down quickly.

But as usual, the wounds on the gossip target remained raw after the political danger had passed. Foley was elected Speaker, but he had not forgotten how it felt to have his sexuality debated in public. When he learned that House members were being allowed to write free overdrafts on the congressional bank, giving themselves interest-free loans, he made only a few clumsy and tentative attempts to stop the practice. The bank was under the control of one of Wright's old allies, and many Foley aides still felt Wright might have been involved in spreading the rumors about their boss. In 1992, when the House bank scandal exploded, a source close to Foley was quoted as saying that the Speaker's office had been reluctant to get involved in a fight that might lead to a revival of the gossip.

Others blamed Foley's own administrative shortcomings for his failure, and when the Speaker lost a re-election bid in 1994, his defeat was due less to rumors about his private life than his opposition to term limits and the anti-incumbent spirit of the moment. But the tenor of political discourse guaranteed that Foley's last days in office would be as painful as possible. During the rancorous re-election campaign, one Spokane talk radio host demanded on the air that the Speaker of the House tell his constituents whether or not he was a homosexual. Foley, who was used to being treated as something of a local hero back home, told friends that day was the low point of his political career.

"If someone's in rehab, the tabloids will find out"

There was nothing new about a politics that specialized in ruined reputations and vicious partisan debate. In the pre–Civil War period, the blood on the floor in the House and Senate had sometimes been literal. But the voters of the 1990s had not been around for the Civil War, and even the rancor of the 1950s was a dim memory, made even dimmer by the fact that the hateful battles of the McCarthy period had been filtered through a media that was more discreet than the wall-to-wall communications technology of the end of the century.

Besides the Internet and cable TV, old forms of communications were re-creating themselves. Radio had become talk radio, and the scandal magazines of the 1950s morphed into supermarket tabloids like the *National Enquirer* and the *Star*. The tabloids used many of the old techniques—checking police records and bribing servants, greedy mistresses and low-level studio employees. In a new wrinkle, they also recruited former patients who spent some time in group therapy with a famous alcoholic or addict. "If someone's in rehab, the tabloids will find out," said entertainment reporter Nancy Griffin. "You can't even go and dry yourself out without having someone at your group meeting sell your story to the tabs. I'd hate to be a celebrity today."

Like their scandal-magazine ancestors, the supermarket tabloids were mainly interested in entertainment celebrities, not politics. The *Star,* which had published Gennifer Flowers's story, also paid a Washington prostitute for a first-person account of her ongoing relationship with presidential adviser Dick Morris, and the story made a huge sensation when it appeared on the stands during the 1996 Democratic national convention. But the attention that such exposés attracted gave the impression that the tabloids were far more concerned with governmental figures than they really were. A politician, to be worth exposing, had to be at the highest level of national fame. Governors, congressmen, and even senators who were not a part of the Kennedy family would have to misbehave in a spectacular manner to draw the tabloids' attention. But the papers happily covered the misfortunes of all entertainers, large and small, down to the sins and embarrassments of the most obscure former actors from long-dead sitcoms. (" 'Webster' Ex-Star Selling Car Wax from His Van.")

The one medium that really preferred *political* gossip was talk radio, where viewers need a topic with a little more meat than Hollywood rumors are likely to carry. "The key is entertaining conversation rooted in something important," said Michael Harrison, the editor of *Talkers Magazine*. "If it seems frivolous or shallow, it doesn't work." On talk radio, President Clinton was always a far bigger draw than Tom Cruise or Julia Roberts. Even the Clintons' uneventful vacation on the Massachusetts coast in the summer of 1997 gave the radio audiences something to chew over. Callers traded rumors that the First Family would be guests at a secret wedding of Barbra Streisand and her boyfriend, argued about how Clinton's sexual harassment defense would play when he got home, and speculated that the president would be playing golf with Tiger Woods. "That had it all," Harrison said with a sigh. "Show business, politics, sports, personalities."

Talk radio really came to life after 1987, when deregulation made it easier for stations to broadcast political opinion without worrying about offering equal time to the other side. "The late eighties was a cold and lonely place. People didn't know their neighbors. Talk radio created an electronic community, a backyard fence," Harrison said. It was a backyard populated almost entirely by conservatives, particularly conservative men. The intimate air of the talk show encouraged many callers to speak as freely, and irresponsibly, as if they were having a gabfest at their neighborhood bar. Obscenities were bleeped, but not questions about "whether it's true that" political figures were gay, adulterers, alcoholics or members of the Mafia. A salacious question, when posed to a talk-radio superstar like Rush Limbaugh, was often enough to launch a thousand new threads of gossip.

"A vanity press for the demented"

If talk radio sometimes sounded like a crowd of regulars gabbing away at the local tavern, much of the Internet political gossip of the 1990s resembled the ramblings of the drunken strangers at the other end of the bar.

"My guess is there is significantly less evidence of Kemp having a gay encounter than there is that Bill and Hillary had Vincent Foster bumped off," typed in one chatter on an average day during the pre-Lewinsky segment of Bill Clinton's second term.

"Many gays I have talked to say that Kemp's homosexuality is known in the gay community," chimed in another, in the age-old tradition of "everybody says . . ." gossip.

Someone else threw in his two cents' worth on the ongoing Internet speculation about Bill Clinton and drugs, sounding remarkably like the country club Republicans of the New Deal era, passing around stories about the president's supposedly insane behavior: "When he burst into endless laughter during Yeltsin's visit, I knew he had inhaled something."

It was still early in the life of the Internet. The traditional media was dismissive or hostile to everything that smacked of the Web. The late Lars Nelson of the *Daily News*, a much-respected reporter of the older generation, used to call it "a vanity press for the demented." At presidential conventions and other big events where print reporters were forced to share space with the then-lowly minions of a newspaper Web site, it wasn't unheard of for veteran political reporters to "accidentally" trip over the wiring and disconnect a Web editor at some critical filing moment.

The worm would turn. But what made the Wild West of the early Internet political sites particularly disturbing was the anonymity and lack of accountability. We don't think of gossip as something that involves much responsibility to begin with—think of all those generations of dinner party conversationalists who passed on fanciful stories about presidential misbehavior, from Grover Cleveland's wife beating to George W. Bush's relationship with cocaine. Still, the other dinner party guests knew where the gossip was coming from. On the Internet, other users couldn't tell whether the person they were talking with on a Republican chat line (say the one who informs them that "Liddy Dole has her lesbian problem licked" or that Bob Dole is joining a professional wrestling league) is really a fellow partisan, a Democratic mole, or a pair of giggling teenagers.

"Who's her girlfriend? Give me her name."

Back when writer David Brock was the sharpest pen on the right (he slimed Clarence Thomas' accuser, Anita Hill, as "a little bit nutty and a little bit slutty"), Brock was doing a talking-heads appearance on CNBC with columnist Jimmy Breslin. The topic was Hillary Clinton and Brock told the moderator that he felt the First Lady was being hurt by gossip that she was a lesbian. "Who's her girlfriend? Give me her name," barked Breslin, dismissively.

Brock's response—that he was only saying there was *talk about* the First Lady's sexuality was, by the mid-1990s, easy to verify. Even after Bill Clinton had won a second term, during the period when his wife's profile had been temporarily reduced almost to a vanishing point, a quick search of the Internet Web sites that solicited chat about politics, conspiracies and celebrities could turn up a steady stream of Hillary-is-a-lesbian postings. There were jokes. Alleged partners were identified. The familiar once-removed authorities were cited. ("A senior network news source told me. . . .") Conspiracy theories were floated. ("Is there a cover-up by talk-radio hosts? Only Liddy has hinted at this . . . are other talk show hosts being paid to keep the issue quiet?") In 1998, Sen. John McCain told a Republican gathering the most well-worn of the jokes, which centered on Chelsea Clinton being the love-child of Hillary and Janet Reno. When the word got out, he apologized to President Clinton—but not to any of the women.

The stories about Hillary Clinton's mythic life as a lesbian were encouraged by the Internet, which allowed people to speculate about the most outrageous and intrusive topics, from whether a long-faded TV actor really had a necrophilia fetish to the possibility that the First Lady preferred sex with women. But the Internet was still the new medium in town. In the 1990s, the tone of the political discourse was set by talk radio, which bandied about the lesbian gossip—even though it preferred the rumors that Mrs. Clinton and White House counsel Vincent Foster were lovers, and that Hillary was somehow involved in Foster's death. Endless investigations confirming that Foster had committed suicide seemed unable to tamp down the stories, which were hyped by talk radio mega-host Rush Limbaugh. When Limbaugh reported (incorrectly) that an obscure financial newsletter was claiming "that Vince Foster was murdered in an apartment owned by Hillary Clinton," the financial markets shivered, and a Lehman Brothers market analyst told *Newsweek* that European traders were particularly worried that "Hillary Clinton was involved in a murder. They hate that."

The murder rumors were pure right-wing conspiracy theory. But the two most sensational themes to the gossip about the First Lady's personal life—that she was a lesbian and that she was Vince Foster's lover—were more spontaneous. The stories came from two different sources. The talk about Mrs. Clinton and Foster began as grassroots gossip that had been whispered around Arkansas long before Bill

Clinton became a presidential candidate. Foster was Hillary's law partner and close personal friend at a time when Little Rock was humming with stories about Governor Clinton's amorous activities. It was almost inevitable that local political insiders would speculate about whether Hillary might turn to Foster for consolation. Martin Walker, in his Clinton biography, claimed the week before his suicide "Foster heard press gossip that the conservative *Washington Times* had assigned a team of reporters to probe his background and explore the rumors about him and the woman who was now the First Lady." The paper denied it was conducting any such investigation. Reports on Foster's death issued by independent prosecutor Kenneth Starr's Whitewater investigation suggest that depression and job pressures would have been enough to send him into a suicidal tailspin.

The Hillary-is-a-lesbian rumor had a far more venerable pedigree. From the first days that people gossiped about politicians, powerful women have almost always been rumored to be lesbians, and frequently the hosts of lesbian orgies. Aspasia, the common-law wife of Pericles in ancient Athens, nearly lost her life over such gossip. (Pericles' oratory won her acquittal from the death penalty.) Marie Antoinette, who never even said "Let them eat cake" much less sponsored sexual romps with her ladies-in-waiting, really did lose hers. The image of the lesbian orgies seems to have much less to do with sex than the ancient fear of the secrets women knew about the men in their households. It's the vision of a sort of über-gossip session, in which unnatural women get together and swap their dangerous secrets while they plot against helpless males.

4. The Local Angle

"People in very high places have told me . . ."

The Boston-Washington corridor generally considers itself the American political rumor capital, and Southerners often brag that their elected officials—the Huey Longs and the Kissin' Jim Folsoms—spark the most interesting gossip. But the clean-living good-government cities produce many of the wildest stories. (Some of them are based on fact. It was in Cincinnati, for instance, that an up-and-coming city council member resigned when he got caught paying for the services of a prostitute with a personal check, then quickly returned to politics and successfully ran for mayor. He became more famous later as talk-show host Jerry Springer.) Seattle once had a mayoral race in which a candidate was rumored to have murdered a prostitute at a Young Democrats convention. "There was this woman who claimed she had been at the party. She went to another candidate with the story and he sent her to a reporter, who got the sheriff to go and dig where she said the body was," said Bob Gogerty, a Seattle political consultant who was working for the gossip target. "There was no body, and the woman turned out to have been just out of a mental hospital." Gogerty's client won. "But that rumor floated around throughout his political career—it cropped up every time he ran in an election."

The rumors about Mayor Norm Rice were different from what went before only because of the new media that existed to spread them. Rice, who became Seattle's first black mayor in 1990, was so bland that he was nicknamed "Mayor Nice." Nevertheless, almost from the time he took office, there was an undercurrent of talk about a mysterious shooting. Some of the details, like the name of the hospital where he was supposed to have been treated, remained constant. But the central facts kept mutating. Rice had been caught sleeping with his mistress. Or his deputy mayor, Bob Watt. Or some other well-known Seattle male. The shooter was his wife, Constance. Or his son. The wound was in his stomach. Or his shoulder. It was all part of a plot to fill all the city's top political positions with homosexuals. Or to cover up a child-prostitution ring.

The little kernel from which the story grew seemed to be a crank phone call that came to Deputy Mayor Watt in 1991, claiming the mayor had been shot and was being taken to the hospital. The report was quickly dismissed as a hoax, but the rumor of the shooting and cover-up somehow took hold and simmered. Rebecca Hale, who became Rice's press secretary, remembered having to check out the story when she was a reporter. "It was humiliating," she said. "I'd have to phone city hall and say: "I'm sorry but some weirdo just reported the mayor's been shot. . . .' "

In 1993, a disgruntled former city water department employee named Kurt Hettiger began circulating fliers demanding WHO SHOT MAYOR NORMAN B. RICE? In the great tradition of such literature, Hettiger cited unnamed but supposedly reliable sources who vanished when he was required to produce them. A "transcribed testimony of an eyewitness" turned out to be a three-page summary of unsubstantiated allegations put together by an investigator Hettiger had hired. When the aggrieved ex-employee moved to the other side of the state (and filed a suit against another water department), both the mayor's staff and his security guards breathed more easily. "But then he went online," said Hale. "We started getting more phone calls. When you hear something, it's one thing. But when you can print it off the Net, that gives it more weight."

Hettiger's allegations were also picked up by a local talk radio host, Mike Siegel, who kept urging the mayor to come on air and deny the stories. "The mayor just said: 'Who wants to dignify that?' " recalled Gogerty. But in 1996, Rice decided to try running for governor and Siegel hooked up with Spokane talk-show host Richard Claire for a statewide broadcast dubbed "The Truth Squad."

"The accusations surrounding this shooting . . . ," Claire began. "Is there anything that can be talked about, or is that something that's out there hanging with no proof whatsoever and not worth mentioning at all?"

Siegel found it worth mentioning. "It's a rumor," he responded. "We've talked to a variety of people about this. It's not taken lightly. People in very high places have told me something like this occurred." The program featured guests like a fired Seattle police officer, who reported that Rice's wife Constance had been seen with a bandage on her wrist. "It seemed then, it seems now, consistent with a scuffle over a gun," the ex-cop announced. His sources, he said, included "a professional woman in Seattle's black community" and "a city council source."

Gogerty, who was Rice's consultant, started getting calls from the mayor's supporters asking if everything was all right. "One of our key people pulled me aside at a fund-raiser and said: 'You've got to tell me if there's anything to this,' " he recalled. Campaigning around the state, Rice was constantly being asked about his marriage, his wife, and the shooting rumors. "In Seattle, people knew this man. They can make their own decisions about what's true," said Hale. "But clear across the state, they don't know him."

Rice finally agreed to denounce the rumors, and brought out all possible big guns. The press conference was held in a local synagogue. Rice was surrounded by rabbis, priests and ministers, as well as his family. "Rumor and innuendo has found a ready conduit through so-called hot talk radio," said the mayor to local acclaim. The public response was overwhelmingly favorable, (though not strong enough to get Rice the gubernatorial nomination), and the Seattle talk-radio station turned out to be surprisingly sensitive to criticism. "There was no intent to spread something that was rumor and innuendo, and if that happened, I'm sorry," said the talk host, Siegel, who was fired over the incident. He said he had no idea whether any of the gossip about Rice was true.

Addendum

When Rice's office passed out transcripts of the Seattle-Spokane "Truth Squad" talk show, it noted that between demands that Mayor Rice deny the "rampant rumor" about his shooting, the hosts "talk briefly about their challenge to Tom Foley"—who had been out of office since 1994—"to admit that he's a homosexual."

"The town's abuzz about it"

On Election Day in 1996, Mississippi governor Kirk Fordice dismissed his normal escort of state troopers and his driver and got in the car by himself, announcing he was going to Memphis on "family business." Leaving the driver behind turned out to be a bad idea. By the end of the day the newly re-elected sixty-two-year-old Republican was in the hospital with serious injuries, and the *Jackson Clarion-Ledger* had a front-page headline announcing: FORDICE, WOMAN DINED

BEFORE CRASH. The owner of an "upscale Memphis grill" named Three Oaks told the paper that Fordice had lunched with "a middle-aged lady" and that the two had consumed a modest amount of wine. It was a story too good not to recycle for a second day, and under a banner announcing MEMPHIS TONGUES WAG OVER FORDICE WRECK, the paper produced an interview with another of the Three Oak's owners, George Falls. He reported that the restaurant was getting a lot of customers who wanted to "sit in the governor's seat."

"The town's abuzz about it. We've had more business," he added.

The state's first lady, meanwhile, was reported to be in Paris on "a cultural mission."

As all of Mississippi was well aware, Pat Fordice had shown an inordinate commitment to her wedding vows. When her husband was questioned about his relationship with "a Memphis lady" in 1993 and suddenly announced that his marriage was suffering from "irreconcilable differences," Pat released a statement saying she would continue serving as First Lady (and living in the governor's mansion) unless she was forced out. She outlasted her husband's period of discontent, and proved extremely supportive during his re-election campaign. After Fordice's opponent made merry with the "irreconcilable differences" line during a campaign appearance, the governor and his wife created a sensation by walking onstage hand-in-hand to confront him. While Pat stood by supportively, Fordice blasted his opponent for taking "a veiled cheap shot at that forty-year-old marriage," and kissed her on the cheek.

Students of Mississippi politics have commented frequently on the fact that the state has, in modern times, managed to combine an intense commitment to family values with a public tolerance for exceptionally frisky sexual behavior on the part of elected officials. Fordice had as little trouble with the voters as with his wife. And in 1996, when the governor recovered from the car wreck and returned to the capitol he said he could not remember anything that happened the day of the accident and refused to discuss the matter further. That tactic worked rather well, all things considered, reinforcing the general rule that if none of the principals in an affair complain in public, the media will let the matter drop.

But in 1999, Fordice staged another marital meltdown on his own. He bought an expensive house for his term-limited future and spent his weekends there, although Pat acknowledged she had never been invited along. Then he tromped off to Europe with the Memphis lady, who turned out to be a high school sweetheart named Ann Creson. Confronted by reporters on his return, he told a TV correspondent: "I'll whip your ass," and then announced he was seeking a divorce to marry Creson.

Former vice president Dan Quayle, who was then running for the 2000 presidential nomination, swiftly dumped Fordice as his national campaign co-chairman. "The fact of a split, unfortunately, in a marriage that's lasted for 40-odd years doesn't seem to me to negate one's advocacy of family values, which I certainly do," the governor protested.

Pat Fordice turned out to have much more patience than Quayle— or Creson, whose marriage to the ex-governor ended after three years. Fordice died of leukemia in 2004, and during his last days, friends said, it was his former wife who took him to the hospital for his cancer treatments and stayed by his side.

"Demeaning rumors notwithstanding"

In the summer of 1995, rumors swept through New York City's political subculture that there was trouble in Gracie Mansion, the official home of Mayor Rudy Giuliani and his wife, Donna Hanover Giuliani. The stories were no more well-documented than other rumors about previous mayors that had been ignored by the public and the media— all the way back to Jimmy Walker. But the change in the national culture made it almost certain that this time, they would wind up being shared with the city as a whole. The most persistent story involved the mayor's relations with his communication director, Christyne Lategano. It began, anthropologists now agree, with an item in *New York Newsday* in March, reporting that the mayor had been seen helping Lategano shop for a dress. The mayor, a clerk reported, said "Oh that looks fine" no matter what Lategano held up. "Spoken like a well-trained husband, no?" inquired the paper's gossip column.

The *New York Post* followed up with a piece that did everything but beat the readers over the head. "The mayor can't seem to keep on his hand the gold band given to him 11 years ago by his wife . . . ," it began. After pointing out that Giuliani had been wearing the ring on his right pinkie finger for a long time, the paper continued "Now we hear the mysterious matrimonial jumping ring simply shot off the mayor's hand and into a bathroom drain—without poor Rudy even noticing. . . ."

Not to be outdone, the *Daily News* ran an item on the mayor's weekend in Long Island: "The mystery of Mayor Giuliani's latest quickie—er, getaway. . . ."

Although the rumor itself had moved forward not one iota, the pace felt like it was picking up quite a bit. Only a few weeks later, *New York* magazine produced a cover story on Lategano's performance as communication director, which noted that the tabloid stories about her and the mayor "had hinted at their extra-professional relationship." But the magazine virtuously added, ". . . Demeaning rumors notwithstanding, even Lategano critics in City Hall dismiss the idea that she and Giuliani are romantically involved."

The demeaning rumors had been given a great deal of encouragement by the fact that Hanover, who had played an important role in her husband's successful race for mayor in 1993, was seldom seen in his company anymore. A former TV anchorwoman, she had retreated to the apolitical world of the Food Channel when Giuliani ran for office and she campaigned for the candidate she described as "the most virile man . . . so strong and wonderful . . . the most good-looking man in the city as far as I'm concerned."

But when Donna resurfaced just before Giuliani's re-election race in 1997, she announced that she was returning to TV news and planned to stay out of the campaign. In fact, she said, she felt it might be better if she never mentioned her husband's name in public again. That was not the sort of statement likely to put the rumors to rest—particularly when, after the election, Hanover declined to say who she had voted for. Still, the mayoral marriage continued to be a story in search of a defining public moment. Hanover, who dropped her married name, steadfastly refused to speak about anything except her career and her charitable activities. When asked about his marriage, the mayor simply denounced the questioner. In 1996, at the annual show put on by the Inner Circle, an organization of New York City journalists and public relations people, a local TV reporter asked Giuliani why his wife had not been present to witness his breathtaking performance in drag as "Rudy/Rudina." "You have no right to ask that question and you should be ashamed that you asked it!" Giuliani exploded. "There are parts of my life that I can reserve for being private and your asking that question is outrageous and it's a shame that you've stooped to reaching into people's lives to that extent."

In the same week, the *Los Angeles Times* published a rather definitive roundup of the printed gossip. "New York's press hounds are hot on a story that can't be verified—that the mayor's marriage has gone south," said part of the headline. The author, Josh Getlin, reported that the press had staked out Hanover, "trying to determine whether she spends nights at Gracie Mansion. . . ." The piece also opined that Hanover, a California native, seemed too nice for New York.

The City Hall press corps had gotten rather tired of the mayoral matrimony issue. Giuliani had been asked about it repeatedly. Most of the reporters had talked to the same two or three vocal but insistently anonymous sources. Some had staked out the Giuliani home. Then in the summer of 1997, *Vanity Fair* produced what was basically Getlin's story, combined with an attack on the reporters for not going further. "Even members of the mayor's own staff are questioning the objectivity and independence of the local media, which seems content to sit on the marriage story until it's broken elsewhere," wrote Jennet Conant, quoting an unnamed police source as calling the city journalists "cowardly lions." It was an interesting moment in the history of gossip and politics: A national magazine was attacking the ethics of political reporters who had chosen not to expose affairs that they couldn't prove existed and which definitely didn't seem to have anything to do with a politician's performance in office.

In the end, as usual, it was a series of defining public events that brought Giuliani's personal life into the headlines. The mayor started appearing in public with his mistress, Judy Nathan, and then held a bizarre press conference in which he told reporters that he was seeking a divorce before he told his wife. Hanover followed up with her own press availability, in which she accused him of having had a long-running affair with Lategano. The divorce itself was extremely messy, with the mayor and his estranged wife fighting for control of Gracie Mansion. Giuliani's attack-dog lawyer confided in the entire New York press corps that his client was impotent from prostate cancer treatments and claimed that Hanover woke him up by running on the treadmill at five a.m. The public consensus, even in live-and-let-live New York, was that the mayor had behaved like a cad. But when terrorists attacked the World Trade Center, Giuliani became a hero and *Time*'s Man of the Year. His marital misbehavior was utterly forgotten.

"I said I hadn't slept with anybody"

U.S. Senator Chuck Robb was an ex-Marine combat commander, a man his daughters described as so disciplined he would eat exactly three Oreo cookies every evening and never once reach for a fourth. Humorless, stolid, fiscally conservative and borderline sanctimonious, he had been briefly touted as a future presidential possibility when he was first elected to the Senate in 1988. But for a politician who looked so extraordinarily stiff, Robb had a surprising history as a party animal. During the years he had served as governor of Virginia, Robb was a frequent—and solo—visitor to Virginia Beach, the state's hard-core recreation zone. During his first term in the Senate, he had been involved in an embarrassing flap when Tai Collins, a former beauty queen and soon-to-be *Playboy* cover girl, went on NBC to announce that she had once had an assignation with Robb in a New York hotel. In a denial that was more memorable than the allegation, Robb claimed he had been in the room with Collins, but had succumbed only to a massage.

Robb kept claiming he had always been faithful to his wife, Lyndon Johnson's daughter Lynda, but his aides worried about what new stories might come up in the future. Like so many of their peers in American political history, they did not trust their boss to provide full disclosure. They resolved the problem in a way that most other campaign staffers only fantasized about in late-night gripe sessions—they launched their own investigation, traveling to Virginia Beach to question his pals there and flying to Boston to talk with a woman they had heard was bragging about her affair with the senator. The resulting memo concluded that during his gubernatorial years, their employer had oral sex "with at least half a dozen women twenty to twenty-five years his junior at random times."

Inevitably, the memo wound up being leaked, and the *Washington Post* got the story just before Robb was due to make his official announcement of his candidacy for reelection in 1994. In a letter to his supporters, the senator admitted he was "clearly vulnerable on the question of socializing under circumstances not appropriate to a married man." But he denied lying about his behavior. "I previously said I hadn't slept with anyone. I hadn't had an affair. I clearly did not limit anything more than that," he said.

The *Post* described Robb as "the sort of damaged celebrity usually on the cover of tabloids by the checkout line." But in the end, the Virginia voters preferred him to Republican Oliver North, the right-wing star of the Iran-Contra scandal. Robb was reelected in a campaign that may go down in history as the first time American voters were asked to consider the issue of whether oral sex counts.

5. The Lewinsky Era

"Bob Dole's Secret Mistress"

Bob Dole's presidential campaign was dogged by rumors about rumors of sex. Even before the Republican convention made Dole the official nominee to run against Bill Clinton in 1996, his staff was distracted by stories that one paper or another was preparing to run an exposé of one alleged love affair or another. If the campaign had ever gained any real momentum, the constant drain of attention would have been a real problem. But as it was, Dole's candidacy was doomed for reasons having absolutely nothing to do with gossip: the wrong message, the wrong staff, and a candidate too haunted by failed campaigns of the past.

The most potentially damaging gossip about Dole that circulated in the summer of 1996 held that in his younger days, the pro-life Republican had gotten a woman pregnant and arranged for her to have an abortion. Dole said the story wasn't true, but the constant rumors that someone had the story and was prepared to publish it were "all a distraction, like a tailgating car," said a Dole aide. "Some days the headlines were shining in your eyes, sometimes it was a way back." Everyone eventually concluded that the abortion rumors were, indeed, false, but not before at least one young staff member had to sit down and have a serious discussion with the seventy-two-year-old candidate about his sexual history.

Finally, there was Meredith Roberts, a rather retiring sixty-three-year-old Virginian who had, indeed, had an affair with Dole while he was married to his first wife. Roberts was no Gennifer Flowers. She had, in fact, rejected a fifty thousand dollar offer from the *National Enquirer* for an interview about an affair she had had with Dole twenty-eight years earlier. She did finally agree to share her rather extensive documentation of the relationship with a *Washington Post* reporter. But the *Post* decided to kill the story and Roberts eventually wound up exactly where she didn't want to be—on the cover of the supermarket tabloid as BOB DOLE'S SECRET MISTRESS.

Few mainstream papers picked up the *National Enquirer*'s story. The affair had ended a lifetime ago, and many editors felt there was some sort of statute of limitations on these matters. Perhaps more important, the Dole camp had managed to hold off the story for a long time. When it finally did break, Dole was, for all practical purposes, already out of the race. "We're gonna lose—why do this thing to him, too?" one top aide recalled telling a *Washington Post* editor.

When the media declined to make a fuss about the story of Meredith Roberts, critics claimed the editors were depriving the voters of an important insight into a man who claimed to be running on character issues. But the voters did not need to meet Roberts to understand the dark side of Dole's personal life. The public was getting so much information on the private lives of presidential candidates that even a workaholic like Dole got rather thoroughly vetted before the primary season was well underway. The voters had been told that Dole had initiated a divorce from the woman who had married him when he was a crippled veteran and supported him through his long and traumatic effort to get through law school and establish a political career. His first wife's description of Dole's unexplained withdrawal from the relationship, and his abrupt request, "Let's end it," had been reported widely. The candidate's emotional landscape—his austere personal life, his lack of outside interests, his inability to relax and his rather remote relationship with his second wife—had been described thoroughly. Votes who watched the carefully staged Republican convention could get a pretty good idea of Dole's comfort in the role of family man by listening to his daughter Robin attempt to dredge up anecdotes about her father's interactions with her as a child—there was that roller-coaster ride in which Dole was quoted as saying "Wheeee."

"Open auditions for Hee Haw*"*

Meanwhile, on the Democratic side, voters who were interested in issues like sexual fidelity were nothing if not well-informed. Some polls showed that nine out of ten Americans could identify Paula Jones, the former Arkansas state employee who accused Clinton of sexual harassment. In their regular family newspapers and general interest magazines, the public could learn that Jones, a $6.35-an-hour clerk, claimed Clinton had lowered his trousers and said "Kiss it" during a Quality Management Conference at the Excelsior Hotel in Little Rock. The story had gone through all the very largest of the national gossip loops—talk radio (where hosts were hard-pressed to control speculation about what Jones claimed was a "distinguishing characteristic" of Clinton's genitals) to the Internet, to the ultimate mass gossip loop of the late-night talks shows.

David Letterman: "According to a poll, 50 percent of Americans feel President Clinton is concealing something in the Paula Jones case. Think about it. If he'd actually concealed something, he wouldn't be in this mess in the first place."

Jay Leno on Paula Jones' potential trial. "Imagine if they start bringing up the past sexual histories of these two. Oh my God, the witness stand is going to look like open auditions for *Hee Haw*."

It was impossible to imagine a politician whose private life had been more exposed, more subject to debasing jokes, more thoroughly established as being less than what Americans thought of as "presidential" than Bill Clinton's. Still, in poll after poll, during the 1996 campaign, voters said "character" was simply not their chief concern. That may simply have been their way of telegraphing an intention to vote Democratic. No president in American history has ever been thrown out of office at a time when the economy was in as good a shape as it was in 1996. Since the public was unable to convince itself that Clinton's character was the sort they would ideally ascribe to a president, they may have resigned themselves to putting character in second place.

Possibly, Clinton was benefiting from the fact that people react angrily to shocking stories about a famous person's life only when the gossip is out of sync with their image of his or her character. Ingrid Bergman's most famous role, after all, was as a nun. The congressmen who lost office after they were revealed to be homosexual were men who had campaigned on conservative, anti-gay platforms. Clinton, almost from the day he entered the national consciousness, was perceived as "Slick Willie," a man who couldn't be trusted to keep his word, even when it came to his marriage vows. But Clinton's good qualities—his intelligence, his flexibility, his emotional connection with the country's moods, his ability to keep going under extraordinary pressure—gradually became apparent, too.

"You sure didn't tell anybody"

The Monica Lewinsky affair was an almost unbelievably public event. Within months after the story broke, the former White House intern was such a global household name that her picture decorated the podium at an anti-American rally in Khartoum. ("Clinton: Screw Monica, not Sudan," the posters urged.) It certainly seemed as if the nation had been completely transformed since those discreet days when JFK romped with his girlfriends in the White House pool. But in retrospect, it's pretty clear that the difference between the White House of 1998 and the White House of 1962 was neither the moral climate of the country nor the willingness of the media to print stories about the president's personal life. It was all about the post-Watergate era of perpetual investigation. Until the independent prosecutor's office got its hands on Linda Tripp's tapes, the number of Washington insiders who knew about Lewinsky and Bill Clinton was probably smaller than the number who had known about Warren Harding and Nan Britton seventy-five years earlier. "I see politicians saying, 'This is nothing new. We all knew about Clinton,' and I think, 'Well, if you did, you sure didn't tell anybody,' " said Michael Isikoff of *Newsweek*, who spent several years investigating the president's sex life.

Of course everybody, including the voters, was familiar with the rumors about Clinton's past. But he was no Estes Kefauver, howling that he needed a woman at every campaign stop. Many people who worked with Clinton at the White House claimed later that he gave no hint that he wasn't keeping the implicit compact he'd made with the American people to give up the philandering that had gotten him into trouble in the past. Until January of 1998, most of the rumors about Clinton were junk gossip—vague speculation informed by history. It's very possible that Clinton would have been able to finish his term unscathed, Kennedy-style, if it had not been for the legal inquiry triggered by the appointment of the independent prosecutor Kenneth Starr.

In his book, *Uncovering Clinton*, Isikoff reported that Lewinsky's ever-active pal, Linda Tripp, considered giving tapes of her conversations with Lewinsky to the *National Enquirer* or some other supermarket tabloid if she failed to get attention anywhere else. So the president's love affair with the ex-intern would probably have wound up being written about, even absent Starr's wide-ranging probe. But Lewinsky had made it very clear that she was prepared to deny the relationship if the story became public. The traditional media, which was still the arbiter of what stories became part of the national conversation, was loath to write about the sex life of a sitting president without some sort of very official confirmation. Isikoff's book details the reluctance of his former employer, the *Washington Post*, to publish anything about Paula Jones' accusations, even after Isikoff had tracked down several people who were willing to back up her story.

Clinton's disgrace was, obviously, entirely his own fault. But the mega-scandal still depended on a long string of events, which began in 1991 when David Brock wrote an article on Clinton's behavior as governor in Arkansas. Brock mentioned a woman named "Paula" who had visited Clinton in a Little Rock hotel room and later volunteered to be his "girl friend." Without that article, published in the conservative journal *American Spectator*, Paula Jones would not have filed the sexual harassment suit she claimed was necessary to clear her name. Without the Supreme Court's ruling that the lawsuit could go forward even while Clinton served as president, there would have been no Jones lawyers to hear Linda Tripp's story about her friend's affair with the man she called "Handsome." There would have been no deposition, in which the president was asked if he ever had an affair with the former intern. Without that deposition, there would have been no question of perjury or obstruction of justice to permit Starr to look into the Lewinsky affair. Without Starr's investigation, there would have been no 421-page prosecutor's report containing all the now world-famous graphic details of Clinton's Oval Office affair. No impeachment hearings, no twenty-four-hour Monica programming on the cable news channels.

In 1998, as Clinton was slogging through the morass of political and personal crises that the Lewinsky affair had produced, Brock published an open letter to the president in *Esquire* apologizing for ever having brought the matter up. "Surveying the wreckage my report has wrought four years later," Brock wrote, he had to ask himself, "What the hell was I doing investigating your private life in the first place?"

A spokesman for Bill Clinton said the president had read the article and accepted Brock's apology.

"Values, schmalues. I don't get it."

One of the most remarkable parts of the Lewinsky saga was certainly the stubborn determination of the public to continue supporting a president who had been caught having sex in the Oval Office. (Or at least in as close proximity as Warren Harding got during those coat-closet encounters with Nan Britton.) It was a phenomenon that perplexed the nation's chattering class. The people who were supposed to be opinion-makers consistently felt Clinton's behavior was a far more serious matter than the public did. Late in the evening of January 20, 1998, the Monica Lewinsky story broke when the *Washington Post* announced that independent prosecutor Kenneth Starr had tapes of a former White House intern talking about the affair she had with the president. By early the next morning, *Newsweek* columnist Jonathan Alter was being introduced on MSNBC-TV as the man who had first mentioned the word "impeachment" on national television. (Alter clocked in at around eight a.m.) But surveys showed that almost no one, except the third of the country that had hated Bill Clinton all along, wanted to see the President go.

On ABC, conservative Bill Kristol announced confidently that Clinton "could not possibly survive." George Stephanopoulos, now reborn as a TV commentator, suggested that the resistant public was just waiting to see if the story about Lewinsky was actually true before it turned on the administration. David Broder, the venerable *Washington Post* columnist, agreed. "I would not put a whole lot of confidence in today's polls as to where this story is going to be three months from now, six months from now, a year from now," he said.

It became a political version of *Waiting for Godot*. The insiders, outraged by Clinton's defiant demeanor, kept waiting for the public to get angry, too. In August, after the polls showed voters failed to find the president's apology as unsatisfactory as the pundits did, George Will was sure the breaking point would be the graphic details in the Starr report. "There's going to come a . . . yuck factor, where people say, 'I don't want him in my living room,' " he predicted.

"I'm sure things will get worse when we get the full report from Starr," agreed William Bennett.

The Starr report actually seemed to harden public resistance to the idea of impeachment, and at the end of the year it was a sadder Bennett who admitted, "I may have been wrong. I'm not sure enough people care. For the first time in my adult life, I'm not in sync. I don't get it. What about all these conferences I've been invited to? I mean, values, schmalues. I don't get it."

But public opinion was totally in keeping with the transactional attitude toward the White House that had been growing more pronounced throughout the post-Watergate era. "What he's done is a personal thing," a seventy-two-year-old retired schoolteacher in Arizona told pollsters. "It doesn't have anything to do with what he's doing for the country. He's done a very good job for the country." Leading, to many people's minds, meant keeping the economy going strong, negotiating trade agreements, fixing the gaps in Social Security. It did not mean setting a moral example. The *New York Times*/CBS poll in September of 1998, taken right after the release of the Starr report, showed that two-thirds of the respondents felt Clinton did not share their moral values, and two-thirds felt he was an effective leader.

6. Republicans Behaving Badly

"If anyone's got a problem, they shouldn't be in this business"

The highly partisan nature of the impeachment effort mounted against Clinton made it almost inevitable that stories about Republican sexual misconduct would start cropping up, creating one of those tsunamis of political scandal that have dotted congressional history since the Civil War. "If anybody's got a problem—and I'm not talking about one mistake, but a problem over years—maybe they shouldn't be in this business," warned Senate Majority Leader Trent Lott. He turned out to be right in at least one sense. Enough stories emerged to convince already cynical voters that a history of philandering was a job requirement for Congress, like U.S. citizenship. The atmosphere was much like that of the 1970s except that in this case, the sins being exposed had generally taken place long before the politician in question was in office. The magnanimity with which newspaper editors had responded to pleas about Bob Dole's long-gone affair was definitely no longer the mood of the day.

Salon reported that Henry Hyde, the seventy-four-year-old chairman of the Judiciary Committee, had once conducted a long-running adulterous affair with a beautician. In Idaho, the *Statesman* got Representative Helen Chenowith to admit she had engaged in a six-year-long affair with a married rancher. Porn publisher Larry Flynt gleefully entered the fray with testimony from an ex-wife of Representative Bob Barr of Georgia, who said that Barr, a leader of the right-to-life movement, had helped her to get an abortion while they were married. Another Clinton foe, Dan Burton of Indiana, realized that *Vanity Fair* was on his trail and admitted he was the father of an illegitimate child.

Most of the stories had long been gossiped about in the legislator's home districts. The only exception was Hyde's mid-life love affair (which the congressman made the mistake of referring to as a "youthful indiscretion"). That story was passed on to the media by a Florida retiree who was a golfing buddy of the still bitter ex-husband. In every case, the publication that first exposed the long-past sins cited the hypocrisy issue as an excuse for bringing them up. The impeachment hearings were serving as a defining public event for any Republican who made a fuss about the "character" issue. And it did seem as if some politicians were courting exposure, or at least engaging in major-league self-denial. Representative Chenowith ran ads challenging her Democratic opponent to "affirm that personal conduct does count and integrity matters." When Idaho reporters, given the opening, started asking about her rumored affair with the long-married rancher, Chenowith admitted it, but pointed out that she herself had been divorced at the time.

Bob Barr, the first congressman to call for impeachment, once said that he would try to block his wife from having an abortion even if she had been raped. Yet his own second wife, Gail, had had an abortion while they were married. Barr had testified during the divorce proceedings that it was against his wishes, but during the great scandalfest of 1998, Flynt produced an affidavit from the former Mrs. Barr saying her ex-husband had driven her to the clinic and paid for the procedure. She also claimed he had been unsupportive when she came down with cancer and had carried on an affair with the woman who later became the third Mrs. Barr.

"I have, on occasion, strayed."

This was the sort of thing that ought to have caused some concern to the social conservatives who were Barr's strongest backers. (Along with everything else, it turned out that Barr had once raised a $200 donation at a Cobb County Leukemia Society luncheon by agreeing to lick whipped cream off the chests of two women.) But Barr did not seem to lose support of anti-abortion groups or the religious right. And in Indiana, the chairman of the board of the Christian Coalition said he felt Dan Burton had been "very brave" in acknowledging his illegitimate child and recommended "judge not lest ye be judged."

All the members of Congress who were caught up in the scandals of 1998 were re-elected, and none seemed to lose any of their major organizational support. Social conservatives, like most people who try to pressure government for change, have always kept a closer eye on politicians' voting records than their private behavior. Stephanopoulos had once asked Ralph Reed, the former Christian Coalition head, why Reed and his people had preferred Ronald Reagan to Jimmy Carter. Reagan, after all, was a divorced man without any strong attachment to organized religion who was known to have been a less than attentive father. Carter was a devoted family man and a born-again Christian who often spoke publicly about the importance of faith in his life. "We aren't electing a Pope," said Reed, citing Reagan's close adherence to the positions of social conservatives on issues like abortion and taxes.

One of the reasons voters failed to punish any of the exposed Republicans may have been lack of options. (The Democrat running against Burton was a felon who was disavowed by his party after he admitted impersonating a female judge.) Nevertheless, there is no evidence the voters were itching to toss out their humiliated representatives. Once again, the real punishment for exposure of sexual wrongdoing came somewhere other than at the polls. The members of Congress had to endure pain, both in personal humiliation and on behalf of their families—Burton's fifteen-year-old illegitimate son was said to be distraught when his home was suddenly surrounded by reporters. At least one representative also discovered the lesson that

Wayne Hayes and Wilbur Mills had learned in the 1970s—that one's peers can be more judgmental than the public. Robert Livingston, whom the Republicans had just chosen as their next Speaker, found out that he was the next target for smearing. He consulted his colleagues, some of whom made it clear they would toss him to the wolves if he admitted to having committed adultery. On the eve of the House impeachment debate, Livingston rose to announce that "during my thirty-three-year marriage to my wife, Bonnie, I have, on occasion, strayed" and that he was going into political exile and retirement.

7. Into the New Millenium

If the social conservatives were disappointed by the general public's reaction to Bill Clinton, they were enraged by the women. "The feminist movement needs to stand up against any man who would use women like pieces of meat, like our president has," said Linda Smith, the Republican candidate for Senate in Washington. Smith lost to the incumbent, Patricia Murray, who opposed the impeachment movement.

Polls showed that women voters had the same attitude toward their philandering president as men did—they opposed impeachment and regarded Clinton pragmatically, as a good leader but a lousy human being. That was different from their response a decade earlier, when Gary Hart's philandering became public and polls showed that it was especially disturbing to female voters. Harking back to the old concerns from the 1980s, some women had questioned whether a man who behaves like a randy teenager could be trusted with the country. Essayist Barbara Grizzuti Harrison recalled how John Kennedy had described his conquest of a stewardess as "I got into the blonde." Kennedy, she reminded readers, "got into" Vietnam, too.

Hart's disaster had come during the height of American women's fight to reverse thousands of years of tradition regarding the relations between the genders. The battle was one of enormous scope, ranging from equal pay at the workplace to equal rights to enjoy orgasms in the bedroom. Issues of law, sex, politics, and human relations were intermixed. "The personal is political," decreed Gloria Steinem memorably. It was an echo of the way turn-of-the-century heroines related the general plight of powerless women to the bad private behavior of public men. But in 1998, Steinem was one of Bill Clinton's defenders. "Welcome sexual behavior is about as relevant to sexual harassment as borrowing a car is to stealing one," she wrote. The real culprits, she said, were people like Ken Starr and Linda Tripp who were determined to force Lewinsky to go public with her private sex life.

What made the difference? For one thing, women had moved forward. For all the continued inequalities that existed, they were well on their way to equal representation in many professions and fields of business. Few of them had reached the very highest ranks at work, but they were still coming to see themselves less as potential victims and more as political players. They had less concern about the misbehavior of individual men, and more about how to use their power to shape society to their liking. Something like this—on a far more modest scale—had happened after World War I, when women were enjoying new social freedoms along with the spreading right to vote. Their concerns shifted from getting government to crack down on men to keeping government restrictions off their own backs.

Bill Clinton had been reliable in supporting the classic feminist agenda like abortion rights, but his appeal went farther. The bulk of his entire political program had been a reflection of women's concerns, from his talk about V-chips and school uniforms to his focus on maintaining the safety net of Social Security and Medicare. His approach to governing, which seemed to stress good listening skills and a readiness to compromise, also reflected the kind of politics women preferred. In 1996, women re-elected him—the gender gap was 11 percent and Bob Dole won a plurality of the male vote. It was apparently going to take more than private bad behavior to detach their support.

"The character is the person"

The Clinton-Lewinsky scandal inevitably sparked another round of debate about whether voters have any right to know about the private

274

lives of their political leaders. Most Republicans said that the impeachment effort was all about perjury, not Oval Office sex. But that standard tended to slip around a bit. "I'm scared to death of such notions that it doesn't matter what a person does in his private life. The character is the person," said Tom DeLay, the increasingly powerful House leader.

The argument had really not moved much since Gary Hart—or since the Mugwumps debated whether they wanted James Blaine, the devoted family man and crooked Congressman, or Grover Cleveland, the honest official with a love-child in his past. (DeLay would eventually be exposed as a politician very much along the Blaine line, and retire from office.) Michael Isikoff's argument that Clinton's sex life was relevant because it revealed "a pattern of troubling behavior that seemed reckless and out of control" was just like the argument of Hart's pursuers. But Hart had been a little-tested presidential candidate. Clinton had been running the country for more than six years, and apart from his sex life, he did not seem to have been reckless at all.

Chapter 11

Millennial Politics

1. The Election of 2000—All over but the Counting

"We really made an effort"

By the year 2000, the nation was so drenched in information about the private lives of politicians that gossip seemed in danger of becoming irrelevant. The whole concept, after all, is based on the idea of hidden behavior and in America the lines of privacy appeared to be vanishing. The second requirement for gossip, a set of community standards that are only broken behind closed doors, also looked like an endangered species. To many observers, the public's opposition to impeaching Bill Clinton was a sign that the rules about right and wrong had been repealed. It was, conservative writer William Bennett proclaimed, "The Death of Outrage."

Or was it? When the presidential election was over, some people would say that Al Gore lost because Americans were angry about Bill Clinton's improper behavior—not angry enough to want to see the nation turned upside down by impeachment, perhaps, but ready to reject his former vice president when the opportunity came around. Others, with equally passionate conviction, would argue that Gore had turned into just another one of those unhappy elected officials whose self-inflicted wounds were the only serious result when scandal and politics intersected. Gore was so traumatized by the Lewinsky episode, the argument went, that he was afraid to use Clinton as a surrogate and forfeited several swing states where The Great Campaigner could have made all the difference.

Going into 2000, the public was yearning for candidates with personal lives of excruciating boredom. The presidential hopefuls, for the most part, were well educated about how to tamp down firestorms of gossip. But there was still nothing to stop another eruption of scandal if the stars aligned in the right—or wrong—way. Whether they liked it or not, reporters felt obliged to track down leads on a love child here, a drug arrest there. That was particularly true in Texas, where the press corps was worried that out-of-state journalists might come into town and dig up something about Governor George W. Bush. The state's media were determined that if there was anything to be found, they would get there first. Nobody wanted the world to think they had been giving the local favorite son a slide. "We did try," said Wayne Slater of the *Dallas Morning News*. "We really made an effort."

"Prove there aren't any"

Almost every presidential campaign produces one dark-horse candidate who wins journalists' hearts simply by talking like a normal human being. In 2000, John McCain had the honors. McCain spent much of 1999 going from one New Hampshire town hall to another in his bus, the *Straight Talk Express,* holding question-and-answer sessions and hanging out with whatever reporters volunteered to ride around with him. Unlike most people who have occupied the colorful but generally unrewarding role of maverick contender, McCain actually made some headway, upsetting Bush in the New Hampshire primary. On the night of the victory the McCain campaign, giddy with optimism, flew down to South Carolina, where the next crucial balloting would take place among a conservative populace heavy with military families. McCain's campaign was banking on the theory that Carolinians would prefer their candidate, a heroic former POW, to Bush, who avoided the draft with a somewhat lethargic tour in the National Guard.

It was a faulty game plan. McCain never picked up any traction. The senator's aides were dismayed by the polls, and they felt ambushed by a subterranean hit squad of rumormongers. The stories were spread mainly by telephone, sometimes through "push polls," in which a caller claimed to be doing survey research about the election. The most infamous was a nineteenth-century classic—that the candidate was the father of an illegitimate black child. But in McCain's case the rumor was bitterly personal—he and his wife have a dark-skinned daughter, Bridget, who was adopted from a Bangladesh orphanage. "We had no idea who made the phone calls, who paid for them, or how many calls were made," wrote his campaign manager, Richard Davis, in the *Boston Globe*. "Effective and anonymous: the perfect smear campaign." Davis recalled an email that a professor at Bob Jones University sent to "fellow South Carolinians" saying that McCain "had chosen to sire children without marriage." When confronted by reporters, Davis said, the professor demanded to know if they could "prove there aren't any."

Although McCain's supporters always believed the whole thing had been organized—or at least sanctioned—by the Bush forces, no one had ever been able to prove it. And as Davis acknowledged, no one really knew whether the campaign was widespread, or simply the sporadic product of a few strange eccentrics. The entire scurrilous effort almost certainly had more effect on McCain's desperately loyal campaign staff than on the voters themselves. The mere idea that their opposition was stooping to such tactics unhinged some of McCain's aides, at least temporarily. "We started making emotional decisions based on anger," said consultant John Weaver. And in the days after the South Carolina contest ended in a decisive victory for Bush, the McCain forces appeared to have tossed out their remaining game plan as the candidate picked a principled, but utterly distracting, fight with the religious right. The *Straight Talk Express* ran off the highway and Bush marched, triumphant, to the conventions.

"Divorce expunges it"

The South Carolina attacks, while particularly sleazy, were not all that intense by the standards of modern political pile-ons. The proof they had occurred at all was mainly anecdotal, and even many of the senator's staunchest supporters will admit, if pressed, that they probably didn't affect the ultimate results. What's interesting, though, is that despite all the sniping from the far right, there was very little talk about McCain's first marriage. While McCain was a prisoner of war in Vietnam, his wife, Carol, had been involved in a near-fatal automobile accident that left her on crutches, several inches shorter than she had been before. By the time he was released, she no longer looked much like the former model he had married. The marriage continued, shakily, for several years until McCain met a beautiful twenty-five-year-old heiress from Arizona named Cindy Hensley and abruptly divorced Carol to marry her. His political career, financed by his new wife's fortune, began soon after he moved to Phoenix, where his father-in-law gave him a public relations job that allowed McCain to devote his time to making speeches around what would soon become his Congressional district.

It was very much like Bob Dole's own post-war story, and Dole's opponents never seemed to feel tempted to make a big issue about that, either. But a much less dramatic version had undermined Nelson Rockefeller's presidential chances in 1964. Given the nastiness of the South Carolina campaign, it seems surprising that the story did not come up. McCain was possibly being given a pass because it was hard to hold post-Vietnam misbehavior against a man who had suffered two broken arms, a broken leg and a crushed knee when he was shot down, endured extraordinary suffering as a POW, and had turned down a chance to be repatriated ahead of other prisoners due to his father's high rank in the Navy. When asked about his first marriage, McCain usually got a pained look on his face and said that everything that went wrong was his fault. Reporters did not usually feel like pressing. (*Time* columnist Joe Klein found himself asking McCain why he was being so hard on himself.) Another critically important reason the story did not go anywhere was that Carol McCain would not cooperate. "I'm crazy about John McCain and I love him to pieces, but I'm just not going to do any interviews," she said.

Of course, Nelson Rockefeller's former wife had not made a fuss either. It was just the fact that he had divorced his wife for another, younger, married woman that made primary voters angry and suspicious. But the world had changed a lot in the thirty-odd years since then. Divorce had become ingrained in the culture. It was not so much the proportion of marriages that wound up broken, although the rate had certainly gone up. It was that people had gotten used to it. Divorce had become accepted as a normal part of life's progression. No longer a scandal, it was now seen as the end of a mistake, a wiping clean of the domestic slate and the official onset of a new life. Whatever bad behavior went before no longer quite counted.

It was a change in the rules that had not gone unnoticed in Little Rock, Arkansas. One prominent Democrat remembers being in the governor's mansion in 1991, when Bill Clinton was sitting with some advisors, trying to plot a route to the White House through the tangle of his own personal problems. "We're saying: 'What about the rumors?'" said the Democrat, who asked not to be identified. "He's saying: 'There's nothing to them.'" Suddenly, the man recalled, Hillary Clinton spoke up. "She said: 'You know, if we divorced right now, no one would ever raise those things. Divorce expunges it. And then if we remarried before the Inauguration, it would be one of the great love stories.'"

"What I did as a child"

It's unlikely that the Bush campaign would have bought the theory that things were quieting down when it came to political gossip. The stories about the governor of Texas spanned the gamut of virtually everything short of cannibalism: love child, abortion, drugs, drink, covered-up arrests. There was also an ongoing rumor—shades of Senator Tower—that somebody had a picture of a buck-naked young

George dancing on top of a bar. (The photo, though apparently mythical, made it onto the *Tonight Show* opening monologue. "Did you hear what his excuse was today?" Jay Leno asked his audience. "He said it was casual Friday.")

George W. Bush had a good deal of experience in handling gossip explosions—it was he who had attempted to defuse rumors about his father, by telling reporters that "The answer to the Big A question is an N.O." He and his aides readily admitted that Bush had, at one point, drunk too much. But, they said, at his wife's urging he had renounced alcohol on his fortieth birthday and had, with the help of a revived Christian faith, stayed sober ever since. "When I was young and foolish I was young and foolish," Bush said. Critics pointed out that Bush's period of youthful oat-sowing was still underway when he was 39. (They snickered even more when, in response to a question about marijuana, Bush said: "I'm not going to talk about what I did as a child.") But the public seemed accepting. The idea that it is never too late to turn one's life around was one that Americans were extremely comfortable with, and the fact that Bush credited his faith for helping him succeed made it even more resonant for the social conservatives who would become his most important political base.

What worked with drinking did not necessarily work with drugs, however. Rumors that Bush had, in the past, used cocaine were racing through politically attuned communities around the country by the old-fashioned route of word of mouth. "They bounced from the Washington, D.C., party circuit to . . . (a) nonpolitical gathering on the west coast," said the *Wall Street Journal* in May of 1999. "A gossip-circuit favorite: That Mr. Bush, the top contender for the Republican presidential nomination, bought coke on a Washington street corner and was high at his father's inauguration." The paper told its readers that "even people spreading the rumors admit they have nothing to back them up."

Ever since members of the baby boom generation began running for president—and particularly since Bill Clinton made the disastrous corner-trimming argument about not having inhaled—candidates had been asked about drug use, under the theory that (1) It involved law-breaking, and (2) If they had been in college after 1965, the chances were very good that there was something to hide. Conservatives who take strong stands against recreational drug use naturally have a tougher problem answering these questions than less judgmental liberals. Al Gore had acknowledged using marijuana when he was young; the only controversy had been a minor dust-up when a former friend claimed the smoking in question had been heavy rather than sporadic. His hometown paper, the *Tennessean,* dispatched a team of reporters who interviewed forty old acquaintances of the candidate, and came up with nothing more than Gore had already admitted.

When George W. Bush ran for governor of Texas in 1994, he was asked by a reporter from the *Houston Chronicle* whether he had ever used illegal drugs. "Maybe I did, maybe I didn't. What's the relevance?" he retorted. "How I behaved as an irresponsible youth is irrelevant to the campaign." Things did not go much farther than that; perhaps because his opponent, Gov. Ann Richards, was a recovering alcoholic who had always refused to discuss the issue of illegal drug use herself. While declaring the question off limits, Bush made a stab at defining the always-tricky dividing line between a candidate's privacy and voter's right to know. His theory, according to the *Chronicle*, was that "questions about a candidate's personal life should not be raised as a campaign issue unless they deal with their fitness to hold office or reveal hypocrisy in their rhetoric. As a theoretical example of what would be relevant, Bush cited a politician who preaches morality but enjoys a hedonistic lifestyle." The hypocrisy test can be a dangerous standard for politicians. They toss it out thinking about Elmer Gantryish ministers who denounce sin from the pulpit and then seduce the Ladies Sodality president, or legislators who decry homosexuality by day and pick up teenage boys by night. But the test can just as easily be applied to someone who, say, bought and consumed cocaine as a young adult without suffering any consequences and then started advocating tougher jail sentences for drug dealers. It can, under the broadest interpretation, make any candidate who runs a campaign based on character fair game for an exposé of past bad behavior.

At any rate, Bush quickly dropped the hypocrisy standard and when he entered the presidential race, he went back to talking about the irrelevance of his foolish youth. But this time, the issue did not go away. Instead of running against a recovering alcoholic, in the primaries Bush was pitted against a field of Republicans that included several professional clean-livers. In general, they seemed rather pleased by the whole controversy. "I think it would be wrong for any possible Republican presidential nominee to refuse to say clearly and distinctly that they've not used drugs," declared Gary Bauer, the Christian conservative. The *New York Daily News* asked the twelve contenders from both parties if they had ever used cocaine and eleven of them said no. Bush did not respond.

The *Wall Street Journal* counted thirty-seven articles and editorials in newspapers or magazines that raised the drug issue "mostly noting that Mr. Bush declines to answer questions about drug use or other youthful misdeeds." What Bush did provide was an ever-expanding list of reasons for not answering. He said he was trying to elevate campaigning, which was sending "a signal to people that politics is ugly and therefore I don't want to participate." He said he was doing it for the children: "If I were you, I wouldn't tell your kids that you smoked pot unless you want them to smoke pot. I don't want some kid saying, 'Well, Governor Bush tried it.' " In the summer of 1999, Bush won one of the earliest tests of the presidential campaign season—the deeply unscientific Iowa Republican straw poll. He went back to Austin expecting a tad of triumphal welcome. Instead, his next press conference was dominated by questions about cocaine. "You know when that happens, somebody floats a rumor and it causes you to ask a question," he said with some agitation. "And that's the game in American politics and I refuse to play it. That is a game, and you just fell for the trap, and I refuse to play."

On a campaign swing through the Midwest, Bush was asked how he would respond to the questionnaire that federal employees have to fill out, which asks whether they have used illegal drugs in the previous seven years. Bush first dodged the question—his aides said he had not understood it. But he came back to it later, saying he was happy to tell the reporters that if he *were* answering such a questionnaire, his response would be "No." It seemed like a good way to reaffirm the campaign's reckless-youth bottom line. Then on second look, things seemed less satisfactory. Bush was in effect vouching that he had not used cocaine since he was in his mid-forties, which gave the impression that there was something to hide in the fairly recent past. The candidate then volunteered that he could have passed the same test when his father was sworn into office in 1989. And, his aides pointed out later, back then the window of vulnerability was fifteen years, not seven.

It was now a high-stakes game of Twenty Questions. Before the fortieth-birthday-reformation? Before your marriage? In your thirties? At Yale? Bush, who had been vigorously arguing that this stuff was nobody's business, now claimed that he had provided all these new hints because "It was a relevant question about how I would handle background checks if I were president." The whole episode actually turned out to be a very handy way for the candidate to send out a clear but coded message to any voter who cared: Bush had used drugs of some kind in his twenties but not later. And the campaign was adamant about not saying explicitly what had been implied with such specificity. It seemed as if he was insisting on an almost meaningless distinction—between a clearly spoken admission of long-ago drug use and a carefully contrived series of markers that only made sense if the drug use had indeed occurred. But he and his campaign understood voter psychology very well. Refusing to confirm that he had once used drugs was, for Bush, a tacit show of respect for the large number of Americans who regarded even experimentation with marijuana as a dangerous and sinful thing. These people wanted to feel sure that a candidate supported their position, and shared their overall view of things, even if the price was a good deal of hypocrisy. What he *said* really was in many ways more important than what he had *done*.

> "*It was before he was married. It was before he had children.*"

Getting caught under an embarrassing spotlight had become almost a rite of passage in a national campaign. Even Gary Bauer had a turn during the 2000 primaries, when two former aides announced they had resigned to protest the candidate's "inappropriate" behavior with his female deputy campaign manager. The aides did not claim Bauer had had an affair—they charged he was guilty of holding private meetings with a woman not his wife. "As a pro-family and pro-life leader, Gary is held to a higher standard. Meeting hour after hour alone, as a married man, candidate and as a pro-family pro-life leader, he had no business creating that kind of appearance of impropriety," Charles Jarvis, the former campaign chairman, told the *Washington Post*.

It was hardly a major news event. For Bauer's campaign, a good primary night was one in which the candidate got a full percentage point of the vote and his most high-profile moment may have been when he fell off the platform during a pancake-flipping demonstration in New Hampshire. (CNN reported that Bauer seemed "strangely energized" by the mishap.) But the inappropriate meetings crisis does point to an important political fact about the United States at the edge of the 21st century. When it came to moral values, there was very little national consensus. Some voters didn't want a president who met alone with female staff members. Some didn't care if the chief executive had sex with an intern in the Oval Office as long as he performed his day job well. Some parts of the country had no problem with homosexual politicians; other parts could overlook clearly racist remarks by their elected representative. There was probably no single congressional district that would tolerate both.

As a result, in millennial politics, the issue became not the sin, but the cover-up—the hypocrisy, the deception. Americans had no universal view of what kinds of behavior were wholesome, permissible or just plain wrong. One of the few things—short of murder—that everyone agreed about was that lying was bad. So most misdeeds wound up being put in the context of some larger pattern of denial. "The issue is not smoking dope but the measure of a man who would browbeat a friend into covering up," said John Warnecke, a former friend of Al Gore's. (Warnecke created a minor stir during Gore's first presidential campaign in 1987, when he retracted earlier descriptions of Gore as an occasional user of marijuana after his return from Vietnam. He and Gore had smoked grass *hundreds* of times, Warnecke claimed, and he now needed to clarify the record as part of his own psychiatric rehabilitation.)

Bush had labored heroically to avoid getting caught in any lies about his past while also avoiding any confessions that would offend his Christian conservative base. But then at the very end of the campaign, two television stations in Maine produced evidence that he had been convicted of driving while under the influence of alcohol twenty-four years earlier. The candidate called the revelation "dirty politics" and said he had never mentioned the incident because he didn't want to serve as a bad role model for his two daughters. It was an excuse that inspired the press corps—pleased to have the seemingly endless and rather dull campaign take such an interesting turn so late in the game—to ask whether Bush felt Bill Clinton would have been right in concealing the truth about Monica Lewinsky in order to shield Chelsea.

The fact that a fifty-four-year-old presidential candidate had pleaded guilty to a misdemeanor driving charge nearly a quarter of a century before hardly seemed earthshaking. But Bush had also broken the prime directive on handling questions about private misbehavior: he had specifically denied it, and gotten caught in a lie. Wayne Slater of the *Dallas Morning News* had asked Bush in 1998 whether he had ever been arrested after his college days, when he was picked up for disorderly conduct after stealing a hotel Christmas wreath as a fraternity prank. Bush said no, but Slater said he seemed prepared to add more information when they were interrupted by Karen Hughes, the press secretary. When Slater tried to follow up, he was put off.

After the arrest record was made public, the presidential campaign plane was the scene of one of those complicated back-and-forths between Hughes and the reporters in which the press secretary denied Bush had ever lied and claimed, under questioning, that a DUI conviction when he was thirty could be counted among his "mistakes as a youth" because "It was before he was married. It was before he had children." The story did not go much farther. But some of the central players on both sides believed that, in the end, it made a difference. Gore strategists argued that the DUI story had been enough to tip undecided voters to Gore, who won the popular vote by more than

500,000 ballots. Until it broke "all our internal polls showed it was literally a dead heat," said Chris Lehane, Gore's press secretary. Bush's political strategist, Karl Rove, believed Christian conservatives decided to stay home rather than make a commitment at the polls to a man who suddenly appeared to be morally lax and slightly dishonest. If either one of them is right, George Bush would be one of the relatively few prominent politicians in history whose electoral success was significantly altered by an issue of personal behavior. The sting must have been ameliorated by the fact that he got to be president anyway.

What the country took away from the 2000 campaign was the new perception that the nation was divided down the middle, into what were designated blue and red camps in honor of the color codes on the election maps during the mesmerizing election-night coverage of the vote count. And Bush's near-disaster convinced the new administration that it needed to be much, much more attentive to what's known as the Christian right, a very critical and extremely judgmental segment of the voting population. Perhaps that's part of the reason the Bush administration wound up being much more conservative than many people had expected.

2. Outing for Fun and Profit

"Apparently not news to many of his colleagues"

The old lethal nineteenth-century gossip about "Negro blood" had been replaced by rumors of homosexuality. It was talk that had less to do with moral corruption than with defining someone as an outsider—the Other. But as large swathes of the country became accepting, or at least used to, the presence of gay men and women in public life, gossip about who was gay took some unexpected turns. It was, for one thing, generally not harmful to the politician who got talked about as long as the talk remained just that. Some extremely conservative cities, congressional districts and states had elected officials who were widely whispered about in private conversation—or blabbed about on the Internet—as homosexual, but their constituents seemed happy to ignore the gossip, in much the same way that social conservatives were willing to ignore George W. Bush's verbal gymnastics about drug use as long as he did not specifically acknowledge it. The "don't ask, don't tell" policy that Bill Clinton instituted for gays in the military may not have been a profile in executive courage, but it was a very close reflection of red-state American attitudes at the turn of the new century.

While the willingness not to ask seemed virtually universal among American voters, there did not seem to be any great desire to elect people who had already told. By 2000, only one openly gay politician had gone before the voters as a non-incumbent and gotten elected to Congress—Tammy Baldwin, a Democrat whose Madison, Wisconsin-based district was unusually liberal on social issues. On the other hand, the electorate generally seemed willing to stick by lawmakers who came out of the closet after they were already in office. It was if, having already gotten to know them in a different context, the public was able to see beyond their sexual orientation. Rep. Gerry Studds (D-Mass) came out in 1983, in what the *Washington Post* said was "apparently not news to many of his constituents" and became the first openly gay member of Congress. It was not exactly a voluntary admission. At the time, Studds had been named in a scandal involving House members having sex, some years in the past, with Congressional pages. Studds was re-elected five times after the incident. (A male House member who was accused of having an affair with a seventeen-year-old female page, Republican Daniel Crane of Illinois, lost his re-election bid. "This is a very, very conservative area," said the Republican chairman of Crane's district. "Something like this would have a drastic effect on anybody . . . people don't approve of this at all.")

Voters in Massachusetts first elected Barney Frank when his sexuality was widely speculated about but never discussed in public. Later, they took his decision to come out as a gay man in stride. They also re-elected him with nearly two-thirds of the vote after he got involved in a messy scandal with a former lover-turned employee who was freelancing by running a male prostitution ring out of Frank's Washington apartment. Steve Gobie, the ex-lover, attempted to sell his story for cash, then claimed to the *Washington Post* that he wanted to go public in order "to show up people in positions of power who abuse other people."

"Painful truths are sometimes understood but unspoken"

Another incumbent, Republican Jim Kolbe, had been serving as representative from a Tucson, Arizona, district for a decade before, in 1996, he decided to reveal to his constituents that he was gay. Almost everyone who knew him had tacitly understood the truth about his sexuality for some time, but no one, including his relatives, ever actually mentioned it. "In a loving, boisterous, but ultimately very private family like ours, painful truths are sometimes understood but unspoken," wrote his brother John, a columnist for the *Phoenix Gazette*. Once his sexual orientation was made public, Kolbe easily survived a re-election campaign despite a few nasty moments—opponents put up posters declaring that he had AIDS. Coming out publicly, he said, was a great relief. But it wasn't voluntary. He was being threatened with exposure by activists who were angry about his vote in favor of a bill to ban federal recognition of same-sex marriage. Jeff Yarbrough, the editor of the gay magazine *The Advocate*, told the Associated Press that it was hypocritical of Kolbe to vote against the bill while living a "semi-open homosexual life" in Washington.

It was a sign of a new and counter-intuitive period in the history of this sort of gossip. Social conservatives seemed, on the whole, indifferent to the question of who was gay in Congress—as long as those matters were kept quiet. It was gay activists and their allies who sometimes exposed, or threatened to expose, lawmakers who wanted their sexual preferences kept secret. The impetus was usually some piece of anti-gay legislation, like the Defense of Marriage Act. But not always. When Sen. James Inhofe, a conservative Oklahoma Republican, told a hometown paper that he would not hire a gay staffer, blogACTIVE, a Web site that made something of a specialty of outing politicians, revealed the name and Congressional phone number of a gay man who worked on Inhofe's committee and urged its readers to call the staffer "and tell him what YOU think of gay men working for right wing homophobes." Steve Gunderson, a Republican who represented a socially conservative district in Wisconsin's dairy country, was outed by members of the radical group ACT UP, who confronted him in gay bars in Washington and then issued press releases about the incidents. Gunderson, who had been a member of the Republican leadership, was supportive of gay rights legislation and lived openly in Washington with his partner, an architect. "Everybody who knew us personally was aware that I was gay. Yet because I didn't stand up in Congress and announce my homosexuality, ACT UP saw me as a hypocritical closet case," he wrote later. In 1994 Gunderson was attacked from the other side, and outed on the floor of the House by Bob Dornan, the Paleolithic representative from California who told his colleagues that Gunderson "has a revolving door on his closet." Dornan later complained to the *Milwaukee Sentinel:* "We've got a homo in the midst of the Republican party" who people like him had "a moral obligation to expose." Gunderson was re-elected anyway.

"I'm not going to be dragged into the gutter"

In 2003, a group of gay journalists in Fort Lauderdale sponsored a panel discussion on the ethics of outing elected officials. Much of the talk centered on Representative Mark Foley. A South Florida Republican, Foley had been outed by the gay press nearly a decade earlier over his vote on the Defense of Marriage Act. But instead of acknowledging his sexuality, Foley changed his position on legislation relating to gay rights. Freed from the hypocrisy issue, he continued to lead his double life, showing up for social events with an eligible woman while living with his long-time male partner in private. "I'm not going to be dragged into the gutter by these rumor mongers," he said when asked directly whether he was gay.

It was a comment that certainly offended many gay Floridians, but Foley's socially conservative constituents seemed willing to accept his protestations the same way they accepted George W. Bush's coded discussion of past drug use. By refusing to acknowledge he was gay, and denouncing the people who tried to out him, Foley was clearly placing himself on the side of those who believed there was something shameful or unwholesome about homosexuality. To conservative voters, that was far more important than whatever he did in his private life.

Three years later, of course, Foley's sex life became a central issue in the 2006 Congressional elections after it was disclosed that he had sent sexually explicit e-mails to young men who had worked as Congressional pages. Foley resigned, but the Republican leadership was dogged with charges that they had tried to cover up or ignore Foley's behavior. Kirk Fordham, Foley's former aide, said he had warned the office of the Speaker of the House about his boss three years earlier. The talk in the Capitol was that Fordham had acted after the House clerk, who was in charge of the pages, had reported that Foley, possibly intoxicated, had tried to enter the pages' dormitory after hours.

Some commentators argued that the media was at fault in having failed to make it clear to the voters that Foley was lying about his sexuality. If the congressman had been clearly tagged as gay, even the early less-than-sinister signs of trouble, like "over-friendly" e-mails to pages, would have set off warning bells. That made little sense, since everyone in a position to do anything was well aware of Foley's secret life. Edward Wasserman, a professor of journalism ethics at Washington and Lee University who had participated in that panel on outing politicians, decided in retrospect that the story should have been told because it was the only way voters could make any sense of their congressman's behavior. Foley's shifting positions on gay rights issues, and his simultaneous leap to please his conservative constituents with strange crusades like a war against a Florida nudist colony were all connected to his struggle to keep a central fact about his life secret, Wasserman contended. "Foley's public actions were unintelligible unless you knew this backstory. And in failing to tell it, the media failed the public and endorsed a principle of timidity that's sure to fail the public in the future as well," he wrote in the Miami Herald.

It was, at any rate, quite a saga to be unraveling a month before a hard-fought Congressional election. Worried Republicans quickly reminded the media of the Gerry Studds story. And of course, they spun desperately, a White House intern was only one step up from a page, and everybody knew what had happened. . . .

It was indeed true that there was very little new under the sun when it came to sexual misbehavior in Washington. But the Foley story really did break new ground. No one following it could help notice how many of the Republican staffers were gay, including Fordham and the clerk of the House who warned him about Foley's late night rambles.

It was not that the gay staff members had tried to shield Foley. If there were any enablers, they were the heterosexual leaders who were too uncomfortable or too worried about a possible political embarrassment to take action. But the scandal let the general public in on a fact that had been clear to people inside Congress for a long time: Despite the Republican willingness to use opposition to gay marriage as a way to rally conservative voters at election time, many of the talented and hard-working staff members laboring for that party were gay. What was even more startling was how many gay men worked for legislators who seemed downright homophobic. Fordham was gay, and among his past bosses was Senator Inhofe, the man who had vowed never to employ a homosexual. Senator Rick Santorum, who once decried same-sex marriage in a way that appeared to equate it with bestiality, had a gay staff member handling communications. Brian Bennett, who was a gay political consultant at the time of the Foley scandal, had once worked as chief of staff to *Bob Dornan,* for heaven's sake.

For some conservatives, the message was simply that the Other was everywhere. "The secret Capitol Hill homosexual network must be dismantled," said a spokesman for one right-wing group, Accuracy in Media. To others, it seemed to unmask an enormous hypocrisy on the part of Republicans. Another analysis was that the don't-ask-don't-tell coda—which looked like a kind of muted tolerance when it came to the voters—had become a bizarre state of denial on the part of an entire political leadership, something that, as Frank Rich wrote in the *New York Times,* "isn't just hypocrisy; it's pathology."

"I can't believe they're bringing that old thing up again"

The strangest turn-of-the-millenium story about a gay politician was surely that of James McGreevey, the governor of New Jersey. Speculation about McGreevey's sex life had been going on quietly when he was a suburban mayor, then an almost-giant killer who came surprisingly close to toppling Gov. Christie Whitman in 1997. In 2000, when he was very clearly angling for a second try at the governor's mansion, McGreevey, who was preparing to get married for the second time, asked one of his political supporters to sponsor a work visa for a young Israeli named Golan Cipel. When he arrived in the United States, Cipel was given a job handling Jewish outreach for McGreevey's campaign. David Twersky, the former editor of the *New Jersey Jewish News*, found the whole thing peculiar. "Golan didn't really know New Jersey Jews. It didn't make sense," Twersky later told the *Newark Star-Ledger*. Of such matters is gossip born. But the talk absolutely exploded when McGreevey named Cipel the state homeland security adviser. It was not long after the terrorist attack on the World Trade Center, which took the lives of many of McGreevey's constituents, and Cipel, who had no experience in security issues, could not even be granted a security clearance because he was not an American citizen.

"People would say in barroom conversations: 'Hey, McGreevey—I hear he's gay," said Terry Golway, a former political columnist and editorial writer from New Jersey. "I can't tell you how many times people said that to me. Men and women in the street just sort of brought it up." In Trenton, state legislators cornered members of McGreevey's administration, demanding to know if the governor and the homeland security adviser were lovers. McGreevey's public relations advisor decreed that Cipel had to go. "This is about you and Golan being gay," Twersky said he told the governor. "That old thing? I can't believe they're bringing up that old thing again," McGreevey retorted.

But after only a few months, Cipel was transferred to a less high profile job, and by summer he was gone entirely. It would have been interesting to see what happened next if he had simply disappeared from the scene, and the voters of New Jersey went back to the polls in 2005 to decide whether to re-elect a governor whose sexuality was being talked about by everyone from the state senators to the clerk at the local 7-11. American history suggests that if the object of the governor's affection had not been turned into the homeland security advisor the gossip would not have made all that much difference. But

Cipel had been given the job, and Cipel did not go away. In the summer of 2004, he hired an attorney and threatened to file a lawsuit against McGreevey for sexual harassment. Instead, the governor called a press conference, announced he was gay, and resigned.

Addendum

In 2005, New Jersey elected a new governor, in a race between Democratic Senator Jon Corzine and Republican Douglas Forrester. During the campaign it was revealed that Corzine, who was by then divorced, had had an affair with a woman who was an official in a state public employees' union while he was still married. Corzine's former wife opted not to suffer in silence and told *The New York Times* she believed her husband "let his family down and he'll probably let New Jersey down, too." Forrester ran the comment in commercials 24/7 during the runup to what was predicted to be a rapidly narrowing election. Corzine won by 10 percentage points.

3. The War on Terror

"It's just a different time"

In the presidential campaign of 2004, national security was uppermost in everyone's mind. And it expressed itself even in the ways people gossiped. Questions of sexual misbehavior or drug use—and often even the debate over taxes and education—gave way to the very peculiar issue of the candidates' military records in a war that had been over for nearly thirty years.

Both John Kerry and George W. Bush were charged with having shameful secrets. In Bush's case, it was a story that had been chewed over pretty thoroughly in the 2000 campaign, when critics scrambled to prove that he had either pulled strings to keep out of the war, or failed to fulfill his duties to the National Guard while avoiding punishment thanks to his father's influence. Kerry's case was newer and more dramatic—allegations that he had hyped stories about his performance under fire in Vietnam to paint as heroic what was unremarkable or even cowardly behavior.

The attacks on Kerry were well orchestrated. But they had their roots in spontaneous talk by men who had served with him in Vietnam and were later angered by his prominent role in the anti-war movement—particularly the fact that he had denounced widespread "atrocities" committed by American troops. (A few of the central critics also seemed to have a much more recent grievance, in the form of unflattering comments Mr. Kerry made about them to the author of a book about his war exploits.) Kerry's promotion of his war record—beginning with the heavy-handed "reporting for duty" speech at the Democratic convention—undoubtedly seemed like boasting to some people who had also been in combat, and felt they had been demeaned by his anti-war statements. In cases like this, it's not unusual for detractors to start suggesting that there's less to the war hero than meets the eye. And unlike run-of-the-mill gossips, the men who would dub themselves the Swift Boat Veterans for Truth had well-heeled angels who were willing to underwrite a public campaign against Kerry. Texas Republicans donated whatever it took to get the Swift Boat Veterans' campaign started, and the men later made money off a bestselling book providing their contrarian view of Kerry's war record, "Unfit for Command."

It highlighted one of the biggest changes in modern politics. Politicians had been dogged by semi-obsessive critics who were out to expose what they saw as the true story of the great man's failings since the time of Thomas Jefferson. But in the past, they didn't have access to large sums of money to get their point across. (Remember Professor Chancellor, peddling his Warren Harding "family tree" door-to-door across Ohio.) However, by the 1990s, billionaires and near-billionaires like Richard Mellon Scaife, who bankrolled investigations into Clinton's financial and sexual activities in Arkansas, were willing to put their money into the seamier side of political campaigning. (The willingness to pay for that kind of sliming wasn't necessarily confined to right-wing Republicans. In 1999, former Clinton aide Lanny Davis addressed a group of big Democratic contributors who pressed him for gossip about George W. Bush. Davis, who didn't really have any specific stories, asked them whether if he *did* have some dirt—something that didn't reflect on Bush's ability to govern but which might hurt his chances of winning the election—would they ante up to put commercials on television to broadcast it? Hands went up all over the room.)

"What's Kerry got to hide?"

Kerry's supporters believed his war record—he won a Silver Star, a Bronze Star and three Purple Hearts—would set him apart in an age of international terror, not only from the other Democrats but from George Bush and his wishy-washy service in the National Guard. But, strangely enough, as much as Americans admire war heroes, they do not seem to give many points for military exploits when they vote, or punish politicians who had gone out of their way to avoid service. Perhaps the attitude is a residue of the Vietnam era, when a great many otherwise conservative American families plotted energetically to keep their sons away from the war. Even more likely, it was another example of the transactional nature of American voting, in which candidates were rewarded for what they seemed likely to do as president rather than what they were. And when it came to Vietnam, those who fought in the war and those who supported it seemed to prefer the men who had dodged combat but endorsed the *idea* to those like Kerry who had risked their lives in service but later denounced the whole enterprise.

Voters of almost every stripe seemed indifferent to the actual military record of their candidates. The country chose Bill Clinton over the first George Bush, who had been a navy combat pilot in World War II, and then over Bob Dole, whose mangled hand bore testimony to his war injuries. Later, as we've seen, even Republicans in the heavily military state of South Carolina preferred George W. Bush of the National Guard over John McCain, the prisoner of war. McCain himself had supported Sen. Phil Gramm, who had piled up multiple deferments during the Vietnam era, over Bob Dole in the 1996 Republican presidential primary.

Instead of boosting his candidacy, the stress on Kerry's war record derailed it. The Swift Boat Veterans' allegations that he was not really a hero after all rocked the campaign, distracted its staff and threw the candidate off-balance during the critical weeks after the nominating convention. The charges included claims that Kerry's rescue of a fellow crewman who had been blown into the water by an explosion was not a brave action taken under heavy fire, but just a matter of fishing someone out of the drink while no one was shooting at all. Rather than rushing a nest of Vietcong gunners, the Swift Boaters said Kerry had simply shot down one half-naked, wounded teenager. They claimed he had hyped his performance when reporting the incidents in order to pile up commendations. Almost all the fights boiled down to thirty-year-old memories of men whose vision of their war experiences had become set in concrete decades earlier. And on every important matter, the men who had actually served with Kerry supported his version against the recollections of men who had been on other boats at the time of the incidents under dispute.

But the sense that there was *something out there* was fed by the bloggers. The Internet was playing a far more significant role in the 2004 election than it ever had before, and many of the sites became serious, established sources of information—though virtually none made any effort at bipartisan evenhandedness. The Web was for the true believers of both political camps and all factions between. Most of the bloggers made no attempt to verify information they posted the way traditional journalists did. Many felt it was not their responsibility; those who cared about accuracy believed in the self-correcting nature of the Internet, where superior information would simply cancel out what had gone before. Since so many popular sites were run by identifiable figures, the Web lost some of the anonymity that had given it such a weird and unreliable tone during earlier campaigns. But there was still a vast arena for irresponsibility, since the bloggers were not legally liable for the information that their fans posted.

One of the great themes of Kerry's critics was that if the candidate had nothing to hide, he would have signed a Standard Form 180, authorizing public access to his military records. Kerry had said that he would do so, but he never did. One blogger ran an SF-180 countdown clock. The Swift Boat Veterans posted the form on their Web site.

"What's Kerry got to hide?" demanded Jerome Corsi, a co-author of the Swift Boat Veterans' anti-Kerry book. "By not releasing these files, he is creating the impression that there is something there he doesn't want anybody to see. What is it?"

Among the people wondering the same thing were many members of Kerry's own staff, who were constantly fielding questions from the press about one bizarre allegation after another. That he had shot a man in the back. That he had shot himself in order to win a Purple Heart. That he was concealing a case of syphilis. Every new question seemed to require that the candidate retrieve a new document from the Navy, which the staff then posted on the Kerry Web site. It was an endless, confusing process. "We put out the records he gave to us," said Stephanie Cutter, who served as Kerry's spokeswoman during the campaign. When reporters asked why the candidate didn't simply sign the 180 form so they could check the files themselves, "there was no good answer," Cutter said. "It was frustrating."

It was that classic campaign experience we've seen over and over again. A candidate under attack for some alleged character flaw or secret sin. The staff scrambling to answer, but unsure of exactly what the truth is, or what new revelation might be lurking around the corner. The experience was probably not much different from the one George Stephanopoulos and the Clinton campaign staffers had, speculating among themselves about Gennifer Flowers, or all the other miserable aides throughout history who fought to defend their bosses against rumors they were afraid might be at least partly true. American politicians are particularly loath, it seems, to share personal information with the people appointed to speak in their name.

The story had a peculiar ending. Something about losing the election seemed to energize Kerry to defend himself far more vigorously than he had when it mattered most. In May of 2005, he did sign Form 180 and authorized the Navy to send an undeleted copy of his complete record to the *Boston Globe*. There was no smoking gun. What there was, in fact, were commendations from some of the same Navy officers who had attacked him during the campaign. The only piece of information that seemed to cast the least bit of negative light on Kerry was his college transcript. Kerry, who had been universally viewed as the intellectual in the race, had attended Yale at about the same time as George W. Bush and it turned out that he had gotten an almost identical grade average—76, or a mid-C. He had gotten more Ds than Bush, including some in history and political science.

Was it possible that Kerry had endured all that flack and destabilized his campaign out of embarrassment about his college grades? "If there is anything else in there, it hasn't been discovered," shrugged Cutter.

"The Net is like print, not like dinner"

One of the few non-military eruptions of gossip in 2004 began in early February, as John Kerry was dispatching Howard Dean and the other Democratic challengers. Matt Drudge, whose Web site had been the staging ground for Republican rumors for two presidential election cycles, reported that "a woman who recently fled the country, reportedly at the prodding of Kerry" was at the center of a budding scandal being investigated by all the arms of the mainstream media. "A close friend of the woman first approached a reporter late last year claiming fantastic stories—stories that now threaten to turn the race for the presidency on its head!" Drudge announced.

The mystery woman in question was an aspiring young journalist named Alexandra Polier, who had recently moved to Kenya to be with her fiancé. Once her name was introduced by a British tabloid, she found that when she Googled herself, she got more than 1,000 hits. "One site, screwthegovernment.com, had a photo page set up with a naked picture supposed to be of me," she said. Polier, who was very attractive and clearly a good networker, later wrote the story of her fifteen minutes of fame for *New York* magazine. She said that she had introduced herself to Kerry at a cocktail party, and that the candidate had then sent her a free ticket to a fundraiser in New York, where he invited her to join him, his finance director, Peter Maroney, and some others for dinner. "I was surprised to be invited and flattered when I was seated between Peter and the senator," she wrote. "I hoped it was my wit and enthusiasm, not my blonde hair and long legs, that got me a seat at the table."

That may have been a bit overoptimistic, but Polier said that it was Maroney, not Kerry, who began asking her out. The rumors about her and the senator, she said flatly and consistently, were totally false.

Later, when Polier returned to the United States, she attempted to find out exactly how the rumor had gotten started. David Frum, a former Bush speechwriter who wrote about the rumors on the *National Review* Web site, told her that he had "read it in the paper. I heard it gossiped about, but I didn't do anything like reporting. I joked about it on the Internet in a way I would at dinner. Then I learned the Net is like print, not like dinner."

In the end, Polier discovered the story began with one of her oldest friends, who had been present when Polier called Kerry's office and got a very prompt call-back from the Senator. "And I thought *How amazing* and I got excited and I told friends about it," the woman confessed, breaking into tears. The tale made its first transition from dinner party gossip to the printed word on an unheralded Web site, Watchblog.com, in which a poster identified as Son of Liberty announced that Kerry's affair with "a twenty-year-old woman" was about to be revealed in *Time*. Son of Liberty, Polier later determined, was a twenty-five-year-old Atlantan named Stephen VanDyke. VanDyke told her that he wanted to be another James Callender and do to Kerry what Callender had done to Jefferson and Hamilton. "What I tried to break," he told Polier, "was that the rumor did exist. I didn't know whether it was true or not. I know now it's not."

Addendum

This seems like the right place to leave the story—with a young blogger who wants to be like the guy who tried to take down Thomas Jefferson. Once again, the country is full of ambitious political junkies whose writings just won't pay the rent; this time in the form of bloggers hoping lightning will strike in the form of national fame and a book contract. For all the worries about terrorism, the impulse to speculate about elected officials' private behavior seems to be strong as ever in the new millenium. When George Bush's second term hit the skids, stories that he was drinking again surfaced immediately. (*The National*

Enquirer, citing anonymous "family sources," claimed the disaster of Hurricane Katrina had the president hitting the bottle while his horrified wife yelled "Stop, George!") Hillary Clinton's rise to presidential candidate was quickly followed by speculation about whether her husband was seeing other women, along with the ever-popular hints that she was a lesbian. ("The Truth About Hillary," a popular screed against the New York senator, written by Edward Klein in 2005, contained more than a dozen less-than-subtle suggestions.) Movie stars continued to have far more power to keep their private lives private and control their public images than politicians did—although Tom Cruise and Mel Gibson demonstrated that some of them weren't making use of their advantages. Politicians continued to be willing to do almost anything to get attention, exposing themselves to ridicule in ways that their predecessors would have found shocking, or possibly insane.

If the last few decades have taught us anything about the American electorate, it's that voters put very little stock in questions of politicians' private misbehavior—even in times when "family values" are campaign watchwords. When it came to Congress, at least, conservative voters were mainly concerned that their representatives support their agenda, and vote to ban abortion or gay marriage. If, in the process, a legislator secretly arranged to have an inconvenient pregnancy terminated in his own family, or lived quietly and comfortably with a gay lover after work, all they asked was that they not be told the details. Even when it came to the presidency, most people were far more interested in effectiveness than good behavior behind closed doors. All the magic words that pollsters and the media toss around during an election season—"leadership," "values," "character"—seemed to boil down, in the end, to public performance. (In May of 2006, a CNN poll found that when asked which of the two most recent presidents was more honest, 46 percent picked Bill Clinton and 42 percent picked George Bush.) The scorpion tongues of political gossip have the power to sting a target's heart, but they're unlikely to be fatal to anyone who looks capable of getting the job done.

Bibliography

Interview

The chapters about the World War II era and beyond are based in part on the memories of journalists, politicians, and other witnesses who helped me with this book. I've also included some of my own observations from the presidential campaigns of 1988 and beyond, which I covered, in various capacities, for the New York Daily News, New York Newsday, and The New York Times. The sections about Bill Clinton's 1992 campaign are based mainly on my own notes.

A list of people who generously helped me by confirming facts, offering anecdotes, or advising me on historical issues is included at the end of this book. The following people agreed to longer interviews, in which they described events they had been part of or witness to. The numbers in parentheses refer to the chapters in which their information was used:

Russell Baker, columnist, *New York Times* (1,7,8)
Joel Connelly, national correspondent, *Seattle Post-Intelligencer* (10)
Stephanie Cutter
Bob Donovan, retired Washington bureau chief, *Los Angeles Times* (6,7,8)
Charles Fontenay, former political reporter, *Nashville Tennessean* (7)
Austin Fox, Buffalo historian (4)
Representative Barney Frank of Massachusetts (9,10)

Bibliography

Max Frankel, columnist and former executive editor, *New York Times* (8)

Robert Gogerty, Seattle political consultant (10)

Tevry Golway, *New York Times*

Rebecca Hale, press secretary to Seattle mayor Norman Rice (10)

Morton Halperin, senior vice-president, the Twentieth Century Fund and former National Security Council staff member (9)

Michael Harrison, editor, *Talkers* magazine (11)

Steve Hess, Brookings Institution (7)

Murray Kempton, the late newspaper columnist and author (1,5,6,7,8)

Ed Kosner, writer and former editor, *Esquire* (8,9)

Chris Lehane

Senator Joseph Lieberman of Connecticut (9, 11)

Jay Malcynsky, managing partner, Gaffney, Bennett & Associates, and former aide to the late Congressman Stewart McKinney (9)

Margaret Marquez, Hyde Park, New York, town historian (6)

George McGovern, former South Dakota senator and presidential candidate (8)

Lars-Erik Nelson, columnist, New York *Daily News* (1,10,11)

Tom Oliphant, columnist, *The Boston Globe* (9)

Rex Reed, writer and critic (8)

Warren Rogers, former Washington correspondent, *New York Herald Tribune* (7,8)

Wayne Slator, *Dallas Morning News*

Liz Smith, syndicated columnist (6,7,8,9)

Helen Thomas, UPI White House bureau chief (7,8,9)

John Weaver

Chapter 1

Bartlett, Irving. *Daniel Webster*. New York: Norton, 1978.

Bok, Sissela. *Secrets*. New York: Oxford University Press, 1984.

Boller, Paul. *Presidential Campaigns*. New York: Oxford University Press, 1984.

Bowra, C. M. *Periclean Athens*. London: Weidenfeld & Nicolson, 1971.

Dunbar, Robin. *Grooming, Gossip and the Evolution of Language*. Cambridge: Harvard University Press, 1996.

Garment, Suzanne. *Scandal*. New York: Random House, 1991.

Leonard, Thomas C. *The Power of the Press*. New York: Oxford University Press, 1980.

Marbut, F. B. *News from the Capital*. Carbondale: Southern Illinois University Press, 1971.

McGerr, Michael. *The Decline of Popular Parties*. New York: Oxford University Press, 1986.

Moore, Barrington. *Privacy, Studies in Social and Cultural History*. New York: Sharpe, 1984.

Bibliography

Mott, Frank Luther. *American Journalism, a History: 1690–1960*. New York: Macmillan, 1962.

Nunnelley, William. *Bull Connor*. Tuscaloosa: University of Alabama Press, 1991.

Ritchie, Donald. *Press Gallery—Congress and the Washington Correspondents*. Cambridge: Harvard University Press, 1991.

Rotabaugh, W. J. *The Alcoholic Republic*. New York: Oxford University Press, 1979.

Russell, Francis. *The Shadow of Blooming Grove*. New York: McGraw-Hill, 1968.

Sabini, John, and Maury Silver. *Moralities of Everyday Life*. New York: Oxford University Press, 1982.

Schickel, Richard. *Intimate Strangers: The Culture of Celebrity*. Garden City, N.Y.: Doubleday, 1985.

Schlesinger, Arthur, Jr., ed. *A History of American Life*. New York: Scribner's, 1996.

Schudson, Michael. *Discovering the News—A Social History of American Newspapers*. New York: Basic Books, 1978.

Spacks, Patricia Ann. *Gossip*. New York: Knopf, 1985.

Summers, Mark Wahlgren. *The Press Gang*. Chapel Hill: University of North Carolina Press, 1994.

Tebbutt, Melanie. *Women's Talk?* London: Scholar Press, 1995.

Trefousse, Hans. *Andrew Johnson, a Biography*. New York: Norton, 1989.

White, William Allen. *Masks in a Pageant*. New York: Macmillan, 1928.

Wilcoxon, George Dent. *Athens Ascendant*. Ames: Iowa State University Press, 1979. *Birmingham News*, Jan. 4–6, 1952.

Chapter 2

The Founding Fathers

Anthony, Carl Sferrazza. *First Ladies*. New York: Quill, 1990.

Brodie, Fawn. *Thomas Jefferson, an Intimate Biography*. New York: Norton, 1974.

Brown, Walt. *John Adams and the American Press*. Jefferson, N.C.: MrFarland, 1995.

Bryant, William Cullen. *The Embargo*. Gainesville, Fla: Scholars' Facsimiles & Reprints, 1955.

Coyle, David. *Ordeal of the Presidency*. Washington, D.C.: Public Affairs Press, 1960.

Durey, Michael. *With the Hammer of Truth: James Thomson Callendar and America's Early National Heroes*. Charlottesville: University Press of Virginia, 1990.

Gordon-Reed, Annette. *Thomas Jefferson and Sally Hemings: An American Controversy*. Charlottesville: University Press of Virginia, 1997.

Gould, Lewis, ed. *American First Ladies*. New York: Garland, 1996.

Hendrickson, Robert. *The Rise and Fall of Alexander Hamilton*. New York: Van Nostrand Reinhold Co., 1981.

Lebergott, Stanley. *Manpower in Economic Growth: The American Record Since 1800*. New York: McGraw-Hill, 1964.

Bibliography

Leonard, *The Power of the Press*.

Miller, Hope Ridings. *Scandals in the Highest Office*. New York: Random House, 1973.

Mitchell, Broadnus. *Alexander Hamilton*. New York: Oxford University Press, 1976.

Mott, *American Journalism*.

Pollard, James. *The Presidents and the Press*. New York: Macmillan, 1947.

Schachner, Nathan. *Alexander Hamilton*. New York: Perpetual, 1946.

Schwartz, Barry. *George Washington—the Making of an American Symbol*. New York: The Free Press, 1987.

Sennet, Richard. *Oligarchy in Colonial American Politics*. New York: Pageant, 1968.

Tebbell, John, and Sarah Miles Watts. *The Press and the Presidency*. New York: Oxford University Press, 1985.

Wharton, Anne Hollingsworth. *Social Life in the Early Republic*. Philadelphia: Lippincott, 1902.

Periodicals

Brodie, Fawn. "The Great Jefferson Taboo." *American Heritage*, Vol. 23, No. 3, June 1972.

Freeman, Joanne. "Slander, Poison, Whispers, and Fame: Jefferson's 'Anas' and Political Gossip in the Early Republic." *Journal of the Early Republic*, Spring 1995.

Graham, Pearl. "Thomas Jefferson and Sally Hemings." *The Journal of Negro History*, Vol. 49, No. 2, Apr. 1961.

Jellison, Charles. "That Scoundrel Callender." *The Virginia Magazine of History and Biography*, Vol. 47, No. 3, July 1959.

Richmond (Va.) *Recorder*, Sept. 1-Dec. 15, 1802.

U.S. Department of Commerce. "Historical Statistics of the United States, Colonial Times to 1970." Bureau of the Census, 1975.

U.S. Department of Labor. "History of Wages in the United States from Colonial Times to 1928." Bureau of Labor Statistics No. 604, 1934.

The Election of 1828; Andrew Jackson and Peggy Eaton

Adams, James T. *The Adams Family*. New York: Literary Guild, 1930.

Anthony, *First Ladies*.

Bassett, John Spencer. *Correspondence of Andrew Jackson*. Washington: Carnegie Institution, 1928.

Boller, *Presidential Campaigns*.

Brown, *John Adams and the American Press*.

Caldwell, Mary French. *General Jackson's Lady*. Nashville: Kingsport Press, 1936.

Clark, Bennett. *John Quincy Adams*. Boston: Atlantic Monthly Press, 1932.

Coit, Margaret. *John C. Calhoun*. New York: Houghton Mifflin, 1950.

Colman, Edna. *Seventy-five Years of White House Gossip*. New York: Doubleday, 1925.

Bibliography

Coyle, *Ordeal of the Presidency*.

Curtis, James C. *Andrew Jackson and the Search for Vindication*. Boston: Little, Brown, 1976.

Davis, Burke. *Old Hickory*. New York: Dial, 1977.

Eaton, Margaret. *The Autobiography of Peggy Eaton*. New York: Scribner's, 1932.

James, Marquis: *Andrew Jackson, Portrait of a President*. New York; Garden City Publishing, 1940.

Klein, Philip Shriver. *President James Buchanan*. University Park: Pennsylvania State University Press, 1962.

Leary, Lewis. *The Book-Peddling Parson*. Chapel Hill, N.C.: Algonquin Books, 1984.

Lindsey, David. *Andrew Jackson and John C. Calhoun*. Woodbury, N.Y.: Barron's Educational Series, 1973.

Morse, John, Jr. *John Quincy Adams*. Boston: Houghton Mifflin, 1882.

Mott, *American Journalism*.

Nagel, Paul. *Descent from Glory*. New York: Oxford University Press, 1983.

Nevins, Allan, ed. *The Diary of John Quincy Adams*. New York: Frederick Ungar, 1928.

Phillips, Leon. *That Eaton Woman*. Barre, Mass.: Barre Publishing, 1974.

Pollard, *The Presidents and the Press*.

Remini, Robert. *The Election of Andrew Jackson*. Philadelphia: J. B. Lippincott, 1963.

———. *The Life of Andrew Jackson*. New York: Harper & Row, 1988.

———. *The Revolutionary Age of Andrew Jackson*. New York: Harper & Row, 1976.

Schlesinger, Arthur, Jr. ed. *History of American Elections*, Vol. 2. New York: McGraw-Hill, 1971.

Shephard, Jack. *Cannibals of the Heart*. McGraw-Hill, New York: 1980.

Smith, Margaret Bayard. *The First 40 Years of Washington Society*. New York: Frederick Ungar, 1965.

Summer, William Graham. *Andrew Jackson as a Public Man*. New York: Haskell House, 1968 (first printed 1882).

Tebbell and Watts, *The Press and the Presidency*.

Weed, Thurwood. *The Autobiography of Thurwood Weed*. Boston: Houghton Mifflin, 1883.

Weston, Florence. *The Presidential Election of 1828*. Philadelphia: Porcupine Press, 1974.

Wharton, *Social Life in the Early Republic*.

Periodicals and Pamphlets

Advocate and Monthly Anti-Jackson Expositor. Cincinnati: Lodge, L'Hammedieu and Hammond, 1828.

Barbee, David Rankin. "Andrew Jackson and Peggy O'Neale." *Tennessee Historical Quarterly*, Vol. 15, No. 1, Mar. 1956.

Bemis, Samuel Flagg. "The Scuffle in the Rotunda." *Proceedings of the Massachusetts Historical Society*, Vol. 71, 1953–57.

Challinor, Joan. "A Quarter Taint of Maryland Blood: An Inquiry into the Anglo/

Maryland Background of Mrs. John Quincy Adams." *Maryland Historical Magazine,* Vol. 80, No. 4, 1985.

Eriksson, Erik McKinley. "Official Newspaper Organs and the Campaign of 1828." *Tennessee Historical Quarterly,* Vol. 8, Oct. 1924.

Farrell, Brian. "Bellona and the General." *History Today,* Vol. 7, July 1958.

Green, Fletcher. "Duff Green, Militant Journalist of the Old School." *American Historical Review,* Vol. 52, No. 2, 1947.

Hill, Isaac. "A Brief Sketch of the Life, Character and Services of Major General Andrew Jackson." Concord, N.H., 1828.

Lowe, Gabriel, Jr. "John Eaton, Jackson's Campaign Manager." *Tennessee Historical Quarterly,* Vol. 11, No. 2, June 1952.

Nevin, David. "The Petticoat War and How It Grew." *The Smithsonian,* May 1992.

Read, Allen Walker. "Could Andrew Jackson Spell?" *American Speech,* Vol. 38, Oct. 1963.

Roswell, March. "The Life of Charles Hammond." Steubenville, Ohio: Steubenville Herald, 1865.

Smith, Culver. "Propaganda Technique in the Jackson Campaign of 1828." *East Tennessee Historical Society's Publications,* Vol. 6, 1934.

Smith, Elbert. "Now Defend Yourself, You Damned Rascal!" *American Heritage,* Vol. 9, Feb. 1958.

Smith, William Henry. "Charles Hammond and His Relationship to Henry Clay and John Quincy Adams." *Chicago Historical Society,* 1884.

Weisenburger, Francis. "A Life of Charles Hammond, the First Great Journalist of the Old Northwest." *Ohio Archeological and Historical Society,* Vol. 43., No. 4, Oct. 1934.

Chapter 3

Bartlett, *Daniel Webster.*

Barzman, Sol. *Madmen and Geniuses: The Vice Presidents of the United States.* Chicago: Tollett, 1974.

Bode, Carl. *The Anatomy of American Popular Culture, 1840–61.* Berkeley: University of California Press, 1959.

Boller, *Presidential Campaigns.*

Brodie, Fawn. *Thaddeus Stevens: Scourge of the South.* New York: Norton, 1959.

Chesnut, Mary Boykin Miller. *A Diary from Dixie.* Boston: Houghton Mifflin, 1949.

Clark, Clifford, Jr. *Henry Ward Beecher, a Spokesman for Middle-Class America.* Urbana: University of Illinois Press, 1978.

Coyle, *Ordeal of the Presidency.*

Crockett, David. *The Life of Martin Van Buren.* Philadelphia: Robert Wright, 1836.

Curtis, George Ticknor. *Life of James Buchanan.* Freeport: Books for Libraries, 1883.

Bibliography

Davis, Burke. *Old Hickory*. New York: Dial, 1977.

Eaton, Margaret. *The Autobiography of Peggy Eaton*. New York: Scribner's, 1932.

James, Marquis. *Andrew Jackson, Portrait of a President*. New York: Garden City Publishing, 1940.

Klein, Philip Shriver. *President James Buchanan*. University Park: Pennsylvania State University Press, 1962.

Leary, Lewis. *The Book-Peddling Parson*. Chapel Hill, N.C.: Algonquin Books, 1984.

Lindsey, David. *Andrew Jackson and John C. Calhoun*. Woodbury, N.Y.: Barron's Educational Series, 1973.

Morse, John, Jr. *John Quincy Adams*. Boston: Houghton Mifflin, 1882.

Mott, *American Journalism.*

Nagel, Paul. *Descent from Glory*. New York: Oxford University Press, 1983.

Nevins, Allan, ed. *The Diary of John Quincy Adams*. New York: Frederick Ungar, 1928.

Phillips, Leon. *That Eaton Woman*. Barre, Mass.: Barre Publishing, 1974.

Pollard, *The Presidents and the Press.*

Remini, Robert. *The Election of Andrew Jackson*. Philadelphia: J. B. Lippincott, 1963.

————. *The Life of Andrew Jackson*. New York: Harper & Row, 1988.

————. *The Revolutionary Age of Andrew Jackson*. New York: Harper & Row, 1976.

Schlesinger, Arthur, Jr. ed. *History of American Elections*, Vol. 2. New York: McGraw-Hill, 1971.

Shephard, Jack. *Cannibals of the Heart*. McGraw-Hill, New York, 1980.

Smith, Margaret Bayard. *The First 40 Years of Washington Society*. New York: Frederick Ungar, 1965.

Summer, William Graham. *Andrew Jackson as a Public Man*. New York: Haskell House, 1968 (first printed 1882).

Tebbell and Watts, *The Press and the Presidency.*

Weed, Thurwood. *The Autobiography of Thurwood Weed*. Boston: Houghton Mifflin, 1883.

Weston, Florence. *The Presidential Election of 1828*. Philadelphia: Porcupine Press, 1974.

Wharton, *Social Life in the Early Republic.*

Periodicals and Pamphlets

Advocate and Monthly Anti-Jackson Expositor. Cincinnati: Lodge, L'Hammedieu and Hammond, 1828.

Barbee, David Rankin. "Andrew Jackson and Peggy O'Neale." *Tennessee Historical Quarterly*, Vol. 15, No. 1, Mar. 1956.

Bemis, Samuel Flagg. "The Scuffle in the Rotunda." *Proceedings of the Massachusetts Historical Society*, Vol. 71, 1953–57.

Challinor, Joan. "A Quarter Taint of Maryland Blood: An Inquiry into the Anglo/

Curtis, *Andrew Jackson and the Search for Vindication.*

Donald, David. *Charles Sumner and the Coming of the Civil War.* New York: Knopf, 1960.

Duberman, Martin. *About Time—Exploring the Gay Past.* New York: Meridian, 1986.

Dunlap, Leslie. *Our Vice-Presidents and Second Ladies.* Metuchen, N.J.: The Scarecrow Press, 1988.

Fischer, Roger. *Tippecanoe and Trinkets Too.* Urbana: University of Illinois Press, 1988.

Fuess, Claude. *Daniel Webster.* New York: Da Capo Press, 1968.

George, Sister Mary Karl. *Zachariah Chandler: A Political Biography.* East Lansing: Michigan State University Press, 1969.

Goldhurst, Richard. *Many Are the Hearts, the Agony and Triumph of Ulysses S. Grant.* New York: Reader's Digest Press, 1975.

Hart, James. *The Popular Book, a History of America's Literary Taste.* New York: Oxford University Press, 1950.

Hesseltine, William. *Ulysses S. Grant, Politician.* New York: Dodd, Mead, 1935.

Jordon, David. *Roscoe Conkling of New York.* Ithaca: Cornell University Press, 1971.

Josephson, Matthew. *The Politicos.* New York: Harcourt Brace & Co., 1938.

Kasson, John. *Rudeness and Civility: Manners in Nineteenth Century Urban America.* New York: Hill & Wang, 1990.

Katz, Jonathan. *Gay American History.* New York: Thomas Crowell Co., 1976.

Klein, *President James Buchanan.*

Larsen, Arthur, ed. *Crusader and Feminist: Letters of Jane Grey Swisshelm.* St. Paul: The Minnesota Historical Society, 1934.

Leach, William. *True Love and Perfect Union.* New York: Basic Books, 1980.

Marbut, *News from the Capital.*

McCulloch, Hugh. *Men and Measures of Half a Century.* New York: Scribner's, 1889.

McFeely, William. *Grant.* New York: Norton, 1981.

Meyer, Leland Winfield. *The Life and Times of Colonel Richard M. Johnson of Kentucky.* New York: AMS Press, 1967.

Miller, Charles Grant. *Donn Piatt: His Work and His Ways.* New York: Beelman Publishers, 1974.

Miller, Neil. *Out of the Past.* New York: Vintage Books, 1995.

Nevins, Allan. *Frémont, Pathmarker of the West.* Lincoln: University of Nebraska Press, 1992.

Pollard, *The Presidents and the Press.*

Rolle, Andres. *John Charles Frémont: Character as Destiny.* Norman, Okla.: University of Oklahoma Press, 1991.

Rorabaugh, *The Alcoholic Republic.*

Ross, Ishbel. *Proud Kate.* New York: Harper, 1953.

Ross, Shelley. *Fall from Grace.* New York: Ballantine Books, 1988.

Sachs, Emanie. *The Terrible Siren.* New York: Harper, 1928.

Schlesinger, Arthur, ed. *A History of American Life.*

———. *History of American Political Elections,* New York: Chelsea House, 1971.

Shaplen, Robert. *Free Love and Heavenly Sinners.* New York: Knopf, 1954.

Smith, Gene. *High Crimes and Misdemeanors: The Impeachment of Andrew Johnson.* New York: William Morrow, 1977.

Smith-Rosenberg, Carroll. *Disorderly Conduct—Visions of Gender in Victorian America.* New York: Knopf, 1985.

Steele, Janet. *The Sun Shines for All.* Syracuse: Syracuse University Press, 1993.

Summers, Mark W. *The Press Gang.* Chapel Hill: University of North Carolina Press, 1994.

Swanberg, W. H. *Jim Fisk.* New York: Scribner's, 1959.

———. *Sickles the Incredible.* New York: Scribner's, 1956.

Swisshelm, Jane. *Half a Century.* Chicago: Jansen, McClurg, 1880.

Thompson, E. Bruce. *Matthew Hale Carpenter, Webster of the West.* Madison: State Historical Society of Wisconsin, 1954.

Trefousse. *Andrew Johnson.*

Trollope, Frances. *Domestic Manners of the Americans.* London: Whittaker, Treacher & Co., 1832.

Updike, John. *Buchanan Dying.* Knopf, New York, 1974.

Waller, Altina. *Reverend Beecher and Mrs. Tilton.* Amherst: University of Massachussets Press, 1982.

Periodicals and Pamphlets

"John C. Fremont's Record." Anonymous pamphlet, 1856.

Klotter, James C. "Sex, Scandal and Suffrage in the Gilded Age." *Historian,* Vol. 42, Feb. 1980.

MacCracken, Brooks W., "Althea and the Judges." *American Heritage,* Vol. 18, No. 4, 1967.

Roberts, Gary L. "In Pursuit of Duty." *The American West.* Vol. 7 No. 5, Sept. 1970.

Stearns, Bertha-Monica. "Reform Periodicals and Female Reformers." *American Historical Review,* Vol. 37, No. 4, July 1932.

"Who is John C. Fremont?" Pamphlet "By one who has long known him socially, financially and politically," 1856.

Newspapers

"Amalgamation." *Lexington Intelligencer,* July 7, 1835.

Henderson, Thomas. "Col. Johnson." *The Washington Globe,* July 7, 1835.

"Let It Drop." *The New York Times,* Dec. 5, 1873.

"Senator Carpenter." *The New York Times,* Dec. 2 1873.

"Take Your Choice." *Chicago Times,* Apr. 15, 1876.

"Gov. Sprague's Troubles." *The New York Times,* Aug. 12, 1879.

"The Narragansett Mystery." *The New York Times,* Aug. 13, 1879.

"Censorship and Flunkeyism." *The New York Times,* Aug. 21, 1881.

Chapter 4

Grover Cleveland and the Election of 1884

Armitage, Charles. *Grover Cleveland as Buffalo Knew Him.* Buffalo: Buffalo Evening News, 1926.

Armstrong, William, ed. *The Gilded Age Letters of E. L. Godkin.* Albany: State University of New York Press, 1974.

Boardman, Fon W., Jr., *America and the Gilded Age.* New York: Henry Z. Walck, 1972.

Cashman, Sean Dennis. *America in the Gilded Age.* New York: New York University Press, 1984.

Clark, *Henry Ward Beecher.*

Hoover, Irwin Hood. *Forty-two Years in the White House.* Boston: Houghton Mifflin, 1934.

Hudson, William. *Random Recollections of an Old Political Reporter.* New York: Cupples & Leon, 1911.

LeFevre, Benjamin. *The Campaign of '84.* Chicago: Baird & Dillon, 1884.

Lynch, Denis. *Grover Cleveland: A Man Four-Square.* New York: Horace Liveright, 1932.

McElroy, Robert. *Grover Cleveland, the Man and the Statesman.* New York: Harper, 1923.

McGerr, *The Decline of Popular Parties.*

Merrill, Horace Samuel. *Bourbon Leader: Grover Cleveland and the Democratic Party.* Boston: Little, Brown, 1957.

Miller, *Scandals in the Highest Office.*

Morgan, H. Wayne. *From Hayes to McKinley.* Syracuse: Syracuse University Press, 1969.

Muzzey, David Saville. *James G. Blaine, a Political Idol of Other Days.* New York: Dodd, Mead, 1934.

Nevins, Allan. *Grover Cleveland, a Study in Courage.* New York: Dodd, Mead, 1932.

———, ed. *Letters of Grover Cleveland, 1850–1905.* Boston: Houghton Mifflin, 1933.

Pollard, *The Presidents and the Press.*

Rosebloom, Eugene, and Eckes, Alfred E., Jr. *A History of Presidential Elections,* 4th ed. New York: Macmillan, 1979.

Schudson, Michael, *Discovering the News.*

Summers, *The Press Gang.*

Tebbel and Watts, *The Press and the Presidency.*

Tugwell, Rexford. *Grover Cleveland.* New York: Macmillan, 1968.

Bibliography

Welch, Richard E., Jr. *The Presidencies of Grover Cleveland*. Lawrence: University Press of Kansas, 1988.

White, *Masks in a Pageant*.

Periodicals and Pamphlets

Chase, Philip Putnam. "The Attitude of the Protestant Clergy in Massachusetts During the Election of 1884." *Massachusetts Historical Society Proceedings*, Vol. 64, Oct. 1930–July 1932.

"Grover Cleveland and Buffalo." Buffalo & Erie County Historical Society, Vol. 11.

Public Opinion: A Comprehensive Summary of the Press Throughout the World. Vol. 1, Apr.–Oct. 1886.

Rice, William Gorham. Papers.

Rosenberg, Marvin and Dorothy. "The Dirtiest Campaign." *American History*, Vol. 13, No. 5, Aug. 1962.

Tell the Truth, or The Story of a Working Woman's Wrongs. New York: Popular Press, 1884.

"A Terrible Tale." *Buffalo Evening Telegraph*, July 21, 1884.

Twining, Kinsley, et al. *Cleveland's Moral Character: Some Facts It Would Be Well to Know*. Buffalo, 1884.

Newspapers

Cincinnati Commercial Gazette, July 1884.

Cincinnati Post, July 1884.

Cincinnati Penny Post, July 1884.

The New York Daily Tribune, July–Nov. 1884.

New York Evening Post, July–Nov. 1884.

New York Sun, July–Nov. 1884; Apr.–June 1884.

The New York Times, July–Nov. 1884; "Dr. James King, 71, Physician in Buffalo," Mar. 11, 1947.

Frances Cleveland and the Celebrity Culture

Anthony, *First Ladies*.

Dibble, R. F. *John L. Sullivan*. Boston: Little, Brown, 1925.

Ford, Paul Leicester. *The Honorable Peter Stirling*. New York: Henry Holt, 1894.

Gamson, Joshua. *Claims to Fame*. Berkeley: University of California Press, 1994.

Geller, G. G. *Sarah Bernhardt, Divine Eccentric*. New York: Frederick A. Stokes Co., 1933.

Gerson, Noel. *Because I Loved Him: The Life and Loves of Lillie Langtry*. New York: William Morrow, 1971.

Gould, *American First Ladies*.

Hart, *The Popular Book*.

Isenberg, Michael. *John L. Sullivan and His America*. Urbana: University of Illinois Press, 1988.

Kroeger, Brooke. *Nellie Bly*. New York: Times Books, 1994.

McArthur, Benjamin. *Actors and American Culture, 1880–1920*. Philadelphia: Temple University Press, 1984.

Middlemas, Keith. *Edward VII*. London: Weidenfeld & Nicolson, 1972.

Mott, *American Journalism*.

Pearson, John. *Edward the Rake*. London: Weidenfeld & Nicolson, 1975.

Sullivan, John L. *I Can Lick Any Sonofabitch in the House*. London, Proteus Publishing, 1980.

Wallace, Irving. *The Fabulous Showman*. New York: Knopf, 1959.

Newspapers and Periodicals

The Cleveland Marriage

Bishop, Joseph. "Newspaper Espionage." *The Forum*, Vol. I, 1886.

Hirsch, Mark. "A Gallant Lady." *New York History*, New York State Historical Association, April, 1946.

"Paul Leicester Ford." *Bookman*, Vol. 10, Feb. 1900.

"A Wedding at the White House" and "Keyhole Journalism." *Public Opinion*, Vol. 1., No. 8, Apr.–Oct. 1886.

The New York Times

"A Bride for President Cleveland." Nov. 16, 1884.

"Is Mr. Cleveland to Be Married?" Nov. 20, 1884.

"The President's Wedding." June 2, 1886.

"Mr. Ford's Able Political Novel." Nov. 11, 1894, .

New York Daily Tribune, Apr. 14–June 6, 1886, including:

"Will Mr. Cleveland Marry or Not?" May 27, 1886.

"After the Wedding." June 6, 1886.

"A Beastly Scandal." June 7, 1888.

"The President's Attack on Women." July 17, 1888.

New York Sun: Apr. 15–May 27, 1886, including, "Is Mr. Cleveland to Be Married?" Apr. 15, 1886.

"Social Life in Washington." Apr. 18, 1886.

"Is He Going to Be Married?" Apr. 23, 1886.

"More About Miss Folsom." May 2, 1886.

"The Mother or the Daughter?" May 19, 1886.

New York Evening Post: "Wicked and Heartless Lies." June 8, 1888.

John L. Sullivan

The New York Times, Mar. 28, June 7, July 28, 1882; Sept. 19, 1883; Sept. 16, Nov. 18, 1884; Jan. 20, 1885, Sept. 15, 1886; Sept. 9, 18, 1892; and:

"A New Attraction." May 30, 1883.

"Slugger Sullivan's New Bar-Room." Aug. 9, 1883.

"Sullivan's Triumphant March." Oct. 14, 1883.

"Tired of the Prize Ring." Nov. 21, 1883.

"The Big Sluggers." Sept. 16, 1884.

Editorial, Dec. 17, 1884.

"John L. Wants to Be a Gentleman." Jan. 15, 1885.

"The Boston Renaissance." Sept. 13, 1885.

"Mr. Sullivan in New-York." June 27, 1886.

Chapter 5

The New Women and the New Gossip

Blocker, Jack. *American Temperance Movements.* Boston: Twayne Publishing, 1989.

Borden, Ruth. *Women and Temperance.* Philadelphia: Temple University Press, 1981.

Coyne, *Ordeal of the Presidency.*

Josephson, Matthew and Hannah. *Al Smith: Hero of the Cities (a political portrait drawing on the papers of Frances Perkins).* Boston: Houghton Mifflin, 1969.

Klotter, James. *The Breckinridges of Kentucky.* Lexington: University Press of Kentucky, 1986.

Lender, Mark Edward, and James Kirby Martin. *Drinking in America.* New York: The Free Press, 1987.

Rorabaugh, *The Alcoholic Republic.*

Ross, *Fall from Grace.*

Sklar, Kathryn Kish. *Florence Kelley and the Nation's Work.* New Haven: Yale University Press, 1995.

Smith-Rosenberg, *Disorderly Conduct.*

Tebell and Watts, *The Press and the Presidency.*

Periodicals and Pamphlets

Klotter, James. "Sex, Scandal and Suffrage in the Gilded Age." *Historian,* Vol. 42, Feb. 1980.

MacCracken, Bruce, "Althea and the Judges." *American Heritage,* Vol. 18, No. 4, 1967.

"The Celebrated Trial Madeline Polard vs. Breckinridge." American Printing and Binding Co., 1894.

Newspapers

The Breckinridge Trial

The New York Times:
"Col. Breckinridge's Marriage a Surprise." July 23, 1893.
"A Congressman in Trouble." Aug. 13, 1893.
Coverage of the Breckinridge/Pollard trial, Mar. 10–Apr. 15, 1894.
"Breckinridge Before the Church." May 7, 1894.
"All Met to Condemn Breckinridge." May 15, 1894.
"No Sympathy with Breckinridge." Aug. 23, 1894.
"Urged to Defeat Breckinridge." Sept. 11, 1894.
"Kentucky Blood May Flow." Sept. 15, 1894.
"Decency Wins in Kentucky." Sept. 16, 1894.
"Miss Pollard Wants the Money." Dec. 27, 1894.

Congressmen Behaving Badly

The New York Times:
"Ex-Senator Brown Shot." Dec. 9, 1906.
"Arthur Brown Very Low." Dec. 10, 1906.
"Senator Brown Dead." Dec. 13, 1906.
"Ex-Senator Brown's Will." Dec. 22, 1906.

Patent Office Sex Scandal

Louisville Courier Journal:
"Shot." Mar. 1, 1890.
"The Inquest." Mar. 13, 1890.
"Acquitted." Apr. 9, 1891.
"Times Reporter Bloodied Stair." Feb. 14, 1952.
Washington Evening Star:
"Shot at the Capitol." Feb. 28, 1890.
"The Taulbee Affair." Mar. 1, 1890.
"Not Out of Danger." Mar. 3, 1890.
"In Danger of Death." Mar. 4, 1890.
"Taulbee and Kincaid." Mar. 6, 1890.
"Mr. Taulbee Dying." Mar. 10, 1890.
"The Taulbee Tragedy." Mar. 12, 1890.

Kincaid trial, Mar. 28–Apr. 9, 1891.
The Washington Post:
"Kincaid is Not Guilty." Apr. 9, 1891.

First Family Gossip

Beer, Thomas. *Hanna.* New York: Knopf, 1929.

Collier, Peter. *The Roosevelts: An American Saga.* New York: Simon & Schuster, 1994.

Coyle, *Ordeal of the Presidency.*

Morgan, Howard Wayne. *William McKinley and His America.* Syracuse: Syracuse University Press, 1963.

Tebbell and Watts, *The Press and the Presidency.*

Newspapers

The New York Times, Oct. 3, 18, 24, 1905; Feb. 11, June 1, 21, 26, Sept. 29, Dec. 22, 1906; Apr. 23, July 5, Aug. 2, 17, Sept. 28, Oct. 27, 31, 1908; and:

"Miss Roosevelt a Merry Bride." Feb. 18, 1906.

"Mr. and Mrs. Roosevelt Brave the Northeaster." Sept. 4, 1906.

"Archie Roosevelt Sinks, Then Rallies." Mar. 8, 1907.

"Archie Roosevelt Better." Mar. 11, 1907.

"Pete the Bulldog Gets a Victim." May 10, 1907.

"Rubberneck Irreverence." June 3, 1907.

"A New White House Dog." June 6, 1907.

"Kermit Fled From Petting." Sept. 6, 1907.

"Ethel Roosevelt Drives Fast Train." Apr. 5, 1908.

Theodore Roosevelt's Drinking Problem

Bishop, Joseph B. *Theodore Roosevelt and His Time, Shown in His Own Letters,* Vol. 2, New York: Scribner's, 1920.

Jaffray, Elizabeth. *Secrets of the White House.* New York: Cosmopolitan Books, 1927.

Lender and Martin, *Drinking in America.*

Morris, Edmund. *The Rise of Theodore Roosevelt.* New York: Coward, McGann & Geoghegan, 1979.

Selections from the Correspondence of Theodore Roosevelt and Henry Cabot Lodge, 1884–1918, Vol. 2: New York: Scribner's, 1925.

Periodicals

Abbott, Lyle. "The Roosevelt Libel Suit." *The Outlook,* Vol. 104, June 14, 1913.

The American Review of Reviews, Vol. 48, July 1913.

"Mr. Roosevelt's Beverages." *The Literary Digest*, Vol. 46, June 7, 1913.

"Mr. Roosevelt's Libel Suit." *Current Opinion*, Vol. 55, July, 1913.

"What I Know About Saloons." *The Independent*, Sept. 10, 1908.

Newspapers

The New York Times, May 27–June 3, 1913, and:

"President Drinks Wine." Oct. 3, 1907.

"Roosevelt's Drink Stirs Up Preachers." Oct. 7, 1907.

"Roosevelt Drinks Too Much Milk." May 21, 1912.

"He Must Not Drink Milk." May 22, 1912.

"The Lactic Peril." May 23, 1912.

"Protesting Too Much." July 13, 1912.

"Roosevelt Suing for Criminal Libel." Oct. 26, 1912.

"Myths and Real Evidence." May 22, 1913.

"Roosevelt Intends to Lay Bare His Life." May 26, 1913.

Woodrow and Edith Wilson

Anthony, *First Ladies*.

Bok, Edward. *Twice Thirty*. New York: Scribner's, 1925.

Gould, *American First Ladies*.

Hatch, Alden. *Edith Bolling Wilson, First Lady Extraordinary*. New York: Dodd, Mead, 1961.

Heckscher, August. *Woodrow Wilson*. New York: Scribner's, 1991.

Lawrence, David. *The True Story of Woodrow Wilson*. New York: George H. Doran, 1924.

Link, Arthur. *Wilson, Campaigns for Progressivism and Peace*. Princeton, N.J.: Princeton University Press, 1965.

———. *Wilson, Confusions and Crises, 1915–16*. Princeton, N.J.: Princeton University Press, 1964.

McLean, Evalyn Walsh. *Father Struck It Rich*. Boston: Little, Brown, 1936.

Saunders, Frances Wright. *First Lady Between Two Worlds: Ellen Axson Wilson*. Chapel Hill: University of North Carolina Press, 1985.

Shachtman, Tom. *Edith and Woodrow*. Thorndike, Maine: Thorndike Press, 1981.

Smith, Gene. *When the Cheering Stopped*. New York: William Morrow, 1964.

Periodicals

Weaver, Judith. "Edith Bolling Wilson as First Lady: A Study in the Power of Personality, 1919–1920." *Presidential Studies Quarterly*, Vol. 15, No. 1, 1985.

Williams, Joyce. "The Resignation of Secretary of State Robert Lansing." *Diplomatic History*, Vol. 3, No. 3, Summer 1979.

Bibliography

Newspapers

The New York Times, Feb. 11, 14, Mar. 5, June 18, July 8, 1920, and:
"President Wilson Weds Mrs. Galt." Dec. 19, 1915.
"Lansing Out." Feb. 14, 1920.
"Sees President Near Recovery." Feb. 11, 1920.
"Wilson Impatient; Wants to Play Golf." Mar. 5, 1920.

Chapter 6

The Election of 1920 and the New Discretion

Adams, Samuel Hopkins. *Incredible Era.* Boston: Houghton Mifflin, 1939.

Beale, Betty. *Power at Play.* Washington: Regnery, 1993.

Britton, Nan. *The President's Daughter.* New York: Elizabeth Ann Guild, 1927.

Chancellor, William Estabrook. *Warren Gamaliel Harding, President of the United States.* The Sentinel Press, 1921.

DeBarthe, Joseph. *The Answer to the President's Daughter.* Marion, Ohio: The Answer Publishers, 1928.

Knebel, Fletcher. "The Placid 20's." *Dateline Washington,* Cabell Phillips, ed., 1949.

Russell, *The Shadow of Blooming Grove.*

Tannenbaum, Frank. *Osborne of Sing Sing.* Chapel Hill: University of North Carolina Press, 1933.

Ward, Geoffrey. *A First-Class Temperament.* New York: Harper & Row, 1989.

Whitaker, Wayne Richard. "Warren Harding and the Press." Ph.D diss. Ohio University, 1972.

White, *Masks in a Pageant.*

Williamson, Joel. *New People: Miscegnation and Mulattoes in the United States.* New York: The Free Press, 1980.

Wilson, Edith. *My Memoir.* New York: Bobbs-Merrill, 1939.

Periodicals and Pamphlets

Adams, Samuel Hopkins. "A Case of Bibliocide." *The New Yorker,* Vol. 15, Oct. 21, 1939.

Boroson, Warren. "America's First Negro President." *Fact,* Vol. 1, Jan.–Feb. 1964.

Broun, Heywood. "It Seems to Heywood Broun." *The Nation,* Oct. 5, 1927.

Cohen, Gary. "The Lady and the Curse." *Vanity Fair,* No. 444, Aug. 1997.

Downes, Randolph. "The Harding Muckfest." *Northwest Ohio Quarterly,* Vol. 39, Summer 1967.

————."Negro Rights and the White Backlash in the Campaign of 1920." *Ohio History,* Ohio Historical Society, Vol. 75, Nos. 2 and 3, Spring–Summer 1966.

Duckett, Kenneth, and Francis Russell. "The Harding Papers." *American Heritage,* Vol. 16, Feb. 1965.

Madame Marcia. "What the Stars Told Mrs. Harding." *Collier's,* May 16, 1924.

Ohio Journalism Hall of Fame. "Proceedings of 3rd Annual Dinner-Meeting, Oct. 31, 1930." Columbus: Ohio State University Press Journalism Services, No. 9, 1931.

Russell, Francis. "The Four Mysteries of Warren Harding." *American Heritage,* Vol. 14, Apr. 1963.

————."The Shadow of Warren Harding." *The Antioch Review,* Vol. 36, Winter 1978.

"They Honor Harding." *The Nation,* June 24, 1931.

Newspapers

Marion Independent:
"We Have No Desire . . ." May 20, 1887.
"Some Persons Drew . . ." May 24, 1887.
Cincinnati Enquirer:
"Deceit Is Alleged in Ohio as Bitter Fight Nears End." Nov. 1, 1920.
"Discredit Cast on Chancellor." Nov. 1, 1920.
"Women at Ohio Polls Today." Nov. 2, 1920.
Cincinnati Times-Star: "Writer Ousted." Oct. 30, 1920.
Baltimore Sun: H. L. Mencken, "Saturnalia." July 18, 1927.
The New York Times:
"Roosevelt Charges Libel, Orders Suit." Oct. 26, 1920.
"Caffey Reveals Rathom Admissions." Oct. 28, 1920.
"Lay Navy Scandal to F. D. Roosevelt." July 20, 1921.
"Preserved Harding Papers." Jan. 11, 1964.
"Harding Letters Held Up by Court." July 31, 1964.
"Copies Are Made of Harding Notes." Aug. 4, 1964.
Auburn (N.Y.) Citizen:
"Roosevelt Brings Big Libel Suit." Oct. 26, 1920.
"News Faking by Rathom Is Shown." Oct. 28, 1920.

The New Discretion

Felsenthal, Carol. *Alice Roosevelt Longworth.* New York: Putnam, 1988.
Fowler, Gene. *Beau James.* New York: Viking, 1949.
Josephson, *Al Smith.*
Martin, Ralph. *Cissy.* New York: Simon & Schuster, 1979.

Bibliography

Teichmann, Howard. *Alice.* Englewood Cliffs, N.J.: Prentice Hall, 1979.

Walsh, George. *Gentleman Jimmy Walker, Mayor of the Jazz Age.* New York: Praeger, 1974.

Washington Merry-Go-Round. New York: Blue Ribbon Books, 1931.

Periodicals

Broun, Heywood. "It Seems to Me." *New York World-Telegram,* Jan. 27, 1932.

The New Distractions

Allen, Frederick Lewis. *Only Yesterday.* New York: Perennial Library, 1964.

Eyman, Scott. *Mary Pickford, America's Sweetheart.* New York: Donald Fine, 1990.

Griffith, Richard, et al. *The Movies.* New York: Simon & Schuster, 1981.

Katz, Ephraim. *The Film Encyclopedia.* New York: HarperCollins, 1994.

McArthur, *Actors and American Culture.*

McGerr, *The Decline of Popular Parties.*

Pickford, Mary. *Sunshine and Shadow.* New York: Doubleday, 1954.

St. Johns, Adela Rogers. *Love, Laughter and Tears.* Garden City, N.Y.: Doubleday, 1978.

Snyder, Robert. *The Voice of the City.* New York: Oxford University Press, 1989.

Windler, Robert. *Sweetheart: The Story of Mary Pickford.* New York: Praeger, 1973.

Newspapers

Olive Thomas

"Paris Probes Death of Olive Thomas." *New York Herald,* Sept. 11, 1920.

"Investigate Death of Olive Thomas." *The Washington Post,* Sept. 11, 1920.

"Thomas Tragedy Loosens a Storm of Criticism on Paris as Modern Babylon." *The Washington Post,* Sept. 11, 1920.

"Will Hold Autopsy over Olive Thomas." *New York Sun,* Sept. 12, 1920.

"Pickford Depicts His Wife's Agony." *The Washington Post,* Sept. 13, 1920.

"Olive Thomas Dies a Poor Little Rich Girl." New York *Daily News,* Sept. 21, 1920.

Fatty Arbuckle

New York *Daily News,* Sept. 11–15, 28, 1921; and:

"Movie Papers Warn 'Stars' to Cut Out the Rough Stuff." Sept. 16, 1921.

"Studio Official Reveals How Exaggerated Ideas Have Ruined Careers of Many Popular Film Stars." Sept. 17, 1921.

"Millions in Hush Money Paid Blackmailers to Cloak Revels of Screen Players." Sept. 18, 1921.

"Women Toss Flowers in Arbuckle's Path." Sept. 30, 1921.

"Women Testify Miss Rappe Had Abdominal Pains." Nov. 26, 1921.

The New York Times:

Sept. 12, 13, 29, Nov. 29, 1921; and:

"Stepmother a Charwoman." Sept. 14, 1921.

"Miss Rappe's Fiancé Threatens Vengeance." Sept. 14, 1921.

"Shoot Up and Burn Fatty Arbuckle Film." Sept. 18, 1921.

"Arbuckle Film Not Burned." Sept. 22, 1921.

"Jurors Seem Almost a Race Apart." Feb. 6, 1922.

"Acquitted but Still to Be Tried." Apr. 14, 1922.

Wallace Reid

New York *Daily News:* Oct. 21, Dec. 18, 20, 1922; Jan. 22, 1923; and:

"Writhing Terror of Dope's Clutches Holds Filmland in Fearful Vise." Nov. 23, 1922.

"Movie Idol a 'Dope.' " Dec. 17, 1922.

"Stage Stars Named in Exposé of Drug Ring." Dec. 17, 1922.

"Dope Kills Reid." Jan. 19, 1923.

"Majority of Film Stars Use Dope." Jan. 24, 1923.

New York Herald Tribune: "Wallace Reid Dies After a Long Fight." Jan. 19, 1928.

Los Angeles Times: Dec. 18, 21, 22, 1922; Jan. 12, 19, 1923; and:

"Narcotics Given Up." Aug. 16, 1922.

"Wallace Reid Interested in 'Burial' Plan." Oct. 23, 1922.

"Wallace Reid Improved." Dec. 23, 1922.

"Hold Reid Physician." Jan. 2, 1923.

"Narcotics Agents Raid Reid Drug Cure Retreat." Jan. 8., 1923.

The New York Times: Dec. 19, 1922; Jan. 19, 1923; and:

"The Screen." June 28, 1923.

Eleanor and Franklin

Collier, Peter, with David Horowitz. *The Roosevets: An American Saga.* New York: Simon & Schuster, 1994.

Cook, Blanche Wiesen. *Eleanor Roosevelt, Vol. 1.* New York: Viking-Penguin, 1992.

Davis, Kenneth S. *FDR, the New Deal Years, 1933–7.* New York: Random House, 1979.

Faber, Doris. *The Life of Lorena Hickok.* New York: William Morrow, 1980.

Freidel, Frank. *Franklin D. Roosevelt: A Rendezvous with Destiny.* Boston: Little, Brown, 1990.

Gabler, Neal. *Winchell.* New York: Vintage, 1994.

Gallagher, Hugh Gregory. *FDR's Splendid Deception.* New York: Dodd, Mead, 1985.

Gellman, Irwin. *Secret Affairs: Franklin Roosevelt, Cordell Hull and Sumner Welles.* Baltimore: Johns Hopkins University Press, 1995.

Goodwin, Doris Kearns. *No Ordinary Time*. New York: Simon & Schuster, 1994.

Lait, Jack, and Mortimer Lee. *Washington Confidential*. New York: Crown Publishers, 1951.

Lash, Joseph. *Eleanor and Franklin*, New York: Norton, 1971.

————. *Eleanor: The Years Alone*, New York: Norton, 1972.

————. *Love, Eleanor: Eleanor Roosevelt and Her Friends*. New York: Doubleday, 1982.

Parks, Lillian Rogers, with Frances Spatz Leighton. *The Roosevelts: A Family in Turmoil*. Englewood Cliffs, N.J.: Prentice Hall, 1981.

Pilat, Oliver. *Drew Pearson*. New York: Harper & Row, 1973.

Potter, Jeffrey. *Men, Money and Magic. The Story of Dorothy Schiff*. New York: Geoghegan, 1976.

Smith, Merriman. *Merriman Smith's Book of Presidents*. New York: Norton, 1972.

Theoharis, Athan. *From the Secret Files of J. Edgar Hoover*. Chicago: Iva R. Dee, 1991.

Ward, *A First-class Temperament*.

Wolfskill, George, and John Hudson. *All but the People: Franklin Roosevelt and His Critics*. New York: Macmillan, 1969.

Periodicals

Britt, George. "Poison in the Melting Pot." *The Nation,* Vol. 148, Apr. 1, 1939.

"The Case of Sumner Welles." *Commonweal,* Vol. 38, No. 21, Sept. 10, 1943.

Childs, Marquis. "They Hate Roosevelt." *Harper's Magazine,* Vol. 172, May, 1936.

Early, Stephen T. "Below the Belt." *The Saturday Evening Post,* June 10, 1939.

Fleeson, Doris. "Missy to Do This." *The Saturday Evening Post,* Jan. 8, 1938.

Martin, John. "The Truth About How FDR Died." *Behind the Scenes,* Nov. 1955.

Sidey, Hugh. "Upstairs at the White House." *Time,* May 18, 1987.

"They Still Hate Roosevelt." *The New Republic,* Vol. 96, Sept. 14, 1938.

Time, Sept. 22, 1941; May 22, Oct. 16, 23, 30, 1944.

Ward, Paul, "Campaign Dirt." *The Nation,* Vol. 143, Nov. 7, 1936.

"Washington Notes." *The New Republic,* Vol. 77, Jan. 10, 1934.

"Whispers: Unfounded Gossip About the President's Health Comes into the Open." *News-Week,* Vol. 6, No. 3, July 20, 1935.

Newspapers

Atlanta Journal: "Aubrey Williams Is Sure Roosevelt Will Not Run." Mar. 26, 1944.

The New York Times:

"President's Health Called Better Than Ever." Jan. 29, 1944.

"Roosevelt Was Ill of Bronchitis, but Says That He Is Feeling Fine." Mar. 29, 1944.

"Roosevelt Goes South for Two Weeks to Rest and Recuperate in the Sun." Apr. 1, 1944.

"President Returns from Month's Rest on Baruch Estate." May 8, 1944.
New York Sun: "If It Were Bricker or Truman for President." Oct. 13, 1944.

Chapter 7

The Fifties

Halberstam, David. *The Fifties.* New York: Fawcett, 1993.
Lait and Lee, *Washington Confidential.*

Eisenhower

Allen, Craig. *Eisenhower and the Mass Media.* Chapel Hill: University of North Carolina Press, 1993.
Ambrose, Stephen. *Eisenhower, Vol. 1.* New York: Simon & Schuster, 1983.
Anthony, *First Ladies.*
Barry, Lucy Barry. *Co-Starring Famous Women and Alcohol.* Minneapolis: CompCare, 1986.
Beale, *Power at Play.*
Cheshire, Maxine. *Maxine Cheshire, Reporter,* Boston: Houghton Mifflin, 1978.
David, Lester and Irene. *Ike and Mamie.* New York: Putnam, 1981.
Eisenhower, Julie Nixon. *Special People.* New York: Simon and Schuster, 1977.
Eisenhower, Susan. *Mrs. Ike.* New York: Farrar, Straus and Giroux, 1996.
Miller, Merle. *Plain Speaking: An Oral Biography of Harry S. Truman.* New York: Putnam, 1973.
Morgan, Kay Summersby. *Past Forgetting.* New York: Simon & Schuster, 1976.
Neal, Steve. *The Eisenhowers, Reluctant Dynasty.* New York: Doubleday, 1978.
Smith, *Merriman Smith's Book of Presidents.*

Periodicals and Pamphlets

Buckley, Tom, "Past Forgetting." *The New York Times Book Review,* Feb. 13, 1977.
Daniell, Raymond. "He Is Our Eisen and This Is Our Hour." *The New York Times Magazine,* Nov. 1, 1942.
"The Presidency: About a Cold." *Time,* Mar. 12, 1953.
"The Story of Mrs. Eisenhower's Health." *U.S. News & World Report,* Mar. 25, 1955.
"They Hate Ike." *Time,* May 5, 1952.
"They Lied About Ike's Girl Friday." *Inside Story,* Mar. 1955.
"The Truth About Those Mamie Rumors." *On the Q.T.,* Aug. 1955.
"Why Mamie Stays Home." *Newsweek,* Feb. 8, 1960.
"Why Mamie 'Takes It Easy.' " *U.S. News & World Report,* May 13, 1955.

Bibliography

Newspapers

The New York Times:

"Eisenhower's Wife Finds Wait Tough." Oct. 17, 1943.

"George VI Honors 1,070 in Civil Life." Jan. 3, 1945.

"Eisenhower Honors Wac Aide." May 5, 1945.

"From Theatre of War to Theatre of Entertainment." May 17, 1945.

"Two Parties in Clash on Mrs. Eisenhower." May 9, 1955.

"Eisenhowers Fly to Phoenix Today." Feb. 23, 1958.

"25,000 Welcome the Eisenhowers at Phoenix." Feb. 24, 1958.

"Mrs. Eisenhower Returns to Capital." Mar. 12, 1958.

"Eisenhower Letters Hint at Affair With Aide." June 6, 1991.

Safire, William. "Indeed a Very Dear Friend." June 6, 1991.

Scandal Magazines

Betrock, Alan. *Sleazy Business: A Pictorial History of Exploitation Tabloids, 1959–74.*
   Brooklyn: Shake Books, 1994
———. *Unseen America: The Greatest Cult Exploitation Magazines, 1950–1966.*
   Brooklyn: Shake Books, 1990.
Sanders, Coyne Steven, and Tom Gilbert. *Desilu—The Story of Lucille Ball and Desi
   Arnaz.* New York: Quill, 1993.
Spoto, Donald. *Notorious—the Life of Ingrid Bergman.* New York: HarperCollins,
   1997.

Periodicals

Time:

"Sewer Trouble." Aug. 1, 1955.

"Lid on the Sewer." Sept. 19, 1955.

"Confidential Wins a Round." Oct. 17, 1955.

"Ssh!" Apr. 2, 1956.

"Gutterdammerung?" Mar. 11, 1957.

"Confidential Revisited." Mar. 18, 1957.

"The Woes of Confidential." July 22, 1957.

"Putting the Papers to Bed." Aug. 26, 1957.

"Disorderly Charge Against Tab Hunter." *Confidential,* Sept. 1955.

"The Dolls That Dulles Couldn't Handle." *Tip-Off,* June 1956.

"The Lusty Lovelife of Marshal Tito." *Uncensored,* Jan. 1956.

"Michigan Governor, Pardon Johnny Ray." *Lowdown,* Aug. 1955.

"The O'Dwyer Story." *Confidential,* Dec. 1952.

"We Accuse Sumner Welles." *Confidential,* May 1956.

Bibliography

"Why Jackie Kennedy Went to Rome." *Uncensored,* Feb. 1963.

"Why Liberace's Theme Song Should Be 'Mad About the Boy.' " *Confidential,* July 1957.

"The Wild Whiskey and Women Scandals Rocking Rockefeller." *Confidential,* Aug. 1963.

Wolfe, Thomas. "Public Lives: Confidential Magazine." *Esquire,* Apr. 1964.

Newspapers

The New York Times: May 5, Aug. 10, 18, 31, Sept. 4 1957; Jan. 16, Feb. 22, July 2, 16, 1958; and:

"Sinatra Version of Raid Disputed." Feb. 28, 1957.

"Detective Tells Inquiry He 'Checked Out' 150 'Scandal' Articles for Confidential." Mar. 1, 1957.

"Magazine Policy Cited by Witness." Aug. 14, 1957.

"Movies to Hit Back." Aug. 23, 1957.

"Agreement Set on Confidential." Nov. 8, 1957.

"Accord Approved for Confidential." Nov. 13, 1957.

Drinking and Congress

Daniel, Clifton. *Lords, Ladies and Gentlemen.* New York: Arbor House, 1984.

Fontenay, Charles. *Estes Kefauver.* Knoxville: University of Tennessee Press, 1980.

Gorman, Joseph. *Kefauver: A Political Biography.* New York: Oxford University Press, 1971.

Lender and Martin, *Drinking in America.*

Pilat, *Drew Pearson.*

Tower, John. *Consequences.* Boston: Little, Brown, 1991.

Periodicals

Baker, Bobby, and Larry King. "Wheeling and Dealing." *Playboy,* June 1978.

"Estes Kefauver, RIP." *Commonweal,* Vol. 15, No. 8, Aug. 27, 1963.

Moore, William Howard. "Was Estes Kefauver 'Blackmailed'?" *The Public Historian,* Vol. 4, No. 1, Winter 1982.

Adlai Stevenson

Allen, *Eisenhower and the Mass Media.*

Beale, *Power at Play.*

Graham, Katherine. *Personal History.* New York: Knopf, 1997.

McKeever, Porter. *Adlai Stevenson, His Life and Legacy.* New York: William Morrow, 1989.

Theoharis, *From the Secret Files of J. Edgar Hoover.*

Periodicals

"How That Stevenson Rumor Got Started." *Confidential,* Aug. 1953.

Seebohm, Caroline. "The Remarkable Marietta Tree." *Vanity Fair,* No. 445, Sept. 1997.

Theoharis, Athan. "How the FBI Gaybaited Stevenson." *The Nation,* May 7, 1990.

John Kennedy

Anthony, Carl Sferrazza. *First Ladies, Vol. 2.* New York: Quill, 1991.

Bradlee, Ben. *A Good Life.* New York: Simon & Schuster, 1995.

Collier, Peter, and David Horowitz. *The Kennedys, An American Drama.* New York: Summit, 1984.

Hersh, Seymour. *The Dark Side of Camelot.* New York: Little, Brown, 1997.

Horne, Alistair. *Macmillan vol. 2, 1957–1986.* London: Macmillan, 1989.

Thomas, Helen. *Dateline: White House.* New York: Macmillan, 1975.

Reeves, Richard. *President Kennedy.* New York: Touchstone, 1993.

Reeves, Thomas. *A Question of Character.* Rocklin, Calif.: Prima, 1992.

Periodicals

Barcekkam, Ernest. "New Man in the White House." *Today's Health,* Feb. 1961.

"The Blauvelt Campaign." *Newsweek,* Sept. 24, 1962.

"Those Whispers About Jack Kennedy." *Confidential,* Oct. 1960.

"Medical Facts on President Kennedy's Mysterious Malady." *Confidential,* July 1962.

Newspapers

The New York Times:

"Johnson Backers Urge Health Test." July 5, 1960.

"President's Back Strain at Tree Planting Is Disclosed." June 9, 1961.

"Kennedy Still on Crutches." June 13, 1961.

"President's Physician Describes His Condition as a Common One." June 14, 1961.

"Virus Disables President." June 23, 1961.

"Excerpt from News Conference by President's Physician." June 23, 1961.

"He Cut It Slicing Bread." May 9, 1963.

"Kennedy's Back Better." May 19, 1963.

Chapter 8

Nelson Rockefeller and the Election of 1964

White, Theodore. *The Making of the President 1964.* New York: Atheneum, 1965.

Periodicals

Newsweek, Nov. 27, 1961; Apr. 29, May 20, 1963; Aug. 31, 1964.
U.S. News & World Report, Dec. 4, 1961; May 6, 1963; Jan. 13, 1964.
Time, Apr. 26, May 10, 17, June 7, 1963; Oct. 9, 1964.
"New Hampshire: First Test for Big Divorce Issue." *Life,* Feb. 7, 1964.

Newspapers

The New York Times:
"Gov. Rockefeller and His Wife Part." Nov. 18, 1961.
"Governor Took Initiative in Separating from Wife." Nov. 19, 1961.
Knowles, Clayton. "Rockefeller's Future." Nov. 20, 1961.
"Governor Assays Impact of Divorce." Feb. 15, 1962.
"Views of Press on Rockefeller." May 7, 1963.
Albany (N.Y.) *Times-Union:*
"Rockefeller 'Certainty' in 1962." Nov. 19, 1961.
"Politicians Divided on Effect of Wedding." May 5, 1963.
"Minister Faces Discipline for Marrying Rockefellers." May 9, 1963.

Walter Jenkins

White, *The Making of the President 1964.*

Periodicals

"As the Morals Issue Took a New Turn." *U.S. News & World Report,* Nov. 9. 1964.
"Down to the Wire." *Newsweek,* Nov. 2, 1964.
"From Washington Straight." *National Review,* Nov. 3, 1964.
"Jenkins Case: Unanswered Questions." *U.S. News & World Report,* Nov. 2, 1964.
Wainwright, Loudon. "What Road Back from Ruin?" *Life,* Oct. 30, 1964.
"What the FBI Found in the Jenkins Case." *U.S. News & World Report,* Nov. 2, 1964.

Newspapers

The New York Times, Oct. 15, 16, 1964.

Bibliography

All-Purpose Celebrity

Deakin, James. "The Dark Side of LBJ." *Esquire,* Aug. 1967.

Hayes, Harold, ed. *Smiling Through the Apocalypse.* New York: Delta, 1971.

Reed, Rex. "Ava: Life in the Afternoon Talese." *Esquire,* May 1967.

Talese, Gay. "Frank Sinatra Has a Cold." *Esquire,* Apr. 1966.

George McGovern and Thomas Eagleton

Crispell, Kenneth, and Carlos Gomez. *Hidden Illness in the White House.* Durham, N.C.: Duke University Press, 1988.

Crouse, Timothy. *The Boys on the Bus.* New York: Ballantine, 1972.

Weil, Gordon. *The Long Shot.* New York: Norton, 1973.

White, Theodore. *The Making of the President, 1972.* New York: Atheneum, 1973.

Newspapers

The New York Times:

"Eagleton Illness Known to Associates." July 26, 1972.

"Eagleton Tells of Shock Therapy." July 26, 1972.

"Candidates' Staffs Wage Below-Surface Struggle." July 31, 1972.

"The McGovern Image." July 31, 1972.

"Troy Would Not Vote for Ticket." July 31, 1972.

"Eagleton Withdraws at Request of McGovern." Aug. 1, 1972.

Carl Albert

The Washington Post:

"Albert's Car Hits Two Others." Sept. 11, 1972.

"Albert: Drink Not Cause of Accident." Sept. 12, 1972.

"Two Students Say Albert Was Drunk." Sept. 13, 1972.

"Congressmen, Cars, Laws and Favortism." Sept. 18, 1972.

The New York Times:

"A Voice in Naming Ford." Oct. 13, 1973.

"Muckraker." *Newsweek,* June 27, 1966.

Sherrill, Robert. "Running from the Presidency." *The New York Times Magazine,* Dec. 9, 1973.

Wilbur Mills

The New York Times:

"Wilbur Mills Offers Sober Testimony to an Alcoholic Past." Dec. 4, 1978.

"Mills, Back in the Capital, Gives Tax Advice Again." Dec. 30, 1978.

The Washington Post:

Oct. 10–14, Nov. 4–6, Dec. 5, 26, 31, 1974; and:

"Arkansas High School Students Grill Mills About D.C. Incident." Oct. 19, 1974.

"The Incident at the Tidal Basin." Oct. 20, 1974.

"Mills Appears on Stage with Stripper." Dec. 2, 1974.

"Hill's Reform Democrats Make Gains." Dec. 3, 1974.

"Tired Wilbur Mills Under Fire." Dec. 3, 1974.

Von Hoffman, Nicholas. "Wilbur Mills and Journalistic Malaise." Dec. 9.

"Rep. Mills Gives Up Hill Post." Dec. 11, 1974.

Duke, Paul. "Private Lives and Public Responsibilities." Dec. 20, 1974.

Wayne Hays

Newsweek: June 7, 14, 21, 1976.

Time: June 7, 14, 21, 1976.

Cleveland *Plain Dealer:*

"Drop Second Shoe, Hays!" June 4, 1976.

"Hays May Have Taken 10 Times Normal Dose." June 12, 1976.

"How Did Poor Boy Wayne Hays Rise So Far?" June 14, 1976.

New Orleans Times-Picayune:

Weiss, Kenneth. "Lawmakers Off Duty—Do We Need to Know?" June 6, 1976.

The New York Times: May 15, Aug. 14, Sept. 2, 3, 1976; and:

"Rep. Hays and Secretary Marry." Apr. 15, 1976.

"Rep. Hays Defers Trip, Denies Aide's Accusation." May 24, 1976.

"Hays's District Calm over Alleged Mistress." May 25, 1976.

"Hays, in Reversal, Admits Affair with Staff Member." May 26, 1976.

"Hays Asserts Woman Got $1,000 Through Threats." May 27, 1976.

"Despite Scandal, Hays Is Still 'Old Wayne' to Voters." Apr. 9, 1978.

Congress

Christian Science Monitor:

"This One's on the House(boat)." June 16, 1976.

"Straying Solons." Dec. 8, 1976.

Congressional Quarterly:

"Congressional Immunity." July 31, 1976.

"Ethics: Lots of Scandals, Little Action." Oct. 30, 1976.

Dallas *Times Herald:*

"Texas Congressman in New Sex Scandal." June 11, 1976.

"Rep. Young Asks for Probe into Sex Scandal Charges." June 12, 1976.

"Mrs. Gardner Expected to Give Probers Tapes." June 13, 1976.

"Congressman May Quit After Utah Sex Arrest." June 14, 1976.

New Orleans Times-Picayune:

"Rep. Breaux Vigorously Denies Romance Charge." June 4, 1976.

"Police Records Say Waggoner Picked Up." June 18, 1976.

"Waggoner Back Home; Senators Give Support." June 19, 1976.

Weiss, Kenneth: "Washington Watch." June 20, 1976.

The New York Times:

"Congressman's Ex-Aide Links Her Salary to Sex." June 11, 1976.

Wicker, Tom. "Congress, Sex and the Press." June 22, 1976.

"Arrests Studied as Capital Policy." July 11, 1976.

"Howe Repeats His Intention to Run Despite Conviction." Sept. 4, 1976.

"Rep. Young's Wife Is Apparent Suicide." July 15, 1977.

Playboy:

Jenrette, Rita. "The Liberation of a Congressional Wife." Apr. 1981.

The Washington Post:

"Voters Seem Tolerant of Members of Congress Who Stray." Oct. 24, 1974.

"Rep. Robert Leggett: Life of Immense Complications." July 18, 1976.

"No Prosecution Seen in Rep. Young Case." Aug. 17, 1976.

Cheshire, Maxine. "Onassis's Traumatic Holiday: The Jerry Ford Suite." Sept. 9, 1979.

Detroit News:

"Riegle Tapes Reveal Talks with Girl Friend." Oct. 17, 1976.

"Riegle Charges News-Esch 'Plot.' " Oct. 18, 1976.

Ashenfelter, David. "Riegle: 'No New Skeletons.' " Oct. 19, 1976.

"Michigan Congressman Admits to Affair in 1969." United Press International, Oct. 19, 1976.

Gordon, Lou. "Gordon Lashes News as 'Rotton' on Riegle." Oct. 20, 1976.

"Expose of Riegle Affair Hit." Oct. 22, 1976.

Girard, Fred. "Motives Behind Riegle Story." Oct. 24, 1976.

Gordon, Lou. "Here's More on Riegle-News Controversy." Oct. 24, 1976.

Kantor, Seth. "Riegle's Affair Piques Press." Oct. 27, 1976.

President Kennedy

Hersh, *The Dark Side of Camelot.*

Reeves, *President Kennedy.*

Periodicals

Time: "JFK and the Mobsters' Moll." Dec. 29, 1973.

JFK's Love Affairs. New York: National Mirror, 1976.

Newsweek:

"A Shadow over Camelot." Dec. 29, 1975.

"Hoover's Kennedy File." Dec. 29, 1975.
"Lady-in-Waiting." Jan. 26, 1976.
"More Pillow Talk." Mar. 1, 1976.
"JFK's 'Close Friend.'" Sept. 18, 1978.
"What JFK Meant to Us." Nov. 28, 1983.
People:
Kelley, Kitty: "The Dark Side of Camelot." Feb. 22, 1988.
Vanity Fair: Smith, Liz. "The Exner Files." Jan. 1997.

Newspapers

"Dog Days at the White House." *Chicago Tribune,* July 20, 1975.
"A Dog's-eye View of White House Life." *The Washington Post,* July 17, 1975.
Ephron, Nora. "Dog Days at the White House." *The New York Times Book Review,* Aug. 3, 1975.
Reeves, Richard. "13 Days in October." *The New York Times,* Oct. 8, 1997.
Safire, William. "The President's Friend." *The New York Times,* Dec. 15, 1975.

Chapter 9

Gary Hart

Bradlee, Benjamin C. *A Good Life: Newspapering and Other Adventures.* New York: Simon & Schuster, 1995.
Germond, Jack, and Jules Witcover. *Whose Broad Stripes and Bright Stars?* New York: Warner Books, 1989.
Simon, Roger. *Road Show.* New York: Farrar, Straus and Giroux, 1990.
Taylor, Paul. *See How They Run.* New York: Knopf, 1990.

Periodicals

"Miami Woman Is Linked to Hart: Candidate Denies Any Impropriety." *The Miami Herald,* May 3, 1987.
The Miami Herald, various stories. May 5, 1987.
"The Gary Hart Story: How It Happened." *The Miami Herald,* May 10, 1987.
"Infidelity." *The Nation,* May 16, 1987.
"Donna Rice, the Woman in Question." *People,* May 18, 1987.
Time, May 18, June 8, 1987.
U.S. News & World Report, May 18, 1987.
Newsweek, May 18, 1987; Nov. 21, 1988.
"On the Zipper Beat." *The New Republic,* May 25, 1987.
Hertzberg, Hendrik. "Sluicegate." *The New Republic,* June 1, 1987.

"New Morality, New Journalism." *National Review,* June 5, 1987.

"Chronicle of a Ruinous Affair." *People,* June 15, 1987.

Von Hoffman, Nicholas. "Should the Press Play Vice Cop." *The Nation,* June 20, 1987.

Harrison, Barbara Grizzuti. "X-Rated Politicians." *Mademoiselle,* Sept. 1987.

Henkel, Oliver, Jr. "The Press, the Process and Gary Hart." *Vital Speeches of the Day,* Vol. 53, Sept. 1, 1987.

Sheehy, Gail. "The Road to Bimini." *Vanity Fair,* Sept. 1987.

Barnes, Fred. "Monster from the Id." *The New Republic,* Jan. 18, 1988.

Handelmann, David. "Campaignus Interruptus." *Rolling Stone,* Mar. 24, 1988.

Wills, Gary. "How Pure Must Our Candidates Be?" *American Heritage,* May–June, 1988.

The Gossip Standard of Probable Cause

Celeste, Christopher. "Political Voyeurism." Honors thesis, Stanford University, 1977.

Hertzberg. "Sluicegate."

"No Hart Problem, Says Celeste." Cleveland *Plain Dealer,* June 2, 1987.

"Celeste Womanizing Worries Aides." Cleveland *Plain Dealer,* June 3, 1987.

"Survey: Celeste Affairs Nobody's Business." *Cincinnati Enquirer,* June 4, 1987.

"Newspaper Links Celeste to 3 Women." *Cincinnati Enquirer,* June 4, 1987.

"Dagmar Celeste Cites Forgiveness." Cleveland *Plain Dealer,* June 4, 1987.

"PD Criticized over Article." Cleveland *Plain Dealer,* June 4, 1987.

"Are the Sex Lives of All Politicians Now Fair Game?" *U.S. News & World Report,* June 15, 1987.

"Clinton's Health Care Cheerleader." *Congressional Quarterly,* Vol. 51, Oct. 16, 1993.

Jack Kemp

Rollins, Ed. *Bare Knuckles and Back Rooms.* New York: Broadway Books, 1996.

Newspapers and Periodicals

"Gentlemen's Agreement." *Esquire,* Nov. 1985.

Newsweek, Dec. 2, 1985.

"Rep. Kemp Angry over NBC Question on Homosexuality." *The Washington Post,* Mar. 14, 1986.

Evans, Rowland, and Robert Novak. "No Surprises for Kemp." *San Diego Union-Tribune,* Mar. 17, 1986.

"The Fish Bowl." Associated Press, May 9, 1987.

"California Roots: Kemp Is Out to Tackle State's Forgetfulness." *Los Angeles Times,* June 2, 1987.

Dowd, Maureen. "Is Jack Kemp Mr. Right?" *The New York Times Magazine,* June 28, 1987.

"Morris Plotted Gay Rumor—Hooker." New York *Daily News,* Sept. 14, 1996.

Celebrities

"Hollywood Still Directs Its Coverage." *The New York Times,* June 1, 1992.

"They're Hot! They're Not!" *The New York Times,* Aug. 1, 1993.

"Cruise Bristles." *USA Today,* Aug. 11, 1993.

"With Awards Season . . ." *Daily Variety,* Nov. 22, 1993.

"The Jackson Jive." *Vanity Fair,* Sept. 1995.

Ronald Reagan

Burford, Anne. *Are You Tough Enough?* New York: McGraw-Hill, 1985.

Cannon, Lou. *Reagan.* New York: Putnam, 1982.

———. *President Reagan: The Role of a Lifetime.* New York: Simon & Schuster, 1991.

Davis, Patti. *Home Front.* New York: Crown, 1986.

Deaver, Michael. *Behind the Scenes.* New York: William Morrow, 1988.

Kelley, Kitty. *Nancy Reagan, the Unauthorized Biography.* New York: Simon & Schuster, 1991.

Reagan, Maureen. *First Father, First Daughter.* Boston: Little, Brown, 1989.

Reagan, Michael. *On the Outside Looking In,* New York: Zebra Books, 1988.

Reagan, Nancy. *My Turn.* New York: Random House, 1989.

Regan, Donald. *For the Record.* San Diego: Harcourt Brace Jovanovich, 1988.

Speakes, Larry. *Speaking Out.* New York: Scribner's, 1988.

Stockman, David. *The Triumph of Politics.* New York: Harper & Row, 1986.

Von Damm, Helene. *At Reagan's Side.* New York: Doubleday, 1989.

The New York Times:

Buckley, Christopher. "Washington Memoirs: Bombshell or Bust." Oct. 1, 1989.

Korda, Michael. "Prompting the President." *The New Yorker,* Oct. 6, 1997.

Henry Cisneros

Maraniss, David. "The Tumult of Mayor Cisneros." *The Washington Post,* Oct. 24, 1988.

Morrison, Patt. "Cisneros' Grand Opera." *Los Angeles Times,* Nov. 10, 1988.

"San Antonio Mayor Leaves Office with Tarnished Reputation." Reuters, May 29, 1989.

"San Antonio's Cisneros Still a Hero." *San Diego Union-Tribune,* May 21, 1992.

Gra, Marty. "Her Life In Ruins, Cisneros Former Mistress Says." *Houston Post,* Aug. 8, 1994.

"Cisneros Admits Apparent Contradiction on Payments to Ex-Mistress." *The Dallas Morning News,* Sept. 22, 1994.

Gugliotta, Guy. "Has She Been Branded with a Scarlet 'A'?" *The Washington Post,* as published in *Los Angeles Times,* Oct. 20, 1994.

Guerra, Carlos. "A Blonde and a Latin Lover." *Newsday,* Oct. 30, 1994.

Burka, Paul. "Hard Times for Henry." *Texas Monthly,* Vol. 22, No. 11, Nov. 1994.

"I Feel Some Shame." *USA Today,* Mar. 16, 1995.

"Many See Cisneros as Symbol." *The Dallas Morning News,* Mar. 23, 1995.

"Cisneros Quits as HUD Chief." *The Dallas Morning News,* Nov. 22, 1996.

Stewart McKinney

"Rep. Stewart B. McKinney Dies of AIDS Complications." *The Washington Post,* May 8, 1987.

"McKinney Dies of Illness Tied to AIDS." *The New York Times,* May 8, 1987.

"Honoring a Memory: Aiding AIDS Victims." *The New York Times Connecticut Weekly,* May 8, 1987.

"Conn. Lawmaker's AIDS Death Sparks Debate over Gay Report." *Atlanta Constitution,* May 11, 1987.

"Friends Hope AIDS Won't Obscure McKinney Legacy." *The Washington Post,* May 11, 1987.

"McKinney Recalled as Fighter for the Poor." *The New York Times,* May 15, 1987.

"McKinney's Aides Pursuing His Policies." *The New York Times,* June 7, 1987.

Dreifus, Claudia. "And Then There Was Frank." *The New York Times Magazine,* Feb. 4, 1996.

John Tower

Lender and Martin, *Drinking in America.*

Rorabaugh, *The Alcoholic Republic.*

Tower, *Consequences.*

The New York Times:

"Rebutting Witnesses, Tower Flatly Denies a Drinking Problem." Feb. 2, 1989.

Kolata, Gina. "Alcohol Is a Problem When It's a Problem." Feb. 12, 1989.

"Is John Tower Judged by a Double Standard or Just an Appropriately Higher One?" Feb. 25, 1989.

"Tower Takes Vow He Will Not Drink If He Is Confirmed." Feb. 27, 1989.

"Emotional Tower Asks the Senate About Standards." Mar. 2, 1989.

"Senators Mark Congress's Rich Past Before Facing the Painful Present." Mar. 3, 1989.

"FBI Report on Tower Provokes Bitterness." Mar. 3, 1989.

"Mud on the Senate Floor." Mar. 5, 1989.

"Senate Rejects Tower, 53–47." Mar. 10, 1989.

Hall, Trish, "A New Temperance Is Taking Root in America." Mar. 15, 1989.
"FBI Document on Tower Cited 'Pattern of Alcohol Abuse.' " Mar. 17, 1989.
Buckley, William F. "On the Fitness of Tower." *National Review,* Mar. 24, 1989.

Chapter 10

Bill Clinton

Maraniss, David. *First in His Class.* New York: Simon & Schuster, 1995.
Rosenstiel, Tom. *Strange Bedfellows.* New York: Hyperion, 1994.
Stephanopoulos, George. *All Too Human.* Boston: Little, Brown, 1999.
Walker, Martin, *The President We Deserve.* New York: Crown, 1996.

Newspapers

"Governor Getting Mileage Out of Publicity Over Bad Speech." Associated Press,
    July 28, 1988.
"Clinton Speaks Again." *St. Petersburg (Fla.) Times,* July 30, 1988.
"Lemons to Lemonade." *Arkansas Democrat-Gazette,* July 30, 1988.
"From Doghouse to White House?" Associated Press, July 31, 1988.
"As Entertainment, This Campaign Is Not So Bad." *The New York Times,* Mar. 31,
    1992.
"Clinton Tries to Regain New York Poise." *The New York Times,* Apr. 5, 1992.
"Woman from St. Charles Says She Had Affair with Clinton." *St. Louis Post-Dispatch,*
    July 18, 1992.
Waldman, Amy. "The Decline of Loyalty in Modern Politics." *The Washington
    Monthly,* Sept. 1996.

George Bush

Taylor, *See How They Run.*
Cooke, Janet. "Anatomy of a Rumor." *The Washington Post,* March 22, 1981.
Anderson, Jack, and Dale Van Atta. "Bush Friend Gingerly Investigated." *The Wash-
    ington Post,* Apr. 17, 1990.
"Former Bush Aide Fined for Customs Violations." *The Washington Post,* Apr. 18,
    1990.
"State Dept. Charges Longtime Bush Aide." *The Washington Post,* Aug. 8, 1990.
"What Hillary Wants." *Vanity Fair,* May 1992.
"Bush Angrily Denies Report of an Affair." *The New York Times,* Aug. 12, 1992.
"Bush Angrily Denounces Report of Extramarital Affair as 'a Lie.' " *The Washington
    Post,* Aug. 12, 1992.

"The Press' Merry Chase of the Jennifer Question." *The Washington Times,* Aug. 17, 1992.

"Tale of the Tape." *Newsweek,* Aug. 24, 1992.

"Spy Magazine to Fold." *The Washington Post,* Feb, 19, 1994.

"State Dept. to Probe Access to Personnel Files." *The Washington Post,* Sept. 3, 1994.

Don Imus

"Unexpectedly, the Clintons Are Skewered at a Dinner." *The New York Times,* Mar. 23, 1996.

Dowd, Maureen. "The Last Laugh." *The New York Times,* Mar. 24, 1996.

Transcript of Don Imus remarks at Radio-TV Correspondents Association Dinner, Washington, D.C., Mar. 21, 1996. Federal Document Clearing House Inc.

Reliable sources, CNN. Transcript, Mar. 24, 1996, 9:30 P.M. ET.

Tom Foley

Nelson, Lars-Erik. "Newt Tastes Blood and Has Feeding Frenzy." New York *Daily News,* June 5, 1989.

"Anatomy of a Smear." *U.S. News & World Report,* June 19, 1989.

"Why Foley Stood Idle." *Time,* Apr. 13, 1992.

The New Indiscretion

"Rush & Molloy: Gender Bender." New York *Daily News,* Oct. 16, 1996.

Seattle

"Springer Testifies in Ky. Vice Probe." *Cincinnati Enquirer,* May 2, 1974.

"Unsilent Springer." *People,* Jan. 24, 1994.

"Who Shot Mayor Norman B. Rice?" *The Seattle Water Department Solidarity Newsletter,* undated.

"Who Shot Mayor Norman B. Rice?" AOL posting, Mar. 5, 1995.

"Rice to Denounce 'False' Rumors." *Seattle Post-Intelligencer,* May 1, 1996.

"Rice Wins Apology over Rumors." *Seattle Post-Intelligencer,* May 14, 1996.

"Siegel Apologizes for Rice Rumors." *Seattle Post-Intelligencer,* May 14, 1996.

"In Washington State, a Candidate Strikes Back at Talk Radio." *The New York Times,* May 14, 1996.

"Talk Show Host Siegel Is Fired." *Seattle Post-Intelligencer,* May 30, 1996.

Bibliography

Burniller, Elizabeth. "Mayor's Wife to Sit Out Campaign." *The New York Times*, July 2, 1997.

"Affair Story Dogs Rudy." New York *Daily News*, Aug. 9, 1997.

Golway, Terry. "Covering Mating Habits of the Rich and Famous." *New York Observer*, Aug. 11, 1997.

Kelly, Keith. "Scene and Heard: He's the Wrong Guy!" New York *Daily News*, Aug. 12, 1997.

Conant, Jennet. "The Ghost and Mr. Giuliani." *Vanity Fair*, Sept. 1997.

Bob Dole

"Dole's 'Emergency' Divorce." *The Washington Post*, Aug. 7, 1996.

Ledbetter, James. "Who Do You Trust?" *The Village Voice*, Nov. 5, 1996.

"Dole, the Other Woman and the Press." *The Boston Globe*, Nov. 7, 1996.

Auletta, Ken. "Inside Story." *The New Yorker*, Nov. 18, 1996.

"Print Report of Dole Affair?" *Sacramento Bee*, Nov. 24, 1996.

Rusher, William. "Now We Know Why Dole Didn't Use 'Character.' " *Human Events*, Jan. 17, 1997.

Bill Clinton

"Clinton v. Paula Jones." *Newsweek*, Jan. 13, 1997.

"Page Six: We Hear . . ." *New York Post*, July 4, 1997.

Crichton, Judy. *America 1900: The Turning Point*. New York: Henry Holt, 1998.

Isikoff, Michael. *Uncovering Clinton*. New York: Crown, 1999.

Morton, Andrew. *Monica's Story*. New York: St. Martin's Press, 1999.

Newspapers and Periodicals

Ayres, Drummond. "Extramarital Penalty, Indiana Style." *The New York Times*, Jan. 17, 1999.

Bennett, James. "Clinton Accepts Apology from Maker of First Sex Life Inquiry." *The New York Times*, Mar. 11, 1998.

Bennett, James. "Who's Mr. Clean?" *The New York Times*, Sept. 6, 1998.

Brock, David. "The Fire This Time." *Esquire*, Apr. 1998.

Carr, Rebecca. "A Week of Crisis." *The Atlanta Constitution*, Dec. 20, 1998.

Cocco, Maria. "Barr Got Message, Missed Point." *Newsday*, Jan. 17, 1999.

Goodman, Ellen. "Clinton Not Only One with Sordid Past," *Peoria Journal Star*, Sept. 14, 1998.

Grove, Lloyd. "Under Fire in a Glass House." *The Washington Post*, Sept. 18, 1998.

Neiwert, David. "Lives of the Republicans, Part Two." *Salon*, Sept. 16, 1998.

Neuman, William. "Flynt: We Were Hustlers of Dirt." *New York Post*, Dec. 18, 1998.

Schneider, Mary Beth. "Burton Learned of Son Years Later." *The Indianapolis Star*, Sept. 6, 1998.

Steinem, Gloria. "Feminists and the Clinton Question." *The New York Times*, Mar. 22, 1998.

Stuteville, George. "A Telling Day." *The Indianapolis Star*, Sept. 5, 1998.

Talbot, David. "This Hypocrite Broke Up My Family." *Salon*, Sept. 16, 1998.

Warren, James. "Coping with the Washington Mudslide." *Chicago Tribune*, Sept. 20, 1998.

Wehrman, Jessica. "Burton's Remarks Not Wise, Analysts Say." *The Evansville Courier*, Sept. 4, 1998.

"Why we ran the Henry Hyde story." *Salon*, Sept. 16, 1998.

Vobejda, Barbara. "Scandal's Legacy." *The Washington Post*, Feb. 12, 1999.

"This Week," ABC-TV, Jan. 25, Feb. 1, Aug. 23, 1998.

Chapter 11

The Election of 2000

Klein, Joe. *Politics Lost*. New York: Doubleday, 2006.

Frontline. The Choice 2000: Al Gore editors note *www.pbs.org*

Newspapers

Mike Allen. "Bush Seeks to Minimize DUI Fallout." *Washington Post*, Nov. 4, 2000.

Felicity Barringer. "When an Old Drug Question Becomes New News." *The New York Times*, August 22, 1999.

Richard Davis. "The Anatomy of a Smear Campaign." *Boston Globe,* March, 21, 2004.

Thomas Edsall. "Ex-Aides to Bauer Speak Out." *Washington Post*, Sept. 30, 1999.

Nicholas Kristof. "POW to Power Broker." *The New York Times,* Feb. 27, 2000.

Ellen Joan Pollock. "Behind Rumors about George W. Bush Lurks a Culture of Washington Gossip." *The Wall Street Journal*, May 14, 1999.

R.G. Ratcliffe. "Drugs 'Irrelevant' to Race, Bush Says." *Houston Chronicle*, May 3, 1994.

Jim Yardley. "Bush, Irked at Being Asked, Brushes Off Drug Question." *The New York Times,* August 19, 1999.

Outing

Gunderson, Steve and Morris, Rob. *House and Home*. New York: Dutton, 1996.

"Kolbe Opponents Admit to Posting False AIDS Signs." *National Journal's Congress-Daily*, Oct. 31, 1996.

Bibliography

Newspapers

Bill Dedman. "TV Movie Led to Prostitute Disclosures." *Washington Post*, Aug. 27, 1989.

John Kolbe. "A Wall of Privacy Crumbles." *Phoenix Gazette*, Aug. 5, 1996.

Josh Margolin. "McGreevey's Reclusive Israeli Aide Steps Down." *Newark Star-Ledger*, Aug. 15, 2004.

Mark Mueller and John Martin. "How It All Unraveled." *Newark Star-Ledger*, Aug. 15, 2004.

Arthur Rotstein. "Arizona GOP Congressman Acknowledges He is Gay." Associated Press, Aug. 2, 1996.

Sandra Evans Teeley. "Politicians Assess Future of Studds, Craine, in Wake of Sex Report." *Washington Post*, July 16, 1983.

The War on Terror

Michael Dobbs. "Swift Boat Accounts Incomplete." *Washington Post*, Aug. 22, 2004.

David Halbfinger. "Campaign 2004: The Military Records." *The New York Times*, Aug. 29, 2004.

Michael Kranish. "Yale Grades Portray Kerry as Lackluster Student." *Boston Globe*, June 7, 2005.

"Kerry Allows Navy Release of Military, Medical Records." *Boston Globe*, June 7, 2005.

Jennifer Luce and Don Gentile. "Bush's Booze Crisis." *The National Enquirer*, November 22, 2005.

Marc Morano. "Navy Contradicts Kerry on Release of Military Records." CNSNews.com, Sept. 16, 2004.

Alexandra Polier. "The Education of Alexandra Polier." *New York* magazine, June 7, 2004.

Ellen Joan Pollock. "Behind Rumors about George W. Bush Lurks a Culture of Washington Gossip." *The Wall Street Journal*, May 14, 1999

Kate Zernike. "Kerry Pressing Swift Boat Case Long After Loss." *The New York Times*, May 28, 2006.

Kate Zernike and Jim Rutenberg. "Friendly Fire: The Birth of an Attack on Kerry." *The New York Times*, Aug. 20, 2004.

Acknowledgments

Hundreds of people helped me write this book—thousands if you start with my ancestors, who thoughtfully left Europe for a land that contained a more manageable amount of political history, and end with the sushi guy who delivers late. My thanks to them all. But not to whoever invented the computer program that ate Chapter 7.

Carolyn Brook was my researcher for a year and a half, and is the only person in the world who shares my obsession for finding out who was the real father of Grover Cleveland's baby. For that, as well as unearthing so much of the information in this book, I will be eternally grateful. She gets credit for most of what's accurate and none of the mistakes. Karen Avrich, who came on board later, collected a great deal of the gossip that's in here, and a lot more that I'm saving for the next project. Particularly Peaches Browning. My thanks to Maureen Muenster for all of the lunch hours she spent looking for stories about Theodore Roosevelt's family and Fatty Arbuckle's trial.

People who are much smarter about history than I were very kind about sharing their expertise. My particular thanks to Joanne Freeman of Yale University, John Catanzariti, the editor of the Jefferson papers

Acknowledgments

at Princeton University, Stephen Oates of the University of Massachusetts, Elizabeth Blackmar of Columbia University, William Leach and biographers Doris Kearns Goodwin, Richard Reeves, Bill Nunnelly, and Charles Fontenay. Donald Ritchie, associate historian of the U.S. Senate, was an all-purpose source. My thanks to all state historical societies for simply existing, but the one in Kentucky deserves special gratitude both for helpfulness and having such good gossip. Director Jim Klotter and Ron Bryant were informative about both poor Congressman Taulbee and the silver-tongued William Breckinridge. Debbie Henley, the managing editor of the *Louisville Courier Journal*, is one of the few people I can thank constructively, and I am deeding her newspaper my Taulbee files for all eternity.

Thanks to everyone who works at New York City's research library, to the librarians at *The New York Times* and, on behalf of Carolyn Brook, to the librarians and staff at New York State Library and library at the State University of New York at Albany.

One of the best things about this project was discovering the amazing bits of history people are carefully preserving out there. Jim Connor gave me the big Jim Folsom song; Alan Betrock told me about scandal magazines in the 1950s. Thanks to Michael Harrison for explaining talk radio and Patricia Tobias for straightening me out about Fatty Arbuckle.

Bob Donovan, Max Frankel, Warren Rogers, Helen Thomas, Liz Smith, and Russell Baker were particularly kind about giving me their time and recollections. A few other people who didn't want to be quoted by name gave me helpful background for which I'm eternally grateful. They know who they are. My friend Murray Kempton took me out to dinner and explained in great detail how evil and soul-destroying gossip is. He then proceeded to tell me some of the best stories, only a few of which were entirely printable. Murray died before the book was finished. I miss talking to him as much as I miss reading him.

I also want to thank all the others who answered questions, gave me leads, told me anecdotes, and showed me, very frequently, when I was wrong. I could never list all of them, but they included R. W. Apple Jr., Joni Balter, Elizabeth Bumiller, Ron Casey, Joel Connelly,

Acknowledgments

Maureen Dowd, Jim Dwyer, Timothy Egan, Jack Elliott Jr., Austin Fox, Bob Gogerty, Nancy Griffin, Ed Hayes, Rick Hertzberg, Joe Klein, Ed Kosner, Steve Kotchko, Gene Mustain, Tom Oliphant, Eleanor Randolph, Rex Reed, Frank Rich, Marla Romasch, Kevin Sachs, Bob Semple, Terry Tang, Paul Taylor, Curtis Wilkie, Steve Weisman, and Barbara Wilson.

My parents, Roy and Rita Gleason, my sisters, Mary Ann and Patricia, and my sisters-in-law Kathleen and Laura, and my brother Gary all helped me find people who knew things I didn't know, and forgave me when I stopped answering phone calls.

Thanks to Adam Nagourney and his message function, which got me through many crises, and to my co-workers at the *New York Times* editorial department for putting up with me, particularly Howell Raines.

My particular thanks to Trish Hall and Gail Gregg, who read earlier versions of this book and offered both their suggestions and encouragement.

Thanks to the people at William Morrow, including Henry Ferris, and especially my ever-vigilant agent, Alice Martell, for always sounding optimistic. Finally, thanks to my husband, Dan, for editing, for not complaining about the lack of a summer vacation, for listening to all those stories about Grover Cleveland, and for giving me all my best lines.

343

Index

Abbott, Lyman, 109
ABC, 269
abolitionists, 34, 54, 55, 66, 123
abortion, 264, 271–272, 274
Accuracy in Media, 293
ACT UP, 291
Adams, Abigail, 25
Adams, Annie, 103
Adams, Charles, 30
Adams, George, 30
Adams, John, 20, 23, 24–25, 27, 30
Adams, John Quincy, 13, 30–31,
    36–38, 41, 43–44, 243
Adams, Louisa, 30, 36–37
adultery, 26–27, 33, 34–35, 51, 158,
    160–161
  and murder, 49–50
  trials for, 67–70
  see also affairs; womanizing

Adventures of a Nobody, 30
Advocate, The, 290
affairs, 196–200, 202
  of congressmen, 22, 61–62,
    97–99, 133–134, 200–203,
    264–265, 270–273
  murders over, 49–50, 102–104
  of presidential candidates,
    173–174, 207–214, 262–263
  of presidents, 2–6, 7, 9–11,
    21–22, 26–27, 78–79,
    113–114, 129–132, 149–150,
    160–163, 175, 176–177, 205,
    234–243, 241, 266–270,
    273–275, 277–278, 287
  reporting on, 13–15, 132–133
Agnew, Spiro, 190, 193
AIDS, 17, 171, 226–227, 290
Aiken, George, 164

Index

Albany Argus, 13

Albert, Carl, 192–193, 200

alcohol, alcoholism, 18, 55, 112, 165
   George W. Bush and, 6, 22, 282, 287
   Congressional, 166–167, 171, 192–196
   Mamie Eisenhower and, 3, 11, 163–165
   Ulysses Grant and, 59–60, 62
   Andrew Johnson and, 56–58
   Nicholas Longworth and, 134–135
   Franklin and Eleanor Roosevelt and, 11, 144–145
   Theodore Roosevelt and, 11, 20, 108–111, 112–113
   social drinking and, 165–166, 228, 229–230, 231–232
   temperance movement, 20, 96, 111–113
   John Tower and, 228, 229–230, 231–232

Alexander, Czar, 13, 37, 243

Allain, Bill, 21

Allen, Robert, 134

Alter, Jonathan, 269

American Spectator, 268

Anderson, Jack, 190, 199, 202, 240–241, 242

Anthony, Susan B., 67, 68

anti-war movement, 247, 296

Antony, Mark, 6–7

Apple, R. W., Jr., 174

Arbuckle, Fatty, 11, 18–19, 140–141

Aristotle, 8

Armandt, Lynn, 209

Army Counter-Intelligence Corps, 153

Arnaz, Desi, 158

Arnold, Thomas, 35

Aspasia, 254

Associated Press, 145, 164

Association for the Prevention of Cruelty to Animals, 17

Atlanta Journal, 147

Augustus, Emperor, 6–7

Baker, Russell, 12, 166, 168

Baldwin, Tammy, 289

Ball, George, 78–79

Ball, Lucille, 158

Baltimore Patriot, 50

Barr, Bob, 271–272

Battistella, Annabella (Fanne Foxe), 194–195

Bauer, Gary, 284, 285–286

Bauman, Robert, 202

Beale, Betty, 164, 174

Beatty, Warren, 186, 187, 212

Beecher, Catherine, 67

Beecher, Eunice, 67, 68

Beecher, Henry Ward, 66, 67–70, 74–75, 80

Beecher, Isabella, 67

Bennett, Brian, 293

Bennett, William, 269–270, 277

Benton, Thomas Hart, 38

Bergman, Ingrid, 159, 266

Bernstorff, Johann von, 115

Biden, Joseph, 246

bimbo eruptions, 234

Birmingham News, 118

Bissell, Wilson, 93

Index

Black, Shirley Temple, 186–187
blackmail, 26, 64, 65
blacks
  abolitionists and, 34, 54, 55, 66, 123
  descendence from, 11, 20, 28–30, 123–127
  in local politics, 255–257
  as mistresses, 20, 28–30
  see also slavery
Blaine, James, 73, 75, 78, 82–83, 84, 275
Boobs, the Musical, 236
Borah, William, 133, 134, 145
Boston Globe, 3, 212, 213, 279, 299
Bowen, Henry, 68
Bowen, Mrs. Henry, 68
Bradlee, Ben, 175, 179
Bradley, Andrew, 98
Bradley, Anna, 102–103
Brandeis, Louis, 117
Brazile, Donna, 241
breach-of-promise suits, 97, 98–99, 118
Breckinridge, Louise Scott Wing, 96
Breckinridge, William C. P., 96, 97–99, 100–101
Breslin, Jimmy, 252
Britton, Elizabeth, 131
Britton, Nan, 130–131, 132, 267, 269
Broadhurst, William, 209
Brock, David, 252, 268
Broder, David, 269
Brown, Arthur, 102–103
Brown, Isabel, 102
Brown, Jerry, 235, 244

Bryant, William Cullen, 29
Buchanan, James, 36–37, 49, 50, 51–52
Buffalo, New York, and Grover Cleveland, 71, 73, 75–77, 78–79
Buffalo Courier, 77
Bullitt, William, 151, 152
Bumiller, Elizabeth, 213
Burch, Dean, 184
Burchard, Rev. Samuel, 83, 84
Burr, Aaron, 46
Burton, Dan, 271, 272
Bush, Barbara, 243
Bush, George H. W., 227, 239–243, 297
Bush, George W., 241
  2000 campaign and, 277–288
  2004 campaign and, 293–300
  alcohol and, 6, 22, 282, 287
  drugs and, 252, 282–285, 287–288, 289, 291
  as governor of Texas, 283–284
  National Guard service, 279, 297
  youthful activities, 10, 281–285
Butler, Paul, 164, 165
Byron, George Gordon, Lord, 18

Caceres, Cesar, 227
Caesar, Julius, 6–7
Calhoun, Floride, 43
Calhoun, John, 42–43
Callender, James, 26, 28, 29, 301
Campbell, Judith, 177, 203–206
Cannon, Lou, 222
Carnegie, Andrew, 86
Carpenter, Matthew, 63–64, 211
Carson, Johnny, 244

Index

Carter, Jimmy, 242, 272

Carville, James, 236

Cassini, Igor, 176

Cassini, Oleg, 176

Castro, Fidel, 204

Catholicism, 48, 83

celebrities, 11, 17–20, 85–87,
    88–89, 136, 137

  First Families as, 90–94,
    105–108, 174–175,
    250–251

  First Ladies as, 2–6, 9, 22,
    90–94, 252–254

  homosexual, 170–171, 220

  magazines about, 157–158

  politicians and, 186–187

  publicists and, 219–220

  see also movie stars

Celeste, Richard, 215–216

censorship, 125

Chambers, Anne Cox, 242

Chancellor, William Estabrook,
    125, 126, 127, 130

Chandler, Zack, 62

Chase, Salmon, 61

Chavez, Dennis, 166

"Checkers" speech, 19

Cheney, Dick, 6

Chenoweth, Helen, 271

Cheshire, Maxine, 164

Chestnut, Mary Boykin, 53–54

Chicago Times, 63

Childs, Marquis, 172

Chinn, Julia, 53–54

Christian Coalition, 272

Christian right, 272, 287, 288

Christian Science Monitor, 216

CIA, 204

Cincinnati, 255

Cincinnati Enquirer, 91, 109, 124

Cincinnati Gazette, 34

Cipel, Golan, 294–295

Cisneros, Henry, 223–225, 235

Cisneros, John Paul, 224

Cisneros, Mary Alice, 223, 224, 225

Civil War, 42, 43, 55–56, 59, 60–61,
    249

Claire, Richard, 256

Clay, Henry, 11, 48

Cleaver, Eldridge, 187

Cleveland, Esther, 93

Cleveland, Francis (Frank) Folsom,
    77, 78, 84, 90–94

Cleveland, Grover, 11, 22, 71, 82,
    85, 86, 94, 121, 210–211, 212,
    237, 252

  courtship and marriage of,
    90–93

  illegitimate child of, 72–77, 275

  presidential campaign of, 77–78,
    83–84

  sexual conduct of, 78–80

Cleveland, Oscar Folsom, 74–77

Cleveland, Rose, 85

Cleveland, Ruth, 90, 93, 94

Clifford, Clark, 184

Clift, Montgomery, 171

Clinton, Bill, 1–2, 4, 5, 14–15, 110,
    225, 230, 250–251, 281, 302

  1992 elections and, 233–243,
    297

  affairs of, 2–3, 9, 10, 21–22,
    234–239, 266–270, 273–275,
    277–278, 287

  character issues and, 265–270

  "don't ask, don't tell" policy, 289

drugs and, 251, 282–283
as governor, 233–234
impeachment effort, 6, 7, 9,
    21–22, 268–271, 273–275
Don Imus and, 244–247
lamp story, 2–6, 9, 22
presidential campaigns of, 239,
    242, 263–264, 299
Whitewater and, 239, 254
Clinton, Chelsea, 233, 253, 287
Clinton, Hillary, 1–2
Vincent Foster and, 253–254
Don Imus and, 246–247
lamp story, 2–6, 9, 22
marriage of, 4, 5, 22, 234–235,
    237–239, 242, 246–247, 281
as presidential candidate, 301
sexuality of, 239, 252–254
CNBC, 252
CNN, 243, 244, 246–247, 286,
    302
Cobb, Howell, 52
Cody, Buffalo Bill, 87
Cohn, Roy, 171
Colbert Report, 19–20
Collins, Nancy, 218, 219
Collins, Tai, 262
Communists, 170
Compton, Betty, 132
Conant, Jennet, 261
Confidential, 157–158, 159, 170,
    171–172
Congress, U.S.
affairs of congressmen, 22,
    61–62, 97–99, 133–134,
    200–203, 264–265, 270–273
alcohol and, 166–167, 171,
    192–196

homosexuality and, 289–291,
    292
House bank scandal, 249
media and behavior of members,
    22, 166–167, 247–249
Conkling, Roscoe, 61–62, 73, 102
Connelly, Joel, 247–248
Coolidge, Calvin, 133, 136
Correspondents Association, 246
corruption, 16, 26, 33
Corsi, Jerome, 299
Corzine, John, 295
Costello, Frank, 168
Couric, Katie, 6
Cox, James, 126, 128
Crane, Daniel, 289
Crauford-Stuart, Charles, 119, 120
Crawford, William, 121
Creson, Ann, 259
Crime in America, 168
Crockett, Davy, 48, 168
Cronkite, Walter, 14
Cruise, Tom, 302
C-SPAN, 246
Cuomo, Mario, 246
Curtis, Charles, 131
Cutter, Stephanie, 299
cynicism, 238–239

Dallas Morning News, 278, 287
Dana, Charles, 59, 60
Daniel, Clifton, 165
Daniel, Margaret Truman, 165
Daugherty, Harry, 131
Davenport, Alice, 141
Davis, Lanny, 296
Davis, Richard, 279
Dayton Journal, 126

Dean, Howard, 300
deaths
    of movie stars, 139–140
    by suicide, 253–254
    see also murders
Defense of Marriage Act, 290–291
DeLay, Tom, 275
Democrats, Democratic party,
        15–17, 21, 43, 100, 168, 239,
        247
    1884 elections and, 75, 82–83,
        84
    1894 elections and, 100–101
    1920 elections and, 124–128
    1992 elections and, 233–243,
        297
    2000 elections and, 241,
        277–288
    and television, 156, 243–244
denials, 5, 234–236, 241, 287
Detroit News, 200
Dewey, Tom, 155
Dickenson, Angie, 4, 177, 205
Dickerson, Nancy, 195
Dickinson, Charles, 32, 33
DiMaggio, Joe, 158
Dirkson, Everett, 166
divorce, 21, 173, 182, 221, 280–281
Dodd, Christopher, 213, 227
Dodge, Miss, 103
Dole, Bob, 218, 241, 252, 263–265,
        270, 274, 280, 297
Dole, Elizabeth, 252, 265
Dole, Robin, 265
Donahue, Phil, 238–239, 244
Donaldson, Sam, 231, 246
Donelson, Andrew Jackson, 42
Donelson, Emily, 42

Donovan, Bob, 150, 178
Dornan, Bob, 291
double standards, 78
Dowd, Maureen, 246
Dows, Alice, 135
drinking
    social, 165–166, 228, 229–230,
        231–232
    see also alcohol, alcoholism
Drudge, Matt, 300
drugs, 145
    George W. Bush and, 252,
        282–285, 287–288, 289, 291
    Bill Clinton and, 251, 282–283
    Al Gore and, 283, 286–288
    movie stars and, 141–142
duels, 32
Dukakis, Michael, 216–217, 241,
        243–244
Dulles, John Foster, 158

Eagleton, Thomas, 188–190
Eaton, John, 35, 40–43
Eaton, Peggy O'Neale Timberlake,
        40–43
editors, newspaper, 14, 34, 35–36,
        37
Edwards, Edward, 209
Edwards, India, 179
Eisenhower, David, 161
Eisenhower, Dwight, 4, 20, 154,
        156, 173, 180
    affair of, 160–163, 172
    Mamie's drinking and, 3, 11,
        163–165
Eisenhower, Julie Nixon, 161
Eisenhower, Mamie, 3, 4, 11, 156,
        161, 163–165, 172, 173

Eisenhower, Susan, 164

Eliot, George (Mary Ann Evans), 98

e-mail, 2, 14, 279, 292. *See also* Internet

entertainers, 17–20, 250. *See also* movie stars

Erie Railroad, 64, 65

Esquire, 187, 218, 220, 223, 268

ethics, of outing, 291

Evangelist, The, 80

Evans, Rowland, 219

Evening Telegraph, 73–74, 81, 82

Exner, Dan, 206

Exner, Judith. *See* Campbell, Judith

"Faddle," 175, 205

Fairbanks, Douglas, 137, 138–139

Falls, George, 258

Farrow, Mia, 188

Faulkner, James, 109, 124

FBI, 127, 153–154, 185, 230–231

feminists, 273–274

"Fiddle," 175, 205

Fiedler, Tom, 208, 209

First Families, as celebrities, 90–94, 105–108, 174–175, 250–251

First Ladies, as celebrities, 2–6, 9, 22, 90–94, 252–254

Fisk, Big Jim, 64, 65, 66

Fitzgerald, Jennifer, 239–243

Flood, James, 64

Flowers, Gennifer, 235–239, 242, 250, 264, 299

Flynn, Errol, 159

Flynt, Larry, 271

Foley, Heather, 248

Foley, Mark, 291

Foley, Thomas, 247–249, 257

Folsom, Emma, 77, 90

Folsom, Francis. *See* Cleveland, Francis (Frank) Folsom

Folsom, "Kissin' Jim," 160, 254

Folsom, Oscar, 76

Fontenay, Charles, 167, 168–169

Ford, Gerald, 193, 196

Fordham, Kirk, 292

Fordice, Kirk, 257–259

Fordice, Pat, 258, 259

Forrester, Douglas, 295

Fortas, Abe, 184

Foster, Vincent, 251, 253–254

Founding Fathers, 10–11, 24, 28

Fowler, Gene, 132

Foxe, Fanne (Annabella Battistella), 194–195

France, 8, 24

Frank, Barney, 226, 248, 289–290

Frankel, Max, 184, 193

Franklin, Benjamin, 27

Frémont, John, 46–47, 48, 51

Freneau, Philip, 28

Frum, David, 301

Gable, Clark, 19

Gage, Lyman, 94

Galt, Edith Bolling. *See* Wilson, Edith Bolling Galt

Gardner, Ava, 187, 188

Gardner, Colleen, 199–200

Garfield, James, 108

gays. *See* homosexuality

Gebhard, Frederick, Jr., 89

Geffen, David, 17–18

Gere, Richard, 17

Getlin, Josh, 261

Index

Giancana, Sam, 204, 206
Gibson, Mel, 302
Gilded Age, 64, 66, 75
Gingrich, Newt, 247, 248
Giuliani, Donna Hanover, 259–262
Giuliani, Rudy, 259–262
Glass, Frank, 118–119
Glenn, John, 230
Gobie, Steve, 289–290
Godkin, E. L., 79
Gogerty, Bob, 255–257
Goldwater, Barry, 183, 185
Goldwater, Barry, Jr., 197
Golway, Terry, 294
Gooding, Richard, 243
Goodwin, Doris Kearns, 149, 150
Gore, Al, 245
    2000 elections and, 241,
        277–280
    drugs and, 283, 286–288
gossip columnists, 19–20, 245
Gould, Jay, 65, 83
governors, 233–234
graft, 65
Graham, Katherine, 173
Gramm, Phil, 297
Grant, Ulysses, 20, 58–60, 62
Gravel, Mike, 197
Gray, Kenneth, 197
Grayson, Cary, 121
Great Britain, 24
Great Depression, 143
Greece, ancient, 6, 8, 254
Greeley, Horace, 51, 61, 67
Green, Duff, 36
Green, Rufus, 79
Grey, Edward, 120
Griffin, Nancy, 250

Guggenheim, Alicia Patterson, 174
Gunderson, Steve, 291

Haig, Alexander, 223
Hale, Rebecca, 255–257
Halperin, Morton, 230
Halpin, Maria, 73–78, 81–82, 84,
    236
Hamilton, Alexander, 26–27
Hamilton, Elizabeth, 26
Hamlin, Hannibal, 57
Hammond, Charles, 34, 35–36
Hanover, Donna, 259–262
Harding, Florence, 129–130, 131
Harding, Warren, 11, 14, 16–17,
    128, 136, 296
    affairs of, 129–132, 176, 234,
        267, 269
    racial background of, 123–127
Harkin, Tom, 235
Harrington, Michael, 1–2
Harrison, Barbara Grizzuti, 273
Harrison, Benjamin, 27–28, 93,
    105
Harrison, Caroline, 105
Harrison, Michael, 15, 250–251
Harrison, Robert, 157, 159
Harrison, William Henry, 46,
    47–48
Hart, Gary, 133, 186, 207–214,
    215, 234, 235, 237, 242,
    273–275
Hart, Lee, 213
Hatfield, Mark, 166
Hayes, Pat Peake, 198–199
Hayes, Patrick, 132
Hays, Wayne, 196–200, 203,
    272–273

Index

health
  of congressmen, 226–227
  mental, 188–190, 216–217
  of presidents, 121–122, 145–148, 177–180
  venereal disease and, 20, 120–121, 139, 140
Hemings, Sally, 21, 28–30
Hendricks, Thomas, 63
Henry Street Settlement, 96
Hensley, Cindy, 280
Herald Tribune, 194
Herbert, Bob, 238
Hersh, Seymour, 206
Hertzberg, Hendrik, 210, 215
Hess, Steven, 161
Hettiger, Kurt, 256
Hickok, Lorena, 114, 144
Hill, Althea, 102
Hill, Anita, 252
Hill, Isaac, 37, 38, 243
Hinson, Jon, 202, 203
Hintleman, Lisa, 220
history, kaleidoscope theory of, 10–12
Hoffman, Abbie, 187
Hoffman, Dustin, 200
Hollywood, 11, 17–20, 139, 142–143, 158–159, 250. *See also* movie stars
Holum, John, 237
homophobia, 17–18, 291
homosexuality, 20, 21, 51–53, 158, 169–170, 202, 217–218, 247–249, 251, 266
  AIDS and, 226–227
  celebrities and, 170–171, 220
  Congress and, 289–291, 292
  as Internet topic, 252–254
  Walter Jenkins and, 183–185
  outing, 288–295
  Franklin Roosevelt and, 11, 128–129
  Adlai Stevenson and, 171–173
  Sumner Welles and, 151–152
Honorable Peter Stirling, The, 77
Hoover, Herbert, 135, 137
Hoover, Ike, 115
Hoover, J. Edgar, 144, 151, 152–153, 172, 245
Hopper, Hedda, 143
House, Edward, 114, 118
Houston Chronicle, 283
Howe, Allan, 201–202
Hudson, Rock, 171
Hudson Street Baptist Church, 78
Hughes, Charles Evans, 119
Hughes, Karen, 287
Hulbert, Mary Allen Peck, 11, 113–114, 116–117, 118
Hull, Cordell, 151, 152
Hull House, 96
Humphrey, Hubert, 197
Hunter, Tab, 170
Hurricane Katrina, 236, 302
Hush-Hush, 157
Hyde, Henry, 271

illegitimate children, 11, 25, 27, 47, 233–234, 235, 271, 272, 279
  of Grover Cleveland, 72–77, 275
  of Thomas Jefferson, 28–29
I Love Lucy, 155
immorality, 75. *See also* morality
impeachment, 6, 7, 9, 21–22, 268–271, 273–275

Index

Imus, Don, 244–247

Independent, The, 112

Indianapolis Star, 17

infidelity. *See* adultery; affairs; womanizing

Inhofe, James, 290, 291

Inner Circle, 261

Internet, 4, 14, 249, 251–253, 252–254, 298

interracial dating, 158

Iran-Contra scandal, 263

Iron Ore, The, 110

Isikoff, Michael, 275
    Uncovering Clinton, 267–268

I've Got a Secret, 156, 186

Jackson, Andrew, 11, 13, 16, 20, 21, 22, 31, 52, 53, 237
    marriage of, 33–36, 38–39
    presidential campaign of, 32–33, 35–36, 37–38
    Peggy Timberlake and, 41–42

Jackson, Jackie, 216

Jackson, Jesse, 216, 234

Jackson, Michael, 220

Jackson, Rachel Donelson Robards, 33–36, 38–40, 237

Jackson Clarion-Ledger, 257–258

Jacobson, Max, 179, 180

Jameson, Henry, 164

Jarvis, Charles, 286

Jefferson, Thomas, 21, 24, 25, 28–30, 296, 301

Jenkins, Walter, 183–185

Jennings, Peter, 246

Jews, 144

JFK's Love Affairs, 205

Johnson, Andrew, 11, 46, 55, 56–58, 59

Johnson, Lady Bird, 183

Johnson, Lyndon, 176, 179, 183, 185, 187–188

Johnson, Richard, 53–54

Jolly Reefers, 76

Jones, Charles, 102

Jones, Paula, 265–268

Journal-Courier, 104

Kalb, Bernard, 246–247

kaleidoscope theory of history, 10–12

Kansas City Star, 131

Kefauver, Estes, 167–169, 267

Kelley, Kitty, 206, 221

Kemp, Jack, 217–218, 219, 251

Kempton, Murray, 9, 119, 152, 161, 166

Kennedy, Caroline, 91

Kennedy, Jacqueline, 4, 138, 174–175, 176, 177

Kennedy, John F., 4, 14, 138, 155, 172, 173, 211, 273
    affairs of, 4, 10, 203–206
    health of, 177–180
    as womanizer, 174–175, 176–177, 205

Kennedy, Joseph, 149

Kennedy, Robert (Bobby), 156, 177, 179

Kennedy, Ted, 188

Kerrey, Bob, 235

Kerry, John, 295–301

Key, Phillip Barton, 49, 50

Khrushchev, Nikita, 179

Kincaid, Charles, 103, 104

King, Ben, 107
King, Carol, 186
King, William, 51–52
Klein, Edward, 302
Klein, Joe, 280–281
Kling, Amos, 124
Kolbe, Jim, 290
Kolbe, John, 290
Kopechne, Mary Jo, 188
Koppel, Ted, 209
Korean War, 20
Kosner, Ed, 220
Kristol, Bill, 269

Ladies War, 42–43
Langtry, Lillie, 88–89
Lansing, Robert, 119
LaRouche, Lyndon, Jr., 217
Lash, Joseph, 144, 153–154
Lategano, Chistyne, 259, 260, 262
Laugh-In, 19, 186
Lawrence, David, 114, 118
League of Nations, 120, 121
LeFevre, Benjamin, 80
Leggett, Robert, 202, 203
legitimacy, 46. *see also* illegitimate
    children
LeHand, Missy, 144, 149–150
Lehane, Chris, 288
Lehman, Henry, 140
Leigh, Janet, 205
Leno, Jay, 4, 265–266, 282
lesbianism. *see* homosexuality
Letterman, David, 6, 210, 245, 265
Lewinsky, Monica, 7, 21, 266–270,
    274–275, 278, 287
libel suits, 110–111, 159
Liberace, 159

Lieberman, Joseph, 231
Life, 182
Limbaugh, Rush, 3, 251, 253
Lincoln, Abraham, 11, 46, 53,
    55–56, 59
Lincoln, Mary, 56
Lincoln, Robert, 56
"Lincoln Catechism, The," 55
Lives of the Caesars (Suetonius), 7
Livingston, Bonnie, 273
Livingston, Robert, 273
Lockwood, Daniel, 77
Lodge, Henry Cabot, 183
Lombard, Carole, 19
Long, Huey, 254
Long, Russell, 166
Longworth, Alice Roosevelt, 105,
    106, 112–113, 133–134
Longworth, Nicholas, 106, 133,
    134–135
Los Angeles Daily News, 17
Los Angeles Times, 141, 218, 261
Lott, Trent, 270
Louisville Times, 103
Louis XVI, 8
Lowdown, 170–171

McAdoo, William, 107–108, 116
McCain, Carol, 280–281
McCain, John, 253, 278–281, 297
McCarthy, Joseph, 170–172
McCartney, Paul, 17
McClellan, George, 55
McClendon, Sarah, 229
McCormick, Ruth, 134
McCune, Charles, 77
McCurry, Mike, 246
McEvoy, John, 213

McEvoy, Nan Tucker, 174

McGee, Jim, 207

McGovern, George, 186, 188–190, 212

McGreevey, James, 293–294

McIntire, Ross, 147

McKee, Baby, 105

McKinley, William, 11, 95

McKinney, Lucy, 227

McKinney, Stewart, 226–227

MacLaine, Shirley, 186

McLean, Evalyn Walsh, 115–117, 131

McLean, Ned, 115, 131

Mafia, 167–168, 177, 204, 206, 251

magazines, 137
  scandal/tabloid, 157–159, 249–250
  see also specific magazines

Magnuson, Warren, 166

Mailer, Norman, 187

Malcynsky, Jay, 226

Mansfield, Jayne, 205

Mansfield, Josie, 65

Marie, Queen of Romania, 132

Marie Antoinette, 254

Marion (Ohio), Harding's mistresses in, 129–131

Marion (Pa.) *Pioneer,* 36–37

Marion Star, 124

Maroney, Peter, 300–301

Marquez, Margaret, 150

Marshall, George, 153, 162

Means, Gaston, 131

media. *see specific media types and media properties*

Medlar, Linda, 223–226

mental illness. *see* health, mental

Meyer, Mary Pinchot, 205

Miami Herald, 207–209, 214, 292

Middle Ages, 8

midwifery, 8

military heroes, 46

Miller, Earl, 150

Miller, Merle, *Plain Speaking,* 162, 172

Mills, Wilbur, 194–196, 203, 211, 272–273

Milwaukee Sentinel, 291

miscegenation, 53–55, 123–125

Mondale, Walter, 215

Monkey Business (yacht), 209–210

Monroe, Marilyn, 155, 158, 177, 205

Montgomery, Robert, 156

Moore, Owen, 138

morality, 15–17, 21, 24, 64, 75, 76, 100–101

Morris, Dick, 250

Morris agency, William, 220

Morton, Oliver, 63

Morton, Thurston, 166

motion pictures, 87, 137, 159. *see also* Hollywood; movie stars

Motion Pictures Industry Council, 159

Mott, Frank Luther, 36

movie stars, 11, 17–18, 137–138, 158–159, 250, 302
  deaths of, 139–140
  drug addictions of, 141–142
  media coverage of, 142–143
  murder trials and, 140–141
  see also specific movie stars

Moynihan, Pat, 246

MSNBC-TV, 269

MTV, 245
muckrakers, 16
Mugwumps, 67, 73, 275
mulattoes, 54–55, 123–125
murders, 9, 49, 50, 65, 102–105,
    140–141, 253–254, 286
Murphy, George, 159, 182, 186
Murray, Patricia, 273
Murrow, Edward R., 155
Myers, Dee Dee, 5

Nagourney, Adam, 241
narcotics, 141–142. *see also* drugs
Nash, Ruth Cowan, 164
Nashville Tennesseean, 167
Nathan, Judy, 261–262
Nation, The, 79, 210
National Enquirer, 205, 249–250,
    264, 267, 301
National Review, 169, 301
Navy, 128–129
NBC, 6, 243, 246, 262
Nelson, Lars-Erik, 248, 252
Nesbit, Evelyn, 142
New England Courant, 25
Newett, George, 110–111
New Hampshire Patriot, 37
New Hampshire primary, 235
New Jersey Jewish News, 294
New Republic, 210, 215, 247
New Rochelle, 81
New Rochelle Pioneer, 81
Newsday, 182, 244
newspapers, 5, 12–13, 16, 81
    during 1920s, 135–136
    during Civil War, 60–61
    editors, 14, 34, 35–36, 37
    on Thomas Jefferson, 28–29

    as mass entertainment, 87–88
    scandal as topic in, 13–14
newsreels, 137, 143
Newsweek, 5, 145, 197, 205, 213,
    218, 241, 253, 267, 269
New York American, 39
New York City, 132, 259–262
New York Daily News, 141, 142,
    171, 248, 252, 260, 284
New York Dispatch, 50–51
New York Evening Post, 79
New York magazine, 260, 300
New York Newsday, 259
New York Post, 243, 260
New York Sun, 62, 74, 80
New York Telegraph, 132
New York Times, 4, 62, 64, 89, 96,
    101, 106, 109, 117–118, 127,
    128, 161, 174, 196, 199, 222,
    241, 293, 295
New York Times/CBS poll, 270
New York Tribune, 13–14, 51
New York World, 57, 74, 78, 82, 87
Nicodemus, Margaret, 93
Niebuhr, Reinhold, 182
Nixon, Richard, 156, 166, 175, 186,
    188, 189
  "Checkers" speech, 19
  Watergate, 12, 16, 191–192, 200
Nob Hill, 64
North, Oliver, 263
Novak, Kim, 177, 205, 219
Nunn, Sam, 229

Oakley, Annie, 87
Obenehain, Ralph, 142
O'Connell, Linda Matys, 223
Offie, Carmel, 151

Ogle, Charles, 47
O'Hara, Maureen, 159
Oliphant, Tom, 213
O'Neill, Tip, 146
On the Q.T., 157
organized crime, 167–168, 177,
    204, 206
Overton, John, 35, 53
Owens, William, 100, 101

Packwood, Robert, 100
Palmer, A. Mitchell, 121, 131
Palmer, Mrs. A. Mitchell, 131
Parsons, Louella, 19, 143
Past Forgetting, 162
Patterson, Cissy, 133–134, 152
PBs. *See* Professional Beauties
Pearson, Drew, 134, 147, 152, 171,
    193, 217
Peck Mary Allen. *see* Hulbert,
    Mary Allen Peck
"Peggy O'Neale, or the Doom of
    the Republic," 43
Penny Post, 75
People, 206, 215
Perdue, Sally Miller, 238–239
Pericles, 6, 254
Perkins, Frances, 102
Person to Person, 155
Phillips, Carrie, 129–130
Phillips, Jim, 129
Phillips, Stone, 243
Phoenix Gazette, 290
Photoplay, 137, 139
Piatt, Donn, 60, 62
Pickford, Jack, 139
Pickford, Mary, 11, 138–139
Pierce, Franklin, 46

Pierce, Samuel, 222
Pinckney, Charles, 24
Plain Dealer, 215, 216
Plain Speaking (Merle), 162, 172
Platt, Thomas, 13–14
Playboy, 17, 197, 262
Plymouth Congregational Church,
    66, 68–69
Pocahontas, 117, 118
Polier, Alexandra, 300, 301
Polk, Sarah, 51
Pollard, Madeline Breckinridge,
    96–99, 101, 236
pop culture, 186
poverty, 66, 101–102
Power House, The, 243
Pratt, Trude, 153
presidents, U.S., First Ladies as
    celebrities, 2–6, 9, 22, 90–94,
    252–254
presidents, U.S.
  affairs of, 2–6, 7, 9–11, 21–22,
    26–27, 78–79, 113–114,
    129–132, 149–150, 160–163,
    175, 176–177, 205, 234–243,
    242, 266–270, 273–275,
    277–278, 287
  First Families as celebrities,
    90–94, 105–108, 174–176,
    250–251
  health of, 121–122, 145–148,
    177–180
  impeachment, 6, 7, 9, 21–22,
    268–271, 273–275
  see also specific presidents
President's Daughter, A, 132
President We Deserve, The
    (Walker), 239–240

Index

Presley, Elvis, 156
Primary Colors, 235
Prince of Wales, 87, 88–89
Professional Beauties (PBs), 88
Prohibition, 111
Providence Journal, 62, 128
Pryor, Richard, 141
publicists, 219–220
Pulitzer, Joseph, 74, 87
Putin, Vladimir, 8

Quayle, Dan, 259
Quillan, Ronnie, 158

Rabin, Yitzhak, 243
race
  miscegenation, 53–55, 123–125
  as political issue, 123–127
  see also blacks
radio, 136–137, 143. *See also* talk
  radio
Radio and Television
  Correspondents Association,
  245–246
Raphaël, Sally Jesse, 238
Rappe, Virginia, 11, 140
Rathom, John, 128
Ray, Elizabeth, 196–200, 235
Ray, Johnny, 170–171
Rayburn, Sam, 155
Reagan, Maureen, 221
Reagan, Michael, 221, 222
Reagan, Nancy, 221, 223
Reagan, Patti, 221
Reagan, Ronald, 159, 187, 217,
  218, 221–223, 272
Recession, 47, 84
Redford, Robert, 200

Reed, Ralph, 272
Reed, Rex, 187, 188, 219
Reeves, Keanu, 17–18
Reeves, Richard, 175, 178
Regan, Donald, 223
Reid, Dorothy, 141, 142
Reid, Wallace, 18–19, 141–142
Reno, Janet, 225, 253
Republican National Committee,
  130
Republicans, Republican party,
  15–17, 20, 21, 67, 73, 130,
  156, 187, 239, 247, 270–273
  1884 elections and, 73, 74, 83–84
  1920 elections and, 126–129
  1964 elections and, 181–185
  1992 elections and, 233–243,
  297–298
  2000 elections and, 241,
  277–288
Reston, James, 184, 200
Reynolds, James, 26
Reynolds, Maria, 26, 27
Rice, Constance, 255, 256
Rice, Donna, 186, 209–210, 215
Rice, Norm, 255–257
Rich, Frank, 293
Richards, Ann, 283
Richmond, Fred, 202, 203
Riegle, Donald, Jr., 200–201, 211,
  235, 238
Riis, Jacob, 108
Ritchie, Donald, 149
Ritchie's Enquirer, 38
Rivers, Mendel, 193
Robards, Lewis, 33–35
Robb, Chuck, 262–263
Robb, Lynda, 262

Index

Roberts, Cokie, 247
Roberts, Meredith, 264–265
Roberts, Roy, 131
Rockefeller, Margaret "Happy"
    Murphy, 181, 182, 183
Rockefeller, Mary, 182
Rockefeller, Nelson, 181–183, 280,
    281
Rodes, James, 98
Rogers, Warren, 166, 175,
    178–179, 194
Rollins, Ed, 218
Rome, ancient, 6–7
Roosevelt, Alice. See Longworth,
    Alice Roosevelt
Roosevelt, Archie, 106, 107
Roosevelt, Eleanor, 11, 114, 143,
    144, 145, 157–158, 176
  Joseph Lesh and, 152–154
  marriage of, 148–150
Roosevelt, Ethel, 106
Roosevelt, Franklin, 11, 137, 143,
    153–154, 245
  alcohol and, 144–145
  health of, 145–148
  as homosexual, 11, 128–129
  marriage of, 148–150
  Sumner Welles and, 151, 152
Roosevelt, Kermit, 105, 106, 107
Roosevelt, Quentin, 106, 107
Roosevelt, Theodore, 75, 145
  alcohol and, 11, 20, 108–111,
    112–113
  family of, 105–107
  temperance movement and,
    112–113
Roosevelt, Theodore, Jr., 105, 106,
    107

Rose, Charlie, 244
Rosselli, Johnny, 204, 206
Rossellini, Roberto, 159
Rove, Karl, 288
Rusher, Howard, 157
Russert, Tim, 246
Russia, 8, 13, 37, 243
Ruth, Babe, 11
Rutherford, Lucy Mercer, 149

St. Johns, Adela Rogers, 141
Salinger, Pierre, 91, 175
same-sex marriage, 290–291, 293
San Antonio, Henry Cisneros in,
    223–226
Santorum, Rick, 293
Saturday Evening Post, 149
Saturday Night Live, 6
Savage, James, 207
Sayre Institute, 97
Scaife, Richard Mellon, 296
Scripps, Robert, 124
Seacord, James, 81
Seattle, 12, 255–257
Seattle Post Intelligencer, 247–248
Seberg, Jean, 187
Secret Service, U.S., 2–6, 9, 22, 127
Semple, Robert, 192
September 11, 2001, terrorist
    attacks, 15, 262, 293–294
settlement houses, 96
sex, sexuality, 17–18, 25, 78–80,
    266–270. See also adultery;
    affairs; homosexuality;
    womanizing
sexual revolution, 20
Shales, Tom, 244
Shamir, Yitzhak, 221

Index

Sharon, William, 102
Shays, Christopher, 227
Shearman, Thomas, 66
Sheehy, Gail, 239
Shnayerson, Michael, 17–18
"shock-jocks," 19, 238, 244–247
shoptalk, gossip as, 6
Sickles, Daniel, 49–51
Sickles, Teresa Bagioli, 49, 50–51
Siegel, Mike, 256
Simon and Garfunkel, 186
Sinatra, Frank, 158, 177, 187, 188, 221
Sitting Bull, 87
60 Minutes, 239
Slater, Wayne, 278, 287
slavery, 20, 21, 28–30, 34, 53–55, 66, 123
Sloan, James, 108
Smith, Al, 132
Smith, Linda, 273
Smith, Liz, 19, 142, 176, 206
Smith, Margaret Bayard, 42
Smith, Merriman, 148, 184
Spacey, Kevin, 220
Sparkman, John, 190
Speed, Joshua, 53
Sperling, Godfrey, Jr., 216, 234
Sprague, Kate Chase, 61–62
Sprague, William, 61
Springer, Jerry, 255
Standard Form, 180, 298–299
Stanton, Elizabeth Cady, 67, 68
Star, The, 235–238, 249–250
Starr, Kenneth, 254, 267–270, 268, 274
Starr report, 269–270
Statesman, 271

Steel, Ronald, 175
Steinem, Gloria, 274
Stephanopoulos, George, 5, 236–237, 269, 272, 299
Stern, Howard, 238
Stevens, Thaddeus, 48, 58
Stevenson, Adlai, 20, 156, 168, 171–174, 186, 190
Stevenson, Ellen, 171–172
stock market crashes, 66
Stone, Lucy, 78
Stowe, Harriet Beecher, 18, 67
Streisand, Barbra, 1, 186, 250–251
Strong, George Templeton, 49
Studds, Gerry, 289, 292
studio system, 19, 158
Suetonius, 7
suffrage, women's, 96, 116, 136
suicides, 253–254
Sullivan, Ed, 159
Sullivan, John L., 85–87, 88
Summersby, Kay, 160–163, 172
Sumner, Charles, 55, 57
Sunday Capital, 60, 62
Swanson, Gloria, 149
Sweet Potato Pie Man, 233–234
Swift Boat Veterans for Truth, 296–299
Swisshelm, Jane, 54–55
syphilis, 20, 120, 139, 140

tabloids
    magazine, 157–159, 249–250
    television, 3–4, 10, 12
Talese, Gay, 187
Talkers Magazine, 250–251
talk radio, 1–2, 3–4, 10, 12, 14, 19, 249–251, 255–257, 265

Index

Tammany Hall, 49
Taulbee, William Preston,
    103–105, 211
Taylor, Paul, 210
Taylor, Zachary, 46
television, 155–156, 167, 243–247
    cable, 14, 19–20, 249, 268
    news programs, 14
    tabloid, 3–4, 10, 12
*Tell the Truth, or the Story of a
    Working Woman's Wrongs,*
    81–82
temperance movement, 20, 96,
    111–113
Tennesseean, 283
terrorism
    terrorist attacks (September 11,
        2001), 15, 262, 293–294
    war on terror, 295–302
Texas mafia, 176
Thomas, Clarence, 252
Thomas, Helen, 178, 179, 183
Thomas, Olive, 139–140
Thompson, Kate, 52
Thomson, Suzi, 202
Tiberius Caesar, 7
Tillotson, Mary, 243
Tilton, Elizabeth, 67–68, 70
Tilton, Theodore, 67–70
Timberlake, John, 40
Timberlake, Peggy O'Neale,
    40–41, 42
Time, 147, 205, 210, 219, 262,
    280–281
Today show, 218, 219
Tonight Show, 282
Top Ten List, 6, 210
Tower, John, 166, 227–232

Tower, Lilla, 229
Tower, Lou, 228, 229
transvestites, 21
Travell, Janet, 178, 179
Tree, Marietta, 173
Tripp, Linda, 7, 267, 268, 274
Troy, Matthew, 190
True American, A, 86
Truman, Harry, 20, 92, 162, 165
Tsongas, Paul, 235, 244
Tumulty, Joseph, 124, 125
Twain, Mark, 64
Twersky, David, 294
Tyler, John, 54, 55
Tyree, Frank, 108
Tyson, Laura, 2–3

Uncensored, 158
Uncle Tom's Cabin, 67, 86
Uncovering Clinton (Isikoff),
    267–268
United States Telegraph, The, 35,
    36, 54

Vail, Tom, 216
Vallee, Rudy, 137
Van Brocklin, Karen, 248
Van Buren, Martin, 11, 16, 42, 43,
    46–48, 55
Van Court, Arthur, 217
Vanderbilt, Cornelius, 64
VanDyke, Stephen, 301
Vanity Fair, 17–18, 242, 261, 271
venereal disease, 20, 120–121, 139,
    140
Victoria, Queen, 89
Vietnam, 11–12, 16, 237, 247,
    295–299

Index

Von Hoffman, Nicholas, 196,
210–211

Waggoner, Joe, 201, 202
Walker, Jimmy, 132–133, 182, 259
Walker, Martin, 156, 239–240, 254
Wall Street Journal, 282, 284
Walters, Barbara, 22, 165
Warnecke, John, 286–287
War of 1812, 32
Washington, George, 5, 23–28
Washington, Martha, 25
Washington Confidential, 151–152,
170
Washington Fringe Benefit, The,
197
Washington Globe, The, 54
Washington Herald, 134, 152
Washingtonian, The, 5–6
Washington Merry-Go-Round, 134
Washington Monthly, 2–3
Washington Post, 5, 100, 115, 175,
192, 197, 200, 202, 210, 213,
215, 227, 240–241, 242, 263,
264, 267–269, 286, 289–290
Washington Times, 4–5, 103, 193,
217, 254
Wasserman, Edward, 292
Watergate, 12, 16, 191–192, 200
Watt, Bob, 255–256
wealth, 66
Weaver, John, 279
Web blogs, 3, 298, 301
Webster, Daniel, 11, 54–55
Weems, Parson, 31
Weil, Gordon, 189
Weisman, Steve, 4, 222
Welles, Sumner, 151–152, 158

Well of Loneliness, The, 169
West, J. B., 146
Weyrich, Paul, 229
Wherry, Kenneth, 170
White, Fanny, 49
White, Stanford, 142
White, Theodore, 181, 185
White, William Allen, 71, 129
Whitewater, 239, 254
Whitman, Christie, 294
Whittier, John Greenleaf, 67
wife-beating, 93, 95
Wilkie, Curtis, 212
Will, George, 269
William Morris agency, 220
Williams, Aubrey, 147
Williams, Harrison, 166–167
Wilmington News Journal, 212
Wilson, Earl, 203
Wilson, Edith Bolling Galt, 9, 124,
125
    courtship and marriage of,
        114–116, 117–119
    husband's stroke, 119–120, 121
Wilson, Eileen, 114, 118, 119
Wilson, Margaret, 107
Wilson, Nell, 107–108
Wilson, Woodrow, 9, 11, 21, 95,
107, 108
    affair of, 113–114
    courtship and marriage of,
        114–116, 117–119
    Warren Harding's background
        and, 124–125
    stroke and illness of, 119–121
Winchell, Walter, 245
Windsor, Duke of, 155
Wise, Henry, 47

womanizing, 20, 61, 168–169, 215–216, 218, 273–275
   arrests for, 201–202
   of Bill Clinton, 234–239, 266–270
   of John Kennedy, 175, 176–177, 205
   of Wilbur Mills, 194–195
   of Adlai Stevenson, 173–174
   see also adultery; affairs
women
   1890s and 1920s activism of, 95–96, 101–102, 116, 136
   abortion and, 264, 271–272, 274
   William Breckinridge and, 100–101
   feminists, 273–274
   influence on social agenda, 14
   midwifery and, 8
Women's Christian Temperance Association, 96
Women's Journal, 78

women's movement, 101–102, 273–274
women's rights, 20. *See also* suffrage, women's
Woodhull, Victoria, 68–69, 70
Woodhull, Zulu Maude, 70
Woodhull and Claflin's Weekly, 68
Woods, Tiger, 251
World Trade Center terrorist attacks (2001), 15, 262, 293–294
World War I, 11, 20, 107, 125
World War II, 20, 143, 147, 160–163
Wright, Betsy, 234
Wright, Jim, 247–249

Yarbrough, Jeff, 290
Yeltsin, Boris, 251
Young, John, 199, 200, 203
Young, Mattie, 92

Zebra Room, 192